Memories of a Brooklyn Boy

Memories of a Brooklyn Boy

Sol Schwartz

Copyright © 2018 by Sol Schwartz.

Library of Congress Control Number: 2018902399
ISBN: Hardcover 978-1-9845-1013-6
Softcover 978-1-9845-1012-9
eBook 978-1-9845-1011-2

All rights reserved. No part of this book may be reproduced or transmitted in any form or by any means, electronic or mechanical, including photocopying, recording, or by any information storage and retrieval system, without permission in writing from the copyright owner.

This is a work of fiction. Names, characters, places and incidents either are the product of the author's imagination or are used fictitiously, and any resemblance to any actual persons, living or dead, events, or locales is entirely coincidental.

Any people depicted in stock imagery provided by Getty Images are models, and such images are being used for illustrative purposes only.
Certain stock imagery © Getty Images.

Print information available on the last page.

Rev. date: 03/08/2018

To order additional copies of this book, contact:
Xlibris
1-888-795-4274
www.Xlibris.com
Orders@Xlibris.com
770941

ACKNOWLEDGMENTS

FOR MY CHILDREN and grandchildren, with whom I wish to share memories of my life experiences that may help them understand who I am.

To my most patient nephew, Sheldon Schwartz, who I have to thank for all his assistance in helping me select the photographs of our family from his vast collection.

To my cousin Barry Tunkel, who tirelessly constructed our family tree to help identify who is who among the many "Sams" and "Roses" in the family.

Lastly, I want to thank my soul mate, Meta Smith, for her suggestions and criticisms, which she delivered with loving devotion.

AS I APPROACH my eightieth birthday (one I never dreamed I would reach), I will once again try to reconstruct the chronology of the years I have lived. I have attempted to do this on other occasions, usually after a significant tragic event in my life, but I have never succeeded in following through. I may not succeed this time either, but I find I have a strong need to try again.

I am not entirely certain of what possible interest this writing can or will be to anyone other than myself. If I succeed in completing it, perhaps my children or grandchildren will one day find it of some interest, should they become curious about their recent ancestry. I know that much of the history of my father's family is lost to me. I regret not becoming curious during his lifetime, when I could have learned more about my paternal past.

By the time I was born in 1925, my father, Sam Schwartz, had already purchased a house at 492 Hegeman Avenue in the East New York section of Brooklyn. At the time, the area must have been considered an up-and-coming one, about an hour-long subway ride from Manhattan. The house occupied the corner of Georgia and Hegeman Avenues. It was of brick construction, and because it was on the corner, it was one of the more desirable houses on the block. It boasted a small front yard, which was home to a crab apple tree that produced a large crop of crab apples every other year and only a modest crop during the off years. Sharing the yard was a shade tree that made it very pleasant to sit on the wooden bench protected by the tree. The house was two stories, consisting of four bedrooms and a small bathroom on the second floor. On the first floor, there was an enclosed porch that contained assorted chairs and a wooden swing that squeaked as it swung to and fro. The porch was the entrance to the rest of the house and shared a common wall with the porch next door. The wall contained windows so that visual communication was possible between the two porches. Our porch led to a hallway through a small vestibule that allowed access to the kitchen, the dining room, and the living room. The kitchen led into a small dinette surrounded by windows. You could climb through some of these windows and gain access to a flat garage roof that stretched the full length of the rest of the property. Three of the garages were built before I was born, and the other was constructed after my birth. The garages were an investment in order to produce extra income, but we utilized the garage roof as our sometimes bedroom on hot summer nights long before we were introduced to air-conditioning or even electric fans. The hallway also led to a flight of stairs that was the access to the second story. It also contained a door that led down a flight of stairs to the cellar, which housed a heating system and coal storage area before the system was converted to oil some years after I was born. The basement also contained a washtub, where my mother spent almost every Monday handwashing bedsheets, shirts, and all the other laundry for the occupants of the house.

Clotheslines stretched across the cellar on which the laundry was hung up to dry.

Sam Schwartz, he was married, lived in the house with his mother, Rebecca; his brother, Harry Schwartz; and his sister, Tillie. When Sam married Rose Siegel, my mother, she came to live there; and it was in that house that she gave birth to three children. The oldest, my sister, Beatrice, was followed by my brother Leonard and then me. By the time I was born, Uncle Harry Schwartz had married Aunt Rae Kaplan and moved out. After I was born, seven people occupied that house; and although the cast of characters frequently changed, there were never fewer than seven occupants living there until the house was sold many years later.

My earliest recollections were happy ones. Sam Schwartz operated an apparently successful business named the Atlantic Sash and Door Company—a firm that made wooden products, including windows and doors. Eventually, the company suffered the fate of many businesses after the 1929 crash. But for the first four or five years of my life, I was only aware of what appeared to be a harmonious and happy household. Being the youngest of three children, I recall being showered with attention. Being "cute"—as old photographs seem to indicate—did not hurt much. I recall visiting the Atlantic Sash and Door Company and being fascinated by the typewriter in the office. I was allowed to press the keys and spell my name out.

Summers were spent at a "kuchalaine" in Fallsburg, a village in the Catskills. The "kuchalaine" was an old farmhouse consisting of many bedrooms that were rented out to families who came to the country to escape the heat of the city. The renters shared a common kitchen and cooked for themselves. I remember that the owner's name was Bellish. The farmhouse was located on property very close to the railroad tracks, and it was a favorite activity of the children to run close to the tracks when they heard the train whistle blowing and wave to the train engineer. He would always wave back as the train passed. On Friday evenings, we would all go down to the railroad station and anxiously await the arrival of the train, which usually carried the fathers coming in from the city for the weekend. I have no recollection of any planned activity for the children. Uncle Harry Schwartz and Aunt Rae Kaplan—who had only one child, Lester—were also renters at the Bellish farmhouse. Uncle Harry Schwartz erected a tent on the property, and the children played around the tent. I have a photo of myself standing in front of that tent. I can't remember any of the games we played, but my memories of those early summers were pleasant.

There was disharmony that existed within the family, which I was shielded from, and that centered on serious disagreements between Rose and Tillie. When Rose married Sam Schwartz, she was welcomed by her mother-in-law, Rebecca. However, as time went on, Rose was more and more relegated to the tasks of that of a servant. She cooked, shopped, cleaned, and did the laundry. Apparently, Tillie helped little with those chores. She performed the tasks of a mother in areas other than providing basic needs. Tillie spoke, wrote, and read English; and she would go to school for us when it came time to talk to a teacher. She provided love and affection when Rose was too busy with her household chores.

My recollections of Tillie are a mixture of love and hate. I loved her very much, but I also have memories of experiences with her that were not constructive in my formative years. On occasion, when we were alone at home, she would suggest that we play a game called "play with my feet." She would lie on the bed, and I would play with her "feet." I have no specific recollection that my playing with her feet was not limited to that. In later years, I began to think that my probing between her legs was more than I allowed myself to remember.

On a number of occasions, an officer who patrolled the beat in our neighborhood was invited in for coffee. I have this image of him sitting at our dining room table and me standing next to him, intrigued with the holstered pistol hanging from his waist. Tillie reprimanded me, telling me not to bother him and to go play with my own toy gun. But coupled with this reprimand was a punishment that entailed being led into the dark cellar and tied to a pole and left alone for what seemed like hours. I remember crying hysterically during this ordeal, and only years later did I begin to understand that during this interval, they were having sex upstairs.

I don't know how many such encounters Tillie participated in. I do know that one such affair was with a laundryman who used to come to visit with his horse and laundry wagon. It turned out he was married and had a wife and children and was instrumental in impregnating Tillie, ultimately leading to an illegal abortion. We children were told some phony story about what was going on. These escapades resulted in constant friction and fights between Rose and Tillie.

On October 24, 1927, my paternal grandmother, Rebecca, passed away. Although I have vague recollections of her, I cannot recall any details of her funeral. However, her death made a bedroom available in our home.

On March 2, 1930, Rose's youngest sister Lena died of a brain tumor, leaving her husband, Sam Tunkel, a widower with two small children, Raymond and Daniel. At the time, Daniel was about five years old, and Raymond was about nine. The tragedy was accentuated because there was no way for the family to stay together. Sam Tunkel had to go to work, and there was the problem in caring for two young children. There was no question that the entire family had to find a solution to the problem. The ultimate decision arrived at was that Daniel would have to live with Dora Alpert, Rose's older sister who was married to Sam Alpert. They had two small children of their own, Bessy and Adele. Adele was seven years old at the time, and Bessy was about nine years old. They all lived in a two-bedroom apartment, and there was really no bedroom for Daniel. For all the years he lived there, he slept on a folding bed in the kitchen. Sam Alpert made his living as a window washer, which required him to get up at 4:00 a.m. each morning to go to work. Daniel was awakened as Sam Alpert entered the kitchen and prepared breakfast for himself. After Sam Alpert left, Daniel was left with the task of trying to fall back asleep.

Sam Tunkel and Raymond came to live with us. They shared a room. Tillie and Beatrice shared a second bedroom, Leonard occupied a third bedroom that was originally Grandma Rebecca's, and I was shifted to a bed in my parents' room.

Shortly thereafter, my maternal step-grandmother died, leaving Marcus Siegel, my mother's father, living alone in Williamsburg. Soon Marcus also came to live with us. Marcus

Siegel had sired six children in his native land of Romania. Salya was the oldest, followed by Jake, Dora, Rose, Max, and Lena. The children were quite young when Marcus's wife, Basa, died; but he married again. His new wife was named Rose, the same name as my mother. The second wife I knew as my maternal grandmother.

Marcus and his family migrated to America in stages, leaving Salya behind because she was already married with a family. Marcus made his living as a shoemaker and lived with his wife in Williamsburg until Rose passed away. Shortly after her death, Marcus came to live with us. Marcus was given the room Leonard was occupying, and he joined me in our parents' room. Grandfather Marcus's bedroom also became his workshop, where he repaired shoes for some of our neighbors.

Marcus was probably not as tall as I seem to remember him, but the image I have is one of a very tall and thin man with a well-trimmed beard. He was Orthodox and attended synagogue each Sabbath dressed in a dark suit, overcoat, and a derby hat. He carried a cane, but I am not certain whether it was for effect or for support. I remember him as a very serious man, and for the years that he lived with us, our home centered on his Orthodoxy. I was required to go to the synagogue with him. I remember with awe his repairing shoes by placing a handful of nails in his mouth and removing them one at a time as he hammered them into the shoe under repair. The speed and accuracy with which he performed this task bewildered me.

The friction between Rose and Tillie persisted, and finally, Rose demanded that Tillie move out of the house. She gave Sam Schwartz an ultimatum that either Tillie leaves or she would take their children and leave. Left with no alternative, Sam Schwartz was faced with having to decide that Tillie would have to go. I don't remember the actual exodus, but she went to live temporarily with her older sister Chaia, who was married, had children of her own, and lived in the Bronx. Sam was devastated because he had promised his father that he would always see to it that Tillie would be taken care of, and now he was forced to choose between his wife and children and his sister.

ELEMENTARY SCHOOL

THE NEIGHBORHOOD PUBLIC school, PS 190, was the school we went to. About a mile away, there was another public school, PS 202, which was reachable either by walking or by public transportation—namely, a trolley car that ran along New Lots Avenue. Although the distance was not astronomical, the neighborhood that housed PS 202 was less "Jewish" than the PS 190 neighborhood. Many families were of Italian extraction.

PS 202 had a number of experimental programs going. One was a "sight conservation" program for children with vision problems. As it turned out, Beatrice was the first of us to be diagnosed with a bad case of myopia, more commonly known as "nearsightedness." The powers that be chose to have her transferred to PS 202. Not long after that, Leonard was also diagnosed with myopia and was also transferred to that school. I attended PS 190 through second grade. I had been pushed ahead through first grade, apparently because I was bright enough and found the work too easy.

My reaching second grade coincided with the trauma I believe I suffered when Tillie was forced to leave our home. At the same time, I was diagnosed with myopia and was also transferred to PS 202.

The sight conservation program was one that restricted the children in the program from reading books with small print. It also restricted reading any material printed on glazed paper. We were not allowed to use glazed paper to write on and could only use thick lead pencils, never fountain pens.

There were two sight conservation classes. Ms. Stalory was the teacher for one class and Mrs. Jones for the other. The children in these classes all had vision problems. The sight conservation class was more like a homeroom class. The children would attend classes with the "normal" children of their particular grade; but when it came to lunch, physical training, or recreation, they would return to their home sight conservation class. We were not permitted to participate in activities that were deemed harmful to our sight. When we were attending classes with normal children, we were seated in the front rows of the class but could not avail ourselves of any normal textbooks that the other children had. My performance did not live up to earlier expectations of what I could achieve. I believe the sight conservation restrictions on my being able to read normal books hindered my ability to develop rapid reading skills, and I found this devastating in later years.

The trauma of Tillie being forced to leave wreaked havoc with my emotional stability. I remember that Tillie used to come to wait for us outside the school to see us, and it had to remain a big dark secret. On one such occasion, she came and began crying that she had no money. What exactly she expected us to do was not clear, but I remember feeling that I should do something to rectify the situation.

I know that my father was severely torn by his promise to his father to take care of his sister and his responsibility to his wife and children. In his own naive way, my dad tried to doctor up his paycheck, reducing the amount he earned. Although nobody ever said anything to me, I knew he took money out of his pay to give to Tillie, attempting to fool my mother by altering his paycheck stub. I didn't believe that he could get away with this, but I never heard anything about my mom making a fuss about his reduced earnings.

My early years at PS 202 put me in touch, for the first time, with non-Jewish children. Our sight conservation class brought together kids from a number of different neighborhoods, and the neighborhood surrounding the school had a strong mixture of families of Italian, Irish, and Jewish extraction. In the main, we got along well together, although there was an occasional incident that acquainted me with anti-Semitism. When we had fire drills, for instance, and we had to leave the classroom, we were assigned partners and left the room two-by-two holding hands. My partner was a cute little blond girl named Anne whose hair was cut in bangs. She always wore a delightful light perfume, and I was always thrilled to hold her hand as we left our room. She was friendly until, one day, I came to school wearing a pin issued by the Jewish National Fund, which was given to people who contributed to the fund. I attended Hebrew school in the afternoons, and one of the tasks at that time was to collect money for the JNF. To the best of my knowledge, these funds were used to purchase land in Palestine for Jewish settlement. On the day I came to school wearing the pin, Anne noticed it and asked me if I liked that. I replied that I did; but when I asked her if she liked it, she replied with an "ich." From that day on, she was no longer friendly and would no longer be my partner. I never got to hold her hand again.

Not all my recollections of those days were unpleasant. At Christmastime, the sight conservation classes had Christmas trees, and we were all given an opportunity to decorate them. Since Beatrice was older and was in Mrs. Jones's class while Leonard and I were in Ms. Stalory's class, each Christmas, our mother would bake two cakes—one for each class for us to bring to school. All the children would have cake and lots of Christmas candy was passed around, and we would go home with enough candy to last us through the holiday.

Several of my sight conservation classmates left lasting impressions. Joe was a tall lanky boy who wore glasses with very thick lenses. One day while we were playing in the school yard, he accidentally knocked my glasses off my face. They fell to the ground, and one of the lenses shattered. I was unfortunate enough to be wearing tinted lenses that were prescribed in an attempt to help me with a migraine condition. The tinted lens cost $3.50 each and could, at that time, only be obtained from an optician in downtown Brooklyn, entailing a subway ride that added to the cost of lens replacement. I had a history of breaking my glasses frequently. To replace the lens represented a half day of my father's pay, an amount the family could not afford.

I became very upset, and I told Joe that I was afraid to tell my parents about it. Joe said that he felt responsible and told me we should meet the next morning and he would help me get the money necessary for the lens replacement. I made myself very scarce for the rest of the day, and early the next morning,

I met Joe. He was wheeling an old carriage containing several old overcoats and a large stack of newspapers. Together, we went around collecting more newspapers; and after several hours, we went to a used-clothing store, where Joe exchanged the coats and all the newspapers for $1.25. He gave me the money. I was very impressed by the way Joe handled the transaction, and I saw him as a boy who was making his way by knowing how to live on the streets of the neighborhood.

I ran home and confessed to my mother about the terrible accident that had befallen me and gave her the money Joe had given me. It lightened the blow somewhat, but all I remember of the incident was the effort that Joe put in. I had no further contact with Joe after leaving PS 202, but I have never forgotten his name. Several years ago, I read something about a minor union official going to jail. His name and his age coincided with the age of the Joe I knew. I never found out whether it was really him.

I learned to play chess in the sight conservation class from another classmate, Harold K. Harold was entirely different from Joe. It was obvious that Harold was an intellectually gifted boy. He would eventually be college bound. It was obvious that Joe would never go to college. I am not certain that he ever finished high school. Harold and I became very good friends, and he introduced me to the Boy Scouts. He was in Troop 53, and he suggested that I attend a meeting. The troop met on Vermont Street, a short walk from Georgia Avenue, in a finished basement that was decorated like a ship. The basement was the meeting home for a Sea Scout troop, and Troop 53 was allowed to use the facility as its meeting place.

I became enthusiastic about scouting and was instrumental in bringing my cousin Daniel and a neighborhood friend, Harold G., to join the troop. Daniel and I were jealous of the other scouts who had official Boy Scout uniforms. We couldn't afford to buy them, so we attended scout meetings without a uniform. After a while, we saved enough money to buy a Boy Scout shirt and neckerchief, but it wasn't until a family event that took place at the home of Uncle Jake and Aunt Ida that we were able to buy the rest of the uniform.

The event was the culmination of a saga that began years earlier. It was circa 1930 when many banks failed, among them the bank my grandfather had his modest savings in. Those were the days before the Federal Deposit Insurance Corporation, and as a result, he lost all his money. However, some years later, circa 1937, after my grandfather's death, there was a partial recovery of the funds. My parents, along with my aunts and uncles and all their children, gathered at Uncle Jake's home in Long Branch, New Jersey, where the recovered funds were distributed to all the members of our family. My share, as well as Daniel's, was five dollars. We used the money to purchase what we needed to permit us to have an official Boy Scout uniform. I was very proud of that uniform. I diligently studied and worked and quickly rose through the ranks of tenderfoot, second-class scout, and first-class scout.

During this time, I was also preparing for my bar mitzvah as well. I found I had some questions about the Boy Scout pledge.

"On my honor, I will do my duty to God and my country . . ." I was having some real questions about the existence of God, but not seriously enough to rebel against the oath.

Daniel and I were real excited about our first overnight hike to Englewood Cliffs, New Jersey. Our troop took the subway to the George Washington Bridge. There we began our hike across the bridge and the several miles to our campsite. We had the tasks of pitching our tents and arranging for the construction of a fire pit on which we cooked our meals.

Daniel and I prepared a simple breakfast of fried eggs and hot chocolate. My friend Harold K. was very busy frying bacon (still a forbidden food for us). The smell of bacon frying made us very jealous of Harold—whose home, apparently, was not kosher. Hence we were introduced to Jewish boys that came from homes that did not necessarily adhere to the laws of keeping kosher.

Daniel attended elementary school at PS 190, a very short walk from where he lived. For Beatrice, Leonard, and me, getting to school from where we lived entailed walking from our house one long block to New Lots Avenue, where we would wait for a streetcar that would take us the twenty blocks to Berriman Street, and then we would walk another long block to the school. Walking that block to catch the streetcar was no easy task for me in those days. I would walk along with Beatrice and Leonard, but the problem was that I could not walk as fast as they could since I had much smaller legs. In addition, I was always wearing Leonard's cast-off shoes, and they were too big even after stuffing them with newspaper. On one occasion, we were late and we had to run down the street in an attempt to make up the time. Beatrice and Leonard were running ahead of me, and in the process of trying to keep up with them, one of my shoes fell off; but I kept running. When Beatrice turned around and saw that I was partially shoeless, Leonard had to run all the way back to retrieve the lost shoe. We missed the streetcar we were trying to make. In retrospect, I can't remember what the problem was since the streetcars ran on a five-minute schedule. The 8:15 a.m. trolley was operated by Charlie, whom we all liked very much. The 8:20 a.m. trolley was operated by Skinny, whom we didn't like so much. Perhaps that was the reason. We knew the names of all the operators, and they knew ours. They were very friendly to us kids. After all, we rode with them twice a day for years.

As a child, I became aware of the economic hardships we began to encounter after my father had to liquidate his business. The Great Depression was in full swing in 1930, and little or no construction—which was the heart of Sam Schwartz's business—was in progress. His partner suggested that they load up a truck with all their inventory of lumber and go to the Catskills and build bungalows. My father, perhaps unwisely, refused to do that. His partner went ahead and developed a nice rental income over the years. My dad remained and sought work unsuccessfully for a long time. I remember when we had to give up our telephone because we could no longer pay the bill. Eventually, he did obtain employment at a company in Long Island City. He had to rise at five o'clock each morning to make the trek to the subway to get to work on time. My mother would wake with him to fix his breakfast and lunch. He would return from work at seven in the evening, and he always looked tired and depressed.

During those early years, my life centered on the neighborhood and, more specifically, around Georgia and Hegeman Avenues. There were many boys my age around the block, and the center of gathering was the corner candy store, which was located diagonally across the street from my house. Most of the boys and girls attended PS 190 and had a common school experience. My being transferred to PS 202 afforded me another experience, but when I returned home after a day at school, I would have to find common ground with the boys who could generally be found hanging around the candy store.

But there were girls also! I fell in love very early. Falling in love is a very serious matter, especially when you are five or six years old. Don't laugh! It could be very painful at that tender age when the loved one not only doesn't return the love, but is not even aware of your love.

Dorothy F. was pretty. Her blond hair complimented her peaches-and-cream complexion. She was smart, and her self-confidence was reflected in the way she walked and carried herself. She lived on Georgia Avenue, and occasionally, we played house together along with Ruth B., Leo M., Lenny, and Estelle C. When we used to pair off to make believe we were all grown up into mommies and daddies, I always hoped that Dorothy F. and I would be a "pair." Lenny and Estelle C. would supply a touch of realism to our play by arguing who could tell whom about what to do. Estelle C. thought that she could tell Lenny C. what to do. Estelle and Lenny were twins, but Estelle had the good fortune to be born first, so she was older by about twenty minutes or so, much to Lenny's chagrin.

Dorothy F. was a full fourteen months older than me, and I agonized over the bad fortune of being born later than she because, after all, daddies or husbands are always older than mommies or wives. How was I ever going to overcome that handicap?

We grew older (8-9-10-11), and our worlds expanded. She had other friends and so did I, but I wanted to be with her, go to the movies with her, and fantasize that she was Ginger Rogers and I was Fred Astaire. But it seemed as if she continued to be unaware of my interest. How can I attract her attention? How can I awaken her interest? I imagined hitting a home run with the bases loaded or snagging a high fly ball that would surely have been a home run during a stickball game as she passed by.

I invented a car that sprouted wings and could take off and land in front of her house, and she would notice, and I would take her for a ride. I would become her hero. I was Superman and she my Lois Lane; I saved her life a hundred times from as many different dangers that she encountered. But these were only fantasies, and my true feelings continued to remain my secret.

No miracles occurred that made her aware of how I felt about her. I was angry at myself for being too young, too small, too weak, and too inferior. The frustration that accompanied the anger was so great that it led me to do a terrible thing for which I was and am to this day terribly ashamed.

As I look back, there are a number of terrible things I did as a child that continue to haunt me from time to time. One such thing I remember vividly was an injured bird that lay on the sidewalk in front of the garages adjoining my house. My brother and I were trying to figure out what to do about the bird. Leonard told me to watch the bird while he went into our basement to get a box to put the bird in. I recall that his absence seemed like an inordinately long period of time, so I walked over to the fence that surrounded our yard and from which I could look into our basement window to find out why it was taking so long. In that short interval of time, a cat came from out of nowhere and snatched up the bird. I remember chasing the cat but to no avail, and I remember being reprimanded by my big brother for not protecting the bird when he returned. But most of all, I remember the shame and guilt I felt and still feel for not protecting the bird.

However, the terrible thing I did occurred one day as I entered my front yard and saw my cousin Adele playing Monopoly with Dorothy F. The Monopoly game was mine, and it was homemade because I didn't have fifty cents to buy one. Monopoly was the rage at the time. I fashioned it after the bought Monopoly game owned by my friend and next-door neighbor Leo M., who did have fifty cents to buy the game. The board was made from a corrugated box painstakingly measured out and drawn up to scale. The houses and hotels were little wooden blocks that my father made for me in two sizes to depict the difference between houses and hotels. The Chance and Community Chest cards were made from oak tag. And the tokens were made from plaster of Paris that I poured into little clay molds, which I made by taking Leo's real Monopoly tokens and impressing them into clay. Each token was painted to match the original colors. The money was made from school and notebook paper, and I recall being annoyed that I couldn't match the money colors that the original set used.

I was real proud of that Monopoly set, and when I entered my yard and saw Adele and Dorothy F. playing, I was elated because I felt for sure I would join the game and in this way get some attention from Dorothy. When I requested permission to play, I was told that the game was too far in progress; and besides, they were going to stop as soon as the game was over. My frustration and anger reached a breaking point requiring some kind of release, and the only thing I knew to do was to grab the Monopoly board and scatter all the houses and hotels, money, and Chance and Community Chest cards all over the yard. I can still see the hurt, unbelieving look on Dorothy's face.

We didn't speak again for many years, mostly because I was ashamed of what I had done. But I continued to worship her from afar.

We continued to advance in age (12-13-14). She matured sooner, and the blond-haired child with the peaches-and-cream complexion blossomed into a beautiful young woman who began to attract the whistles and admiring glances of men and boys alike. I suffered in silence, knowing that my love was still pure and not motivated by her recently acquired feminine attributes.

I am not quite sure when I finally overcame the agony of this suppressed secret love, but it was eventually replaced by other relationships.

THE NEIGHBORHOOD

THE CANDY STORE—FIRST owned by a man and his wife, Mr. and Mrs. Berg—was a dark and dingy place. There was a counter when you first entered the store, where all sales were handled: ice cream, soda, candy, newspapers, and so on. Mrs. Berg was never known to smile. She always walked around in house slippers. I don't ever remember seeing her in shoes. In the back of the store, there were several tables where Mr. Berg hosted card games in the evenings. I knew all the card players who would assemble after dinner and play rummy for money. I imagine that Mr. Berg was compensated for the use of his premises.

Outside, there could be twenty-five or so boys hanging around. Their ages would span about twenty years. These boys could be broken into three age groups. In the summertime or when the weather became warm, our street hosted frequent stickball games. The older guys usually had preference over the street. Sometimes they would select some of the younger boys and allow them to play with them, but this honor was reserved for those younger boys who were good athletes. I was never so privileged. I was never good at athletics. I had trouble hitting a ball and suffered pangs of disappointment when I was supposed to catch a ball and was never near the ball properly. Years later, I learned that I had difficulty focusing properly on one image, which did not permit me to bat or catch well. The big joke among my then peers was that when it came time to choose up teams, I was usually chosen only in a pinch and only if there was no one else to choose.

However, there were other games we used to play in which poor eye fusion did not play a role and I could even excel. We played hide-and-seek, ring-a-levio, stealing the white flag, and a whole slew of other games that did not entail spending any money for props. Few of us had any money to speak of, although there were some who did. I still have many flashbacks to those days, and I include some of them here.

I look out of my bedroom window, and other than the streetlights, the only lights that are visible come from Marvin's grocery store across the street. He is juggling cases of milk and empty milk bottles in front of the store. I fall back asleep.

I have just entered first grade. I'm called into the pantry because my father has a surprise for me. I am asked to close my eyes. Pop's hands are behind his back. Then I'm asked to open my eyes, and Pop's hands, now in front of him, are holding my first school briefcase. I shout gleefully, but I am aware of the amputated four fingers of my father's left hand as he holds the briefcase.

I walk into the candy store. Mrs. Berg comes out from behind the counter. She is wearing house slippers and looks tired. In back of the store, a group of men are sitting around the table playing rummy. Mr. Berg is playing while a cigar stub is hanging from his lips. Mr. Sheid is also playing, but his cigar is in an ashtray. My uncle Sam Tunkel—who has a nickname and is known to his peers as "Kotchka"—is the third player. He doesn't smoke, but he is surrounded, as are all the other kibitzers, by a cloud of cigar and cigarette smoke.

The candy store is sold to Harry and Harriet L. The store is renovated, and booths replace the dark rear end of the store where the card games were played each night. A jukebox and a pinball machine are installed. The card game is now rotated among the homes of the players. This evening, the game is in the Sheid kitchen. Now there are no kibitzers, only players. I come in with my friend Seymour Sheid just as the game is getting close to terminating. Mr. Sheid says, "It's time to quit and make a little whoopee." Mrs. Sheid, embarrassed, smiles and says, "Shut up, Irving."

Normy Field, one of the older boys, is sitting on the newspaper stand outside the candy store holding a copy of the *Daily News*. He is doing the crossword puzzle and asks if anyone knows the name of a city in Turkey with six letters. He can't look up the answer because the answer to the crossword puzzle are not in this issue. It is a special crossword puzzle contest. If you fill out the entire puzzle correctly, you win a carton of cigarettes. Normy Field won several cartons already; but he doesn't smoke, so he sells the cigarettes and has some extra pocket money.

Normy Field, Sid Cohen, and I are in the same Hebrew class even though I am about ten years old and they are about twelve. Our teacher is Mr. Lerner. Normy Field and Sid decide to play hooky from Hebrew School, and I follow the leader; but later, Normy Field decides he has a better idea. He eats several cloves of garlic and then says, "Let's go to class." We go, but I'm afraid we will have our ears pulled or our hands slapped or our knuckles squeezed if we come late, but Normy Field and Sid Cohen don't seem to be afraid. When we enter the classroom, Mr. Lerner asks, "Why are you late?" Normy Field gets up real close to Mr. Lerner's face and breathes garlic breath at him as he makes some lame excuse. Mr. Lerner turns his head away and says, "Sit down already!"

I am about five or six years old, and I come out on my porch and look through the wall of glass that separates my porch from the Baliches'. Ruthie B. is sitting on her swing. She asks, "Do you want to play house?" I walk out on my stoop and transcend the low wall into her yard and run onto her porch. Now we are both sitting on her swing, making believe we are grown up.

I'm about six years old. Grandfather Marcus (Zayde) is going to shul, and I am waiting for him outside. There is a sickly looking kitten meowing and apparently abandoned. I go over to play with it. When Grandfather Marcus emerges from the house, dressed in his starched white shirt and black tie, carrying his cane, he sees me playing with the kitten and berates me for touching it while he shoos away the kitten with his cane. I feel he is cruel and lacking in compassion, although I am not able to express it at that age.

Zayde is busy repairing a pair of shoes for a neighbor. Sylvia Krepp, the daughter of Mrs. Krepp, has brought a pair of shoes for resoling. I show her to Zayde's room. He says it will cost seventy-five cents to repair the shoes. Zayde says this in Yiddish, and Sylvia doesn't understand what he said, so I translate for her. She says that she only has fifty cents. I tell this to Zayde, and he agrees to do the job for fifty cents.

I cross over to the candy store. Next to the newspaper stand is a double nut dispenser. One dispenser is filled with sunflower seeds and the other with Indian nuts. The sidewalk is covered with empty shells from the sunflower seeds that have been consumed by the guys that put their pennies into the machine to extract a handful of sunflower seeds. They are very adept at cracking the shells between their teeth, extracting the seed with their tongues, and spitting out the shell. Their hands and tongues are so dexterous that it doesn't take long to consume the whole handful of seeds. Ike is consuming seeds. He has his handkerchief tied around his neck, and he is talking to Steiny and Mick. He sees me. I am wearing thick pink glasses because the eye doctor thinks it will help my migraine headaches. Ike says, "Hey, pink eyes, go tell your father to return our ball." I'm scared of Ike. He is big and one of the older guys and very tough. I pray that when they play stickball, the ball does not go into our yard and disturb anybody who is sitting on the bench. I would like to tell Ike that if the ball came into the yard when my father was there, he would return it; but it was not my father who took it. It was my uncle Sam Alpert, and I can't make my vindictive uncle Sam return it. I don't answer Ike because I'm afraid, so I just try to make myself scarce.

I am about twelve years old, and I am playing Chinese handball with Carl Gooz against Mrs. Nagel's wall next to the candy store. We can't hurt the wall any, but Mrs. Nagel doesn't want us to play against her wall. She screams out of her open window at us. We ignore her unreasonableness and tease her by continuing to play. She pours a pitcher of water out the window, getting us wet.

I am seven or eight and I play potsy with Ruthie, Estelle, and Lenny. I throw my potsy in the correct square and begin to hop and skip to the square containing my potsy, pick it up, and continue on my way. I am not aware that I am practicing coordination and distance judgment. I worry that people might think this is a game for sissies, but I like to play potsy anyway.

He's a milkman. His wife stays home and is screwing around. This evening, the argument between them spills out on the street and somehow involves his brother Al who lives with them. When all quiets down, Al comes out to hang around the corner. No one says anything, but I wonder if he is embarrassed by the scene that was just played out. Soon they move away from the neighborhood.

There is a crowd of guys clustered near the candy store. I cross over to see what is happening. The guys are surrounding a man with a brand-new kind of yo-yo. It doesn't just go up and down. This yo-yo goes down and stays down until the man gives his middle finger, around which the string is tied, a little jerk, and up comes the yo-yo. Then he demonstrates other tricks like "around the world" and "the cradle." We are very impressed with his skill. After his demonstration, he offers to sell us yo-yos for ten cents each, but nobody buys one because no one has ten cents. The man walks on, seeking his fortune elsewhere.

Tony and Laura live on Georgia Avenue and are married. Jimmy is an ex-boxer, and his nose shows it. One summer day, I see them walking down the street. Lena is wearing a housecoat, and Jimmy is shirtless. I am amazed at how completely covered with tattoos his arms and chest are. Jimmy is one of the few non-Jews living on the block.

The Garbelli family lived on the block and had two children, Sal and Mary. Sal, one of the guys a few years older than me, shocked the block by developing leukemia and dying young. I go to Sal's wake. I have never been to a wake before. Mrs. Garbelli is sitting in front of the open coffin. Billy Gonusky, one of Sal's best friends, comes in. Mrs. Garbelli says, "Look at your friend, Billy," and she bursts into tears. Billy looks pale and confused as Mrs. Garbelli escorts him to the coffin. Mrs. Garbelli is wearing appropriate mourning clothing. After Sal's death, I never saw her in any other clothing. She mourned until the day she died.

John ran the coffee shop near the New Lots BMT subway station. He and his wife had several children. They never hung around the candy store. It was rumored that John's busiest day of the year was Yom Kippur, when all the men who would usually eat breakfast at home couldn't do so on this holy day. So during a break from prayers, they sneaked out for breakfast at John's.

I am about eleven years old, and I'm the only one of my family still attending PS 202, my sister and brother having graduated. I take the trolley car home from school as I do almost every day. I get off at Georgia and New Lots Avenues and walk the one block from New Lots Avenue to Hegeman Avenue, but before I reach the corner, Itchy blurts out, "Sussy [my nickname], come look what happened to your house." He grabs me by the hand and leads me the rest of the way as if I have never walked this street before. The first thing I see as I approach the corner is the large bay window on the side of the house that is usually painted green. Now it is black, having been completely covered with soot. I let go of Itchy's hand and begin to run to the house. When I come to the front door, I encounter a fireman standing guard. I don't have to ask him what happened. I see for myself. The entire downstairs has been burned out. The smell of burned wood permeates the house. We sleep in the house because the bedrooms are not burned, but my parents immediately rent an apartment on New Lots Avenue for us to live in until the house gets repaired.

I am about twelve years old and lying in bed on New Year morning. Suddenly, I hear a very loud noise outside my bedroom window. I immediately look out in time to see an airplane crashing down into the building housing the candy store and falling to the street. All the occupants are killed.

I am twelve years old. A new drugstore opens on Hegeman Avenue corner of Alabama Avenue. The pharmacist's name is Mr. Pector. I go in and ask for a job. I am hired. I work seven days a week delivering prescriptions, walking to McKesson & Robbins to get chemicals for Mr. Pector, dusting the shelves, and putting out inventory. Mrs. Pector comes to the store sometimes. She addresses him as "Pector," as if that were his first name. Each day for lunch, Mr. Pector opens a can of skinless and boneless sardines and eats it with a roll. At the end of the week, I figure out that I worked twelve hours a day, seven days a week. I earned my pay. Mr. Pector hands me a silver dollar, and I run home to show it to my mother with pride. She puts the silver dollar away, and I don't see it again for fifty years when she returns it to me shortly before she passes away.

I am about fourteen years old. I am hanging around the candy store alone after supper, waiting for some of the guys to congregate and maybe go for a walk on Linden Boulevard and see if we can pick up some girls. I am approached by a man I have never seen before, and he asks me, "Where can I find a piece of tail?" I try to act sophisticated. I think "a piece of tail" must be slang for "a girl." I tell him to try walking on Linden Boulevard. He says, "How about you?" I don't show him that his proposition frightened me. I just say no and walk away.

Construction for the Thomas Jefferson ball field is underway on Pennsylvania Avenue near Livonia Avenue. There are construction workers. It is summer and very hot. Someplace I find an old baby carriage and a large pail. I go to the soda distributor on Hegeman Avenue between Alabama and Malta Avenues and buy a case of mixed flavored soda. The soda cost $0.03 per bottle plus a $0.02 deposit. I give the man $1.20 and put the case of soda in the pail in the baby carriage. I wheel the carriage back to the ice dock on Hegeman Avenue corner of Alabama Avenue and buy a $0.05 block of ice, which I chop up and put into the pail. The iceman gives me a sack to cover the pail so the ice shouldn't melt so quickly. I wheel my carriage and merchandise to the construction site only to find that I have a competitor who has the same idea, but he got there first.

We are on my porch. Bitto, Maxie, Mickey, and I are trying awkwardly to practice the Lindy. We are going to a gathering on Saturday night. Glen Miller's "In the Mood" is playing on our wind-up phonograph. The guys all chipped in to buy the record, which costs $0.35. "Remember," sage

Maxie says, "when you do a slow dance and you are holding a girl close, your right hand should find the button on her bra."

Phone calls are a nickel at the public phone, but if you are a gambler, it might only cost you a penny. I walk to New Lots Avenue and watch for an approaching trolley car. Just before it comes, I put a penny on the track and wait for the trolley wheels to pass over it. If I am lucky, the penny will get flattened out enough so that it becomes the size of a nickel and will be accepted in the phone slot. If I am not lucky, the penny will come out oval-shaped and I have nothing but a souvenir. Risky investment!

Brad and Fran own the candy store now. Harriet L. is going to have a baby. The only way Harry can avoid being drafted is to go to work in a defense plant, so he sells the candy store to Brad. But Brad is more interested in the horse races than he is in the candy store, so he hires Jack Lemurt to work in the store after school while he goes to the race track. Jack is my friend, and I'm glad he works in the candy store. I think maybe he won't kick me out if I don't spend money, but he kicks me out with everyone else that don't spend money. I'm jealous of Jack because on the counter is an open pack of cigarettes. Anytime he wants, he takes a cigarette and lights up. But I'm not jealous just because Jack gets his cigarettes for free. I'm really jealous because he's smoking out in the open and not afraid to be seen. I'm still smoking on the sly because I know that Mom and Pop won't approve of my smoking. So my cousin Daniel and I are partners in a Bugler cigarette roller gadget, and we make our own cigarettes in the cellar and take long walks on Linden Boulevard when we want to smoke. Sometimes we don't have money to buy Bugler tobacco, so we walk around and pick up discarded cigarette butts from the street and break them open and get a mixed blend of tobacco.

Daniel is looking at the fire alarm in front of the house of Teddy G. I stand there with him. Suddenly, he reaches up and pulls the handle. The alarm goes off, and Daniel and I run like hell across the street into my house. We hear fire engines, and we are scared. We go down into the cellar to hide behind the furnace. We stay there for a long time after the fire engines come and go. We never go near that fire alarm box again.

These flashbacks have little meaning to anyone other than myself. They are about people I knew and, with a few exceptions, have little to do with my life. And yet they are incidents that have made a marked impression on me. How else can I explain that I recall them?

Some of these people I did get to see after many years as the result of my making a serious effort to locate them, but more about that later.

My best friend during my early years was my cousin Daniel Tunkel. After his mother died and he went to live with Aunt Dora, Uncle Sam Alpert, Bessie, and Adele, I rarely remember seeing him smile. He felt like an orphan and must have had many problems coping with the idea that his father came to live in our house with his older brother, Raymond, while he was relegated to be separated from the rest of his surviving family. As I indicated earlier, he was never fortunate enough to have a bedroom of his own. His bedroom was the kitchen in the apartment that Sam Alpert and Dora Alpert occupied with their two daughters. Daniel would have dinner at Aunt Dora's apartment and then come over to our house to see his father and brother. Daniel and I played together, did nature projects together, planted and attended flower gardens together in the small patch of ground around 492 Hegeman Avenue, saved our pennies to purchase a first aid kit to be used to tend to injured cats and birds, walked the streets collecting discarded cigarette wrappers so that we could strip the silver paper and add it to our "silver ball," searched the streets for old milk and soda bottles to return to the store and claim the deposit, and built push mobiles from discarded wooden boxes and old roller skates that still had good wheels. And when we were old enough, we would emulate our older brothers, Leonard and Raymond who experimented with chemistry and photography. We were inseparable. And when, at a very early age, Aunt Dora asked me, "Who are you going to marry when you grow up?" My response was "Daniel."

Sometime around 1933, Linden Boulevard was being constructed. Linden Boulevard became a major thoroughfare through Brooklyn and Queens. Our house on Hegeman Avenue was one block from Linden Boulevard. Beyond Linden Boulevard, there was nothing but empty lots. Apparently, some of those lots were slated to have houses built on them because they had been excavated; but in those years, nothing had been built on them. As youngsters, we frequently went to the lot nearest our block, descended into the excavated area, and built a fire to roast potatoes. Sometimes, if we were lucky to obtain marshmallows, we would toast them. That was a warm-weather activity. In the winter, when there was snow in the lot, we would frequent it with our sleds or even with corrugated boxes and slide down the slope. We had no opportunity to ski in those days.

For a short period of time each summer, a band of gypsies would suddenly appear from out of nowhere, and they would occupy that lot. They would not be there one day, and the following day, there were tents mounted and fires going, cooking food. Women in very colorful skirts sat in their tents. My mother identified these gypsies as "Romanian," and she was convinced that they were capable of telling your fortune. I recall being frightened of these strange people, but my mother soon eased my concern. She—along with my sister, my brother, and me—visited the lot on such an occasion, and I would be left outside the tent, attended to by my older sister, while my mother entered the tent to have her fortune told. Then one day, these gypsies mysteriously disappeared as suddenly as they made their appearance, and the lot become "ours" again.

Death was something I became acquainted with early. Although I have little recollection of Grandma Rebecca's death in 1927, I was aware of Aunt Lena's death in 1930, mostly because I was able to relate to my cousin Daniel suddenly becoming an orphan and because of the upheaval it caused in the new living arrangements. I do not have any recollection of Aunt Lena's funeral. When my maternal step-grandmother passed away shortly thereafter, it again caused an upheaval in the family living conditions since that was when Grandfather Marcus (Zayde) came to live with us. However, in 1933, when Grandfather Marcus died, he was laid out on our dining room floor with a cover over him. I remember being aware of his toes making their impression on the covering sheet while his head, although covered, made its impression at the other end. The funeral procession, following Jewish custom, walked around the shul and then walked past our house before proceeding to the cemetery for burial.

When I was about four or five years old, the atmosphere at home was heavily influenced by Grandfather Marcus, whom we called "Zayde." He was Orthodox and attended shul and prayed regularly. My mother, although uneducated in the Jewish tradition, followed the rituals for all the Jewish holidays. One of the traditional customs before Yom Kippur—the holiest of holy days in the Jewish calendar aside from the Sabbath—required that we rid ourselves of all our sins accumulated through the past year. The way to do that was to say certain prayers while holding a live chicken over your head. The ceremony was called "shlug kapoorus." By so doing, your sins are passed on to the chicken. In later years, this ceremony was performed substituting money for the chicken and then donating the money to the local shul.

Some weeks before the holiday, Mom would purchase several baby chicks and raise them in our cellar. These chicks would grow and be ready for slaughter for the holiday meal. I became attached to these little chicks. I would go down to the cellar and play with them (that is, as much as one can play with baby chicks). I grew particularly attached to one chick as it grew. One day, I saw several dead chickens on our kitchen sink. I became hysterical and screamed at my mother, "You killed my chicken!" Mom tried to alleviate my hysteria by telling me that these were not my pet chickens. She had exchanged them for others. She lied! I knew she had lied! I became aware for the first time that grown-ups lie. The experience was traumatic and had dire consequences. I never ate chicken again until I was a grown man. I unconsciously punished my mother for years after by refusing to eat chicken. She catered to my abstinence by cooking something else for me while the entire family ate chicken.

My father died in 1948, and with rare exceptions, I knew him as a kind and loving man. I believe he was depressed—a condition that probably began with his business failure and the need to find work. I have images of him, day after day, going off in the morning and coming back at night after a day of searching for a job. He was a darn good carpenter, although he may have been a careless one. He had suffered an industrial accident in which he had amputated four fingers of his left hand. This accident occurred before he had married my mother, and it was never mentioned or spoken about, so I have no details as to how the accident happened.

During the period of my father's unemployment, things at 492 Hegeman Avenue changed somewhat for the worse, although we kids were mostly shielded from them. Certain luxuries began to disappear. Our telephone was removed. Hand-me-down clothing became more prevalent. I wore many of the clothes my brother had outgrown. I specifically recall inheriting a pair of his shoes, which were too large and had need of resoling. Grandfather Marcus was a shoemaker, but he was dead by the time I inherited the shoes, so my mother improvised by making cardboard soles and inserting them in the shoes.

Although we were in our own home, a luxury by the standards of many of our peers, we considered ourselves poor but not without sustenance. We always had enough to eat.

Vacations in the summertime became a thing of the past, and I spent my summers around our neighborhood. Once there was a day camp that I attended but that lasted just one day because I wouldn't eat what was served for lunch and the counselor tried to force the bowl of soup on me and spilled it all over me.

When my father finally found employment in Long Island City, it meant that he would rise each morning at about 5:00 a.m. My mother would rise with him to prepare his breakfast. He then walked to the subway for the trip to the job, and we would not see him until his return at about 7:00 p.m. I remember he always looked tired when he came home. He had problems with his feet, and the job called for him standing all day. When he finally arrived home, he was usually exhausted.

Then one day when I was about thirteen years old, I was preparing to go to school, and I was home alone with my mother. The doorbell rang, and when I answered it, a young man was there and informed us that there was a phone call for Mrs. Schwartz at the public phone in the candy store across the street. I went across to answer for my mother, who was busy preparing lunch for me to take to school. The caller informed me that my father had an accident at work and that he was taken to the hospital. The caller identified the hospital for me, and I returned home to tell my mother, who was, at that moment, frying an egg. We dropped everything and went off to the subway to go to the hospital. We were both in a state of shock. At the hospital, we learned from the doctor that a blade on a machine my father was operating had broken and had struck him in the eye. He was lucky to be alive, but it was unlikely that his eye could be saved. His eye was removed and ultimately replaced with an artificial glass eye. With four fingers missing from his left hand and his right eye gone, that was the end of my father's working life.

I believe he did receive some form of disability compensation. When added to the small stipend Uncle Sam Tunkel contributed for his and Raymond's room and board and the rental from the garages behind our house, we were able to almost scrape through—but not quite. My mother began taking in sewing from a small factory owned by Mr. Behar, who was willing to have her produce skirts on a piecework basis. She did this on a manual sewing machine for a while until Mr. Behar suggested that she buy an electric machine. He sold it to her and permitted her to pay it off from her earnings. Her production increased after the acquisition of the machine. My father helped her as best he could; but in the main, he was a destroyed man, feeling totally inadequate and helpless.

In June 1938, I graduated from elementary school. There was no big celebration or party. I remember going to the movies with my cousin Adele after we returned home from the graduation ceremony. I was two months short of turning thirteen, and I had been practicing for my bar mitzvah for over a year; it would take place in September. It became a dual celebration, and I recall going to the photographer to take pictures in my graduation blue blazer jacket and white trousers as well as my bar mitzvah suit.

Graduation presented a problem of choice of high school to attend in the fall. During my last semester at PS 202, Ms. Stalory, my sight conservation teacher for the past six years, was on sabbatical. She was replaced by a substitute teacher, Mrs. Bullock, with whom I had no previous relationship. There was no guidance from her on how to choose a high school. I felt that if Ms. Stalory had been there, she would have helped me make a wise decision. As it were, I made my own decision. I chose the East New York Vocational High School because I felt that I could learn about radio mechanics. I had become intrigued with the intricacies of the radio when a radio repairman had come to our house to repair our dysfunctional radio. I felt that radio mechanics would be an appropriate trade to pursue.

Most of my peers chose to attend Thomas Jefferson High School. My choice was a horrible mistake, as I soon found out. The East New York Vocational High School turned out to be a school attended by boys who were required to attend school until they were sixteen and old enough to obtain working papers, after which they would leave school and try to get a job. I attended school there for one semester, during which time I learned how to shoot dice and how to handle a lead pipe. This knowledge I acquired from my fellow students and not from the teachers. I recall that there was a class in auto body repair and one in carpentry. If there were any academic classes, the memory of them completely escaped me. I felt totally ill at ease at that school. I had become friendly with a boy whose last name was Catano. We called each other by our last names. For about a week, we were very close. Then one day, without any provocation, he approached me and hit me. I was shocked and dumbfounded, and I asked him why he did that. He responded that it was because I was Jewish. Somehow I was no more Jewish that day than I had been on previous days. I could only conclude that someone had pointed out to him the fact that I was Jewish and that being friendly with me was in some way being disloyal to his other friends.

With great difficulty, I lasted one semester, and then I transferred to Thomas Jefferson High School and enrolled in the commercial course, which was another mistake. I had absolutely no guidance. I don't know where I got the idea that I would like my education to go beyond high school. College was never encouraged at home, and there was no reason to expect that, after high school, I would do anything other than go to work. Higher education did not seem an option. If higher education had been my goal, I should have worked toward an academic rather than a commercial diploma. The commercial path deprived me of most science courses such as chemistry, biology, and mathematics.

Although I still had an interest in the radio and, ultimately, electronics, I had no idea where a commercial diploma would lead me. In retrospect, I might have saved myself a lot of time after high school making up courses in order to attend college.

My bar mitzvah, coinciding with my elementary school graduation, took precedence in the minds of my mother and father because they paid much more attention in preparing me for that than they did in preparing me for high school. For years, I attended Hebrew school at the local Talmud Torah along with many other boys in the neighborhood. I learned to read Hebrew. I learned about the Jewish holiday rituals. I heard, over and over again, the myths and stories in the Bible. Although I know how to read Hebrew, no one helped me understand what I was reading. I learned how to recite the prayers, but I never learned what they meant. I knew that one prayer was said to be thankful for the bread I ate, another for the wine I drank. There was a prayer thanking God for allowing me to awake in the morning, but the actual meaning of all the words I never knew.

In preparation for my bar mitzvah, I complained to my mother that I was not learning at the Talmud Torah. She heard my plea and paid for a man from the shul to come to teach me. Each morning, he would come to my house. My mother would place a cup of coffee before him, and he would open the sider (prayer book) and direct me to read. As I read from the sider, he read from the *Morning Forward*, a Jewish newspaper that accompanied him each morning. Sometimes I would catch him dozing as I read. Other times, I would deliberately make mistakes just to see if he was paying attention to what I was reading. He rarely corrected me. However, it was very difficult to be critical of him since his compensation was only twenty-five cents per lesson.

I complained to my mother that I really was not learning anything, pointing out to her that he read the newspaper while I labored on reading stuff that had no meaning to me. My mother heeded my concern and dispensed with the man's services. Not to be discouraged, she went about and located a new teacher, Mr. Benjamin, whom I took to immediately. He was a little man with a well-trimmed white beard, eyes that glistened, and a smile that was friendly and welcoming. He also spoke English, so it was easy to communicate with him. He proceeded to teach me grammar and vocabulary. I learned, for the first time, how to conjugate verbs. He was properly preparing me for my bar mitzvah. He taught me my Haftorah and taught me to translate it so that I could understand every word. Together, we prepared my bar mitzvah speech, which I memorized in both Yiddish and English.

More important than any of the lessons he taught me was the many conversations we shared. We spoke at great length about the miracles God had performed. I specifically recall his explanation of how God uses his concept of the hole. "Think of how the hole is used. You breathe through your nose holes, you speak and eat through your mouth hole, and at the same time, a hole in the wrong place can be your death."

Then I would question him about God. I told him that I was having a great deal of trouble believing in God as I was taught to envision him. He was wise enough to instruct me that the concept of God was one that I would have to figure out for myself. He never attempted to force the Judeo-Christian concept on me. Mr. Benjamin was paid seventy-five cents per lesson, and he was worth every penny. He was attentive during our lessons, and I loved him.

Mr. Benjamin saw me through my bar mitzvah with flying colors. I do believe I was successful in making my mother and father proud of me on that occasion. I reveled in the approval I received, and I continued to study with Mr. Benjamin after my bar mitzvah, and out of respect for him as well as my parents, I put on my tefillin (phylacteries) each morning and attended Sabbath services.

One morning, I was awaiting the arrival of Mr. Benjamin for my lesson and was disappointed to find that he did not arrive as usual. I did not understand why he had not come, so after school that afternoon, I went to his house and learned that he was sick and in bed. He asked me to come in to his bedroom, and I sat at his bedside for a while. He did not focus on his illness, but instead, we talked as if we were having our usual conversation about worldly matters. I visited him frequently during the next several weeks, but one day, I was informed that he had died in his sleep. With his death, I was left on my own to struggle with all those religious and worldly concepts that we used to share.

High school was a real struggle. I found that I had to work harder than any of my peers just to get through my daily homework. My cousin Daniel never got great grades in school, but neither did he put in much effort. He never had the mind-set to go to college, and high school was just something he had to live through and then move on to a job. My grades were not much better than his, but I worked hard to achieve just average marks. I attribute that to the failed experiment of the sight conservation experience that I was a part of at PS 202. We had been discouraged from reading any books with small print, especially if they were printed on glossy paper. As a result, I believe that I had to learn to "learn" by listening rather than by reading. That worked in elementary school, but in high school, I was forced to do my school work with the same kinds of books that I was forbidden from using previously. I had to learn to read. I could only read very slowly. It was one word at a time. Reading groups of words was difficult for me. As a result, it would take me much longer to read and absorb an assignment. Thus, while my friends had long since finished their homework and were out in the street playing, I continued to struggle to finish mine. I did not graduate high school with honors in June 1942.

THE WAR YEARS

ON SUNDAY AFTERNOON of December 7, 1941, I was busy carrying boxes of fruit and vegetables into Max's store. Max operated a "green store" on New Lots and Georgia Avenues. He used to employ some of us guys to set up the boxes of fruit and vegetables outside the market and again to carry them back in when he was ready to close the store. My friend Dave A. had the job, but sometimes he would "contract" out the task if he had something else he wanted to do. So it was that on December 7, 1941, I was busy filling in for Dave when I heard on the radio playing inside the store that Pearl Harbor had been bombed. When I finished my tasks, I ran home to find out more about what had happened. Everyone was in a state of shock and did not know what to make of it. I couldn't wait until the next day when I would be attending my history class to see what Mr. Thomason, my history teacher, had to say.

His analysis was that the country was in a state of shock as a result of this unprecedented attack. But even though we suffered severe losses, he was convinced that if we weren't defeated within six months, we would ultimately win this war. By the time I graduated in June 1942, many of my friends in the neighborhood had either gone off to the service or were about to. However, I was not yet seventeen years old in June 1942 and thus was not yet eligible for the draft. I had over a year to wait, and during that time, I had to find a job.

Going to college full time after high school graduation was not an option for me for several reasons. First, my grades were not good enough to permit me to matriculate and attend a city college without tuition. Second, even if I were able to matriculate, it was really necessary for me to start bringing home some money because the finances at home were tenuous with my mother and father trying to scrape together some dollars on my mother's piecework skirt production.

I did, however, enroll at City College for evening courses to pursue a possible degree in accounting. The college was located on Twenty-Third Street and Lexington Avenue, and my first courses consisted of business law and basic accounting theory.

I found employment with a furrier, and I spent the next few weeks soaking pelts and nailing them to boards. I never really learned the remainder of the process these pelts went through before becoming fur coats, nor was I particularly interested. I simply knew that although I did not know what I wanted to pursue in the way of a career or, more aptly, my life's work, I knew that I would not be a furrier.

As tough as things were, I left the fur trade behind me and looked for another job. I found employment with a small jewelry company in downtown Brooklyn. The name of the company was GC&G Jewelers. The *G*s stood for the two Goldberg brothers, and the *C* stood for Cohen, a brother-in-law. One Mr. Goldberg was the president of the company. I learned that he was married to an Irish woman.

His wife's sister was employed by the company, and I became friendly with her. She taught me all I ever learned about the manufacturing process that the company was involved in. She taught me to use a very primitive machine, a device into which a rubber mold that contained an impression of a ring was placed in a spring-loaded arm. Hot wax was poured into the mold through an opening on the top. The arm was then wound up like an alarm clock and quickly released, causing it to spin around, forcing the hot wax to find its way to all the crevices in the mold. When the arm stopped spinning, the mold was removed, opened, and out came a wax impression of the ring. I understand that the wax mold was then used to create another mold into which gold, silver, or platinum was cast, producing the ring from the precious metal. Two or three men sat all day long with files removing metal burrs from the rings before they were polished.

I became adept at making the wax rings and at bringing up lunch for all the people working there. After watching and working there for a while, it became apparent to me that I had no interest in becoming one of the jewelers sitting hunched over with a file in his hand, removing burrs from the rings. I had to move on.

I searched and found employment as a shipping clerk with a company that distributed tablecloths and napkins, cork place mats, and various and sundry other household items. I had absolutely no experience as a shipping clerk, but I was quick to develop the skills associated with making up cartons, placing the prepared orders in the cartons, sealing them, and preparing the proper shipping documents. I became very adept at doing these tasks. I was paid $14 per week.

The warehouse was located on Twenty-Eighth Street and Lexington Avenues, and it was very convenient to get to City College on Twenty-Third and Lexington on time for my evening classes. I remained at this job for quite a while, mostly because it was very convenient. However, I saw no future in the packaging of tablecloths.

Although we had no way of knowing how long the war would last, our country was gearing up for a protracted war. Automobile plants were being converted for the production of military vehicles, radio and electrical appliance manufacturing facilities were converted for the production of military communications equipment, apparel manufacturers were beginning to make military uniforms, and the entire nation's production capabilities were directed toward the war effort. The need for manpower—severely curtailed during the 1930s as the result of the Great Depression—suddenly exploded. People who hadn't been able to find work for years were suddenly in demand. The need for workers with particular skills became essential, and the government had to pay attention to these requirements.

One way they tackled the problem was to form the National Youth Administration (NYA). It was the function of the NYA to train volunteer young people to perform certain skills that were needed in the defense plants. They would pay the trainees $50 per month for the full extent of the training course, which lasted six months, after which they would place the trainee in a full-time job. This concept was unheard of. Until then, anyone who wanted to learn a skill would have been glad to work for nothing for the opportunity of learning the skill. It was like a dream come true for me. I chose to apply for training in an electronic course, responding to an old personal interest in radios and electronics. The school where the training took place was located at Thirty-Third Street and Lexington Avenue. School hours were from 8:00 a.m. to 2:00 p.m.

As soon as I was accepted into the program, I informed my employer that I had to leave my job because I was going to attend the NYA program. When I explained that school let out at 2:00 p.m., I was immediately offered the opportunity to work part-time from 2:30 p.m. to 5:30 p.m. I was told that I was such a good packer and shipping clerk that they did not want to lose me and that they thought I could do more work part-time than they were getting from other full-time clerks. They even increased my hourly wage, somewhat.

So it was that for the next six months, I would attend classes at the NYA, rush from Thirty-Third Street to Twenty-Eighth Street, work there until 5:30 p.m., rush to a local greasy spoon for a bacon-and-egg sandwich and a cup of coffee, rush to Twenty-Third Street to attend classes at City College, and then catch the 10:00 p.m. subway back to Brooklyn. It was a long day.

At the NYA, I learned a great deal about electronic circuits, vacuum tubes, resistors, capacitors, transformers, and a host of other electronic components that, when put together, made up electronic equipment that seemed miraculous. Radios, transmitters, and television became very intriguing to me and reawakened an interest that I first became aware of when a radio repairman came to fix our radio years earlier. We were taught to use soldering irons and all sorts of other tools that would be helpful in the manufacturing processes that we would soon be involved in after completion of our training.

My class consisted of women as well as men. One woman stood out above the others. Her name was Sylvia, and one day, at lunch, I mentioned to her that I had just seen the film *Casablanca* and that I was very impressed with it. Sylvia surprised me by commenting that she could not understand Ilsa falling in love with Rick when she had such a wonderful husband that had wonderful ideals. She left me with the impression that, for her, love was based more on one's political beliefs than on physical or chemical attraction. She was apparently not taken in by the Hollywood concept of love. Some years later, I learned that Sylvia was politically involved with left-wing causes when I ran into her at a political rally that I had, by that time, also become involved in.

After completing my training at the NYA, I was immediately hired by a very small company: Control Parts Inc. Mr. Treptau—who had been an instructor at the NYA—knew me from the school, and he hired me along with a number of other graduates from the course to work on the first contract this company had. It was a start-up company. Our work consisted of building a transmitter-receiver for the government. What made it most interesting for me was that we were involved with building the entire piece of equipment from start to finish. First, we were involved in preparing the chassis by installing the tube sockets along with all the other mounted components and then wiring the chassis, soldering all the contacts, and performing the final testing and inspection before completing the task.

I worked at Control Parts until we completed the contract. Then we were told that there were no other contracts to follow, so we were free agents to find employment elsewhere. We were also told that a company called BCG Radio had a large government contract and that they were hiring people. I quickly applied for employment and was hired as an inspector. I was paid $0.70 per hour. BCG Radio had a contract for what seemed like thousands of trans-receivers for the navy. The factory was large and broken up into many different departments. Each department was responsible for a small segment of the manufacturing process. This was my first encounter with assembly-line production. The inspection process was also broken down into sections. I was assigned a certain section of the equipment that I was to inspect and to become thoroughly familiar with. I perfected that task quickly, becoming quite adept at it and also quite bored.

I had, by this time, passed my eighteenth birthday and had registered for the draft. My brother Leonard and my cousins Raymond and Daniel were already drafted, and many of my buddies were either already in the service or about to go. Like most of us at the time, I was very anxious to go as well. When I was finally called down for my physical, I was fearful about only one problem. I was concerned that I might not be accepted because of my poor eyesight. I had heard about people being rejected because of it. I recall standing in line waiting for my turn to have my eyes tested. The eye chart was there, and I knew I would have to read it without my glasses. I also knew that I could not see the chart without my glasses, so I quickly memorized the chart while I was standing in line. When it came my turn, I was asked to remove my glasses and to proceed to read the chart. I read it from memory, only to find that they had changed the chart to an entirely different one and none of what I read made any sense. I was quickly discovered and sent home with a 4F classification. I carried that stigma throughout the war years. I still carry it to this day when people ask if I was in the service and I have to answer that I was rejected because of poor eyesight. The irony that I have never been able to live down was that my friend Joey M. had only one eye. The other one was glass. He was accepted into the service the same day I was rejected.

I was devastated by this rejection. It was a total negation of any claim I thought I had to manhood. How was I going to face anyone? When I came home, I hid in my bedroom. I cried hysterically. I wanted to see no one and would not speak to anyone. It felt like the end of the world for me. When my father came into my bedroom, I was totally ashamed. I told him that I had been rejected, and he broke out in relieved laughter. "One son in the army is enough," he said. I yelled at him for his lack of sensitivity as to how I felt, but my argument carried very little weight in overcoming his relief that he would not have to deal with another son in the service.

I returned to work at BCG Radio. I could no longer stand the boredom of my job. The factory building with its drab gray walls were depressing. Mr. Burns, the plant superintendent, had been getting on my nerves for some weeks now. He would wear gray trousers and a gray sweater, camouflage himself against the gray walls, and spy on us.

My immediate supervisor was a man named Jack. I got along well with him, as did everyone else in the department.

I approached him and asked if he could arrange a transfer for me to another department so that I could do something a little more interesting. I requested a transfer to the testing department, where I would have an opportunity to learn how to test the trans-receivers we were manufacturing. Jack approached Mr. Burns, but he turned down the request.

My department was some distance from the bathrooms. In getting to the bathroom, you had to pass a number of workstations where workers performed a number of different operations. Each time I would go to the bathroom, I would pass this man who worked at filing excess welding metal from a small box that was used as a shield in the trans-receiver. Day after day, he would stand at this station and file away the excess metal. On one occasion, I approached him and asked him if he ever got bored doing the same thing day in and day out. He looked up at me and said, "You must be a Jewish boy." I was taken aback by his remark, and I defensively replied that I was Jewish but it had nothing to do with the fact that I thought what he was doing was boring. What was really on his mind? Jewish boys won't do menial tasks? Jews think they are special and superior to others? I never pursued the conversation any further.

Working on military contracts at that time entailed a form of slavery. One could not just decide to quit one's job and go search out another without obtaining a release from the company one was working for. I understand today that the rule was intended to stabilize a labor force, but it also kept workers from seeking a job that perhaps paid a little more money.

When I was turned down for a transfer to the testing department, I requested a release from my job, but Mr. Burns refused to grant me the release. I felt trapped.

The bathroom in this terribly old building was not fit for human use. The toilet consisted of a number of individual booths, and the toilet bowls were interconnected by an open trough where water would periodically flow to wash away the waste. This interconnection permitted a wise guy to light a wad of toilet paper and float it down to the next stall where someone was on the toilet. If the prank was successful, you would suddenly hear a scream from the stall as the victim felt heat on his behind.

If you were a supervisor or other lowly official, you would be entitled to a key to another bathroom, which was cleaner and usable. My supervisor would lend me his key when I needed to use the bathroom, for which I was grateful. However, on one occasion, I happened to run into Mr. Burns in the bathroom, and he asked me what I was doing in this bathroom. I retorted, "Mr. Burns, when duty calls, I prefer to use a bathroom, not a pigsty." He reprimanded me and told me that this bathroom was off limits to me.

From that point on, I decided to embark on a campaign to get myself a release—and if not, I would make it so that I would get fired. Whenever I saw Mr. Burns propped against the gray wall spying on us, I would blurt out, "Look at that SOB spying on us." He would walk away. I slowed down in the performance of my job, and Jack would plead with me not to affect the work of the department, but I told him that I wanted out and would do almost anything to get myself fired. Finally, Mr. Burns saw the light and agreed to release me from employment.

I was fortunate enough to be able to talk myself into another job at J. H. Bunnell & Co., located a short distance from BCG Radio. The person that interviewed me had previously worked for BCG and was very sympathetic when I told him that I could not work effectively in an environment where I was being spied on. He had a similar experience, and I was hired on the spot.

My new job placed me in the inspection and test departments, which afforded me new work experience utilizing test equipment that I heretofore had no contact with. I became intrigued with the technology, and I was beginning to find some direction in the pursuit of a career in electrical engineering. To qualify for entrance in any engineering school, I first had to go back to evening school and take advanced math and science courses that I was deficient in as the result of pursuing commercial courses in high school. When I completed these studies, I enrolled at Brooklyn Polytechnic Institute.

In my spare time, my life still centered on the neighborhood. Most of my buddies were in the service, but the few that were not became more closely knit. Al Alcosser, Marty Wellin, Zwc Reibman, and I became almost inseparable. We went to parties together, joined a youth discussion club where we discussed political issues, and in the summertime, we went to camps. It was during this time that I began to become interested in political matters. Our discussion group, entitled

Current Issues Committee, brought up matters relating to topics pertinent at the time.

My social life was also enhanced by a desire to learn to play the guitar. At many of the social events I attended, there was always the singing of folk songs. People like Pete Seeger, Paul Robeson, Harry Belafonte, and Josh White became idols.

Until that time, my only exposure to musical instruments occurred when I was about twelve years old and the swing era was at its height. I was enthralled with band leaders like Glen Miller, Benny Goodman, Artie Shaw, Tommy Dorsey, and Jimmy Dorsey, among others. The idea of playing a musical instrument was totally out of reach until I saw an ad from Wurlitzer offering ten introductory clarinet lessons for five dollars. Wurlitzer would also provide a clarinet on loan. I convinced my mother to sacrifice and permit me to take the lessons. I took the lessons seriously and was beginning to play songs like "Begin the Beguine." The lessons lasted over a period of ten weeks. At their conclusion, I was faced with the necessity of purchasing a clarinet and continue with lessons that were far more expensive than ten for five dollars. The cost at the time was prohibitive, and that was the end of my musical training until I decided to learn how to play the guitar. I took lessons, purchased a guitar, and over the years, learned many folk songs, some of which I later shared with anyone who would listen. Sometimes I had captive audiences of children consisting of my own nieces, nephews, and neighbors.

I became part of a folk singing group. We called ourselves the Freedom Singers. The group was made up of Roz Kuras, my friend Victor's wife; Eddie Muse, my first African American friend; his girlfriend Estelle Fuchs; and me. Later, other people joined the group. As we became more professional, we began to entertain at schools, parties, and political rallies.

My tenure at J. H. Bunnell lasted a little over a year until their contracts were completed. They apparently were not awarded additional contracts, and as a result, many employees were laid off. It was very close to the end of the war, which may have been why they received no new contracts. In the meantime, I had to seek new employment. I found it at a company whose name escapes me. Their main function was to receive surplus military components and prepare them for resale on the commercial market. I was quickly hired, and I spent the next year or so identifying, testing, and preparing these components for shipment. I never quite knew how they were distributed. I do know that a slew of surplus dealers sprang up like mushrooms in retail stores and warehouses. One such surplus dealer was Charles Avnet. He grew his business and, together with his sons, became a very successful publicly traded company on the New York Stock Exchange.

The war ended, and those of us at home were ecstatic. We were looking forward to the return of our buddies and to the end of reports of how many of our boys were killed. We were happy to see a stop to the banners that sprung up in the windows of apartments and homes depicting that a serviceman who lived in that apartment or home would never return home alive.

I felt extremely lucky. My brother Leonard and my cousins Daniel, Raymond, and Larry had all been in the service, and they had all come back alive.

Celebrations were prevalent everywhere. Block parties could be found every single night in the neighborhood. Everyone was welcome to come join in and eat and drink. It was a wonderful time to be alive and young. Those of us that had lived through the war with a 4F status were especially glad because with our boys coming home, we would not have to feel guilty when someone would ask us why we weren't in uniform.

My social life during the war was limited to a few friends who suffered the same fate as I did. They did not qualify for the service for a variety of reasons, and we formed a bond. Al Alcosser, Martin Wellin, Zwe Reibman, and a few others comprised the nucleus of our group. We, of course, were very interested in girls; and girls were interested in us because we were the "only act in town," so to speak. I dated a number of girls during the war. The major social activity consisted of "gatherings" of boys and girls, usually at someone's home, and sometimes there would be parties at cellar clubs. At one of these gatherings, I met Teresa Meshover. She preferred to be called Teddi, and I almost forgot that her name was Teresa. She lived on Jerome Street, a short distance from Georgia Avenue. I was immediately attracted to her. She was pretty, had a beautiful smile, lovely dimples, and eyes we used to call "bedroom eyes." Besides all her attractive physical attributes, she had a charming way of being a great communicator. She was also a very good listener. We became close friends, and when the war ended, we visited one block party after another, joining in the celebrations that were prevalent all over our neighborhoods. *Teddi* became a lifelong friend.

During the war, my brother Leonard was never stationed too far from home, and he never went overseas. He met and married Cynthia Freidman, which was one of the bright events of that period. Uncle Sam Tunkel spent much of the war away from home working at shipyards out of town, so his room was empty. He had shared his room with his son Raymond in the early years, but as Raymond grew older, he went to live with his Aunt Ray Tunkel, who had become a widow when her husband, Rudolph, who was Uncle Sam Tunkel's half brother, died. Raymond was not happy living there, but he tolerated the situation. When he returned from the service, he came to live at our house. He did not remain there too long because he soon met Irene. They married and took an apartment for themselves. When Daniel came home, he too came to live at 492 Hegeman for a short time; and as soon as he was able, he rented a furnished room on Georgia Avenue.

Shortly after the end of the war, many factories temporarily shut down their facilities since they were geared up for military production, and they strove to convert their facilities for commercial products. During that transition, many jobs disappeared, and many people were left unemployed. I was one of the victims. Seeking new employment was no easy task. However, after many unsuccessful attempts, I was offered a job working for Mr. Behar, the local subcontractor who gave my mother piecework to be done at home. My job was to be at the factory before any of the workers arrived, to lubricate the sewing machines and get the work ready for the employees. The production consisted of inexpensive skirts and jackets. When I was not busy with maintenance, I was taught how to operate the machine that made button holes and the machine that blind-stitched the hems on skirts and even a little sewing. The work was boring, and I sometimes wondered how people could continue to come to work day after day. I knew that people had to earn a living, and that was the obvious motivation that kept them going.

With my brother Leonard home and married, he had to find a way to earn a living. We talked about going into business and becoming a subcontractor like Mr. Behar. We went around and appraised the possible acquisition of sewing machines and other necessary equipment to start up a sewing operation. In addition to the little experience I had acquired working for Mr. Behar, Leonard had a lot more experience acquired during his years in the service, where he supervised the repair and alteration of the soldiers' uniforms and other wearing apparel.

We searched around for a loft where we could set up our operation, but we never got far enough to consider where we would obtain work. One day, Leonard came to me feeling very guilty because he was offered an opportunity to become partners with Cynthia's uncle Paul. Paul had experience in the dry-cleaning business, and he wanted to buy a business and build it up. He offered Leonard the opportunity to become his partner. Leonard felt bad because he thought he was deserting me and our dream to become partners in a business. I tried to console him, telling him that his decision to go with Paul was the correct one for him and not to worry about me.

POSTWAR ADVENTURES

AT THIS POINT, I must introduce another part of our family not heretofore mentioned. My father Sam's side of the family was quite small compared to my mother's side, the Marcus Siegel side. Sam had a cousin named Sadie. I'm not certain whether Sadie's mom or dad was the blood relative. Sadie was married to Sam Hirsh (yet another Sam in my life). They had two children; the older girl was named Ruth, and the younger was named Shirley. Sam earned his living as a waiter and did so for many years. Ruth married a very handsome man named Peppino (nicknamed Pep) DeLuca around 1940. Pep's father owned an Italian food market, and Pep cut his teeth on the retail business working in his father's store. Pep and Ruth were very adventurous, and shortly after they married, they decided to move to Hollywood, California, where they opened the first Italian restaurant in Hollywood. They named it Pep's Vesuvio, and it was an instant success. It became the "in" place for the Hollywood bigwigs.

Shortly after Ruth and Pep married, Shirley met and married Ephraim Horowitz. Ephraim worked as a photographer and was quite good at it. Following in her sister and brother-in-law's footsteps, Shirley and Ephraim migrated to Hollywood, where Ephraim was successful in becoming employed by Technicolor, which was just coming into its own in the mid-forties.

Sam and Sadie Hirsch followed shortly thereafter, and Sam went to work as the headwaiter at Pep's Vesuvio. The restaurant continued to prosper. Pep was a charming, good-looking man, and success went to his head. While Ruth handled the business aspects of the restaurant, Pep developed powerful ambitions to become a movie star. A film was being made on the life of Rudolph Valentino. The year was 1946 or 1947.

Pep's success as a restaurateur led him to open an even fancier Italian restaurant; but unfortunately, it was on Ruth's shoulders that the burden had fallen since Pep had become too enamored with his becoming part of the Hollywood scene. Separately, Ruth and Pep returned to New York—he to his father's grocery business and she to setting up an employment agency.

Shirley and Ephraim remained out West for a few more years, but they also returned; and Ephraim eventually purchased a meat delivery business that catered to restaurants.

Many people from all over the country migrated to California after World War II. Some went to seek employment opportunities. Some went to escape the raw winters of the northeast, while others went for adventure.

Nathan and Rifka Rosner were two brave souls that came to this country from Romania, just as the entire Marcus Siegel family did. Like many Jews, they came seeking better economic opportunities and to escape the severe anti-Semitism they experienced in Romania. During World War II, Nathan worked in the needle trades, producing army uniforms and other military ware. Now that the war was over, he—like many garment workers—was laid off. Employment in New York was hard to find, and Nathan looked toward Los Angeles, where small clothing factories were opening. He and Rifka made the move. They rented an extremely modest house in Boyle Heights, a low- to middle-class area of Los Angeles, and Nathan went to work for one of these small clothing contractors doing "piecework," just as my mother did for Mr. Behar. His earnings were modest, but so were his living expenses. Nathan and Rifka loved California. They loved the weather and the slower lifestyle, and they worked very hard at encouraging their old friends to come to the West Coast. They were successful in convincing Sam and Dora Alpert to allow Adele, their daughter, to go out for a visit and serve as an advanced guard to look the situation over. Nathan and Rifka offered to have Adele stay with them, and they would look after her while she was out there. Adele was a recent recipient of a "Dear John" letter from a young man she had been seeing before he was drafted into the service. Throughout the war, Adele was convinced that when the young man returned, they would get married. Just as the war was ending, Adele received fewer and more infrequent letters from him until, finally, he informed her that he was sorry, but he had to marry a girl whom he had made pregnant.

In Adele's time of grief, she welcomed the opportunity to make some changes in her life, and she anxiously looked forward to the opportunity to go out to California. When Adele told me that she was going to California, I thought that it would be an excellent idea for me to do the same. After all, I had no steady job. The idea of starting a business with Leonard was dead, and I was pretty anxious to have a change of environment. When I told Adele that I might be interested in going to California, Nathan and Rifka immediately approved of the idea because my going may be the prerequisite for my parents considering making the move also. I was offered the opportunity to stay with Nathan and Rifka. They only had one spare room, and that was for Adele; however, their little house had an unfinished attic that could be improvised as a bedroom.

The idea of making the move was very exciting to me, and I looked forward to it with great anticipation along with much fantasy. Perhaps I could walk down the streets of Hollywood and be picked up by a talent scout. I would fantasize that I was "strictly Hollywood material." I would become famous and rich, and then I would bring out my mother and father to live in California. Perhaps, after sowing my wild oats, I might even go back to New York and ask Teddi to marry me. Our relationship never ever approached that stage, but I certainly had feelings for her. But first, I would have to become successful.

It took some convincing to get my parents to agree to let me go, but ultimately, they did.

Adele had already made train reservations on the same train as Rifka, who happened to be visiting in New York at that time. They would go to Chicago and there change trains for the *El Capitan*, which would go directly to Los Angeles. I could not make reservations on the same train as they took to Chicago, but I was able to reserve a seat on the *El Capitan*. We agreed that we would meet in Chicago and go the rest of the trip together.

The train trip was magnificent and awe-inspiring to a young man that had never ventured outside of New York or New Jersey. Crossing the Rockies on what appeared to be very narrow tracks with no railings to protect us from the deep ravines we were traveling alongside still gives me chills whenever I think about it.

I was very excited about the new adventures I anticipated having. When we arrived at Union Station in Los Angeles, Nathan Rosner met us and escorted us to their modest house on Winter Street, in the Boyle Heights section. Boyle Heights had been a mostly Jewish neighborhood, but by the time we arrived, it was rapidly becoming home to many Mexican families. Adele and I were introduced to the Jewish center, where we quickly made many friends. It was there that Adele met her future husband, Leon Gurnick. I met many young adults, both guys and gals. They were mostly a fun group, and I spent the remainder of the summer enjoying a wonderful social environment. During that time, I attempted to find work. I was willing to try anything and I did. For a week or so, I became a grease monkey at the local gas station. I would pump gas, change oil, and grease autos. When I found that I wasn't too happy doing that, I found a job as a shipping clerk at a distributor of display products, such as manikins and the like.

As summer began to wane, I heard about a hot dog stand that was for sale. Nathan was interested in becoming a partner if we both purchased the stand. He was working, but Rifka would work the stand with me, and he would come in after he completed his day's work in the garment center. The stand was called Hot Diggety Dog and was owned by a woman who operated it herself. The stand was located in one corner of a large lot that housed a gas station on First and State Streets. It was a rather nice structure with five stools outside. The food consisted of hot dogs, hamburgers, tamales, coffee, donuts, and bottled soda. In addition, other miscellaneous things like candy bars and cigarettes were for sale. Across the street from the hot dog stand, there was Pontrelli's Ballroom, where on Friday and Saturday nights, Mr. Pontrelli ran dances. The clientele were mainly young Mexican men and women.

Neither Nathan nor I had any experience in operating a food-dispensing business, but we were gung ho on buying the business. We each invested $2,000. I had to borrow my share from Uncle Harry, who, during the war, was able to accumulate some savings.

I learned a lot about operating the stand, but I was very unhappy and realized that I had made a mistake. I found that I worked many hours and especially at night since we found that the mainstay of the business were the dances on Friday and Saturday nights. This cut deeply into my social life. The stand did not enjoy much of a clientele except on Friday and Saturday nights, and we did not have any ideas on how to grow the business.

During the time we operated the stand, Adele and Leon's courtship had blossomed into a real love affair, and they decided to get married. They returned to New York for the wedding, and I felt deprived because I couldn't attend the wedding. I felt trapped. On top of that, the location of the stand was in a rather rough neighborhood, and one night when I was alone and about to close, I was confronted by two men and robbed of the meager take of the day.

Nathan and I were unhappy with our investment, and I knew that we would never recoup the purchase price. I was willing to take my loss to get out and go on with my life. It was about this time that I heard that my father had become very ill, and it was questionable as to how long he would live. I knew that I had to return home without coming close to achieving my fantasies of becoming a movie star or even a successful businessman. Just as Pep's dream went up in smoke, so did mine. Nathan and I agreed that we should sell the hot dog stand so that I could go home. We found a purchaser who owned another stand in the neighborhood. We swallowed hard and took our loss.

As I was preparing to return to New York, I was having breakfast in a local cafeteria where I saw a sign advertising that a man and his wife were seeking companions to help share the driving of their car. They were returning to Pittsburgh, Pennsylvania, and they were looking for two additional drivers to share the driving and the cost of gas. I immediately called them, as did another young man named Sam, and the deal was struck. We would leave for Pittsburgh in a couple of days.

During my time in California, my mother and sister came to visit me, but my father was not well enough to make the trip. I remember how I enthusiastically told them how great it was to live in California and how much I wished that they were all out here with me. When I left for home, I said my goodbyes to my cousin Adele, her parents, the Rosners, and the many friends I made. I promised that I would return. I could not conceive that I would not.

The journey home was very exciting. It took us about ten days to cross the country, and we made it a real sightseeing trip, visiting the Grand Canyon, the Grand Tetons, Yellowstone National Park, the Painted Desert, and places I had heard about but had never seen.

When we arrived in Pittsburgh, the couple dropped us at the bus station. We said our goodbyes and purchased tickets to New York. The trip was uneventful since I have no recollection of it. I do, however, remember the subway trip home to Brooklyn. It was stifling hot and crowded, and I realized how little I missed New York during the year and a half I had been away.

I had not seen my father for almost eighteen months during my sojourn to California, and during that time, he had deteriorated quite noticeably. I knew that I had returned to await his demise. As it turned out, it didn't happen quickly. I had to find something to do while waiting. During the period of my absence, the electronics industry converted from a wartime economy to the vast potential of commercial television. Electrical appliances that were not available during the war were in great demand, and a profusion of toasters, broilers, radios, record players, tape and wire recorders, and television sets flooded the market. I found employment as a technician with a company called Electronic Instrument Co. Inc. (EICO), a small manufacturer of electronic test equipment. There I met and admired a young man, Bert Miller, who was chief engineer. I was led to believe that he was responsible for the development of the EICO product line, which consisted of such instruments as power supplies, signal generators, tube testers, oscilloscopes, and a host of other products. EICO sold these instruments to distributors of electronic equipment in both completed form and in kits.

I developed a friendship with Bert and, initially, learned from him. In the evening, I attended the City College of New York, where I resumed taking engineering courses. The City College was and still is located at 139th Street and Convent Avenue in Manhattan. EICO was located in Brooklyn, and it was about an hour-long subway ride to get to the school. I did this three nights a week.

Coming home on the subway one night, I met Victor Kuras, whom I immediately recognized, although I had not seen him in more than ten years. Victor and I had both been Boy Scouts in Troop 53. We had enjoyed a nice relationship. We renewed our old friendship. I had also begun renewing other old acquaintances and visited friends. I contacted Teddi, hoping to renew our friendship; however, things had changed during my absence. Teddi had become engaged to a very nice guy, Paul Mozlin. And of course, we could remain friends, but our friendship would now have to include Paul. I wasn't aware of the devastating effect the news of their plans to marry would have on me. I was not ready to make a commitment to marriage, nor did I have any reason to believe that Teddi had any desire to have a relationship with me on any level other than just friendship. It wasn't for some years that I felt ready to make a marital commitment. I silently suffered as Teddi and Paul married, and then I moved on with my life.

I reconnected with old friends in our discussion group and found that the group had moved from discussion to political action. Its name had changed to Young Progressives of America, and it was actively supporting the candidacy of Henry Wallace in the 1948 presidential elections. There was great disillusionment with Harry Truman after years with Franklin Roosevelt, and the group was dedicated to supporting Wallace, a much more colorful candidate. I was in full agreement with the group's aims and took an active role in campaigning for Wallace's candidacy.

Between my job, school, political activity, and chores at home, I had become very involved with life in New York. Returning to California faded into the background. And when my father died in March 1948, when I probably could have gone back, I found that I had become too enmeshed in my active life in New York.

When I returned from California, I found that things had also changed radically at 492 Hegeman Avenue. The four bedrooms in the house were all occupied. My mother and father continued to occupy their room. Sam Tunkel—who, during the war, sometimes lived and worked out of town—was now back in his old room. My old room was now occupied by Uncle Harry Schwartz, who had become widowed while I was in California, when his wife, Rae Kaplan Schwartz, died. My sister Beatrice occupied her old bedroom, the smallest of the four rooms. There was no place for me except to sleep on a folding bed, which was set up in the dining room. I now experienced the sleeping arrangements that my cousin Daniel had lived with the better part of his growing-up years.

Rumor had it that my mother was attracted to Sam Tunkel long ago, but he courted and eventually married her younger sister, Lena. Now, thirty-some odd years later, they married. I don't know whether it was a "love marriage" or a marriage of convenience, but throughout Sam Tunkel's widower years, he spent almost all of his spare time playing cards with his cronies. After the marriage, Sam Tunkel gave up playing cards and became very attentive to my mother.

In 1951, my sister Beatrice was introduced to Joe Katz, a Polish immigrant who had lost his entire family, including his wife and children, in the Holocaust. They carried on a brief courtship and then married. In 1954, Beatrice gave birth to her only child, Susan, who had become the apple of her father's and mother's eyes.

They lived in a rented apartment on Hegeman Avenue until 1959, when they bought a house on Georgia Avenue. The neighborhood was in the throes of drastic changes. Until now, the houses on the street were almost exclusively occupied by white Jewish people. Then a number of houses were sold to African-Americans, and the local real estate agents were pressuring the people on the block to sell. For a while, the people resisted through a block association. They had agreed that they would not give in. But eventually, they were unsuccessful; and little by little, the block became almost exclusively African-American. My sister and her husband, Joe, held out until 1964. They sold their house and purchased a two-family home in Flushing.

In 1960, Sam Tunkel suffered a fatal heart attack after being married to my mother for ten years, making her a widow for a second time. She continued to live in the family house along with my father's brother Harry Schwartz and my cousin Bessy Alpert, whose parents had relocated to Los Angeles. Bessy Alpert never married.

My mother sold the family home at 492 Hegeman Avenue shortly thereafter, and when Beatrice and Joe Katz moved to Flushing, my mother moved into their house. Bessy Alpert moved to California to be with her sister Adele. Uncle Harry Schwartz moved to a furnished room on Alabama Avenue, where he lived until his death in 1962.

My sister and my mother were always very close. In fact, I believe they enjoyed a symbiotic relationship. They were almost always mutually dependent on each other. They all occupied that Flushing house until around 1982, when Beatrice and Joe decided to relocate to Florida. My mother went along and lived with them.

I terminated my employment at EICO when I was able to find other employment with the Munston Manufacturing Corp., where I was hired as a technician. Working there gave me the opportunity to further my electronic experience. I was introduced to many manufacturing processes that would serve me well later. Munston manufactured power transformers, a vital component used in most electronic devices at the time. I became quite adept at making sample transformers for our customers. I was paid $44 per week, and I used most of the money to repay my loan to Uncle Harry. After selling the hot dog stand, I paid him back all of the proceeds I received from the sale, but it was not enough to repay the entire loan. Now I was repaying him the balance still owed.

Although I enjoyed the work at Munston, I was hearing stories about how much my friend Al Alcosser was earning as a salesman for a sweater manufacturer. Some of my friends were working at jobs that paid more than I made. I felt the necessity to move on. I found a job at a small company named XYZ Coil Co. They were in the business of manufacturing coils and transformers for the emerging television industry. They also manufactured coils and transformers for companies that sold kits, or "do it yourself" electronic test equipment. At that time, many private schools came into existence to train young people in the fields of radio and television repair, and these schools required products from coil winders. The company was also in the business of bidding on small government contracts to provide spare parts to the Signal Corps and the US Navy for equipment that they had in the field.

 Charles Levine and Donald Edelberg owned the company. Charles was more involved in sales and procurement of contracts. Donald was the inside man and was responsible for the shop. The company was divided into two departments: commercial and military. The commercial department was headed by Joseph Rubenfeld. He was a survivor of Auschwitz and spoke little English. He came to the company because he was in some way related to Donald and learned his job from the ground up. They were looking for a qualified technician who could run their military department, which required a little more electronic knowledge. Apparently, I was instrumental in convincing them that I was up to the task. The salary being offered me was $60 per week. I accepted the position and then went back to Mr. Edelston of Munston and informed him that I was leaving and gave him two weeks' notice. He asked me what it would take to make me stay, and when I told him how much I was going to receive on my new job, he replied, "That's a substantial increase. I can't match that." Two weeks later, we parted company on friendly terms.

 I went to work for XYZ Coil Co., and in short order, I was able to get the department functioning well. Within a few weeks, after evaluating the backlog of orders, I informed Donald (to whom I reported directly) that I could use several more people if we were going to be able to produce the work on a timely basis. He was very cooperative, and shortly thereafter, I was busy training others to do the work.

Producing components for the military was different in that we were confronted with requirements to meet military specifications. The component parts all had to conform to certain specifications. I had to become familiar with them. I was also responsible for inspecting all purchased material that was allocated for the manufacture of military contracts. In the performance of these duties, I met with Julius Rosenberg, who was one of our vendors. Apparently, Charles knew Julius Rosenberg from when they were both engineering students at City College of New York. At the time I became acquainted with Julius, he had been dismissed from his position with the government and had set up a small machine shop on the Lower East Side of New York in partnership with his brother-in-law, David Greenglass. Some of the work we subcontracted out was the machining of certain coil forms. Julius was given the contract to manufacture these coil forms, and in the process, we had discussions about the specifications under which they were to be manufactured. Neither Charles nor I could have predicted what was going to happen to Julius and his wife, Ethel, not too long after our contact with him.

In June 1950, Julius and his wife, Ethel, were arrested on suspicion of committing espionage. They were accused of passing secret information about the atomic bomb to the USSR. The Rosenbergs maintained their innocence throughout the trial and various appeals; however, they were executed by electric chair in June 1953.

While working at XYZ Coil Co., Joe Rubenfeld and I became good friends. He had been in America a short time, but he was fast becoming "Americanized." Joe lost all of his immediate family in the Holocaust. His grandfather, who was already here, helped Joe come to America. Joe lived with his grandfather in Williamsburg. His family was Orthodox, and in the main, Joe followed the tradition. However, he did make many experimental inroads in his new environment. Joe did work on the Sabbath when it was necessary. He did not abide by the standards of "kashrut" and ate pork products—at least in the early years. I never knew whether his family knew of his "transgressions."

Outside of my job, I continued to participate in political activity. I was becoming more and more identified with working people. I found an outlet in the American Labor Party. There I met many people with common interests and beliefs. I found myself drawn to people who were politically active. My circle of friends shifted away from my old neighborhood buddies. I also began to feel alienated from my family. The more convinced I became that Henry Wallace should be supported, the more alienated we became. My family was dutifully dedicated to the Democratic Party, being lifelong supporters of Franklin Roosevelt, as was I. I could tolerate the difference of opinion on whether to support Harry Truman or not, but what persistently got to me was that they were taken in by the red-baiting and the branding of Wallace as a Communist.

My social life centered on parties and socials where the attendees were all politically motivated, and I found myself rejecting women who were not "progressive." One of the young women I met and dated was Beverly Watnick. I felt very comfortable with her. She was a schoolteacher—I always respected teaching as a profession. I viewed her as someone who shared many of my political beliefs, and I considered her pretty, perky, and unconventional. I found these traits very appealing. There were other young women, but my friendship with Beverly was a lasting one.

The summer of 1949 was particularly memorable because my friends and I spent a lot of time at progressive vacation resorts. A particular favorite was Camp ABC because the environment was friendly, the food was adequate, and although the accommodations were rustic, it was compensated for by the entertainment that was available. The summer was coming to an end, and we heard about an outdoor concert that Paul Robeson was giving in Peeksville, New York, on August 27, 1949; but the concert had been disrupted by riled-up anti-communist mobs. A subsequent concert had been organized and was going to take place on September 4, 1949. With all the publicity generated, thousands of people made it their business to attend in order to protest the opposition to the concert.

The site was a natural amphitheater with a wooden ridge surrounding sloping hills leading down to a large tree where the stage was constructed. A prominent union took the lead in organizing the security for the concert. A civilian army had been formed. When the police showed up later in the day, there was a confrontation, and the police were asked to leave—which, by law, they were required to do since this was a private event on private property. Two thousand men circled the concert area and quite literally stood shoulder to shoulder. Fifteen men were chosen to guard Paul Robeson on the stage. Other teams patrolled the hills and found two sniper nests. The men in them had rifles with telescopic sights. The rifles were destroyed, and the men were roughed up and escorted from the grounds. Police helicopters flying overhead made it difficult to hear the music. State troopers and other police were stationed at intervals along the road. Entry to the grounds was along a narrow local road. Counter demonstrators marched on the same road at the same time, going in the opposite direction. There were frequent verbal assaults and exchanges, but the organized presence of concert guards wearing union and military insignia caused an uneasy standoff.

I attended the concert with several friends. We were at Camp ABC, and we left there to attend the concert even though we hadn't attended the first one. There was no physical violence during the concert. It was when the concert was over that the violence erupted. As we, along with other concertgoers, left the grounds, we were all directed by state police the same way down a small narrow road. There were people along the road waiting with piles of rocks that they threw at each car as we exited. We were forced to leave very slowly, which made us easy targets. Several windows in the car we were in were smashed, and we were showered with glass. It was a never-to-be forgotten experience. I became more convinced than ever of my being on the correct side politically.

Meanwhile, my job at XYZ Coil Co. progressed to the point where I was given an increase in salary without asking for it. I was very pleased with that. However, at the same time, I felt disloyal. There was a movement to organize the workers into a trade union, and while I was supposed to be on the side of management, I felt loyalty to the workers. I did not hide my sympathies from my employer. Shortly after the shop became unionized, I was called into Charles Levine's office and accused of agitating for the union and was summarily fired. This occurred just weeks after receiving my salary increase.

I was sorry to lose my job. It had been the best job I had ever had. Although I had a boss to answer to, I felt that he had enough confidence in me to permit me a large degree of autonomy in the performance of my duties. It was also a job that paid me more money than any I had previously had. In addition, it was a job that I held long enough to earn a paid vacation. At none of my previous jobs did I stay long enough to earn a paid vacation.

Whether my reputation preceded me, I do not know. I applied for employment at several places, but I found that I was not acceptable. I did offer my last employer as a reference, which may have been very naive of me and the reason for my not being hired. I applied for unemployment insurance and continued to seek employment.

Some weeks after my termination of employment, I received a phone call from Joe Rubenfeld. He asked whether I would be interested in going into business with him. His idea was that we would set up a company and do what XYZ Coil Co. was doing. Not having a boss to answer to appealed to me. Besides, I wasn't sure how easy it would be for me to obtain a job with the negative recommendations I would receive from my previous employer. I agreed to think about it.

In a few days, I called Joe and told him that I was willing to go into business with him. If I knew then what I subsequently learned, I probably would have come to a different conclusion. I was not aware of the problems we would encounter and would have to overcome.

Our first step was to draw up a partnership agreement. I only knew one attorney at the time—Martin Friedman, my brother Leonard's father-in-law. I called him and asked whether he could write up a simple partnership agreement. He agreed to do so, and we encountered our first expense in going into business. Joe and I agreed that we would each invest $3,000. We had no idea how much money we would need to get started, but that seemed like a good number to start with.

By this time, I had completely repaid Uncle Harry, and now I would have to borrow the $3,000 because I did not have a penny to my name. Fortunately, my sister Beatrice, who had been working for quite a few years, was willing to lend me the money. I had no idea when I would be able to repay her, but she had confidence in me and asked for no definitive date for the repayment. Joe, I believe, borrowed the money from either his grandfather or his uncle, and together, we pooled our resources and opened up a bank account.

We had decided that the name of our company would be American Coil Company. We searched the real estate section of the newspaper and found a number of lofts for rent. We finally settled on what had once been a railroad flat at 106-108 Broadway in the Williamsburg section of Brooklyn, a short walk from where Joe lived and a longer train ride from where I lived. The rental was $50 per month.

The loft was on the second floor of a two-story building. Beneath us was a company that did metal plating. We did the usual necessary tasks like apply for telephone service, set up gas and electric accounts, and went about purchasing lumber and electrical supplies in order to build workbenches. Joe, being the better carpenter, busied himself building the workbenches. I was occupied with arranging the purchase of our first coil-winding machine and necessary test equipment without which we could not function. I also started to call a number of companies that were doing business with XYZ coil winders and asked them if we could have an opportunity to bid on their work. I found that loyalty was not a virtue, but lower prices were.

My first appointment was with a company whose name I remember as Cascade Inc. Cascade was an exporter of electronic kits. I knew the kind of coils he used, and I asked for an appointment to come to see him and quote on his requirements. He was receptive, and I visited him with quotations, which he compared with the prices he was currently paying. As soon as he made the comparison, he willingly placed an order with me. I took the order and, in a state of elation, returned to our shop to tell Joe the good news.

After a short mutual congratulatory session, reality set in. First, we had to order materials. This entailed contacting at least seven different vendors. It also entailed acquiring a number of machines to perform certain operations. We found that, most often, these material purchases would take from two to three weeks for delivery. In addition, we had no credit with these companies, and we were forced to pay in advance for the materials or have them come in COD. The biggest problem of all was the customer's delivery requirements. We could not wait this long for the receipt of the material and have enough days to perform the labor. It was at this time that we realized that our four hands were insufficient to perform all the hours of labor required to meet our delivery commitments.

It became apparent that as much as we were reluctant to becoming employers of people, we would have to do that. This entailed an educational process that we were entirely unprepared for. My limited knowledge of bookkeeping permitted me to purchase the proper ledgers to set up a simple accounting system. Employing people entailed arranging for unemployment insurance and Social Security matters—none of which we had the slightest idea on how to handle. We hired an accountant, who turned out to know very little about accounting but was able to handle the other requirements for operating as employers.

Our next major shock came when we found that we had underestimated the cost of producing the coils for our very first contract. We understood little about overhead costs. We had no knowledge yet as to what comprised overhead and that it was necessary to calculate a profit if we were to keep our heads above water. We, along with an inexperienced crew, did manage to complete that first contract. We licked our wounds, found that our bank account was sorely diminished, and moved on. We corrected our estimating methods and discovered that we could still be competitive and even generate a very small profit, and gradually, we recouped our losses and closed out our first year with a $3,000 profit. Our inexperienced accountant prepared our tax return, and we learned that we had to pay $1,000 in income taxes. Any accountant with any knowledge would have informed us that we should adjust our inventory downward to eliminate the profit in this first year, when cash was at a premium. He did not remain our accountant for very long. We retained a new accountant who was much more knowledgeable, and he set us straight on how to proceed.

American Coil Company came into existence in 1950, and after our first year, Joe and I were able to draw a salary of $50 per week. By 1952, we had retained a sales representative. He operated on a 5% commission, and he began to bring in work. We were now adjusted to the idea that we could not operate without a staff. I still had problems with the idea of being an employer of labor, and I soothed my conscience by contacting the United Electrical Workers Union, the same union that organized XYZ Coil Co. and signed a contract. I felt a little better about the new arrangement.

American Coil achieved a minor degree of acceptance from companies around the New York area, and we began to receive repeat orders from some customers. Although we did not have any standard products and manufactured only to customer specifications, we began to feel secure enough to invest in an inventory of component parts that we found were used by multiple customers. We found it necessary to maintain an inventory of magnet wire of various sizes and insulations. We stored the wire in one room that adjoined the room we set up as our office. The other inventory was stored on metal shelving in another area of the shop.

Many of the products we were asked to manufacture required machining capability. Joe had some basic knowledge of machining and was able to handle some of our requirements; however, there were times when our needs exceeded his ability. It was at this time that I called on the assistance of my friend Victor Kuras, who was employed as a machinist. He performed many machining tasks for us on a part-time basis. After a while, the workload became such that it was not possible for him to perform them in his spare time. I suggested to Victor that he leave his job and start his own machine shop. We could initially give him enough work to at least earn him the same amount of money that he was earning working for the company where he was employed. Victor had some machine shop equipment that he kept in the basement of his parents' home, which he moved into our facility. He agreed with the partnership arrangement we worked out, and the arrangement worked very well for some time.

Our new accountant, Arthur Zimmerman, recommended we incorporate instead of remaining a partnership. He educated us in the risks we were taking. As a company, Joe and I, as partners, were responsible for all liabilities incurred by the company. Were we to incorporate, we would become employees of the corporation—and hence, we would not be personally liable. We thought it was a good idea, and we asked Martin Friedman to set up our new corporation. There was one hitch. We were unable to incorporate under the name American Coil Company Inc. because the name had already been incorporated by others. We were able to incorporate under the name Automatic Coil Co. Inc.

Shortly after accomplishing this task, we were shocked to hear that Joe received a call from his draft board. We were in the middle of the Korean conflict, and Joe was drafted after not being successful in getting a deferment. So Joe went off to war, leaving me to operate the company on my own. During his absence, sales and earnings continued to grow. Joe and I agreed that I should take an increase in salary to $75 per week. Joe was drawing no money from the company during his term in the service.

One day, as I was sitting in my office talking on the telephone, I chanced to glance into the room where we stored our wire inventory. There were thousands of pounds of wire concentrated in that small room, and I noticed that the floor was beginning to buckle, and the floor and the wall were separating. Beneath that floor sat tanks of acid that our downstairs neighbor used in the metal-plating process. All I could visualize at that moment was a collapse while someone was walking through that room and ending up in a tank of sulfuric acid. I immediately ordered a group of our workers to empty out the room and to spread out the wire reels throughout the shop. That being done, I called our landlord and informed him that I was being forced to move because of the dangerous conditions. Since we were operating on a month-to-month basis, there was no lease to worry about.

I immediately searched out and found another location a short distance from the old shop. This location at 299 Wallabout Street was on the third floor of an old building. Aside from the steps, there was an elevator that was little more than a dumbwaiter about 9 square feet in area. Most of our machinery had to be carried up the stairs because it wouldn't fit in the elevator.

I was young, and no obstacle seemed too forbidding. With the help of Victor and other employees, we were set up and operating in our new location within one week. All our employees stayed with us despite the fact that now they had to walk up to the third floor if they were hesitant about using the elevator, which was capable of transporting just two people at a time.

JULIA

I WAS STILL LIVING at home and sleeping on a folding bed in our dining room. Not only was I uncomfortable with the arrangement, I also felt that it infringed on my social life. In addition, I was feeling somewhat estranged from my family because we did not see eye to eye politically. I felt it was time for me to assert my independence and move into my own apartment. My mother viewed this as a rejection of her. It was not "nice" for a young man to leave his mother's home and move into his own apartment while unmarried. Times were changing, but Mom was not ready to accept the change. The fact that my brother Leonard, before being drafted into the army, lived in a rooming house in Washington, DC, away from the family home and the fact that I lived away from the family home when I lived in California did not appear pertinent. I was in New York and unmarried, and my mother did not approve. I was also twenty-six years old, so my mother knew she was unable to stop me from moving.

Much of my social and political life was shared by my friend Victor. We got along very well. I thought I would explore the idea of sharing an apartment. Victor was still living at home with his mother. When I raised the subject, he took to it enthusiastically. His mother, like mine, also disapproved of his moving out; but that did not deter him.

We began to search for an apartment, which we ultimately found at 5 Debevoise Street, a stone's throw from where we worked. It was a cold-water railroad flat on the fourth floor of a building near the BMT elevated line in Williamsburg. We were very enthusiastic about the place. The apartment was kept warm by gas heaters. It provided us with a kitchen, a living room, a bathroom, and a bedroom for each of us. We searched for secondhand furniture, furnished the apartment adequately, and began to exert our independent living without any assistance from others. Victor and I lived together for many months in relative tranquility. Occasionally, we would have a problem with food choices, but somehow we worked them out. We continued to work together at Automatic Coil Co. Inc., and the business continued to grow.

Attending to the business took much more time than a normal eight-hour day. I found that I did not have enough time to do justice to my studies, and I was forced to discontinue evening college classes. Summers offered us the opportunity to pursue a social life. We would spend weekends at Camp Midvale in New Jersey. There we would meet young women and men with similar political leanings as our own. Camp Midvale was more commonly known as Nature Friends. It was a collection of small independently owned houses and a larger number of cabins used for temporary vacationers. There was a small dining room, and the food served was plain and modest, although usually wholesome. Camp Midvale boasted a beautiful swimming pool in natural surroundings. It was fed by a continuous stream of fresh water, eliminating the need for an artificial filtration system. The water was always cool and refreshing. Campers sat around the pool, leisurely enjoying the outdoors. Playing guitars and singing folk songs was a common activity around the pool.

The camp also ran a nursery school for small children, and I was impressed with the arts and crafts the children produced on what I knew was a very limited budget for art supplies. Each evening, there would be another activity for the adults, such as folk dancing, concerts, or some form of theatrical endeavor. It made for relaxing recreation for me and also gave direction to my life.

One day, I was relaxing near the pool and I saw a small child, about four or five years old, running down the path toward the pool. She ran on tiptoe with a determination that appeared to reflect urgency. She was petite and pretty. I called to her and asked her why she was running in such a hurry.

"I'm not in a hurry. This is how I always walk," she responded with a sweet smile.

"What's your name," I asked.

"My name is Chippy. What's yours?" she asked.

I told her my name was Sol. I thought my name was fairly common, but her name certainly was not. I did not verbalize my observation. Instead, I asked her about herself. She was not the least bit shy in sharing that information with me. She told me that she was spending the entire summer here because her mother was the nursery schoolteacher in camp. They lived in New York when she was not at camp with her mother. She told me about all her friends here in camp and about the day-care school she attended at home. I told her that I was relatively new to Camp Midvale and asked if she would show me around. Chippy became my guide, pointing out the various houses where people she knew lived, and there were few houses she was not familiar with. She showed me the dormitory where people slept. We toured the dining room, and then she took me to the arts and crafts shed, where she introduced me to her mother, Julia Minter. It was obvious from whom Chippy derived her sweet smile. The three of us talked at great length, and I quickly felt a camaraderie with Julia and a warmth from Chippy that immediately won me over. When Chippy and I left the arts and crafts shed, leaving Julia with her class, Chippy now grasped my hand to lead me to other parts of the camp.

That summer, I spent a great many of my weekends at camp. Julia and I became close, as did Chippy and I. I learned that Julia was separated from her husband, who was a union organizer. Their relationship had been deteriorating for a long time.

I learned that Chippy had been born prematurely, weighing in at just over two pounds. Julia worked as a teacher at a local day-care center, which paid poorly. The family lived on E. Seventh Street in Manhattan, in a third-floor brownstone.

Julia and I began to date more seriously—as did Victor, who had met Roz Golub. Their relationship moved along more quickly, and they decided to get married. The marriage took place at the home of Roz's brother, Lenny Golub, who lived in a suburban house with a large backyard. It was the first wedding I ever attended that took place outdoors. I was Victor's best man. After the wedding, Victor, Roz, and I went to Camp ABC, where they spent their honeymoon night. The following day, they left for some place unremembered by me to spend the rest of their honeymoon.

When they returned, the three of us shared the apartment at 5 Debevoise Street until Victor and Roz found an apartment on Washington Street in Brooklyn, and I was then left with the task of finding someone to share the apartment with and to help with the expenses. By coincidence, an acquaintance of mine, Ed Levin, was looking for a place to live. He became my apartment mate, but the relationship wasn't as close as the one I had with Victor.

Automatic Coil Co., Inc. continued its gradual growth at the Wallabout facility, and during that time, I carried on infrequent communications with my partner, Joe Rubenfeld, who was in Korea. When he returned to the States after he was discharged from the army, I welcomed him back and gave him a tour of our Wallabout facility. We happened to be working on a series of jobs that required a great deal of soldering. The process resulted in an overhanging cloud of smoke that resembled a smog cloud. It was not a healthy environmental atmosphere. The solution would have been to install an exhaust system, which would have been extremely costly.

We had been at this location for over a year and a half when Joe returned, and before he could adjust to the new environment, I informed him that we would have to move again. We did not have enough space to handle our expanding business anyway, and it would not make any sense to invest in an exhaust system at this location.

We searched and found an acceptable new factory on Bedford Avenue near Broadway, just around the corner from Automatic Coil Co., Inc. original home. This loft was situated on the third floor of a six-story building, but it was equipped with an elevator and elevator operator. We more than doubled our space, and here we installed an exhaust system that kept the environment smoke-free.

Across the street from our factory was a candy store. One day, I entered to make a purchase, and I noticed a sign that read "Apartment for Rent." I inquired about it and learned that it was a three-bedroom heated apartment on the first floor of a building on Monroe Street in Manhattan. The candy store owner also owned the building containing the apartment. After establishing that the rent was reasonable, I approached my friend Ed Levin and asked him to accompany me to look at the apartment. We liked what we saw. We appreciated the fact that it was a heated apartment, a step up from the cold-water flat on Debevoise Street. In addition, most of our social activity and Ed's job were all in Manhattan, making the location convenient. Since we were not tied down to a lease, we were able to immediately vacate Debevoise Street and move into the Monroe Street apartment. Ed and I shared that apartment during my period of courtship with Julia.

There were many doubts to overcome. First, Julia was eight years older than I was. And she had a child. Neither of those realities sat well with my mother. She, of course, felt that her son could do a lot better than marrying an older woman. I had some doubts to overcome myself. So did Julia. She overcame her aversion at my being so much younger when a friend of hers suggested, "Just think. When Sol will be 100 years old, you will be 108."

I overcame my reservations, partially because I felt very comfortable with Julia, and I really was taken with Chippy.

I don't think I was madly in love with Julia, but we saw eye to eye politically. It was at that time that I recalled a conversation I had with a young woman named Sylvia, who was a fellow student at the National Youth Administration, studying electronics. We were discussing the film *Casablanca*, which we both had recently seen. Sylvia observed that she could not understand how Ilsa could love Rick more than her husband, who was a politically correct hero. Sylvia could never have chosen Rick. Passionate love was a creation of Hollywood. It had no place in real life. I concluded that if it was absent in my relationship with Julia, it was compensated for in other ways.

Julia and I decided to get married. We made our own wedding at Julia's apartment. Our wedding date was March 29, 1953, two months after she obtained her divorce. Julia had to go to Mexico for a few days to legalize the divorce, and we agreed that I would babysit for Chippy during her absence. Chippy seemed very amenable to the idea. We spent those few days entertaining each other. At one point, we were driving somewhere, and I got the feeling that Chippy suddenly became aware of Julia's absence. She wanted to know when her mommy was coming home. It sounded like a feeling of more than just missing her. She was feeling very insecure about the idea that she was being abandoned. After all, she already had those feelings about being abandoned by her father. I tried to comfort her and distract her at the same time. It was at that moment that I invented Mr. Whistleman, a figment of my imagination. Mr. Whistleman was invisible, but he could be heard and talked to. He lived in my car, and he had many responsibilities. He was responsible for pushing the cigarette lighter up after it heated up. He was responsible for holding up the seats in the car. As Mr. Whistleman, I spoke out of one side of my mouth, always tilting my head away some from the passenger seat where Chippy sat. I held conversations with her, and she actually believed in his existence. Mr. Whistleman kept Chippy intrigued so that when Julia came home, Chippy told her about her new friend. At some point, Chippy began to realize that I was Mr. Whistleman, but she continued to play the game for quite some time. Then Mr. Whistleman went off to another home and returned when my grandchildren rode with me years later.

I invited my family to my wedding. My mother; my brother, Leonard, and his wife, Cynthia; my sister, Beatrice; and my aunts and uncles and cousins who lived in Long Branch, New Jersey, attended. They didn't appear to be too enthusiastic about the marriage. Julia's mother, Chaia, came from Florida to attend the wedding. She was a widow and shared an apartment with two other widows in Florida. Julia's sister, Lillian Finn; her then husband, Jack; and their daughter, Judy, also attended. We had quite a few friends that were there also. Chippy acted as our flower girl, and I chose my friend Ed Muse to be best man. At the time, I thought it was politically correct to select my African-American friend as my best man. In later years, I regretted my choice because I felt that I should have chosen my brother instead. I was best man at his wedding. However, at the time, I felt distanced from my family because they disapproved of my marrying Julia, and so I chose Ed. As it turned out, blood was thicker than water. My relationship with Leonard grew better in time, while my relationship with Ed faded.

We were married on March 29, 1953. After the wedding, Julia and I went on a one-night honeymoon, checking into a New York hotel with a shopping bag. We paid in advance for our room. The following day, we slept late and returned home that evening, and both of us returned to work the next day. I moved into Julia and Chippy's apartment on E. Seventh Street and turned my keys to the Monroe Street apartment over to Ed Levin. He was happy to have the apartment to himself.

Meanwhile, working out of the Bedford Avenue loft, Automatic Coil Co., Inc. continued to grow. Now that Joe was back, I was able to spend more time on matters concerning administration and less time in the shop. Outside of work, I was involved with the Freedom Singers, learning folk and work songs. With Ed Muse's input, we "grew" our repertoire of Negro spirituals and began to perform before PTA groups.

As things continued to improve with Automatic Coil Co., Joe and I were able to increase our salaries. We could afford to pay ourselves $100 per week. By that time, I had repaid the money I had borrowed from my sister, Beatrice, and was able to begin saving modestly.

The eighteen months I spent in California seemed a long way off, and it truly was. I was destined to return to Los Angeles on a very sad occasion. Dora Alpert, my mother's sister, became very ill and succumbed to cancer on March 13, 1953. My cousin Daniel and I decided to go to California to attend the funeral. In those days, flying was still an uncomfortable experience. Neither Daniel nor I had ever flown before. We made arrangements to fly out in a two-engine plane. The flight took over eight hours, and it was extremely rocky. We encountered a storm at one point, and I was able to see flashes of lightning outside my window. We arrived just in time for the funeral. It was a very sad reunion with my cousins Adele and Bessie and my uncle Sam Alpert.

During the short time we remained in Los Angeles, I was amazed at how much had changed in the five or so years since I was last there. Many orange and lemon groves had been replaced by a system of freeways.

On June 2, 1953, another tragedy struck when Jack Siegal, my mother's brother, also succumbed to cancer.

Sam Alpert was not the kind of man who could live alone, and so he quickly and unwisely became involved with another woman, who virtually fleeced him of all his savings before he died on June 13, 1954. As far as I can recall, none of the family on the East Coast attended his funeral.

Living on E. Seventh Street was not altogether to my liking. I longed for a more suburban setting. I was brought up in our own home in Brooklyn, and although I enjoyed the freedom and independence I experienced living in my own apartments on Debevoise Street and Monroe Street, I felt different about continuing to live in a brownstone with a wife and child. Julia and I were seduced—like many others of our generation—by the idea of a little house we could call our own.

Julia had a second cousin, Harry Friedman, who lived in Far Rockaway with his wife, Fanny. Harry was in his ninetieth year. He was extremely intelligent and yeshiva educated. He was fluent in ancient Hebrew and was one of the few people who could read and write Aramaic. Politically, he was a strong advocate of left-wing causes and was a supporter of the Soviet Union until the revelations of Stalin's policies toward Jews became evident. After that, he became disillusioned and, for all practical purposes, became apolitical.

Harry Friedman was very close to both Chaia and Julia. It was Harry Friedman who suggested we come out to look at houses in Far Rockaway when he heard that we were interested in moving to the suburbs. We went to look at a few houses. We found one that we became enthusiastic about. It was an old colonial on a large piece of property. We were interested in buying it even though it was much larger than we needed. I asked Martin Friedman—the attorney I had been using to handle any legal matters that arose at Automatic Coil—to come out with me and look at the house. He did but he discouraged us from buying it since he felt that it would require a lot of renovation that would cost more than I could afford. He suggested a smaller house needing less immediate repair. We continued our search and finally settled on a much more modest home. The house was located on McBride Street in Far Rockaway. We purchased it in the spring of 1954 for $14,000 shortly after Julia became pregnant with our daughter Sheila Jane. It was a modest house, but we relished in the quiet of our street and new home. Chippy took to her new environment extremely well and immediately made many friends, some of whom she continues to have a relationship with even today.

On November 6, 1954, we were blessed with the birth of Sheila. Sheila came onto the scene somewhat prematurely, as had Chippy. She was a beautiful baby. The next few years, Julia and I lived together harmoniously and happily with our two children. On December 13, 1956, we were again blessed with the birth of our third daughter, Deborah Anne, who made her entrance into our lives with a head of the reddest hair one could imagine. Julia did not work during those early years. She stayed at home with the children, putting her nursery school training to the test each day.

Automatic Coil Co., Inc. continued to grow, as did the need for more workers. We had continued to sign yearly contracts with our union, with whom we maintained good relations. Salary increases for our workers were modest but in line with what we were able to afford with our level of development.

Tragedy, however, struck in 1957. Martin Friedman—who had been our attorney since we started our business—was stricken with cancer. One day, he called me and asked Joe and me to come visit him at his home. He informed us of his illness and said that he could no longer be our attorney. He turned over all our corporate records that he had in his possession. Shortly after that meeting, I developed pneumonia, and after a week of recuperation, I returned to work, only to find that I had not fully recovered and had a relapse. I was advised by my doctor to take some time off and relax. Julia's mother, Chaia, suggested that I come to Florida and recuperate under her care. I took her up on the offer and went to Florida for a week. When I returned home, I was informed that during my absence, Martin Friedman had passed away. I was not told before because everyone thought it would delay my recuperation.

Upon my return to work, I immediately had to deal with the problem that we had outgrown the space we occupied on Bedford Avenue. We found our next new home outside of Williamsburg, although still in the confines of Brooklyn at 199 Sackett Street. A new lease had to be signed, and we had to find a new attorney to replace Martin. Since we retained Arthur Zimmerman as our accountant, he had joined forces with Reuben Siwek, an attorney, and they began to practice under the name of Siwek and Zimmerman. Arthur introduced us to Reuben when we asked him to suggest an attorney for us. We immediately felt comfortable with him and retained him, and his first service for us was to check our lease arrangement for 199 Sackett Street. This loft was on the third floor of a building that had many windows and gave us a great deal of natural light. We occupied the second floor of an elevated building. For the first time, we were located in what I considered a place where I would not be ashamed of bringing potential customers. Once again, we were faced with the task of moving all our machinery and equipment (some of it quite large) that we had acquired over the past few years while we were on Bedford Avenue. Our business had expanded to include in its customer base companies that manufactured television sets, electronic test equipment, and military communication equipment.

Doing the work for the military, even on a subcontract basis, required that we meet military specifications. This entailed our becoming familiar with the specifications and required that we perform certain manufacturing operations in accordance with these specifications. I believe we grew to the point where we built confidence with many of our customers, who considered us a responsible and reliable supplier. In our new location, we were able to compete better in obtaining larger orders. Occasionally, we were successful in competing favorably with our old employer, XYZ Coil Co., which also grew during this period. They left Brooklyn and relocated to Long Island.

We were also successful in winning over, as a customer, another company for whom I had previously worked: Electronic Instrument Co. Inc. (EICO). EICO was also the forerunner of another spin-off. Their old engineer whom I had worked with, Bert Miller, had left them and started up a new company in competition with EICO. He found a partner who backed him financially, and they set up a company called Exact Precision Corp. Bert was a charming guy who was capable of convincing you that he was a genius. He developed a line of electronic kits, which were really copies of the ones sold by EICO. Stereo and high-fidelity sound systems were the craze, and Bert introduced a high-fidelity amplifier and an AM/ FM tuner. He was also instrumental in convincing some underwriters to underwrite a public offering for Exact Precision Corp. Bert then began to merchandise his products to distributors all over the country, making a big splash with his hi-fi equipment. Shortly after the successful completion of the underwriting, Bert went into full-scale production and began to ship the equipment all over the country. Within a few months, disaster struck. Customers were returning their equipment to the distributors because they were burning up. The design was faulty, and the power transformer could not deliver the required power and started to burn. Thousands of amplifiers and tuners were returned, and the company was ultimately forced to declare Chapter 11. The victims were the stockholders, and many of Bert's suppliers had not been paid. Automatic Coil Co., Inc. was one such supplier.

Bert approached me, suggesting that we purchase the assets of Exact Precision Corp. by offering the creditors five cents on the dollar. The stockholders would, unfortunately, be left holding a lot of worthless stock. Bert convinced me that we could get the company running successfully again. My interest was enhanced by the idea that were we to take over the assets and start the company under a new name—namely, Precise Electronics Corp. We would have the ability to take our joint company public. Precise Electronics Corp. would provide the necessary glamor of being in an industry destined to grow, while Automatic Coil Co., Inc. would provide a history of making profits for the past years—and together, we would have the combination necessary to take the company public. We felt it was necessary to raise additional capital if we were to grow beyond where Automatic Coil Co., Inc. was at that time.

Our offer was accepted, and with the assistance of bankruptcy attorneys, we acquired the assets of the old Exact Precision Corp. Bert convinced us that he knew how to make a talking tube tester. Of course, this was long before computers were able to talk. We thought Bert was a valuable asset. He even went so far as to make a mock-up of the device with a simulated tape recorder implanted. We then demonstrated the model at a trade show, where Bert took many orders from distributors. He quoted prices without having any idea as to actual cost of development or building of the device. He convinced us that he knew what he was doing, and we went along.

Exact Precision Corp. was located in a one-story building in Oceanside, New York. Automatic Coil Co., Inc. was still in Brooklyn. After we took over the assets of Exact Precision Corp., which was now renamed Precise Electronics Corp., I started to spend my time in Oceanside, leaving Joe to run Automatic Coil Co., Inc. Much work had to be done to get the company started again in handling orders for test equipment kits. Inventories were unbalanced, and orders were being shipped missing components. I found that the company had been run haphazardly and it was poorly managed, but I was hopeful that I could put it back on a stable footing.

With an eye toward going public, we thought it advisable to have a name more appropriate and appealing to the public. What we finally decided on, after much deliberation, was one that we knew captured the spirit of the "onics" craze. We set up a corporation known as Designatronics Inc. (DSG) as the parent company, with Automatic Coil Co., Inc. and Precise Electronics Corp. as subsidiaries. In September 1960, DSG acquired all the existing stock of Automatic Coil Co., Inc. in exchange for 150,000 shares of DSG shares. Joe, Bert, and I each became owners of 50,000 shares. I was to be president, and Joe and Bert were vice presidents. The DSG board of directors was made up of Joe, Bert, Julia, and me. We then searched for and eventually found underwriters who agreed to sell 100,000 shares at $2.25 a share. At the time, it represented a lot of money to us. We would still control the company with 150,000 shares among us. Our board of directors was required to add a representative of the underwriters, George Heller.

With the underwriting behind us, I felt I badly needed a vacation. Julia and I had been married for ten years but had never been able to go on vacation. Recreational opportunities had been limited to long weekends now and then in the vicinity of New York with the children. Now for the first time, we were able to go away alone for at least a week. We wanted to go somewhere exotic, maybe even romantic. There was no shortage of suggestions. "Go to France." "Have you been to Israel?" "How about Puerto Rico?" All these suggestions came from friends at a party Julia and I attended. "Listen," said my friend Al Alcosser, "you have only one week, and you have never been out of the country. There is only one place to go that will meet all your requirements. It is exotic. It is very romantic, and you will be thrilled with the artistic environment. And above all, it is very different. Go to Haiti. I can fix you up good. There is a great hotel that you have to stay at. It's called the Hotel Oloffson, and I know the owner. You will have a great time."

I called my travel agent, and she had no trouble making reservations for the flight to Haiti or at the hotel. She readily admitted that she didn't know too much about Haiti. She told us that she was not able to book our return flight when we wanted it, but we were on standby. She assured us that there would be no trouble getting back when we wanted to. After all, "who is going to that place anyway?" Since there was no trouble arranging for the flight to Haiti, she could not envision why there would be a problem getting a return flight, "especially in the summer."

For a whole week before we were scheduled to leave, we shopped for provisions. The freezer was full with an abundance of steaks, chops, frozen dinners, juice vegetables, and ice cream. The house and babysitter were in place, and we were assured that there was nothing to worry about. Our friend Al was full of advice and suggestions as to where to go. He supplied us with a list of people to look up and who would "take good care of us."

The flight to Haiti was uneventful. As a matter of fact, we were almost the only passengers. There were about twenty Haitians traveling, and most Caucasians appeared to be missionaries. Being inexperienced international travelers, we did not think much about the scarcity of fellow passengers.

When the plane made its approach to land in Port-au-Prince, we were very excited. We looked out the window and saw the bare mountains that made up a considerable portion of the Haitian land mass. It seemed to us that the plane was a little too close to the mountain we were flying over, but soon it was behind us, and the airport clearing with its single runway came into view. We were anticipating getting off the plane and setting foot on foreign soil for the first time in our lives.

The plane landed without incident, and as soon as the door opened and the first passenger began to deplane, the music began. Waiting at the entrance of the small building that served as a terminal was a band playing Caribbean music. "How enchanting it all is," I thought as we walked past the band and into the building. A line formed behind a sign that said "Passport Inspection" in French. When our turn came, I presented our passports to the agent. He inspected them carefully and asked us the purpose of our visit and how long we intended to stay. He wanted to know what hotel we were staying at. I answered his questions appropriately, and he stamped our passports, and we proceeded to the baggage-claim area in an adjoining room.

As we waited along with the other passengers for the baggage to be brought from the plane, a young man approached us and introduced himself. "Bonjour, my name is Jacques, and I will help you with your bags when they arrive." I gave him my baggage receipts, and he scrambled among the bags until he found ours. He then carried them to the customs counter, where they were inspected thoroughly—an experience I resented, never having had my baggage inspected before.

Jacques asked if we wanted a taxi. I said yes and we followed him out of the terminal, where we were immediately accosted by many pathetic souls, some without an arm or a leg, some blind, and all begging. An obviously blind man, holding on to the arm of a young boy, had his hand out, palm facing up, and was jabbering in Creole. Another man with a missing arm knew two English words: "money please." I felt a tug on my trouser near my ankle, and I looked down to see the remains of a human being with no legs. All around, we were faced with people who were in the throes of misery, hunger, and deprivation. It was a scene neither Julia nor I had ever witnessed before. Jacques was attempting to push through the crowd to get to a taxi, but Julia called to him and told him to bring our bags back into the terminal. Jacques pushed his way back into the terminal, and we followed. "I want to leave here right now," said Julia. There were tears in her eyes, and she was shaking. Jacques could not understand that Julia's reaction was not fear but shock at the terrible state of what passed for humanity.

Jacques carried our bags back to the ticket agent, and I inquired as to when the next flight to New York would leave. The agent reported that the flight for New York had already left and there would be no other flight until the next day; however, there were no available seats on that flight. As a matter of fact, there were no available seats on any flight to New York or Miami for at least two weeks. We were not to learn the reason for the difficulty until much later that day. Julia paled visibly and asked, "Are there any reservations available on a flight to anywhere?" The agent was very cooperative, and after extensive checking, he found that there were reservations available on another airline that flies to Jamaica in four days, but he suggested that if we wanted them, we had better make the ticket purchase immediately because he could not guarantee that they would still be available an hour from now.

We purchased the tickets and were resigned to remaining in Haiti for at least four days. Jacques, who had patiently waited while we made our arrangements, suggested that we get a taxi. Julia dreaded the thought of having to brave through the scene outside the terminal but resigned herself to it since there was no alternative. Jacques pushed through the crowd as quickly as he could and helped us into a cab and instructed the cabdriver in Creole to take us to the Hotel Oloffson. As the cab pulled away, the driver introduced himself as Carl and asked where we were from and if this was our first visit to Haiti. Carl informed us that he was available to chauffeur us around and take us to the best shopping places where we could buy paintings, sculpture, and other very fine craft items. I told *Carl* that I wasn't sure what we were going to be doing but that he should check with us later.

Proceeding along the airport road, we saw what up to now we had only seen in pictures. A woman on the back of a donkey weighted down with several grayish bags, which we later learned contained charcoal. Women walking along the road with baskets laden with fresh vegetables being carried on their heads. Children, barefoot and in rags, were walking along, chewing on what looked like pieces of wood but was actually sugarcane. Off in the distance, mountains were partially obscured by smoke from many fires, which were not visible. The air was filled with aromas emanating from these fires. Garlic, charcoal, and other familiar and unfamiliar smells permeated the air.

Driving through the streets of Port-au-Prince, we saw for the first time in our lives what poverty really was. The slums we drove through contained shacks constructed from discarded boxes and crates. Some utilized what must have been sheets of rusted metal, and wherever we looked, the streets were teeming with people. Continuing the drive, we went past buildings whose architecture and construction must have dated back to the days of the French occupation.

Finally, the taxi arrived at a large iron gate, which was opened by a young man when the cabdriver honked his horn. As we proceeded along the driveway, the majestic hotel came into view in all its colonial gingerbread elegance. It was a beautiful sight, and Julia smiled for the first time. The taxi came to a stop next to a stairway consisting of several steps before it came to a landing and then, making a sharp U-turn, the steps continued up until they ended at a large veranda. Tables covered with red-and-white starched tablecloths were spaced comfortably so that each enjoyed a degree of privacy. The table settings—consisting of beautiful crystal and polished silverware—suggested that dining here would be a delight.

Inside the gates of the hotel grounds, we felt as if we were in another world. The squalor beyond the gates was invisible, hidden by the stone walls and lush vegetation. The bougainvillea shut out the slum we had seen just a short time ago.

Several boys were immediately available to carry the luggage, which had been removed from the taxi. We climbed the steps and followed them into a small lobby. Off to the right of the lobby was an office. The beauty of the hand-carved desk that was visible from the lobby was insufficient to retain Julia's attention. The chair behind the desk and its occupant immediately drew her attention. From our friend Al's description, we immediately knew that the occupant of the chair had to be Al Seitz, the owner of the hotel. We entered his office and introduced ourselves and, invoking our friend Al's name, we found that Al Seitz had little or no recollection of the previous friendship that my friend Al said would open up doors for us. Al Seitz was very gracious, however; and after signing the register, he arranged for a convenient room and had our bags brought there. Al Seitz asked us to join him at the bar for a complimentary drink before we retired to our room to unpack. Julia and I both felt the need for some serious unwinding and were only too glad to join him. We followed him to the bar and, in Creole, Al addressed the bartender, who stood attentively behind the bar. He ordered rum punches for the three of us. The bartender smiled and prepared the drinks.

The red liquid garnished with an orange slice and maraschino cherry turned out to be an exquisite elixir, and after a few sips, the tension that had built up began to diminish. Talking with Al, we learned that he came originally from Wilkes-Barre, Pennsylvania. Coincidentally, so did Julia, and they began to reminisce about what it was like being Jewish and growing up in a mining town—and by the way, what was a Jewish boy doing running a hotel in Haiti? Al explained that he had been in the tour business and had sent many tourists to Haiti and had come to Haiti many times himself. He became intrigued with the beauty and mystique of the place, and when he learned of an opportunity to lease the hotel, he seized it.

Things went very well for a while; the tourists came in increasing numbers. But then the political situation had deteriorated with the coming of Duvalier, and he said, "I don't have to tell you what is happening." Julia threw me a sideward glance as she "knowingly" nodded. I did the same, but I wondered what exactly was happening that we should know about.

By this time, our glasses were empty, and Al offered another round. Julia was quick to accept, but I, feeling the first drink had its calming effect, declined another. At that moment, the phone rang, and Al excused himself. And Julia, feeling the need to retire to our room, asked Al if it would be all right to bring her drink with her. Al said that would be fine and they would talk again later. We left the bar and walked toward our room. In doing so, we were able to see the pool. Although it was not too large and its rectangular shape was not particularly unusual, it looked invitingly refreshing. I thought it a little odd that there were no guests around the pool although it was a sunny afternoon and very hot.

Once inside our room, I noticed that the ceiling was very high. There were two very tall doors that opened onto a small balcony. The sleigh bed appeared to be very old and probably was an antique. Aside from a matching dresser, only one chair was all the furniture in the room. The bathroom too was old, but the fixtures were functional. On a small shelf over the sink, there was a thermos of ice water and several glasses. A small sign on the shelf indicated that the sink water should not be used for drinking.

Julia, rum punch in hand, tested the bed and found it to her liking, and she decided that a nap was in order. I felt stimulated and decided that I would like to take a walk and survey our environment. I undressed, took a shower, and put on a fresh pair of shorts and a shirt and left Julia to rest. I walked toward the gate, and when the young man who opened the gate when we arrived saw me approaching, he opened it to let me pass. As soon as I was outside, I was immediately surrounded by a group of boys ranging in age from about six to fourteen years old, jabbering away. I understood none of what they were saying, but I guessed that they were requesting money. Then one young man, who was off to the side, yelled something in Creole, and the group melted away. The young man came over and introduced himself as Francois and said that he was going to be my guide. He told me that he had told the other boys that I was a member of the clergy, and that was why they stopped bothering me. He asked me if this was the first time I had been to Haiti, and when I told him it was, he asked me what I wanted to do. He could arrange for a very nice girl, "not too expensive." I told him that I was not interested in a girl, but I wanted to walk around and see the town. Francois was more than anxious to be my escort. It was not a far walk. Francois and I talked as we walked. He told me he was fourteen years old and learned to speak English from the tourists. No, he didn't go to school, and he didn't know where his parents were or even if they were alive. He lived on the street and had no permanent address.

We walked through the quaint streets. Francois told me that we were in the downtown area, and I couldn't help making a mental comparison to what I knew as downtown back home. It was certainly different. All at once, we encountered a group of people marching as if in a parade. I asked what that was about, and Francois explained that today was a holiday and the people were marching to the church. I asked if we could join, and Francois said it was certainly all right. I, the only white person in the parade, marched along with the others; and except for the curiosity I engendered, nobody said anything.

As we marched, many people stood along the side watching the procession go by. A mother holding a baby noticed that I was looking at the baby and smiling at it. She stepped off the curb toward me, and no sooner had she done that than the baby's hand stretched out with its palm up. I thought in all my life, I had never seen so many beggars. A small baby not more than a year old was already indoctrinated in the art of begging.

When we reached the church, I felt that it would not be right for me to intrude on whatever service was to take place, and I felt the need to distance myself from the extreme level of poverty I was again witnessing. I told Francois to escort me back to my hotel because I certainly would not be able to find my way alone. There was no help from street signs since there were none. When we arrived back at the hotel, I gave Francois a generous tip, and he offered to be my guide the next day. I told him that we had a guide with a car. He said that he would be outside the hotel in the morning, in case our guide didn't show up.

I found Julia sitting by the pool chatting with an attractive woman. She was about thirty years old. Julia introduced Helen to me. In the pool, a bearded man, Frank, was introduced as Helen's husband. Helen said that they were beginning to worry about my absence from the hotel for over two hours. I explained where I had been and what I had seen. I must have sounded loud and angry about how terrible I thought conditions were for the people and how awful the Haitian government must be for permitting such conditions to exist. Suddenly, Frank leaped out of the pool and came over to me. "Shut your mouth! You're not at home now." I was taken aback by what I perceived as Frank's rudeness. He hastened to explain that he was with the American embassy and had been living and working in Haiti for more than a year. He and Helen were leaving the next day. As a matter of fact, all embassy employees had been recalled home; and within two weeks, there would no longer be any American personnel in the country. Frank explained that diplomatic relations between the United States and Haiti had deteriorated dramatically, and there was an excellent chance that diplomatic relations would be severed. Frank was shocked to learn that Julia and I had just arrived that day because he felt that Americans were not immune from danger. Many people had mysteriously disappeared recently; some of them were later found dead, while others simply disappeared. This was not the time or place to indicate how one felt about the Haitian government. My absence was a matter of concern to them, and now I understood why.

It was about six o'clock, and Frank and Helen left for their room to get ready for dinner. Julia and I did the same. Once in our room, Julia expressed wonderment at our complete ignorance and naïveté as to what was going on. Al Alcosser certainly didn't indicate any political difficulties that might exist in Haiti. Our travel agent didn't know or didn't tell us about any problems that may have existed between the United States and Haiti. We were upset and hoped for an opportunity to talk to Al Seitz about our concerns.

Julia and I dressed and went to the bar for a drink before dinner. Sitting there, we ordered rum punches and hoped that Al would appear, but he didn't. Other hotel guests did, however, and we engaged them in conversation. We learned that like Helen and Frank, they were employees of the United States government and had been called home. They would all be leaving in the next few days. They indicated that the hotel had very few guests left as they were departing daily and we were the only new arrivals in many days. Julia asked whether it was safe to leave the hotel since we were unable to leave

Haiti for at least four days. We were advised that it would be best if we were escorted. "Hire a car with a chauffeur, and you will probably be safe during the day."

We finished our drinks and excused ourselves and entered the dining area to have dinner. We were enjoying our dinner when we were approached by a slight Haitian man who introduced himself as Aubelin Jolicoeur. He was neatly dressed in a white suit, white shirt, and tie. He said that he was a reporter for the local newspaper and usually interviewed new guests for his paper. He wanted to know our names, where we were from, and why we had come to Haiti. After mundane conversation, he took his leave. Later, we learned that he was actually a spy for Duvalier and was keeping an eye on any new people arriving in Haiti. I also learned that he was the character depicted in Graham Greene's novel *The Comedians*, a book about Greene's experience in Haiti.

After dinner, we walked around the hotel grounds and came near the gate from which you can enter or exit the hotel. Looking out through the gate, we saw Carl, our taxi driver, waiting there; he was trying to attract our attention. He wanted to know if we had decided to hire him tomorrow. We told him yes. We negotiated a price for the day, and Carl promised that he would arrive by ten o'clock the next morning.

It had been a hard day, and we decided to retire to our room. Reading in bed was difficult since the light was insufficient. There was no radio, so we allowed sleep to overtake us.

We were awakened early by the crowing of a rooster. We had never before experienced this, having lived in the city. We tried to go back to sleep but were unsuccessful. We did, however, enjoy just lying in bed, knowing that we really did not have to get up. We knew that whatever unknown experiences we were in for in the next few days, we had absolutely no tasks or chores we were responsible for performing right now. That was a very unusual state of being for both of us.

When we were ready, we got up and went down for breakfast. We enjoyed the tropical fruit that was served and ate freshly baked bread, which we found full-bodied and delicious. We also drank Haitian coffee for the first time and found it full-bodied and enjoyable as well.

Promptly at ten o'clock, Carl was at the gate. We climbed into the back seat of the cab, and as we exited the gate, I saw Francois waiting. I asked Carl to stop for a moment while I spoke to Francois. I explained that our activities for today required a car because we were going some distance from the hotel. Disappointed, Francois asked about the next day, and I had to disappoint him again.

When we finally pulled away from the hotel, Carl offered us a number of options.

"What do you want to see first? I take you to where there is very fine painting. I take you to see very fine wood carving—very cheap. I take you to the artist."

"Where is Petionville?" I asked.

"Oh, Petionville is in de mountains," offered Carl. "Very rich people—very nice house."

"We want to visit someone there," I said, looking at a sheet of paper containing some names and addresses I extracted from my wallet. "His name is Monsieur Etienne, Jean Robert Etienne." I then mispronounced a street name, and when Carl didn't recognize it, I passed the sheet of paper to him. Carl didn't know the street but indicated that he would inquire when we reached Petionville.

It was an all uphill drive over a poorly paved winding road. Along the way, we passed men and women walking up and down the road, many of them carrying buckets of water or baskets of vegetables on their heads. When we arrived in the village, Carl asked several people before he found someone who recognized the name of the street and gave him directions. Carl, after making a number of rights and lefts onto very small streets, finally pulled up in front of a house enclosed by an iron gate. He got out of the cab and approached the gate. A thin Haitian approached the gate from the inside and talked with Carl, who then came back to the cab and said that the man was Jean Robert Etienne's houseboy and that Monsieur Etienne was not at home. Carl asked when he was expected to return, and the man said he did not know. Monsieur Etienne was out of the country.

Getting back in the cab, I asked Carl to try to find Monsieur Phillipe Duvall. Carl finally located Monsieur Duvall's residence, only to learn that he too was out of the country. Two more of Al Alcosser's contacts produced the same results. I was beginning to wonder why all these people were out of the country.

We became resigned to our failure to locate anyone Al promised would "take good care of us." We agreed to allow Carl to take us to visit several art galleries and craft shops, and we had our first exposure to Haitian arts and crafts. We purchased a number of small wooden statues and several paintings. Carl was encouraging us to purchase a lot more because, obviously, he was receiving a commission for bringing us to the shops. But when Julia saw that it was already past 2:00 p.m., she said she wanted to go back to the hotel.

The last shop we visited was on the road to Kenscoff. We did not know anything about Kenscoff other than that it was up in the mountains and the trip back from the last stop was all downhill, and at one point in the descent, I noticed a small sign which said "Hotel Ibo Lele." I asked Carl about it, and he told me that it was a very beautiful hotel, but they were not very busy now. When asked why, Carl shrugged his shoulders and indicated that he did not know. I asked Carl to detour and take us to the Ibo Lele Hotel. He agreed and we drove up another mountain in the direction the sign indicated. It was a very steep and curvy climb, and the cab had difficulty at some points along the way, and it appeared as if Carl had to give the cab a running start in order to climb up the steep parts.

At last we arrived, and Carl parked the cab and led the way along a courtyard surrounded by beautiful plants and trees. Turning left, we entered the lobby where on the walls were autographed photographs of very famous people who apparently had been guests at the hotel. Carl addressed the man behind the desk and told him that we were interested in seeing the hotel. The man smiled and nodded, and Carl led us to a large concrete deck. From there, we could look out and see downtown Port-au-Prince, the airport, and the sea. The view was so startlingly magnificent that Julia had to admit then that this alone was worth all the trauma she had experienced yesterday.

Carl led us down a flight of stairs to another level that housed a kidney-shaped swimming pool, a beautiful mahogany bar, and a lovely outdoor but sheltered dining room. The tables were all set with white starched tablecloths accompanied by starched napkins. Julia asked if we could see one of the rooms, which we fell in love with. It was large with a sitting area containing a sofa, several soft chairs, and a table. There was a door that led out onto a balcony that afforded the occupant a view of the port.

On the way out, we thanked the attendant and thought it was a shame that such beauty was going to waste.

When we arrived back at the Oloffson, Carl asked if we wanted to go see a voodoo ceremony. He would come back after dinner at about 8:00 p.m. and take us to a place called the Peristyle, where they performed "real voodoo." Julia and I exchanged glances, and we said, "What the hell, we might as well do it while we are here. We will never be back, so let's see it."

After Carl left, we went back to our room and put on our bathing suits and took a swim.

At this point, it is necessary to fast-forward about ten years to relate what I learned about Carl. I met him again at a dance one Friday night at the Ibo Lele Hotel. I was having dinner with one of our managers, Jacque Kenol. Carl approached our table, and my manager politely introduced me to Carl as a friend of his. I did not recognize him immediately. After some friendly conversation, I learned that Carl was once in the employ of the Tonton Macoute, Duvalier's private spy network. But that was "long ago." Carl then said that he was driving a cab back then, and he had to report to his superiors any suspicious signs he might see from his foreign passengers. It was then that I realized that Carl had been our driver on my first trip to Haiti. I suggested the possibility that he had been our cabdriver. After a moment, he confirmed that he remembered me because I had given him a pair of yellow shorts that he admired. He then related that he indeed recalled that he reported on his experience with us. From his explanation, the following is the best description I imagined the event had been.

Carl, after dropping us off, immediately drove down the hill and found his way to the National Road, which led him downtown. He turned into a small street and parked his cab in front of an office building. He entered the building and walked up a flight of stairs to an office. He knocked at the closed door and was invited in. Sitting at a desk was a neatly dressed young man with a dark complexion, with his hair cropped short. On the desk was a telephone, a pair of dark sunglasses, and some file folders. Carl addressed him as Pierre. They exchanged greetings, and then Carl said, "Yesterday, I picked up these Americans at the airport and brought them to the Oloffson. Last night, they hired me to drive them today. This morning, I offered to take them to the usual places, but they wanted to visit some people." Carl withdrew a piece of paper from his pocket, which contained the names and addresses of the people we wanted to visit. Carl handed the paper to Pierre, who studied the names and then directed his attention back to Carl.

"What happened?" he asked.

"Well, in each case, the people were not in Haiti. My passengers were very disappointed, but they then permitted me to take them to some of the galleries."

"What do you think?" asked Pierre. "Are they dangerous?"

"I don't know. I don't think so. When I picked them up at the airport, Jacques told me that they were trying to leave Haiti immediately after they stepped out of the terminal. Jacques carried their bags back into the terminal, and they tried to get a flight out immediately. But of course, there were no flights. They have a reservation to leave for Jamaica in a few days. That was the first available flight they could get anywhere. I think they are just tourists."

"Well, keep an eye on them and report anything that is suspicious. Jolicoeur also felt that they were harmless."

"I'm taking them to the Peristyle tonight," Carl reported. "I'll let you know if anything happens."

After our swim, we felt refreshed. We came out, and each of us sat in a reclining chair. When Al Seitz saw us relaxing, he came out of his office and took a chair near us.

"I'm sorry I had to leave you so abruptly yesterday," he said.

I brushed away his apology and asked, "Al, what's going on? We spoke to Frank and Helen briefly yesterday, and they told us that all American embassy personnel were told to return home. He said they all will be gone in the next two weeks. Today we tried to find some people and found they were all out of the country, but their houseboys or caretakers didn't know when they would return."

Al explained that it was not in our best interest to discuss the political situation in Haiti at this time, but it did not appear very good. "Relations between Haiti and the United States are at an all-time low. Tourists have stopped coming, and I am about ready to close down the hotel if I can't find someone to lease it from me. I don't have a choice. I still have a few friends here, but most of them have left. I still have to make a living, and I can't do that here now. The people you tried to find today probably left the country because they felt or knew that they were not safe here."

"Do you feel safe here?" I asked.

"I have stayed clear of politics, and I don't think I am perceived as a threat to anyone, but you never know."

"Do you think it's safe for us to go see a voodoo ceremony tonight?" Julia felt silly asking the question, but Al, treating it as a serious inquiry, indicated that he thought it would be safe.

Carl arrived at 8:00 p.m. The drive to the Peristyle took us on a road heading south along the waterfront through terrible slums, even worse than what we had seen so far. There were masses of human beings on the street outside crudely constructed dwellings with walls made of old metal Coca-Cola signs and roofs covered with thatch or banana leaves. Vendors were selling snow cones and chewing gum. There were no lights other than that provided by candles or charcoal fires. The dogs roaming the streets lethargically were skeletal and obviously starved.

We entered the stadium where the ceremony was to take place. We were the only white people there. The ceremony began with drum sequences and people coming out on the floor, dancing themselves into a frenzy. We were there only about fifteen minutes when Julia felt that the music was getting to her and making her feel peculiar. She wanted to leave, and we did. It wasn't until years later that I was able to witness a full voodoo ceremony.

Carl drove us back to our hotel. We made arrangements with him to drive us to the airport when we were scheduled to leave. The remainder of our stay we spent at the hotel.

When we were finally seated on the airplane taking us to Jamaica, we were relieved, and we vowed never to return to Haiti. I left with the impression that Haiti was a nation of beggars. Little did I realize that less than a decade later, I would be carrying on a love affair with Haiti.

Our flight to Jamaica was short and uneventful. We arrived in Kingston and rented a jeep for our trip to Ochos Rios. We didn't realize that we had arrived just after Jamaica had obtained its independence from England. Some of the Jamaicans—unlike the Haitians we met—appeared hostile to us. We were only going to be there three days, and in that time, we managed to learn to drive on the wrong side of the road and do a little sightseeing on our own before returning to Kingston for our flight home.

I returned to work when we arrived home, and with the underwriting behind us, we now faced new responsibilities to stockholders. We had to learn a lot about how to relate to them, writing reports to stockholders, Securities and Exchange regulations, certified annual reports, and a host of other regulatory requirements that began to take up a lot of my time. On top of that, I had the problem of continuing to pressure Bert to get to work on the talking tube tester, which he continued to procrastinate about. Distributors began to push us on delivery of their orders. We still did not have a design ready. I was beginning to think that Bert had neither the intention nor the ability to design this product.

We were also plagued with the problem of being in two different locations so that it was difficult for me to assist Joe in Brooklyn and he was in no position to assist me in Oceanside. We felt we had no alternative but to consolidate these two facilities under one roof.

We found a 20,000-square-foot building at 76 E Second Street in Mineola for Automatic Coil Co., Inc. and Precise Electronics Corp. Bert was totally useless in helping us make the move. In fact, we found him frequently absent without any explanation. In addition, we also found that he was loose with the company checkbook and began to make purchases without asking Joe and me.

With no authorization, he leased a sporty convertible for himself, and the company was responsible for the payments. We were convinced that he would bring ruin to our company as he did to his previous firm. It was becoming obvious that Bert was a con man and had to move from one con to the next.

Bert came to us to report that he was in touch with a company that we could take over that would prove to be a bonanza for us. He gave us the details about Standard Precision Corp., a company whose stock traded on the American Stock Exchange.

Standard Precision had a subsidiary called Starlite Precision that manufactured precision gears and other mechanical and electromechanical components. They also did work for the military. Standard Precision wanted to sell off the precision gear subsidiary, and we could buy it at a bargain price. The details indicated that it had sales of over $1 million per year. Bert reported to us that they were not profitable because there were no qualified managers. Mr. Cameo was the general manager, and he had other corporate responsibilities, hence the company had only absentee management. Properly managed, the company could be a real moneymaker. Bert pointed to Starlite's chief competitor, Ace Design, a company that was apparently quite profitable. Again we were seduced, finding the idea of a company with a product catalog of hundreds of pages attractive in that it would add to the prestige of Designatronics, increase its sales in one move, and help cover up the fiasco of the Precise Electronics Corp. talking tube tester, which hadn't come to pass.

The proposal was for Designatronics to acquire the assets of the Starlite Precision subsidiary at book value in exchange for 115,936 shares of 4% convertible preferred stock valued at $10 par value. Each share would be convertible into 2.5 shares of common stock at $4 per share. Of course, we would need operating capital, which could be acquired by the sale of convertible debentures. We would sell convertible debentures bearing interest at 6%, which would be due for redemption on December 1, 1974.

Starlite Precision had its factory in Port Washington, New York. The building it occupied contained 15,000 square feet. When I first visited the plant, I was impressed by the quantity of machinery and equipment, and I was concerned because we did not have any knowledge about the product line, which was extensive and included hundreds of different gears, couplings, and a multitude of other components.

Up to now, Joe and I were being swept along. Our underwriters were enthusiastic about the deal because they saw a way of making money through the debenture sale and because they were also seduced by Bert's promises of great things to come. Bert had the ear of the underwriters and the Standard Precision representatives on our board of directors, and it was intended that Bert would go in and run the operation, which would become a division of Designatronics.

All that was left to do was to have a contract drawn up and have a board of directors meeting approving the purchase arrangements. These arrangements entailed establishing the exact sales price, which would be determined by a certified audit by Standard Precision's auditors. The machinery was valued at "book value," and the inventory was taken to establish its value. The total value came to $1,159,360, for which Designatronics would issue and turn over to Standard Precision Corp. that amount in convertible preferred stock Class A as described above. This stock had to be authorized and approved by the Designatronics stockholders. A number of other actions were necessary, and at a special meeting of stockholders that was held on March 6, 1961—attended by Joe, Bert, Julia, George Heller (who now sat on our board as a representative of the underwriters that took our company public), and me—the following actions were taken:

1. Amend the certificate of incorporation of Designatronics to increase the authorized number of common shares to 1 million.
2. Authorize the issuance of $1 million Class A convertible preferred stock.
3. Authorize the issuance of $750,000 Class B preferred stock.

4. Authorize increasing the board of directors to up to nine directors.
5. Approve the sale of up to $300,000 convertible debentures.

Part of the arrangement was that two members representing Standard Precision Corp. would become members of the board of directors. Effectively, that would increase our board to seven members. Once the special meeting of stockholders was completed, the contract to purchase the assets was signed, and Bert divorced himself almost completely from our Mineola facility and made his home base at the newly renamed Sterling Instrument Division in Port Washington. Only $210,000 of the convertible debentures were successfully sold. Then we watched the losses at Sterling Instrument Division begin to mount. In the previous year, under the old management, Starlite Precision Corp. had sales of $1 million and losses of $1 million. That may have been something the old owners may have been able to afford, but it certainly wasn't anything we could handle for very long. Bert did not seem to realize that something had to be done to stem the losses. He insisted that everything was going well; but each month, we had more losses. I wanted to go to the plant to see if there was anything I could do to help the situation, but he forbade me from going in. And on one occasion when I entered when he wasn't there, I found that the personnel had been instructed not to give me any information. In addition, he was spending less and less time at the plant, and rumor had it that he was busy running around with women. His outrageous expense account seemed to confirm that.

After the consummation of the sale, Standard Precision Corp. appointed Roger Heywood and Peter Hewes as directors to represent them on the Designatronics board. I approached these members and informed them that I was unhappy with the way things were progressing and that I think Bert was not doing what had to be done to rescue the operation. My fear was that if I were not able to convince them of the problem, I would be voted down and even fired. This was possible since if the Standard Precision Corp. board members sided with Bert and were able to convince George, the underwriters' representative, to side with them, they would have four votes against our three, represented by Joe, Julia, and me. Fortunately, I was successful in convincing them that I had to go into the plant and put a stop to the way it was being run. I showed them the wasteful practices Bert was engaged in. A board of directors meeting was held, and I proposed firing Bert. After much negotiation, we agreed to allow him to resign. I then went in to run the operation myself.

The Starlite Precision Corp. had a contract with a union, and that contract had to be honored. This union represented the Starlite Precision Corp. workers, while the United Electrical Union represented the Automatic Coil Co., Inc. employees. After my original meeting with the union representative for Starlite Precision. I turned over all union negotiating matters to Martin Hoffman. I knew that I would be too soft to handle these matters. Martin was capable of handling this situation. Joe Rubenfeld handled union matters for Automatic Coil. Being on the management side of employer-employee relations always bothered me. I knew that I could not effectively represent the stockholders of the corporation and the employees at the same time. We were successful over the forthcoming years to enjoy reasonably good relationships with both unions, although I was in frequent conflict with the union representatives on their inability or lack of interest in attempting to organize companies that were our competitors to even out the playing field.

I was terribly naive about the financial arrangements we had made. I was under the impression that we bought the assets of the component division of the Standard Precision Corp. Actually, as I later realized, Standard Precision Corp. could easily take over Designatronics merely by exercising the option to convert their convertible preferred stock into common stock. Were they to do that, they would increase the common stock of the corporation by 289,840 shares—which would have given them more than 50% of the outstanding stock and hence absolute control of the company. They would be able to do anything they pleased. There was just one drawback for them. The preferred stock, when converted at $4 per share, would entail showing substantial losses on the financial statement. As preferred stock, the value on their books would be the total value of the purchase price, while the common stock price would be pegged at the market price, which was below two dollars a share at the time. This was a deterrent to conversion because it would require them to show a substantial loss on the Standard Precision books.

With Bert out of the management, we instituted a lawsuit against him to recover monies that he had been lavishly spending without a legitimate business purpose. At this point, Reuben Siwek began to play a more active role in representing Designatronics. I went into the Sterling facility and began a study of the entire operation. What I found was, in some respects, shocking. I made a study of the sales, which were broken into two categories. Category 1 were sales for standard products as listed in the catalog, and category 2 was made up of subcontracts for nonstandard assemblies. I discovered that our order backlog contained subcontracts that were being sold at a loss. The catalog sales appeared to be potentially profitable. There were 120 people employed and had been for some time. I began to evaluate each person and their function and found that forty people were unnecessary. Forty people were engaged in the subcontracts division that continually generated losses. I found that a great deal of the machinery was outmoded and never used. However, the most shocking thing of all was the condition of a considerable portion of the inventory, which I discovered to be obsolete and unsalable or in such unbalanced quantities that it would take years to sell based on current sales.

It went against my grain when I was forced to lay off so many people, but it had to be done. Within eight weeks, we reduced our workforce by forty people. I began to develop a reputation for being an "axer." In the process of evaluating our personnel, I found Martin Hoffman, who was in the accounting department. I saw in him the potential for helping me turn the company around. Together, we worked to evaluate each job and each worker.

We studied the contracts we had on the books and were able to successfully get out from under many of them by subcontracting them out to other vendors with better capability. We reviewed our purchase orders and vendors and found that we were overpaying for many of our purchases. We learned that our purchasing agent was receiving kickbacks on orders he let. He had to be replaced. We made a study of the machinery and equipment and ultimately decided to arrange for an auction sale of much of the equipment used mostly for the subcontracts division, which was losing so much money. After the auction sale, we realized that we could move the valuable part of the company into our Mineola facility and save on the costs associated with operating another plant. We did just that!

By August 31, 1961, our certified financial statement was a disaster. We had generated net sales of $1,071,326 and showed a bottom line loss of $665,403. Nobody was happy, but we were on the path to making corrections, and in a few months, we began to see the results of all our efforts. It began to reflect itself in the tremendous reduction of losses; and shortly thereafter, we began to show profits.

Our troubles were far from over. We still had a copyright infringement suit to contend with. This suit was being defended by Standard Precision Corp. since the infringement took place on its watch. It was Standard Precision Corp. that issued the catalog that was infringing. We were barred from using the old catalog and feverishly went to work preparing a new one. We ultimately produced a catalog that became an example for others in the industry. Until then, all competitor catalogs depicted the components in two dimensions. Our new catalog showed our components in isometric (or three-dimensional) drawings. Later, other companies followed. Our new catalog eliminated any further difficulty with the infringement, and Standard Precision Corp. paid Ace Design $21,500. And Designatronics paid $3,500 to settle the suit.

As Designatronics's prospects brightened, our stock price rose, raising a new problem. If we were successful in continuing to grow our company, and if it continued to reflect itself in the market price of the stock going up above $4 a share, it might induce Standard Precision Corp. to convert their stock and effectively retake the company. I felt that we were in a catch-22. Grow the company and it is in danger of being taken over. Don't grow the company and prevent us from making anything successful out of it. We were pondering this problem as we continued to make the company more efficient and more profitable.

Our fiscal year ended August 31, 1962, showed a vast improvement in the company's operations. We had managed to increase sales to $1,812,295. Although we did not generate any profit, at least we had contained the extensive losses we had sustained the previous year.

We still had to deal with the problem that we overpaid for the overvalued machinery and equipment and especially the inventory. With Reuben Siwek as our counsel, we sued Standard Precision. They had certified that the inventory was properly valued. At the next audit, they told us that our inventory contained obsolete components running into the hundreds of thousands of dollars. They insisted that we write off that inventory, reducing our profit considerably. It was on this basis that we sued Standard Precision.

During this period, the management of Standard Precision had a shakeup, which resulted in Roger Heywood and Peter Hewes being replaced on our board of directors by F. Kelly and L. Tornel. I immediately sensed their hostility, and I was certain that if we did not shake ourselves loose from them, we would be swallowed up. We had many arguments about how we were directing the company, and they were defensive about the lawsuit we had instituted against them.

In the fiscal year ended August 31, 1963, we continued to improve our financial position. Our sales increased moderately, replacing a lot of unprofitable sales in previous years. Sales totaled $1,906,734 while net profit was $83,136. The more progress we made, the more concerned we were about being swallowed up again by Standard Precision. We fought hard to come to a settlement with them, and we finally did.

In February 1964, all outstanding issues with Standard Precision Corp. were settled. The agreement held that Designatronics would purchase all the outstanding shares of convertible preferred shares in exchange for $150,000 in cash and debenture bonds valued at $775,000, which would bear interest at 4%. This represented a reduction of almost $235,000 in the purchase price we had paid. We felt it was a fair sum after accounting for the reduction in the value of our inventory and adjusted book value for the machinery and equipment we had acquired. In addition, the agreement included the Port Washington building. Of course, this put an additional financial burden on the company because the transaction converted equity, which was in the form of the preferred stock to debt with the issuance of the debenture bonds.

The agreement also called for the resignation of the Standard Precision representatives on our board. With that accomplished, we were no longer in danger of being swallowed up. All we had to do was concentrate on making money to cover our interest payments.

In the fiscal year ended August 31, 1964, our sales dropped as the result of a reduction of military spending. However, our profit margins continued to improve. Sales totaled $1,607,985 and net profit increased to $224,665. Our cash position improved from $276,081 to $685,560.

All this was reflected at our annual meeting of stockholders held on March 23, 1964. The stockholders approved the following resolutions:

1. Approval of the purchase and redemption by Designatronics of all outstanding shares of 4% accumulated convertible stock, 10 cents par value.
2. Approval and authorization of the corporation to issue series 1979 debenture bonds with an aggregate amount of $775,000 pursuant to terms of agreement dated February 27, 1964, between Standard Precision Corp. and Designatronics. To be applied against the purchase price of the 4% cumulative convertible preferred stock, 10 cents par value.
3. Approval of the cancellation of the entire class of authorized outstanding 4% accumulative convertible preferred stock 10 cents par value and to provide for voting rights to debenture bondholders for election of four directors to the board of directors upon occurrence of certain defaults.

With our cash position so drastically improved, we voted to redeem all the outstanding 6% convertible debenture bonds due on December 1, 1974. We were now in a position where our financial statement had been considerably altered.

We were more heavily in debt as a result of the cancellation of the preferred stock in exchange for debenture bonds, but we were rid of the Standard Precision members on our board.

At a board meeting on February 15, 1965, we elected a new board consisting of Joe, Julia, George, Reuben Siwek, and me. We thought that Reuben would be an asset to our company. We were now a five-person board again. In addition, we voted to grant a stock option to Martin Hoffman of 5,000 shares at $2.875 per share, which was the mean price between the bid and asked on that day. He earned it.

The company continued its growth in 1965. We disposed of the Port Washington property through a sale, and we were happy to be rid of it.

A NEW SCHOOL AND A NEW HOME

ALTHOUGH I SPENT a great deal of time getting our business in some semblance of order, at home, there were other problems. The school that Sheila and Deborah were attending kept getting more and more crowded. Classroom space was at a premium, and there was talk about bringing in portable classrooms; but what did happen was the school went to half sessions, eliminating many of the programs. Julia and other parents thought that was shortchanging the children. We became irate, and after much serious soul-searching, we decided we had to find another school for Sheila and Deborah.

We became familiar with Woodmere Academy, a few towns away from where we lived in Far Rockaway, which had an excellent reputation for its educational program. There was one problem. The tuition was expensive. However, Julia was adamant that we make the change. She was willing to go to work to help pay the tuition. I shortly found out that she was not kidding. She immediately prepared to take the exam to become an attendance teacher. After intensive study, she passed the exam and was hired. Her salary did help with the tuition. Although my salary had increased each year and was now at $25,000, we were not living in the lap of luxury.

When we applied for admission, the children were interviewed; and for some reason, the interviewer thought that Sheila should repeat the last grade she attended in the public school while Deborah moved into her next grade, putting her only one year behind Sheila, who was two years older.

As one would suppose, Woodmere Academy was located in Woodmere, New York, a mostly upper-middle-class town. The public schools are located in school district 14, reputed to be one of the best on Long Island. However, in order to attend public school in Woodmere, one was required to be a resident of either Woodmere or Hewlett. The caliber of education was on par with Woodmere Academy. We thought that if we lived in Woodmere, we could have the children attend public school and reallocate the tuition money to upgrade our housing. We began to search for a house in Woodmere or Hewlett that we thought we could afford. We saw an ad in the newspaper by a local real estate broker that seemed adequate for our purposes. It was located on Henry Avenue, a nice quiet street. The agent, Freida, happened to live across the street from the house. It was owned by Mr. Levy, an attorney who lived there with his wife and children. He was "moving up" to a new, more exclusive home in Woodsburgh, an incorporated village in Woodmere. The house seemed adequate for us and was available to be occupied in time for us to qualify to have Sheila and Deborah attend the public school. We agreed to purchase the house for $28,000, and Mr. Levy agreed to vacate before the beginning of the school year.

Although Reuben Siwek was the corporate attorney for Designatronics, he was also an experienced real estate lawyer, and I retained him to represent me in the purchase of the house. We quickly signed a contract, putting down the necessary deposit while we applied for a mortgage. At the same time, we listed our house on McBride Street in Far Rockaway for sale with a real estate broker.

We quickly obtained mortgage approval; however, when we asked Mr. Levy to set a date for the closing, he informed us that he had changed his mind and did not want to go through with the sale. Reuben told me we could take Mr. Levy to court and force him to go through with the sale, but that would take time, and time was of the essence for us in order to be residents of the Woodmere Hewlett school district before the beginning of the school year. I felt that we had no alternative but to go out and find another house. Feverishly Julia and I hunted. We asked Freida to find us another house, but we also did some searching on our own. We ultimately found a listing in the newspaper for a house in Hewlett Neck, an incorporated village in Woodmere, which Julia fell in love with immediately. She said, "You can bury me from this house."

The house at 143 Hewlett Neck Road was empty. It was available for immediate occupancy. The previous owners were divorcing, and the house had to be sold. It was located on a one-third acre of land. It was an all-brick colonial with four bedrooms and two baths upstairs and a living room, dining room, kitchen, den, maids' room, one and one-half baths, and a screened-in porch on the ground floor.

The price was $38,000. It was more than we could afford, but we entered into a contract to buy it anyway. After signing the contract, I instructed Reuben to arrange for the cancellation of the other purchase on Henry Avenue and to get our deposit back. When he approached Mr. Levy, he was told that he had changed his mind and was going ahead with the sale. I was in a state of shock. There was nothing we could do except go ahead or lose our deposit. We closed on the Henry Avenue house also. I found that I was the owner of three houses, more real estate than I needed or could afford. I was burdened with three mortgages, but at that moment, we were so excited about the new house that the reality of the problem hadn't yet fully struck us.

Within two weeks, we moved in on time to register the children in the school district 14 public school, after which I devoted my attention to the disposal of my real estate holdings. I posted a "for sale" sign at the Far Rockaway house and contacted Freida, the real estate broker who sold me the Henry Avenue house, and listed the house with her. Within a few weeks, I was successful in finding a buyer for the Far Rockaway house for pretty much what I had originally paid for it. The Henry Avenue house was another story. Week after week, I consulted with Freida on why she had not found a buyer. I had entered into an exclusive arrangement with her for eight weeks, during which time she had not brought a single customer. I then began to advertise the house on my own and on weekends, waiting for callers to appear. I also turned the listing over to other brokers on a nonexclusive basis. After a period of no success and a feeling of desperation, I offered the house to the brokers to try to rent it if they could not sell it. Mostly, I was angry at Freida because she sold the house to me, and now she could not find another buyer.

One Saturday morning, I received a call from a real estate broker who said that he had found a prospective tenant, Mrs. Denis, who was interested in renting the house. The broker had shown the house to Mrs. Denis, and she liked it very much. She had agreed to the rent and the security deposit, and there was nothing to do but to come down to the office and meet her. The broker could have the lease ready by the time I came. I thought it was too good to be true and told him I would come down immediately. Upon my arrival, I was introduced to Mrs. Denis, who spoke with a French accent and appeared to be very nice. She told me she intended to live in the house with her son and nephew. She was a widow and made her living as a dressmaker and intended to set one room aside to do sewing in the house. I had no problem with that. We signed a two-year lease. I was not too happy about being saddled with the house for two years; however, the rent was enough to cover my mortgage payments, and I could use the financial relief of carrying the upkeep in the house.

I went home to announce the good news to the family. I would no longer have to spend my weekends sitting in the house waiting for prospective buyers. The following afternoon, I received a phone call from Freida telling me that there are Negroes going in the house and did I know anything about that. I said I did not, but it was possible that another real estate broker might be showing the house. Freida voiced concern about the caliber of people going in the house. I told her that I had no problem with blacks so long as they could pay the rent and take care of the property. Furthermore, I told her that she had nothing to worry about since I just rented the house but had not yet told the brokers to stop showing the house. After a few hours, Freida called me again. This time, she informed me that "those people" were still hanging around. I told her I would come down and find out why.

When I arrived I, found Mrs. Denis in the house. I greeted her, and she proceeded to introduce me to her very "black" brother-in-law (whose name I cannot recall); her not quite so "black" nephew, Pierre; and her "brown" son, Antoine. To me, her brother-in-law appeared well-dressed, and Mrs. Denis then told me they were Haitian refugees from the Duvalier regime. Mrs. Denis's brother-in-law had been a judge. I said I was glad to meet them and that I hoped they would enjoy living there.

I had no problem with them, but Freida was another story. I visited her at her home after leaving Mrs. Denis. I told her that the people she saw were my new tenants, and she was irate. "After all, you don't have to live with them," she said. Her remark made me angry, and I retorted with "Well, you had the chance to sell the house to whomever you wished, but you were unsuccessful."

For many weeks after that, I kept getting complaining phone calls about the wild parties occurring in the house. I ignored these calls, attributing them to prejudice. I also received several threatening phone calls; but after a few weeks, all that quieted down. I continued to be satisfied as long as the rent was paid on time, and it was.

With my children now in a good elementary school offering a full day of classes and my real estate problems eased up considerably, I turned my attention to a plan for a well-deserved vacation. I had been promising myself to do a cross-country trip for a long time. For the past few summers, our children had gone to summer camp. This coming summer would be different. Julia and I would rent a camper, and we would travel cross-country and back and spend six weeks doing it.

We spent much of our spare time planning the trip—laying out routes to follow and deciding what sights we were going to see. The Grand Canyon, Yellowstone National Park, the Badlands, Niagara Falls, and a whole list of cities, including Los Angeles, San Francisco, Salt Lake City, and Denver, just to name a few. We were all excited at the prospect. We rented campers for weekend sojourns to nearby camping grounds to gain some experience in preparation for the trip. With the possible exception of some of Julia's complaints about leaving her beautiful home in exchange for cramped quarters in a camper without comfortable cooking and toilet facilities, everything went off quite well. The trip itself turned out to be especially rewarding, and I measure that remark by the fact that my children have fond and vivid memories of it. They point to it as one of the highlights of family togetherness in their growing-up years.

It was late August when we returned from our trip, and little did I know that I would be back in California before a few months passed. During our trip, I had been in touch with my office frequently. August was the end of our fiscal year, and that meant we would undergo a certified audit in preparation for filings with the Securities and Exchange Commission. It also meant the beginning of preparation of our annual report to stockholders. We immediately plunged into the task.

One morning, Martin approached me and reported that he had just finished a conversation with Joe Davis, our California sales representative. Joe Davis told him that

Perfect Gear and Instrument Corp.—whose home base was in Northridge, California—was in financial difficulty and was for sale. Perfect Gear and Instrument Corp. were a small competitor, and we had customers on the West Coast, and it might be advantageous if we had manufacturing capability there. I was interested in investigating the situation. We talked to the principal of Perfect Gear and Instrument Corp. and made arrangements to inspect the facility. Martin and I flew out, and after a few days of negotiation, we decided that we would buy the company.

After obtaining stockholder approval at a Designatronics stockholder meeting in April 1966, we consummated the purchase of Perfect Gear and Instrument Corp. stock and made it a subsidiary of Designatronics. Perfect Gear and Instrument Corp. had accumulated carryforward tax losses the past couple of years, and we felt that we could offset the losses against profits in Automatic Coil Co., Inc. and Sterling Instrument and thereby save a great deal of tax payments, which would help our cash position considerably. In order to take advantage of the losses, we would not be allowed to move Perfect Gear and Instrument Corp. from its existing location. That was acceptable.

The acquisition was successful. We appointed Martin Hoffman president and Joe Davis vice president of Perfect Gear and Instrument Corp. which operated as a subsidiary of Designatronics. Acquiring Perfect Gear and Instrument Corp. turned out to be a good decision. It gave us increased sales and added to our profit picture.

By the end of our fiscal year, August 31, 1966, sales had increased to $2,648,983 and we generated a net profit of

$245,589 (or 66 cents per common share). Perfect Gear and Instrument Corp. began to contribute to our profit picture.

At a board of directors meeting held on January 9, 1967, we had put a profit-sharing plan in place, and the board voted a bonus to Joe, Martin, and me to the tune of $7,500. The stockholders meeting was held on February 15, 1967, and Martin Hoffman would join our slate of directors in place of George Heller, who resigned. Reuben Siwek had previously joined our board.

Our corporate structure was as follows:

Sol Schwartz	President
Joseph Rubenfeld	Executive Vice President and Treasurer
Martin Hoffman	Vice President in charge of Sales
Reuben Siwek	Secretary
Julia Schwartz	Assistant Secretary

Our fiscal year ended August 31, 1967, was a banner year. Sales increased to $4,132,232 and income to $521,876 (or 70 cents per share). It all appeared to be too good to be true. Our stock soared to almost $16 per share. Our salaries had increased, and mine reached $41,500 per year. We were granted stock options. The board proposed to increase the number of authorized shares from 1 million to 1.25 million, and a special stockholder meeting was called to authorize the increase. The purpose was to be able to approve a five-for-four stock split so that more shares could be put in public hands to improve the stock's marketability.

We were very proud of our accomplishments. In six years, from 1961 to 1967, we quadrupled our sales from $1 million to $4 million, and we grew our profit to more than $500,000 from a loss in excess of $600,000.

When my family and I left for a well-deserved vacation to a lakefront house in the Monadnock Mountains in New Hampshire, I was totally unaware of the terrible misfortunes we were heading into. While relaxing one day in early August, I received a phone call from Martin Hoffman informing me that he had received a call from the federal government's General Accounting Office. Their representatives were coming to our plant to survey us with regard to charges that we had been overcharging the government on some of our contracts. Most of our contracts were small, and they were for component parts. They were items listed in our catalog. I had no idea as to the scope of the charges. I immediately cut my vacation short and returned home.

I was present when the representatives of the GAO arrived, and they told us that Congressman Otis Pike, Democrat from Riverhead, Long Island, was making the charge against us and that the Department of Defense and a subcommittee of the House Armed Services Committee was going to investigate and review the direct military contracts of the Sterling Instrument Division. Representatives of the subcommittee entered our premises and surveyed thousands of our invoices for the past three years. During this review, the Defense Department suspended the company from submitting future bids unless they were in the interest of the government. This action would affect our future sales.

We retained Washington counsel to represent us and to contest the suspension order we received. The subcommittee review was still incomplete and inconclusive, and the ultimate disposition of the matter would be made sometime in the future.

By October 1967, the GAO examination of our records was concluded. The Department of Defense had not continued their initial inquiry awaiting the conclusion of the House subcommittee report.

While we were waiting for the report to be issued, I made an appointment to see Congressman Pike. I wanted to know why he was pursuing us. When I was ushered into his office in Washington, DC, the first question he put to me was "Do you have a public relations firm under retainer?" I said no. He then informed me that there was going to be a congressional hearing on the matter and that there was no way I could stop it.

I tried to explain to him that if we had overcharged the government, we were certainly willing to return any monies deemed excessive, but he was more interested in having the investigation go forward than in settling the matter.

As I became more astute in the months that followed, I began to realize that we were the small fish that the congressman could pursue. His later attempt to accuse General Electric and other large military contractors came to naught because they were powerful and had public relations firms working behind the scenes to squelch any attempt to make any of the charges stick. We did not have that kind of influence, so we were an easy target for him. There was a great deal of newspaper publicity about how the government was paying exorbitant prices for toilet seats and other purchases, but they soon quieted down when Congressman Pike was quietly put in his place by influential company lobbyists. However, the damage was done as far as we were concerned. The investigation turned up that we had done a total of $800,000 with the military during the previous three years.

Our own investigation into these sales showed up that, technically and legally, we had been overcharging on many of the items we sold to the Department of Defense. The illegality centered on the fact that every contract had a clause in small print that said that the price bid to the government was to be no more than that charged to other customers. The clause had to be checked off, and it was as a matter of routine. In addition, most contracts called for special packaging and the addition of a preservative to prevent corrosion. This special treatment increased the cost of the product; however, since we sold it under the same part number listed in the catalog and at an increased price to reflect our additional costs, it was calculated as an overcharge. This carried little weight with the investigators when they figured the overcharges. It is true that there were items that were sold at inflated prices through the greed of certain salespeople whom we employed. Since they were receiving a salary as well as a commission, it was to their benefit to charge as much as they could get away with in order to increase the sale, but this turned out to be under $100,000.

The negative publicity was affecting our sales, and although we had no definitive resolution to our problems with the government, the suspension was still in force. We learned that even though the government had not pressed any charges against our company, they were legally able to continue the suspension for eighteen months. And if they saw fit to continue it for an additional eighteen months, they would have to charge us with committing some illegality or release us from the suspension order. Three years is an awfully long time to wait for us to again be able to pursue the mainstay of our business.

The Sterling Instrument Division represented the biggest portion of our sales volume. We had to do something while we waited for the government matter to be resolved. We did a great deal. We had been investigating possibly moving from the NASDAQ to the American Stock Exchange, but we were told that we did not meet the requirements since we did not have enough stock outstanding and in the hands of the public. We took steps to rectify that situation by amending our articles of incorporation so that we could increase the number of authorized shares from 1.25 million to 2.5 million. Subsequently, our board of directors voted to declare a 2-for-1 stock split, with shares to be distributed on January 25, 1968.

We decided that it was not in our best interest to continue to be dependent on work for the military. We had to redirect our business to the commercial market. With that in mind, we went about searching for an engineer who could help us do this. Victor Kuras knew a mechanical engineer whom he had worked with before he joined us. His name was Frank Buchsbaum, and he had a doctorate in mechanical engineering from Columbia University. He came with great credentials. More important than his credentials, he came with a great deal of common sense, imagination, and enthusiasm in undertaking the challenge. He joined us as director of engineering, and after a short time, he presented us with the idea of starting a new division offering mechanical components for the commercial market. These products would be sold through a catalog, just as we sold Sterling Instrument products—but they would be products we did not manufacture. Instead, he would make deals with other manufacturers to manufacture the components, and we would act as a supermarket for these parts. Frank set to work to make these arrangements and came up with the name Stock Drive Products, which we set up as a division of Designatronics. This turned out to be one of the smartest decisions we made.

Our fiscal year ended August 31, 1968, reflected our difficulties with the government. Our sales dropped to $3,622,796 while our earnings fell to $399,188 (or 53 cents a share).

By March 1969, we had been negotiating with the Long Island Trust Company for a loan, the purpose of which was to retire the debentures Standard Precision Corp. held. Those debentures had built into them certain restrictions against borrowing, which hindered our growth. We successfully negotiated a bank loan of $510,000 for a period of eight years, payable in quarter-annual installments of $17,000 plus interest beginning on January 1, 1970, and maturing on March 1, 1977, at an interest rate of 1/2% above the prime rate. By this time, we had redeemed some debentures so that there was only $485,000 still outstanding. We started to negotiate with Starlite to discount the face amount of these debentures for our total redemption immediately. Standard Precision Corp. was aware of our difficulties with the government and no longer had any confidence in our survival. They were anxious to have us redeem the debentures. We ultimately settled on a sum of $445,000—a discount of $40,000. With the redemption of the debentures, we finally and completely severed any further contact with Standard Precision Corp.

Things were not going well with our Sterling Instrument and Automatic Coil Co., Inc. divisions. Although Stock Drive Products held out promise, we were still in the middle of getting the operation started. Automatic Coil Co., Inc. had personnel problems. They were unable to train and keep a skilled workforce because no sooner did we train a worker than he would leave and find a job that paid him more money at some company that was doing defense work. They were able to pay their workers better salaries because they were operating on cost-plus contracts, and it was to their advantage to pay their help more. We felt that if we were going to survive, we would have to find an offshore location where we could train and keep our employees. We were introduced to the advantages of setting up a factory in Puerto Rico.

Joe and I visited Puerto Rico, and we were hosted by an organization known as Fomento, a government agency whose task was to attract industry to come to the island. They showed us a number of factory buildings in and around San Juan. They told us that there were other buildings available outside San Juan that offered us up to thirty years of tax-exempt status. They were trying to encourage industry to go to outlying areas where the unemployment rate was high. We were taken to a small town, Comerio, where we saw a factory already built and ready for occupancy. We were attracted to the idea that we would be the only factory in town and would have our pick of workers. It seemed to have all that we needed: available labor with no other place to go in town, a thirty-year tax exemption, and a building ready to be powered up.

Joe and I returned home enthusiastic about the idea of setting up manufacturing facilities for Automatic Coil Co., Inc. in Comerio. By July 1969, we had approval of our plan from our board, and we began the task of moving machinery and equipment to the island. We set up a new subsidiary that would operate under the name Automatic Coil Company of Puerto Rico.

JULIA'S DEATH

IN SEPTEMBER, I decided to take Julia to Puerto Rico for our vacation. Since our trip to Haiti and Jamaica some years earlier, she had not been out of the country, and we thought it would be an excellent opportunity to relax there. We stayed at the Caribe Hilton, which we thought was a luxurious hotel; and when we were not relaxing at the pool, we explored the island by auto. We visited the factory building in Comerio and realistically talked about the obstacles we would encounter before we got the plant operating successfully. We knew that both Joe and I would have to spend weeks being there while people were hired and trained to perform the work. Joe and I had agreed that we would perform our duties in two-week periods. He would spend two weeks in Puerto Rico and then return home while I took the next two weeks.

It was a pleasant vacation for Julia and me. We didn't realize that we were about to face a crisis neither of us were prepared for. One day, we decided to take a trip to St. Thomas, where we wanted to do some shopping. We took a hydro seal boat. It was the first time either of us was on a boat of this kind. On the way back, the trip was rocky. Julia was leaning against the rail with her arms resting on a ledge. When we arrived back in San Juan, we noticed that black and blue marks appeared on her arms. We didn't think it was serious at that time.

When our vacation ended, we returned home, and I returned to work. Since our fiscal year ended on August 31, 1969, our auditors were at work auditing our books. We had still not heard anything from the Department of Defense. It was already over two years into the suspension and six months into the extended period, and still, no charges had been pressed. However, a new problem entered my life. I learned about an existing Renegotiation Act, and its purpose was to control excess profits made by corporations on government contracts. We were now going to be investigated for making excess profits. Ironically, we were about to learn about the discouraging results from our accountants. Our fiscal year indicated that our sales had dropped to $2,703,497 while we sustained our first loss year since *1961*. Although a loss of *$29,199* was not disastrous, it was an extreme change from the previous year.

The past two years had been traumatic. When Julia and I returned from Puerto Rico, she saw her physician to investigate the black and blue marks on her arms. After some testing, she was diagnosed with chronic leukemia. We were shocked and devastated. We were told it was serious, but it could be treated. For the next four weeks, she visited a recommended specialist for treatment, but we saw no signs of improvement in her blood tests. In December, just before Christmas, she developed terrible coughing spells, and the doctor arranged for her to be admitted to New York Hospital. I spent the next few weeks at the hospital, but not until I had made arrangements to send Sheila and Deborah to California to stay with Julia's sister, Bess Cohen.

In the hospital, endless tests were performed, but Julia grew progressively worse. Her cough was diagnosed as caused by emphysema. The chronic leukemia had rapidly become acute, and Julia died on December 29, 1969.

Bess brought the children back to New York. At the funeral, the rabbi that officiated delivered the following eulogy:

EULOGY FOR JULIA SCHWARTZ

IT IS HARD TO BELIEVE THAT JULIA IS GONE. SO FULL OF STRENGTH, ORIGINALITY, AND KINDNESS, SHE CAST AN EXTRA GLOW OVER EVERYTHING SHE DID.

HER INTELLIGENT INTEREST, INCESSANT VITALITY, AND BROAD RANGE OF CONCERN MADE HER A SOURCE OF STRENGTH IN EVERYTHING SHE TOUCHED AND FOR EVERYONE SHE KNEW.

SHE WAS AN ORIGINAL. SHE WILL NOT BE EASILY REPLACED. THE HUSBAND WHO SHARED SO MUCH OF THE JOYS AND TRIALS OF LIFE WITH HER WILL MISS HER STRENGTH AND COMPANIONSHIP.

THE CHILDREN SHE RAISED WITH SUCH INTEREST AND CONCERN WILL MISS THE UNIQUE SOURCE OF LOVING VITALITY.

SHE WAS STRONG, AND SHE GAVE THAT STRENGTH TO ALL SHE KNEW AND LOVED. AS SHE NEVER LET THE POWER OF DISEASE FLAG HER STRENGTH, SO SHALL YOU STAND STRONG AT HER LOSS.

> AS SHE WAS STRONG AND BRAVE IN THE BEST AND IN THE WORST OF TIMES, SO SHALL YOU BE.
>
> THERE WILL BE A VOID WITHOUT HER, BUT YOU SHALL CARRY ON. SHE SHOWED YOU THE WAY. LET HER STANDARD BE YOUR INSPIRATION. SEEK A LIFE FILLED WITH VITALITY AND MEANING. NEVER END THE SEARCH THAT SHE BEGAN—A SEARCH FOR THE BEST THAT SHE SET UPON YOU. IT IS THROUGH YOU AND WHAT YOU MAKE OF YOURSELVES THAT SHE SHALL HAVE AN ETERNITY.
>
> MAY THERE BE, FOR HER, A FINAL PEACE!

Rabbi Seigel was not a religious man. There was not one mention of God in the eulogy. He knew how Julia and I felt on the subject.

After sitting shiva, during which time our home was filled with relatives and friends, I settled down to take stock of my life. Chippy was attending and living at Stoneybrook University. Sheila (aged 15) and Deborah (aged 13) were living at home with me. My business responsibilities called for me to alternate going to Puerto Rico with Joe Rubenfeld, and I was in the midst of unresolved issues with the Department of Defense and the Renegotiation Board. I was forty-four years old and turning gray. I knew that I could not afford to have a nervous breakdown.

Primarily, I was concerned about Sheila and Deborah. It was not a good time to lose a mother. Not that any time is, but at their sensitive ages, it was especially bad. I was no substitute for Julia, although I tried real hard. They were in need of winter coats. Julia was supposed to shop for them but instead became ill. So here it was January 1970 and very cold, and I was on my virgin journey with my daughters to shop for overcoats. I don't remember how satisfied they were with our choices, but they did not complain.

There were so many obligations and people depending on me. I don't know where I obtained the strength to go on, but I did.

BACK AT WORK

OUR NEW DIVISION— Stock Drive Products, headed up by Frank Buchsbaum—had introduced our new product catalog geared toward the commercial market, and it was an instant success in the marketplace. Customers reacted positively to the new company, and sales began to increase slowly.

Automatic Coil Co. of Puerto Rico was turning into a disaster. Although I immediately hired a housekeeper, it was not possible for me to leave home and spend two weeks in Puerto Rico. As a result, Joe had to remain there for a long time, and it was playing havoc with his home life. When we opened the plant, the entire town of Comerio turned out, led by the mayor, to cut the ribbon on the plant opening. We were able to hire all the people we needed without difficulty. The problem arose when we searched for experienced supervisory personnel and found that there were no such people in the town. Experienced personnel did exist in San Juan, the capital city, but they were not willing to resettle in Comerio—nor were they willing to commute daily since the roads were treacherous at that time and you needed a car. That was a poor combination of details that ultimately made continued operation impossible for us in Puerto Rico. For a while, there were times when inexperienced people managed the plant. We had to find another solution, and we had to find it fast.

Automatic Coil Co., Inc. had recently begun to do business with a large Israeli company. They were building electronic communications equipment for the Israeli army as well as for other companies internationally. This equipment required a great many coils and transformers that we were able to furnish. At the same time, Automatic Coil Co., Inc. was also building the same coils for other companies within the United States. We desperately needed our production capacity to continue uninterrupted. We had to find a quick solution for our Puerto Rican difficulties. Help came in the form of Amos Altman, whom we met in Puerto Rico. He told us of a company in Port-Au-Prince, Haiti, which had an electronics assembly plant owned by Sidney Fields. He would be willing to allow us to use space in his facility, and he would supply people to work for us at a predetermined hourly rate. When we raised the issue of supervision, which was our real problem, he told us that there was a man trained as an electrical engineer but who had gone to Haiti as a missionary and who now needed to either find a way to earn a livelihood there or return home to the United States. This called for a speedy response, and since decisions had to be made quickly, I arranged to have our housekeeper stay for a week with the children, and Joe and I quickly left for Haiti. There we were met at the airport by Sidney Fields, the owner of the company we came to visit. He first escorted us to our hotel; and after checking in, we spent several hours visiting his facility. We explained that we were interested in meeting the engineer turned missionary.

He made a phone call, and shortly, Phil Hanson came to the plant, where we carried on an extensive interview.

We found that he didn't know very much about the specific product, but he could be taught quickly to take over the responsibilities of training a workforce. Joe and I were ecstatic. We spent the next few days continuing to visit the plant and to see what other production Andy was having done there and spending time with Phil Hanson, acquainting him with our products. Sidney's wife, whom we knew as "Mom," was a wonderful hostess. She took Joe and me around the town and acquainted us with various arts and crafts shops, restaurants, and other hotels. We visited the Ibo Lele Hotel, which was situated in the mountains of Petionville and which I remembered from my first trip to Haiti almost ten years earlier. I was just as impressed as I was back then. It was decorated with extensive Haitian art, had an outdoor dining room, and boasted excellent rum punches. The Ibo Lele became the home of all our stateside personnel who later came to visit Haiti.

Within a few weeks, we had our operation beginning to produce while we shut down our facility in Comerio, shipping all our supplies and equipment to Haiti. Phil did a great job of getting us started and also began training a number of people he felt had the potential for being supervisors. As our productivity increased in Haiti, we produced less and less at the Automatic Coil Co., Inc. plant in New York. New York became a shipping point for sending materials to Haiti and having the completed products returned for inspection and, finally, shipment to our customers.

Events happened quickly from this point and on many different fronts. Our fiscal year that ended on August 31, 1970, indicated that our sales continued to drop, as did our earnings. On sales of $2,548,826, we sustained a loss of $322,813. Our board of directors decided that the officers of the corporation should take a reduction in salary until such time as the fortunes of the company were turned around.

After September 1970, three years after our company had been suspended from doing business with the Department of Defense, no charges had been leveled against us. All attempts by our attorneys to get the government to lift the suspension were met with failure, and we were forced to file suit against the US government. The lawsuit began on October 27, 1970, which resulted in a decision in favor of the corporation on December 1, 1970, enjoining the government from continuing the suspension. We then instituted an action against the United States of America for damages sustained as a result of the continued suspension of the company from doing business with the Department of Defense beyond the period set forth in the Armed Services Procurement Regulations.

We, despite all our difficulties, remained optimistic about the future of the company. We knew that things would get worse before they got better, but we also knew that it was necessary to anticipate our future needs to grow successfully. We knew that our Stock Products Division would require space that was not available at our Mineola plant. I carefully evaluated our position. In the past, we always made our moves to larger spaces during a lull in business. That may not be the conventional wisdom, but I always found that we were better off growing into available space. Our Mineola facility contained 20,000 square feet. The next move turned out to be a brazen departure in that we moved to a 50,000-square-feet facility on Denton Avenue in New Hyde Park. There we were able to house all our operations comfortably in addition to allotting future space for Stock Drive Products when it began to produce results.

My family life at home during the first year after Julia died was extremely stressful. I did have business responsibilities, and I was not always able to tend to things at home as I would have liked. We went through a series of housekeepers. The one that originally seemed most promising was a young woman named Shana who had a son, Fred. They spoke French and came from Algeria. Shana told me that she was looking for the kind of placement that would allow her son, who was seven or eight years old, to go to school in a stable environment. I was very excited about the prospect because we had had a number of previous housekeepers who turned out to be unreliable. I thought Shana and Fred would fit in just fine with Sheila and Deborah. For a while, the household functioned satisfactorily. It seemed that Sheila and Deborah bonded with Shana. Fred was enrolled in school, and Shana turned out to be a good cook. We all learned to speak a little French. I really thought we had lucked out.

For several previous summers, we had rented a rustic house on a lake in the Monadnock region of New Hampshire. The house, which had a sign outside it identifying it as Boulder Oaks, belonged to the same man who owned and ran a trailer camp adjacent to the property on which the house stood. Families would rent sites on the premises and park their trailers for the entire summer. There was a swimming pool available for the campers and a social hall where people would gather to dance and socialize. Our family became friendly with many of the campers, and for several summers, we would return and rent the Boulder Oaks house. I had purchased a small motorboat, which I brought to New Hampshire with us, and parked it in front of our house for the entire summer. Our kids learned to water-ski off the boat, as did many of the other children we were friendly with. I would come up every weekend and return to New York on Sunday night except for the two weeks that I vacationed there with the family.

After Julia died, I thought it would be nice if the kids could have another summer at Boulder Oaks, and I spoke to Shana about it. I explained that she would have to remain in New Hampshire for the entire summer along with Sheila, Deborah, and Fred. I would come up on weekends, do whatever shopping had to be done, and try to make their stay as pleasant as it had been in previous years. Sheila and Deborah encouraged Shana by telling her how great it was and that Fred would have a wonderful summer vacation, swimming, camping, and playing with kids his age. She agreed to the plan, and as soon as the kids were out of school, we packed the car and the boat and left for New Hampshire.

Everything went fine for about two weeks. When I came up for the weekend after the second week, Shana informed me that she wanted to go home. Apparently, she had heard from her boyfriend (whom I didn't know existed), and she wanted to be with him. I was furious because she did not tell me that there was a boyfriend in the picture. I had to find an alternative housekeeping arrangement and quickly. Help came when I asked my sister, Beatrice, if she would be willing to come to New Hampshire and "babysit" for a few weeks. She readily agreed, and very quickly, she and her husband, Joe, and daughter, Susan, made arrangements to come up. In the meantime, I left Deborah and Sheila in the care of one of the camper families with whom we were friendly and took Shana and Fred back to New York. When we arrived, I helped her pack her things; and shortly, her boyfriend arrived and took them away. I was shattered at the absence of any kind of notice. After they left, I immediately began my drive back to New Hampshire, where I remained with the kids until Beatrice, Joe, and Susan arrived a few days later. They stayed a number of weeks, and when it became necessary for them to go home, Abe and Ethel Polakoff, good friends of mine, came to take their place.

My search for a housekeeper was extremely frustrating, trying one after another without being able to find anyone reliable. I finally found a very nice woman named Gerty, a native from St. Kitts, who appeared quite reliable. She was not young or flighty, and I felt that she would be good for us.

After Shana, the kids had to make a whole new adjustment. The children were really very "testy." They were feeling insecure as the result of being "abandoned" by their mother and weren't exactly secure about being abandoned by their father. Did I love them? Would I take care of them? What was their future going to be like? These were some of the concerns I knew the children were having.

During this period and for some time after, I was faced with a great deal of acting out on the part of Sheila and Deborah. I had to contend with Deborah running away from home. She had a need to run away from home often in the past. We dealt with that problem by fixing up a room in our basement, which became her bedroom, or "runaway room," if she chose to "run away." Now, however, it was more serious when I received a phone call from a police precinct in Boston informing me that they were holding my daughter. Deborah and a wayward friend had decided that they could make it on their own and did not need parents anymore. They chose Boston because her girlfriend had a brother living there. I told the police to hold her. I would come and get her. The police also informed the parents of Deborah's friend, but they did not think it was necessary to bring her home. Their decision was to put their daughter on a bus to New York. I chose to drive to Boston and bring my daughter home.

When I arrived at the police station, they released Deborah in my custody, and we started the long drive back. We arrived home very late, and I ordered her to go to bed and we would talk about this in the morning. When morning came, I tried to talk to her and find out why she had run away. She responded with a great deal of impertinence and disrespect. For the second time in her life, I hit her. The first time was when she was still in her crib and insisted on trying to climb out. This time, I must have hit her very hard because her eye blackened. Later, I heard that in school, she bragged that her father had hit her. She also told this to other people, and the distinct impression I got was that she ran away in an attempt to get attention, and she was real proud of that black eye because it represented the fact that I really cared and loved her. There were other acting outs—experimenting with drugs and sex, which I could only surmise without being certain.

Sheila competed quite adequately with Deborah in making me miserable and in testing my devotion to them. She began staying out late without letting me know where she was going. One night, I became frantic when it was past 2:00 a.m. and she was not home from a dance at a local college. I drove like a maniac to the campus to try to find her. I cursed Julia all the way for deserting me and leaving me to handle our children alone. Ultimately, Sheila came home, calmly offering some lame excuse. I knew the girls needed help, as did I. I wasn't sure how to singlehandedly raise teenagers. I arranged for all of us to see a therapist. We began to individually see Mrs. Goodman.

TRUDY

CHRISTMAS WEEK 1970 was approaching. December 29 would be the first anniversary of Julia's death. I thought it would be a good idea if the girls and I spent some quality time together. I suggested that we find a warm climate to vacation to, but Chippy had another idea. She was now teaching at a school, and she had heard about a teacher-sponsored skiing trip to Val d'Isere, a resort town in the French Alps. Our family had done some local skiing in Vermont and New Hampshire in previous years, and the girls were all enthusiastic about going skiing again. Even though I was in favor of a vacation in a more moderate climate, I was more interested in being together with my girls. Chippy made the arrangements, and we all geared up, getting our skis, boots, and equipment ready for the adventure. It turned out to be a trip that altered our lives.

We joined our fellow travelers at the airport. Apparently, many of the people were schoolteachers and their friends. There was one young lady that caught my eye. She was dressed in an unusual jumpsuit that showed off her very attractive figure. She was traveling with another young woman. I couldn't help noticing her, but I quickly turned my attention back to my children. We boarded the plane for what was an uneventful flight. The trip, however, was not.

I became sick and ran a rather high temperature, but I kept that to myself during the flight. As we approached our destination, the captain came on to announce that we would be unable to land at the planned airport because of unusual storms. Instead, we would be forced to fly to another airport somewhere in Italy and, from there, take a bus to our destination. What we didn't realize—because we were not told—was that the bus trip would take a minimum of eight hours. I suffered through the rest of the flight and then the grueling bus trip.

When we finally arrived at our hotel, I was in a complete state of exhaustion. I immediately went to bed, but I felt that I was seriously ill with a high temperature. I asked Chippy to check with the hotel management about having a doctor come to my room. That was quickly arranged, and when he arrived, I told him that prior to our departure, I had been vaccinated. He attributed my high fever to a reaction to the serum. He prescribed medication (probably an antibiotic) and a sedative, and I fell into a deep sleep. I slept for twenty-four hours, and when I awoke, I found that my fever had broken. I was feeling much better.

I joined my girls in the downstairs lounge, where I heard the disappointing news that there was no snow on the mountain and that skiing was impossible. I was totally amazed at the concept that there was no snow in the Alps. Back at home, if we were planning to ski Mount Killington or Mount Snow or Hunter Mountain, we would check skiing conditions for a whole week before our scheduled trip, to make certain that there was snow. But who ever thought that it was necessary to do the same for the Alps? As we were contemplating what we should do, the attractive young lady I had seen the day before at the airport joined in our conversation. Together, we all explored the problem. She and her friend turned out to be very friendly. We learned that her name was Trudy Hoffman, and her friend's name was Marian Gold. They were both teachers and lived in Manhattan. After a while, Deborah, Sheila, and Chippy went off to mingle with other vacationers, and Marian eyed a guy whom she pursued. Trudy and I were left alone. We became better acquainted. Trudy was dressed in a very attractive "après-ski" outfit but confessed that she had never skied; and frankly, she didn't care if she didn't ski. She was more interested in social contacts. I learned that she was divorced, had no children, and was not attached. We enjoyed each other's company that evening and got to know more about each other.

The next day, after breakfast, we found that there was still no snow on the upper slopes. Beginners could fool around on almost level ground. My children went off to do whatever they felt like doing; and Trudy, Marian, and I took the cable car up to the top of the mountain because we had heard that they served delicious hot chocolate there. When we came down, I met the girls, and we went for lunch. The weather forecast was not very optimistic about any snowfall for the next few days. Someone suggested that we rent a car and go to Geneva. I had never been to Geneva, and I did have a second cousin, Lesley Brittman, living there with her husband, Marvin. We could go visit them. It might be better than sitting around at a ski lodge with nothing to do. Our family agreed, and Trudy and another young man, Charlie, thought they would like to go also. Trudy's friend Marian chose to remain behind. We arranged for a car rental and set off for Geneva. It was an adventurous trip across mountains, which required some of us to push the car because it couldn't climb up a hill on its own power. I recall that we made fun of it all and did ultimately reach Geneva. Trudy and Charlie went off to see some sights while the rest of us visited with Lesley and Marvin.

We found hotel accommodations as best we could without having reservations. Over dinner, we discussed what our next step should be. In the process of making elaborate plans, we heard a newscast that it was snowing at Val d'Isere. That being the case, we decided to return to our ski lodge the following morning. Most of us did plan on skiing except for Trudy. She was perfectly happy looking lovely in her ski outfit.

We spent the next few days skiing, and I got to know Trudy well enough to think that I would like to pursue that relationship when we returned home. I later learned that she felt the same way.

Returning home, I once again had to face the ordeal of our business fortunes continuing to spiral downward. After winning our suit with the government, we were able to settle their claim for overcharges.

On the positive side, Stock Drive Products Division was ready to release its first catalog. Our operation in Haiti was beginning to produce positive results. Neither Joe nor I had to be there permanently, which made our home lives more pleasant.

One of our largest customers was the Israeli corporation Tadiran. They were very satisfied with the products we were supplying them. Potentially, they could be the source of large orders. As we were completing one such order, their representative came to us with an offer we could not refuse. They promised to place orders with us in the future, but there was a condition attached. Tadiran wanted us to set up a coil manufacturing facility in Israel in conjunction with an Israeli partner. They would place the orders with us and would pay us 20% more for the products we supplied to them from our Israeli plant than we were currently being paid for products from our Haiti or US facility. We asked who our partner would be. We were told that there was a transformer manufacturer—Oram Mfg. Co. Ltd.—that would make an ideal partner. The company president was Joe Mann, an electrical engineer. Oram was presently supplying power transformers to Tadiran, and they thought it would be a compatible match. When we asked why they were willing to pay us 20% more for the product we manufactured in the Israeli facility, they explained that it was really not costing them more since they were paying a duty of 20% on the imported product. The advantage for them was that they had a source close to home and would not be subject to delays in delivery or supply shortages.

We arranged to have Joe Mann visit us in New York. We got along well. The partnership would move forward. We would begin to gather all the necessary machinery and equipment for shipment to Israel. We would occupy a section of Oram's present manufacturing facility in Lud, a city near the Tel Aviv airport. Joe Mann would manage the plant after a short learning period.

By July 1972, Joe Rubenfeld, Joe Keith (who had joined our company as vice president of sales for Automatic Coil Co., Inc.), and I traveled to Israel to begin the training and setting up of the Automatic Coil Co. of Israel. I left Gerty in charge at home. She was not a strict disciplinarian, but I had to hope the children would not act out too badly during my absence.

When we arrived in Israel, Joe Mann met us at the plane and took us to the Oram factory. We found a group of cooperative people who were willing to learn and master everything necessary to become a competent manufacturer of the products. We assisted in helping them set up the workstations and acquainting them with the production methodology we were using in Haiti. We set up assembly lines for the various operations and watched them begin to master our procedures.

On the Sabbath, when no one worked, I decided to search for Aunt Salya, my mother's oldest sister. She was left behind in Romania when the rest of the family migrated to America because she was married and already had children. All through my growing-up years, I heard about her and my Romanian cousins. Periodically, we would receive photographs from them, and we would send them ours. However, there was one photograph that I grew up with. It was a framed picture, and it sat on a table in our dining room. For as many years as I could remember, that photograph never moved from that spot. An exact copy also sat in the living room of Aunt Dora's apartment. My uncles Jake and Max had similar photographs in their homes. The photo was one posed for by my grandfather; step-grandmother; Aunt Salya; her husband, Chaim; Uncle Jake; Uncle Max; my mother, Rose; Aunt Dora; and Aunt Lena. The pictures all traveled from Romania when they migrated.

Having nothing to do on the Sabbath, I asked Joe Keith if he would accompany me on the wild goose search. I told him that I had an aunt in a small town on the border. I knew the name of the town was Kiryat Shmona, and that was all I knew. I was looking for a woman whose name I didn't know other than Salya. I knew that she had five children, and they had all survived the Holocaust. She had become a widow while still in Romania. I was going to look for a needle in a haystack. I had not anticipated having the time to visit her while on this trip, so I didn't come prepared with any further information as to her whereabouts. Joe Keith was not above an adventure of this sort, and having nothing better to do, he agreed to accompany me.

We drove to Kiryat Shmona and found a small village. We looked around for a post office and were unsuccessful in finding it. I asked people on the street where we could possibly find a woman by that name. By some miracle, after a number of failed attempts, we were directed to a series of small barrack-like dwellings, where we asked around for a woman that came from Romania whose name was Salya. The person we asked apparently knew her and pointed out the exact door. Nervously, I approached and knocked. An old woman answered, and I immediately knew that she was a member of my family. I had seen that face before in a photograph.

I asked her in Yiddish if her name was Salya, and when she said yes, I told her that I was Sol (which she pronounced "Solu"), her sister Rose's younger son. She turned pale, and I worried that I had shocked her terribly. After explaining to her again and again that she was not seeing a ghost and that

I was really her nephew from America, I introduced her to Joe, for whom I had to act as translator. She finally invited us in. The dwelling consisted of two rather small rooms. One served as a bedroom and the other doubled as a kitchen and dining room. As she showed us around, I was most taken by the fact that she had an exact duplicate of the family photo sitting on her bedroom dresser. That photo survived the war, the Holocaust, and the trip to Israel from Romania.

She lived very modestly, but she immediately broke out a bottle of whiskey, and the three of us drank. After a while, she took us to another house, where we met one of her daughters, the only one of her children still in Kiryat Shmona. The others had moved to Tel Aviv.

We had a nice visit, talking entirely in Yiddish, and I promised that business would probably bring me back to Israel. And when it did, I would come and visit her again. Joe and I left to find our way back to Tel Aviv. As we drove back, I was aware of how old she looked, and I wondered if I would ever really get a chance to see her again.

My relationship with Trudy continued after we returned from our ski trip to Val d'Isere. We began to date seriously, but I had concerns about the future. While Julia had been eight years my senior, Trudy was twelve years my junior. Trudy was divorced and had no children from her previous marriage. I was a widower with three children, and although I loved children very much, I was looking forward to a time when I could be master of my own time. A time when I might make plans that suited myself instead of being tied down by the needs of children. I was pretty adamant about not wanting to have any more children. I was forty-five years old and thought that I wanted to devote my time to other things. Trudy was only thirty-two years old and could still have children. I couldn't see why she would consider tying herself to a man so much older with three children. She could certainly do better, and I was fearful that our relationship would not last. Her previous marriage to a cardiologist ended in divorce, but she was young and beautiful and could have her pick of a suitable mate. I saw myself as possibly an inappropriate suitor.

Trudy was raised in Brooklyn, or more accurately described as "raising herself" in Brooklyn. Her mother, Alice Ashendorff, grew up in an orphanage and lacked maternal skills. Trudy always felt that she was raising her mother. Her father, Louis, did not fill in for Alice's inadequacies as a mother. Trudy had one sibling, a younger brother named Arthur. Trudy's home life had always been difficult in that she felt she could not rely on her mother. She attended Erasmus Hall High School and worked at numerous jobs to help sustain herself. She put herself through Brooklyn College and worked consistently during that time. When she married at a relatively young age, she had no assistance in making her wedding and had to do it all on her own. Yet she somehow developed sophisticated tastes in style, a love of the art of cooking, and an inquiring mind into the psyche.

As our relationship became more serious, Trudy and I explored my concerns. She did not see our age difference as an obstacle. Years later, we talked about that again; and by then, she had become a psychotherapist and had also undergone years of psychotherapy. She felt that the absence of a maternal presence in her mother's life deprived Alice of learning how to be a mother. Trudy never felt safe or secure enough to feel she could depend on her mother. Trudy did not want to have children. Her brother, Arthur, must have faced the same realities because he did not want to have children either.

That absence of desire to have children on Trudy's part worked well with me. The interesting thing was that she loved the idea of participating in the raising of my children, who were still living at home. During our ski trip to Val d'Isere, Trudy had an opportunity to spend time with my girls, and they seemed to get along quite well. Trudy said that her first awareness of me was when she saw three girls appearing very concerned for a man who was obviously sick when we entered the ski lodge. She thought, "That must be a real nice man to have all those girls hovering around him." She thought it might be worthwhile to find out more about me.

The summer of 1971 was approaching, and Trudy and I thought it would be nice if we could go off and spend some time by ourselves. I had heard that Lake Winnipesaukee in Northern New Hampshire was very lovely and suggested that we try to rent a cabin near the lake. And then, after one week, we would go to Lake George and camp. I thought if we could stand each other under those conditions for that length of time, we might really have something going for us. The problem was what to do with the children while we were away. We turned to our old standby: Boulder Oaks. However, we did not rent the house that summer, and the best we could do was to rent a campsite in the trailer park. I had a very large tent and all the camping equipment necessary, including a cot, sleeping bags, a stove, an ice box, and other necessities to make camping comfortable. The children would be in a familiar environment among people they knew. I asked Gerty, our housekeeper, how she felt about two weeks living in such a rustic environment; and she assured me that coming from St. Kitts, she had lived under much worse conditions. She actually welcomed the idea of spending a few weeks camping. Deborah and Sheila felt OK about it also. I told them that I would phone the camp office every few days to let them know where we were and to see if they needed anything.

We packed the trunk of the car with as much as it would handle, and the remainder we stored in the boat, which we would be hauling up to the lake. Trudy, Gerty, Sheila, Deborah, and I piled into the car for the six-hour drive to our campsite at Mount Monadnock.

We arrived without incident, and after greeting many familiar friends from previous years, we set up the tent, which was large enough to house six people comfortably. I turned over the keys to the boat to a responsible friend and gave him free rein to use it as he saw fit, but to try to let the kids water-ski as much as he had time for. Then Trudy and I said our goodbyes and left. I was never certain how the girls really felt about our leaving. Were they really comfortable with the arrangements?

Trudy and I drove up to Lake Winnepesaukee, about two to three hours away from Mount Monadnock. We came to a town called Center Harbor and found the chamber of commerce, where we asked if they could help us find accommodations at some place by the lake. They told us that we were in luck because there was a vacant house located right on the shore of Lake Winnepesaukee. The woman gave us directions and told us to ask for Colonel Mathews. We drove to the location, which was a large colonial house just off the road. We knocked on the door, and it was answered by a kind-looking man who responded to my inquiry. Colonel Mathews drove us down to the lake, where we saw six houses scattered so that each house seemed to have its own privacy. They were prefabricated homes. We stopped at one of them, and Colonel Mathews led us to the front door of one of the houses. As we entered, we could see right away that it would be a delight to spend time here. The house had two bedrooms and a full kitchen with dishwasher and double oven, pots and pans, silverware, and a set of service for eight dishes and plenty of glasses, including wineglasses. The living room was comfortably furnished, and it boasted a picture window overlooking the lake. The two bedrooms were more than adequate with a generous supply of closet space. We immediately fell in love with the house and the environment. I found that the price of $200 for the week was reasonable. We went back up the road with Colonel Mathews and brought our car down, quickly unpacked, and settled in for a wonderful week.

We got to know the Mathews family and their history. Colonel Matt Mathews was retired from the US Army with the rank of colonel; and his wife, Doris, was a retired army nurse. They lived in the big house at the top of the road with Matt's aged mother and uncle. Matt and Doris had two children, but they did not live at home. After he retired, Matt decided to put the family property to use and had the prefabs constructed. He rented them out to vacationers. We returned to spend several summers there in future years with our children, and we became better acquainted with the Mathews family. Each Sunday, they would throw a cocktail party down by the boathouse for all the guests at his houses. Matt had an army friend, Colonel Jack Raines (also retired from the service), who worked for him. Jack handled any complaints or problems around the property. We became friendly with him and his wife, June, also.

We ate our breakfast and lunch in our comfortable house and went out to dinner every night to restaurants recommended by the colonel. We attended summer stock theater, and while we lounged by the lake, I dabbled with macrame projects that I learned to do, which I found therapeutic and relaxing. We were sorry to leave when the week was up, but we looked forward to our next week at Lake George. Unfortunately, that did not turn out as well. When we got to our campsite on a small isolated island, I set up our small tent, which was not nearly as comfortable as the one we left at Mount Monadnock. The rustic environment was too much for Trudy to handle. She developed cystitis and became very moody. We began to argue over the discomforts we were experiencing. I decided that it would be best if we cut our week short and return home. She was not feeling well, and as a result, she became ornery. We found ourselves fighting, and by the time we arrived at Trudy's apartment, we were not speaking to each other. How could a romantic vacation that had started out so beautifully turn into such a total disaster? It appeared that our relationship was over at that point.

I kept in touch with Gerty and the children without mentioning Trudy and my decision to end our relationship. When the week was over, I drove up to Mount Monadnock to bring Gerty and the children home, and it was not until we were settled back into our routine at home that they became aware that Trudy and I had not been in touch with each other. Deborah seemed very upset when she learned of the breakup, and she apparently called Trudy, and with her urging, we resumed our relationship. Years later, we had different versions as to whether I was the first to call her or whether she took the initiative and called me.

Meanwhile, at work, our fiscal year ended August 31, 1971, saw sales drop to $1.8 million. Our net loss for the year reached $275,000. I knew that things would begin to improve with all the good things we had going for us. Our Haitian facility was beginning to produce positive results, Stock Drive Products sales began to increase as we became more recognized, and even our Sterling Instrument Division—which had been so devastated in the past because it was barred from doing work for the government—began to show some improvement.

When Trudy and I resumed our relationship as a direct result of Deborah's intervention, I was encouraged because I had the impression that the children approved of our relationship and that if we married, the transition would be a smooth one. I was happy about this turn of events, as was Trudy.

We agreed to get married and set a date of March 5, 1972. The wedding would take place in our home at 143 Hewlett Neck Road in Woodmere. Trudy and I would make our own wedding. We both had something in common in that regard. Trudy's first marriage was done entirely by her without any assistance from her parents with the possible exception of a small financial assist, and my first marriage was done by Julia and me with no financial assist whatsoever.

Now Trudy and I both had living mothers, but we made our own wedding without parental involvement. I guess the unwritten rule might be that parents do not get involved in second marriages; but in our case, they did not get involved in our first marriages either.

Over the years, I enjoyed a wonderful relationship with Julia's mother, Chaia. I had a great deal of respect for her and for what she stood for. Politically, we thought pretty much alike. She was living in Florida with two women. They were all widows and got along very well together. For several summers, Chaia and Rose, one of the women she lived with, were employed as ticket takers at a beach club in Atlantic Beach, Long Island. During those summer seasons, Rose and Chaia lived with us in Far Rockaway. We had lots of time to get well acquainted with each other.

Then one day, several years later, Chaia announced that she met this man, Ben Benewitz, a widower also living in Florida. They seemed to hit it off very well, and they decided to get married. Chaia's three children—Julia, Bess, and Lil—all approved.

So it was when Trudy and I decided to marry I felt that I should tell Chaia about my decision and "seek her blessing." I traveled to Miami and stayed with Chaia and Ben for a few days. During that time, I explained that I felt that Trudy would be good for the children as well as for me. Without hesitation, she agreed it would be good for all of us. And if I thought Trudy was the right person, and since she had a lot of respect for my judgment, she approved unequivocally.

Trudy and I were married in a civil ceremony by the city clerk on February 24, 1972. And on March 5, 1972, which we recognized as our anniversary, we took our vows in the living room of our home. It was a beautiful winter day. We had a brunch. An "omelet man" was making omelets; various other food was served, as were champagne cocktails. Trudy's mother and brother, as well as some of her aunts and uncles, attended. My family, including cousins from New Jersey, were all in attendance. This time, my brother was my best man.

The best and most memorable part of that day was the marriage ceremony, which was written by Deborah:

MARRIAGE CEREMONY FOR TRUDY AND SOL

TRUDY AND SOL, YOU ARE BOTH PRESENT HERE TODAY TO UNIFY TWO SINGLE LIVES INTO ONE, YET REALIZING THAT EACH OF YOU ARE INDIVIDUALS WITH YOUR OWN PATHS TO FOLLOW AND STILL SO MUCH TO LEARN. AND YOU MUST GIVE EACH OTHER THE OPTION TO FOLLOW YOUR OWN PATHS, KNOWING THAT YOU WILL COME BACK TO EACH OTHER AND HAVE A LITTLE MORE WISDOM, LAUGHTER, AND TEARS TO SHARE AND ENRICH EACH OTHER.

TRUDY, YOU REALIZE THAT YOU ARE ENTERING AN ENTIRELY DIFFERENT WORLD, AN UNFAMILIAR ONE. NOT ONLY IS THIS MARRIAGE OF A HUSBAND AND WIFE, BUT OF A WIFE AND FAMILY. YOUR RESPONSIBILITIES WILL BE DIFFICULT. BUT YOU WILL NOT BE ALONE, AND THESE RESPONSIBILITIES WILL BE SHARED. THE MAN AND FAMILY WHOM YOU ARE MARRYING WILL POUR ALL OF THEIR LOVE AND KNOWLEDGE OF WHICH THEY ARE CAPABLE TO

MAKE THE UNFAMILIAR AND FRIGHTENING TO BE WARM AND EMBRACING.

SOL, YOU TOO ARE ENTERING INTO A NEW SITUATION WITH MANY TASKS TO BE UPHELD. YOU MUST OPEN YOUR ARMS AND YOUR HEART WIDE TO RECEIVE YOUR WIFE AND DRAW HER TO YOU AND YOUR FAMILY. YOU, AS THE FATHER, MUST HELP CLOSE THE LINKS OF THIS FAMILY CHAIN AND MAKE IT ONE.

LOVE IS THE ONLY FLOWER THAT GROWS AND FLOURISHES WITHOUT THE AID OF THE SEASONS.

AND BOTH SOL AND TRUDY, YOU MUST REJOICE AT YOUR FORTUNE OF FINDING LOVE AGAIN AND ONCE AGAIN COMPLETING YOUR LIVES. AND REMEMBER THE WORDS OF KAHLIL GIBRAN: "MAN CANNOT REAP LOVE UNTIL AFTER SAD AND REVEALING SEPARATION AND BITTER PATIENCE AND DESPERATE HARDSHIPS."

AND AS YOU BOTH PUT IT IN YOUR OWN WORDS, MARRIAGE IS MADE UP OF MANY EMOTIONS AND MEANS MANY THINGS.

TRUDY, THE WORDS YOU HAVE CHOSEN ARE:

GENTLENESS

UNDERSTANDING

PASSION

GROWTH

STRENGTH

ENDURANCE

TRUDY, THESE ARE YOUR VOWS. IF YOU BELIEVE YOU ARE CAPABLE OF FULFILLING THESE VOWS, STATE SO NOW.

SOL, THE WORDS YOU HAVE CHOSEN ARE:
> *CARING*
>
> *GROWING*
>
> *JOY*
>
> *CHALLENGE*
>
> *COMMITMENT*
>
> *DEVOTION*

SOL, THESE ARE YOUR VOWS. IF YOU BELIEVE YOU ARE CAPABLE OF FULFILLING THESE VOWS, STATE SO NOW.

AND WITH THE GIVING AND RECEIVING OF THESE RINGS, YOU DO SO GIVE AND RECEIVE EACH OTHER. THEY ARE A TOKEN OF YOUR UNION, A SYMBOL OF ENDURING LOYALTY. MAY THEY EVER REMIND YOU THAT YOUR LIVES ARE TO BE BOUND TOGETHER BY DEVOTION AND FAITHFULNESS.

AND AS YOU DRINK FROM THIS CUP OF WINE, ALL OF ITS SWEETNESS SHOULD BE THE SWEETER BECAUSE YOU DRINK IT TOGETHER. AND WHATEVER DROPS OF BITTERNESS IT MAY CONTAIN SHOULD BE THE LESS BITTER BECAUSE YOU SHARE THEM.

MAY THE SUN ALWAYS RISE IN THE EAST AND EMIT ITS GOLDEN RAYS ON YOUR PATHS TO BLEND THEM INTO ONE AND SHOW YOU THE WAY.

MAY THE MOON AND THE STARS ALWAYS GLOW AT NIGHT TO KEEP YOU BOTH FROM BEING ALONE AND TO SHOW YOU THAT YOU WILL ALWAYS HAVE EACH OTHER.

In anticipation of our getting married, we planned on having a real honeymoon. We were still not entirely secure about how the children felt about our marriage. Despite the fact that Deborah was responsible for getting us together and that she volunteered to write our wedding ceremony, we still had some doubts. We thought that if we could have them participate in our honeymoon, it would add to our bonding as a family. The plan was that Sheila, Deborah, Trudy, and I would go to Paris and London for a week. Sheila and Deborah would then go home while Trudy and I would go on to Portugal for a week in the Algarve.

We flew to Paris, ate in some very nice restaurants, boated down the Seine, explored the left and right banks, and visited the Louvre. In London, we visited Trafalgar Square and all the typical tourist attractions that we could possibly cover in a few short days. It was a memorable experience that I believe the girls still remember fondly to this day.

After putting Sheila and Deborah on the plane for home, Trudy and I went off to Portugal, where we checked into a plush, comfortable hotel and enjoyed the privacy we needed to make this a real honeymoon.

When we returned home, we tried to settle in as a family. Trudy did her best to bond with the girls, but despite the fact that they seemed to accept her, they did act up quite a bit. We were hosting a dinner party for a number of business associates, and Trudy was busy preparing a gourmet meal with Sheila's assistance. The house smelled wonderful as Trudy went about preparing. When our guests arrived, I served cocktails, and then we sat down to dinner. The guests raved about each course. Everything went beautifully until the dessert was served. A wonderful chocolate mousse was placed before each guest as they continued to talk with each other. Suddenly, a silence fell around the table, and one brave guest announced, "I think there is garlic in the mousse." Suddenly, all the guests seemed to agree. It was a terrible source of embarrassment to both Trudy and me. Trudy could not understand what had happened until she realized that Sheila had prepared the mousse and had probably spiked it with garlic. Sheila didn't admit to it for years.

Another testy incident occurred when Sheila decided to go into the city one snowy Saturday and decided to borrow Trudy's brand-new suede boots. After arriving in Manhattan, Sheila phoned to announce that she made a mistake and did not realize that she was wearing Trudy's boots. Incidents such as these occurred in the early days of our marriage. To Trudy's credit, she handled these situations like a trooper. She was patient and understanding.

Trudy was employed by the City of New York as a guidance counselor. That year, there was a shakeup in the city, and many jobs were lost. Trudy's was one of them. She and I discussed what her next step should be. She had her heart set on becoming a psychotherapist, and I encouraged her to go back to school to get her credentials. She did and it was the best choice she could have made. She turned out to be an excellent therapist, and I believe her innate ability went a long way toward giving her the tools to deal with the acting out of two teenaged girls.

Nothing, however, prepared us for my daughter Chippy's announcement that she was getting married. She announced this shortly after Trudy and I were married, and I suspect it was a direct result of our wedding. In addition, he appeared crude. I was convinced that Chippy was hastily getting herself into a bad situation as a direct result of my getting married. I believed that Chippy was feeling deserted or abandoned by me. I don't believe she ever completely overcame the fact that her blood father left Julia and her. Then Julia died prematurely, leaving her with no blood parents. Now, I too was deserting her. Nothing we could say or do would change her mind.

We attended the civil ceremony that took place and arranged a wedding celebration at our home. I met Chippy's new in-laws for the first and last time at that affair. The marriage lasted approximately five years, and by 1977, Chippy realized that she had made a terrible mistake. Both she and her husband agreed to divorce.

On July 4, 1989, Chippy met Richard Stock, and it wasn't long before they realized that they had a serious interest in each other. On August 26, 1990, they married aboard a ship with family and friends in attendance. Happily, Richard has since become an integral member of my family.

Back at Designatronics, things were getting better but were a far cry from satisfactory. By August 31, 1972, we had managed to increase our sales to $2.6 million and to reduce our losses to $79,000—a substantial improvement but, nevertheless, still not good. However, by August 31, 1973, our sales increased to over $4 million with a net profit of $150,000.

The summer of 1973, I decided to pay a visit to Israel to see how our operation was progressing. Trudy and I would be going. Israel was to be the first leg of a trip that would eventually take us to Turkey, Greece, and a cruise of the Greek islands. However, it was business before pleasure, and as soon as we arrived, I went to visit the plant. I was shocked to see what had transpired since we left here about a year earlier. All our production lines had been dismantled and replaced by workstations that consisted of five workers at each station. Instead of a worker attending to only one operation, he was set to perform several operations. Each worker, I was told, had been rotated so that they all knew how to perform every operation necessary to completely manufacture the component. I asked why they had changed the system, and I was told that the workers could not adapt to the boring routine of performing the same operation all day, as we had taught them. I said to myself that this is the way we do it in Haiti, and we do it successfully in Haiti. Why should it be any different here? I then asked about the productivity, and when I looked at the figures, I found that they were about equal to the productivity we were achieving in Haiti. I had to accept the inevitable, but I did not understand until some time later what the real explanation was.

On a later trip Trudy and I took to Haiti, we decided to visit Cap Haitian, a city in the north that we had never been to. We found the town quaint with many gingerbread houses along narrow streets. We checked into our hotel, where a friendly management greeted us. We were offered a complimentary rum punch before dinner and socialized with a number of other guests. By the time we finished dinner, it had turned dark. Trudy and I decided to take a walk outside and explore our immediate environment. As we walked down the street, we noticed a solitary streetlight in the center of the block surrounded by at least a dozen young boys. As we approached them, we heard them mumbling quite audibly.

Each boy held a book. I approached one of the boys and asked what was going on. He did not speak English, but another boy answered, "We are studying." I asked him why they were studying here and not at home. He replied that they did not have electricity at home, so they come out here where there is some light. I further learned that what they were studying was from a book given to them by the Catholic school they attended. They had to memorize a number of pages for class tomorrow. I asked if they always had to memorize their lessons. He said "of course."

It was then that I was able to understand what I had seen in Israel. At our plant in Haiti, a worker would be taught how to perform an operation. It would take that worker longer to learn how to do it than it would take a worker in the United States; however, after he or she memorized how to perform the operation, productivity would improve astronomically. Having learned the operation, the Haitian worker was not uncomfortable with the repetition. As a matter of fact, he would resent being put on another operation that he would have to memorize all over again. The Haitian worker could tolerate boredom. He preferred it, and I could only attribute it to their early childhood training of learning by memorization. The Israeli worker could not tolerate continued boredom. It would seem that there are indeed more ways than one to skin a cat because when I again compared the productivity of the Haitian worker to the Israeli worker, I found them equivalent.

Trudy and I spent a few more days in Israel, long enough to arrange a family get-together with my aunt Salya and her children. The meeting took place in Tel Aviv. Communication was difficult since Trudy spoke no Yiddish and understood very little. However, it was gratifying to be able to translate for her. I was very happy that I was able to see my aunt once again. I arranged to phone my mother so that my aunt and all my cousins could talk to her. It was not an easy task in the days before cell phones. It was to be the last time I would see my aunt and cousins.

After we left Israel, we were off for Turkey. We had a prearranged reservation at the Istanbul Hilton, a reservation for a car from Avis, and we were looking forward to four exciting days. We arrived at the airport and learned our flight would be delayed several hours. We weren't happy about it, but with no alternative, we decided to make the best of it. We joked around with a number of passengers. One young couple we found were on their way to Istanbul to board the *Orient Express* for an historic train trip. Jack, the young man, was an American; and his wife, Chava, was an Israeli. They lived in New York and had a child. Chava's parents lived on a kibbutz in Israel, and they had left their child with Chava's parents while they went on vacation. Then there was a young Japanese man whose name I never learned; he was backpacking through Europe. It was difficult to communicate with him since my Japanese was totally absent, and I couldn't say much for his English. We tried to communicate with hand motions. We sort of gravitated to each other while we waited patiently for our flight. It ultimately did arrive, about three hours late.

We arrived in Istanbul past midnight, and as we were going through customs, we had a very frightening experience. Trudy's and my passports were confiscated, and we were told that we could not enter the country without being vaccinated.

I was very suspicious of this since no one told us vaccination was required to enter Turkey. The agent placed our passports on a shelf next to him as he tended to other people. I don't know what possessed me, but when I saw that he was distracted for a moment, I snatched our passports from the shelf and told Trudy to run like hell. We did, fully expecting to be followed; but for some reason, we weren't. We then entered the large terminal where many people were mulling around, and we tried to get lost in the crowd. We looked for the Avis rental and found that they had closed. We claimed our baggage, and as we went out to find a cab, we met Jack and Chava and our Japanese friend. They were also lost. Their train would not be leaving until the following morning. They had no Turkish money and no place to exchange any. I suggested that they come with us to the hotel, where I was sure they would be able to exchange money. We finally found a cab, and with a great deal of relief, we left the terminal and headed for the hotel.

When we arrived, I was told that they had no record of our reservation, and they had no vacancies. I produced a confirmation copy, which they had to admit was valid. They then searched and searched, and they finally told me that they would give me the only accommodation they had vacant—the presidential suite. Tomorrow they would move us to our regular accommodations. We found that satisfactory as long as they were not going to charge us extra for it. They confirmed that they would not. I then asked the desk clerk if he would change some money for our friend. He said he would as long as I would verify their identity. He accommodated Jack and Chava, and I left them in the lobby while we were taken to the presidential suite. We entered a foyer that contained another door that opened into a large living room with a wall of windows overlooking the Bosporus Sea. This magnificent space contained a number of sofas and plush chairs arranged in groupings. From the living room, there were two doors leading to two bedrooms, one very large and the other a bit smaller. There was a door adjoining the two bedrooms. The bar in the living room was stocked with an assortment of liquors and liqueurs. We couldn't have been happier with the "misfortune" of their misplacing our reservation.

After surveying our accommodations, Trudy suggested that we certainly didn't need all of it and suggested that we invite Jack and Chava and the young Japanese man to share our space. I wasn't certain that they would still be in the hotel lobby, but when I went down, they were still there trying to figure out what they should do until morning, when they had to catch the *Orient Express*. I told them where we were and suggested that they subtly make their way up to the penthouse and share our quarters. They were very pleased but also skeptical. I went up first, and shortly afterward, they followed. When I let them in, the young Japanese man took one look around and spoke the only three English words I heard from him: "Who are you?" He wanted to know, thinking I must be someone very important to be occupying this suite. We quickly decided that Trudy and I would have the larger of the two bedrooms, Chava and Jack would have the other one, and our Japanese guest could have any couch in the living room. Once we settled on the sleeping arrangements, I mixed drinks, and we had a party. Things were going along very nicely until there was a knock on the door. I went to answer the knock, and there stood a man with a girl on each arm. They were smiling, and I had trouble tearing my eyes away from the girls' see-through blouses. The man spoke to me in Turkish, and I didn't understand a word. I told him that he must be making a mistake. This was my room, and I politely closed the door. Some minutes later, the telephone rang, and I answered it. "Mr. Schwartz, we know you have other people in your room, and they are not authorized to be there. They must leave immediately." I responded that I could have anyone I wanted in my room. I hung up the phone.

Shortly thereafter, there was a knock on the door, and when I responded, two giants stood there. They were there to enforce the hotel rules, and my visitors had to leave. Jack and Chava were immediately concerned with the fact that they were Arabs and Chava was Israeli, and they didn't want any trouble. So our party came to an end. Chava and Jack said that they thought it was too good to be true, and they would just go down to the railroad station and spend the night there. Our Japanese friend left with them, and I never saw or heard from or about him again. Some months later, we hosted an evening at our home for Chava, Jack, and their son.

When things quieted down, we were told we were entitled to one bedroom and that the rest of the suite was not for us. We were relegated to the smaller of the two bedrooms. Shortly after we settled down in our room, we heard a key turn in the outer door. I got up to see who had entered and saw the man with the two half-naked girls enter the other bedroom. They were noisy, and it didn't take too much imagination to figure out what was going on in the next room. We were kept awake, but we were intimidated, so we tolerated the noise. In about an hour, they left, and it became quiet.

The next morning, we were transferred to another room, far more modest, where we spent the next three nights. We did the typical tourist things like visiting the bazaar, taking a tour of the city, and shopping for brass and copper souvenirs. In Greece, we spent several days in Athens visiting the usual sights, and then we boarded a ship and toured some of the islands, including Mykanos and Santorini, where we took a donkey ride up the mountain. It was a treacherous trip. Trudy yelled "help" so loudly and so frequently that the echo is still reverberating around the mountains. Patmos, Crete, Corfu, and Delos were on our tour. In addition, Alexandria, Egypt, was one of the ports of call. We didn't think we would be allowed to get off the ship because of the relationship that existed between Egypt and Israel. Much to our surprise, we were politely welcomed by Egyptian immigration. From the port of Alexandria, we boarded a bus to Cairo. We visited the pyramids, where we were greeted by Egyptian men and their camels offering us camel rides after welcoming us with "huba, huba," an old World War II greeting that was used by Americans and which the camel drivers picked up from American servicemen almost thirty years earlier. Of course, we saw the Sphinx and went to the Cairo museum, where we saw the King Tut exhibit years before it made its way to America.

Many internal problems were waiting for me at the office when I returned. Since our company was composed of a number of different divisions and subsidiaries, with each one headed up by a different manager, there arose serious issues as to how much of our available finances should be allocated to each division or subsidiary. Competition also developed as to the relative importance of the various entities. Which one was generating the most profit? Which one had the most potential? It was about this time that I decided to return to college to fulfill a lifelong ambition of obtaining a degree. I learned about Empire State College, which is part of the State of New York University System. Empire State was a school "without walls." The program did not entail going to conventional classes. Instead, the student was assigned a mentor, and together, they developed a course of study that the student had to accomplish on his or her own. There were reading assignments, papers to write, and in some cases, experiments to perform, depending on the nature of the contract. When the contract was completed, another contract was established with the same or another mentor, depending on the subject matter of the contract.

When I applied, I was given credit for the college courses I had completed years before. And then I had to prepare a portfolio in essay form describing my "life learning experience." A committee of college professors then evaluated the previous college credits and the completed portfolio and determined how valuable the living experience would be considered and, on that basis, establish its value to equivalent college credit. Then they would determine what additional work had to be performed to be equivalent to that of the course work in a conventional college.

Although I had been pursuing a degree in electrical engineering, my life's twisting and turning placed me in a position where I thought it would serve me and my career better to get a degree in business administration. As president and chief executive officer of my company, I was aware of the many "people problems" we were facing. I found that our most difficult tasks were centered on getting people to work together cooperatively. They had to recognize that cooperation was more productive than competitiveness. I began to realize that my role in the company was to manage people and let them manage products. They also had to learn to manage people under them. With this awareness, I was accepted into Empire State College and worked toward a Bachelor of Science Degree in Business Administration. The contracts I elected were geared toward working in and with groups of people. I extensively studied the work of such people as the following:

Identity, Youth, and Crisis by Eric Erickson
Motivation and Personality by Abraham H. Maslow
The Small Group by Michael S. Olmstead
The Structure and Dynamics of Organizations and Groups by Eric Berne
Interpersonal Underworld Development of Power by William C. Schultz
Relationships in Management by John Talbot

These were just a few of the books I was required to study and report on. I had two mentors during my work at Empire State. During our work together, I learned to respect their knowledge and ability.

On December 16, 1973, another family tragedy occurred. My aunt Rose Segall, wife of Max Segall (my mother's younger brother) and mother of Betty and Sarah, my two younger cousins, became ill and died. My living relatives were decreasing in number all too soon.

By August 31, 1974, our sales increased to $5.5 million, and profits were $267,000. Stock Drive Products was demonstrating attractive growth, and Perfect Gear and Instrument Co. in California contributed, as did our operation in Haiti. In Haiti, we were still operating under the aegis of Sidney Fields. We were employing about 200 people. It was looking as if we could do better if we had our own corporation with the ability of employing people without having to pay Sidney Fields his substantial markups on the labor he supplied to us. We retained a Haitian attorney and set up a corporation known as Automatic Coil Co., Haiti. We found an available building in the industrial park not far from the airport, making it convenient to receive and ship materials and finished products to the United States. It also became economical to set up an operation in Florida as a shipping and receiving point. We moved whatever was left of the Automatic Coil Co., Inc. operation in New Hyde Park to a new location in Hialeah, Florida. Joe Rubenfeld would move to Florida to take charge of both the Hialeah and Haitian operations.

I was traveling up and back to Haiti, usually for a week at a time. I became much more familiar with the country, and I realized that my impressions of Haiti and the Haitian people—which I acquired back in 1961 when Julia and I spent four days there—were erroneous. It is true that there was no shortage of beggars and invalids that hung around the airport, but there was another side of Haiti.

I became acquainted with many Haitians and found them friendly and hardworking. Over the next twenty years, Trudy and I spent many vacations in the country. We found being there very relaxing. The accommodations at the hotels we stayed at were comfortable. We enjoyed wonderful cooking and real French service. The beaches were a delight, and most of all, the people we met were great company. True, we were able to avoid the poverty merely by retreating to our hotel and our luxurious swimming pool, but we also often ventured out to visit the native markets and walk the streets of Port-au-Prince. When we had the time, we would visit other cities like Cap Haitian and Jacmel. We attended voodoo ceremonies, folk dances, soccer games, and befriended Haitian nationals who shared their homes and hospitality with us. We were able to experience Haiti as both tourists and guests of nationals. We rode the *tap-taps*, which was the means of public transportation. A tap-tap is a small vehicle the size of a small pickup truck, usually painted and decorated with religious and voodoo symbols and sayings.

The Ibo Lele was home away from home for us, as well as for many Americans and Canadians who came to work in Haiti for short periods of time. The rooms were comfortable and the food more than adequate. On weekends, dances would be held in the nightclub, and the hotel would fill up with visitors, both natives and guests, from other hotels. We drank rum punch, sang and danced, and had a wonderful time while making new friends.

One morning, Trudy and I were having breakfast in the wonderful outdoor dining room, and next to us sat a young man who was alone. We invited him to join us for breakfast. He readily accepted. The first usual question one would ask a visitor to Haiti is "What are you doing in Haiti?" He told us that his name was Ze'ev and that he was an Israeli agronomist. He was sent to Haiti by the Israeli government to assist in an experimental program in a remote farm community near the Dominican border. His task was to organize the farmers into a moshav. When we expressed interest in learning more about his work, he offered to take us to the moshav for a visit. Trudy and I jumped at the chance, and after breakfast, we drove over poorly paved roads to get to this remote farm community.

While we drove, he explained that the farmers barely scraped out an existence, each working on his own. Ze'ev had to first convince the farmers that working together would be to their advantage. He arranged to bring in a tractor, which the farmers shared. He taught them how to fertilize their crops and the benefits of crop rotation. Ze'ev had been coming to Haiti for more than four years, and in that time, the farmers' income increased from $50 per year to over $100 per month. Ze'ev told us that the quality of the produce they were growing had reached export level and could be sold as a cash crop. The farmers became convinced that the moshav concept was working for them. He told us that in the past two years, the farmers had begun to send their children to school, build toilet facilities in their modest huts, and most important of all, placing tombstones on their relatives' graves—something they could not afford until now. This was an essential part of their culture.

The farmers voted and elected a leader of the moshav, and we went to visit his small two-room hut. Inside, we were welcomed by a man who communicated with Ze'ev. Ze'ev told him that we were visitors who were interested in the moshav. The leader was pleased to hear it. A woman was ironing in the next room with an iron that had to be heated periodically on a fire. Above her, on the wall against which she was leaning, was a picture of Martin Luther King. It struck us as very unusual to find that picture in that remote part of Haiti.

We toured the fields and saw how wonderful it was to see so much greenery as compared to the barren land we encountered on our way here. This was like coming to an oasis. We couldn't help feeling a sense of pride that Israel was sending foreign aid to Haiti in the form of agronomists who could do so much to aid in the development of this country.

Meanwhile, Perfect Gear and Instrument Corp., by 1975, had already taken advantage of all carry-forward losses and was no longer obligated to remain in the same location that the tax code required. In addition, a major source of business dried up, and it no longer appeared advantageous for us to have a manufacturing operation in California. We decided to move Perfect Gear and Instrument Corp. to Florida and share the building with Automatic Coil., Inc. We set up Western Components as a division of Designatronics. We offered Joe Davis an opportunity to move to Florida to continue to manage Perfect Gear and Instrument Corp. there but he chose not to go. Instead, he became our sales representative for Western Components.

By August 31, 1975, our growth continued. Our sales reached $6 million, and our net profit increased to more than $300,000.

In the meantime, at home, we had another tragic death to contend with when my aunt Ida died on September 9, 1975. I had very warm feelings for her. I remembered the many times the family met at her home in Long Branch, New Jersey—mostly on happy occasions. Now with her death, only her son, Nathan, remained in her immediate family.

It was also about this time that I began to experience urinary problems. I became a patient of Dr. Peter Puchner, a urologist at Columbia Presbyterian Hospital. It was in the early stages, and he suggested that we just keep an eye on the beginning of an enlarged prostate. I was to see him again in six months. Keeping an eye on an enlarged prostate became more difficult for me since I developed another annoying problem.

About that time, I developed a cataract in my right eye, and it had progressed to the point requiring surgery. I was referred to Dr. Peter Maris, and hence began an episode that was really troubling. The year was 1975, and at that time, cataract surgery required a hospital stay of almost a week. It was before the age of implants. I was given an appointment to have the surgery performed on a Monday morning. That required me to check into the hospital on Sunday to undergo routine tests. That all went smoothly enough until I received a visitor. A man in a ski jacket approached me while I was lying in bed.

"Mr. Schwartz?" he asked.

I said that I was Mr. Schwartz.

"Anesthesiology," he replied.

I waited for more, but all he did was look at my chart.

I inquired, "Does Anesthesiology have a name?"

"Oh, Dr. Curtis."

I thought it was completely inappropriate for him to come and visit a patient dressed the way he was. It appeared as if he had just come off the ski slopes, but I refrained from commenting on that. He then informed me that the surgery would be performed under a general anesthetic. I was taken aback by that because I was told by Dr. Maris that it would be done under a local anesthetic. I told Dr. Curtis that I was under the impression that I was to receive a local anesthetic.

"Oh no," he exclaimed. "This surgery can't be done under a local. What if you move during the procedure and your eye is dislocated out of the socket?"

I became very frightened, and I conjured up an image of my eyeball rolling down the hallway of the hospital. I told Dr. Curtis that I wanted to speak to Dr. Maris. He shrugged his shoulders and said he would tell the nurse to call him. He then left.

When Dr. Maris called me back, I told him of my conversation with the anesthesiologist. He assured me that the surgery would be done under a local anesthetic. I told Dr. Maris that if that man was going to be the anesthesiologist, I was checking out of the hospital right now. He assured me that he would not be the one.

The surgery went off on schedule with a local anesthetic, and after a number of days, I was able to leave the hospital. Dr. Maris discovered a minor complication when I came to his office for an exam. He discovered that my cornea had a "wrinkle" and that I might require a cornea implant if it didn't get better. He prescribed drops I was supposed to use for the next few days, and then I would return to him for another exam. I tried to use the drops and found that they burned, so I didn't use them. When I returned to his office for the exam, he was very pleased with the way the drops worked.

Apparently, my cornea had rid itself of the "wrinkle." I never told him that I didn't use the drops.

By August 31, 1976, sales remained static at $6 million, but we operated on a break-even basis. There were a lot of expenses in connection with the opening of the new facility in Hialeah, and considerable costs were incurred in relocating Perfect Gear and Instrument Corp. from the West Coast. In addition, the cost of setting up our own building in Haiti was extensive. I found that Joe Rubenfeld was in over his head with the responsibilities of managing all these changes. It was to be a very costly period until we adjusted to all the new changes.

I found it necessary to spend time in Florida to help staff our new facility for both Automatic Coil Co., Inc. and Perfect Gear and Instrument Corp., going there Monday mornings and staying until Thursday nights. I would fly back to New York and spend Friday at my office in New Hyde Park and try to catch up on my duties there. It appeared that this commuting would go on for an extended period of time. I found it economical to rent an apartment rather than spend time in motels.

The employees in the Sterling Instrument and Stock Drive divisions were resentful. They felt that they were profitable and their profits were being eaten up by losses in other parts of the company. It took a great deal of work to keep these frictions from getting out of hand.

By August 31, 1977, our sales declined to $5.5 million, and we had a loss of $165,000 for the year. Although it was not apparent in the consolidated results, Stock Drive Products continued to grow. Their profits, however, were mostly eaten up by losses in the other divisions. I was determined to stop the profit drain, but it would take some time before we accomplished it.

In the meantime, I was completing my studies at Empire State. So were a group of other students. At a rare meeting, the students discussed the fact that the college had made no plans for a graduation ceremony. We set up a committee to confront the administration. They told us that they had no plans for a ceremony, and they had no budget for it. We were irate but determined not to be deprived of a graduation ceremony. We agreed among ourselves to finance our own ceremony. We formed a committee to handle food and drink arrangements. We convinced the administration that we were adults and could handle our own graduation. Finally, we got them to agree to participate in distributing our diplomas to us.

I had taken a leadership role in all these arrangements and had won the confidence of my fellow graduates. Friends and relatives of our class numbered several hundred people. They nominated me to make the keynote speech. I include it here for whatever it will be worth:

> DEAN CORWIN, MEMBERS OF THE FACULTY, FELLOW GRADUATES, LADIES AND GENTLEMEN.
>
> UNLIKE OTHER CONVENTIONAL GRADUATING CLASSES, WE HAVE NOT HAD THE OPPORTUNITY TO BECOME ACQUAINTED WITH EACH OTHER THROUGH MUTUAL PARTICIPATION IN CLASSROOM WORK. WE HAVE BEEN DEPRIVED OF THE OPPORTUNITY TO EXPRESS TO EACH OTHER OUR PRIVATE OPINIONS OF OUR TEACHERS, THE ADMINISTRATION, OR OUR

FELLOW STUDENTS. WE HAVE BEEN DEPRIVED OF THE DUBIOUS PRIVILEGE OF SHARING EACH OTHER'S HOMEWORK ASSIGNMENTS OR PASSING ON TEST QUESTIONS AND ANSWERS TO EACH OTHER. WE HAVE ALSO BEEN DEPRIVED OF THE SOCIAL INTERCOURSE THAT IS SO IMPORTANT A PART OF ONE'S OVERALL EDUCATION.

ONE MIGHT EXPECT TO FIND MANY OF US WALKING AROUND SUCKING OUR THUMBS TO COMPENSATE FOR ALL THIS DEPRIVATION—BUT WE DON'T. WE DON'T BECAUSE WE REPRESENT A VERY SPECIAL BREED OF GRADUATE. IN THE MAIN, WE REPRESENT A SEGMENT OF SOCIETY WHO, THROUGH SELF-DETERMINATION, WERE ABLE TO OVERCOME THE FEAR OF RETURNING TO SCHOOL AFTER MANY YEARS. WE REPRESENT A SEGMENT OF SOCIETY WHO CAN MUSTER THE NECESSARY DISCIPLINE TO WORK AND STUDY WITHOUT RELIANCE ON OUTSIDE PRESSURES FROM TEACHERS OR FELLOW STUDENTS. ONLY PEOPLE SO STRONGLY SELF-MOTIVATED AS WE ARE COULD HAVE SUCCESSFULLY SURVIVED THE PORTFOLIO NIGHTMARE EXPERIENCE WITHOUT LOSING HEART. I OFTEN THOUGHT THAT THE REAL PURPOSE IN REQUIRING THE PORTFOLIO IS NOT TO DETERMINE ONE'S LIFE LEARNING EXPERIENCE BUT REALLY TO SEPARATE THE MEN AND WOMEN FROM THE BOYS AND GIRLS. GENERALLY SPEAKING, I AM NOT ACCUSTOMED TO SELF-INDULGENCE OR SELF-PRAISE, BUT I FEEL TONIGHT IS AN EXCEPTION. I BELIEVE I CAN SPEAK FOR MOST OF MY FELLOW GRADUATES WHEN I SAY WE ARE PROUD OF OUR ACCOMPLISHMENTS. WE ARE PROUD OF OUR

DECISION TO TAKE IT UPON OURSELVES TO ALTER OR FURTHER THE COURSE OF OUR LIVES BY RETURNING TO THE TASK OF OBTAINING OUR DEGREES. FOR SOME OF US WHO WERE UNABLE TO COMPLETE OUR COLLEGE EDUCATION YEARS AGO, IT REPRESENTS THE FULFILLMENT OF A LIFELONG AMBITION. TO OTHERS AMONG US, IT REPRESENTS ONLY THE FIRST STEP IN A CONTINUING PROCESS TOWARDS SELF-ACTUALIZATION. TO STILL OTHERS, IT REPRESENTS THE ABILITY TO TURN TO A MORE PROMISING AND SATISFYING CAREER.

YES, WE ARE AN UNUSUAL GROUP OF PEOPLE GRADUATING FROM A MOST UNUSUAL COLLEGE. IT IS TRUE THAT EMPIRE STATE COLLEGE, LIKE MOST CONVENTIONAL COLLEGES, IS PLAGUED WITH BUREAUCRATIC PROCESSES. EMPIRE STATE COLLEGE IS DEPENDENT ON MANY COMPUTERIZED FUNCTIONS THAT ALL TOO OFTEN NEED A LAXATIVE TO MAKE THEM FUNCTION NORMALLY. WHERE EMPIRE STATE COLLEGE HAS NOT RESORTED TO COMPUTERIZATION AND HAS REMAINED RELIANT ON HUMAN BEINGS, IT HAS INHERITED THE DISEASE OF POWER POLITICS. EMPIRE BUILDING AT EMPIRE STATE COLLEGE IS NOT DISSIMILAR FROM EMPIRE BUILDING AT ANY OTHER COLLEGE OR UNIVERSITY. NONE OF THESE CHARACTERISTICS ARE TERRIBLY UNUSUAL. WHAT IS UNUSUAL IS THAT EMPIRE STATE COLLEGE AND THE PEOPLE RESPONSIBLE FOR BRINGING IT INTO BEING DEMONSTRATED THE COURAGE TO TAKE AN UNCONVENTIONAL IDEA AND TURN IT INTO A VERY UNCONVENTIONAL FORM OF EDUCATION AND THEN PROCEEDED TO MOLD AN INSTITUTION AROUND IT.

EMPIRE STATE THEN DISPLAYED THE DETERMINATION TO GAIN RECOGNITION. IT ATTRACTED PEOPLE LIKE OURSELVES, NOT TO MENTION THE MANY VERY FINE AND DEDICATED MENTORS THAT BECAME COMMITTED, EVEN THOUGH WE KNEW THAT EMPIRE STATE COLLEGE WAS NOT YET AN ACCREDITED COLLEGE. WE KNEW THERE WAS SOMETHING HERE WORTHY OF OUR TRUST, TIME, AND DEVOTION. NOW WE ARE ACCREDITED, AND WE CAN TAKE PRIDE IN THE FACT THAT THE REST OF THE WORLD AGREES WITH WHAT WE ALL KNEW BEFORE. NAMELY, THAT THE EMPIRE STATE COLLEGE CONCEPT IS AT LEAST A VIABLE METHOD OF LEARNING, IF NOT SUPERIOR TO METHODS USED IN CONVENTIONAL INSTITUTIONS.

THERE IS STILL MUCH WORK TO BE DONE, MANY IMPROVEMENTS TO BE INTRODUCED. FOR INSTANCE, DURING MY EXPERIENCE AT EMPIRE STATE, I FELT THAT ITS GREATEST SHORTCOMING WAS THE LACK OF CONTACT BETWEEN STUDENTS. MY MENTORS MUST HAVE BEEN AWARE OF THIS NEED OF MINE AND RECOGNIZED IT AS NOT UNCOMMON. THEY ATTEMPTED TO BRING A GROUP OF THEIR STUDENTS TOGETHER FROM TIME TO TIME, BUT THIS WAS ALL TOO INFREQUENT AND SUPERFICIAL. A WORKABLE METHOD MUST BE FOUND TO ESTABLISH COMMUNICATIONS BETWEEN STUDENTS WITHOUT RESORTING TO CONVENTIONAL ROUTINIZED CLASSROOM ATTENDANCE. THIS, AFTER ALL, IS WHAT MAKES EMPIRE STATE SO VERY SPECIAL TO MANY OF US WHOSE FAMILY RESPONSIBILITIES OR JOBS MAKE IT IMPOSSIBLE TO ATTEND CLASSES ON A REGULAR BASIS.

We've tasted of the heretofore forbidden fruit and found it was good. Our appetites are now whetted. Does formalized education now come to an end because there exists no master's programs that do not require routinized classroom attendance? I should hope not. I should hope that before Empire State becomes too complacent or too smug over past successes—and yes, even before we fully solve the many problems still facing us on an undergraduate level—we will begin the difficult struggle to make available master's programs at Empire State. To this end, I am prepared to work with anyone else interested in the same goal.

On behalf of my fellow graduates, I want to extend our appreciation to all our mentors who have given of themselves through encouragement and direction. I want to thank the entire staff personally for responding to my impatience on many occasions with nothing less than angelic understanding. Above all, I want to thank our husbands, wives, and children who had to endure a great deal while adjusting to a new way of life during this period.

I want to thank my wife, Trudy, who was, to me, a constant source of strength. Without her insight, encouragement, and love for me, this evening would not have come to pass.

Thank you for being here tonight to celebrate with us this happy occasion.

By January 1977, we had found adequate premises in Haiti, where we relocated Automatic Coil of Haiti. We were busy moving machinery and equipment from Sidney Field's plant to our own. Most of the personnel moved with us. Inefficiencies occurred during all this upheaval, and it resulted in continued losses during 1977. Sales declined modestly while we had a loss of $165,000.

As we settled into our new facilities in Hialeah, Florida, and Haiti, our efficiencies improved in the next year. We had growth in all our divisions in line with a somewhat better business climate.

By August 31, 1978, we closed out our fiscal year with record sales of $7 million. Net income was $177,000.

Fiscal year ending August 31, 1979, was another growth year with sales reaching $8.4 million and net profits at $327,000.

Our fiscal year that ended August 31, 1980, resulted in record sales of $10.6 million, but profits were only $329,000. It was a year during which inflation ran high, as did interest rates eating heavily into our income.

It was also the year I celebrated my fifty-fifth birthday. Age was gradually creeping up on me, and I began to have urinary difficulties. My urologist told me that I had an enlarged prostate, and it had to be watched. He suggested a semiannual examination. I didn't realize it at the time, but this was the beginning of a "rest of my life" involvement with urinary problems.

This was also the year that Sheila and Marty Cooperman decided to marry. Unlike my negative feelings about Chippy's first husband, I had only one concern about Marty. I found him personable, certainly a more appropriate choice for Sheila. I was somewhat concerned with Marty's need to "cling" to Sheila. It seemed that she could not get three feet away from him without him following her and establishing physical contact. Aside from that, I was unaware of anything to complain about. Trudy and I suggested that we make the wedding in our backyard since the date arrived at for the wedding was in early September. After the ceremony, our guests proceeded to our front yard, where a dance floor had been set up surrounded by tables and chairs. Food was catered, and the wine and liquor flowed. I may be prejudiced, but my recollection of the wedding is that it was a successful affair with everyone enjoying themselves. The only fly in the ointment was that Sheila's maid of honor was her sister Deborah. She came in from California for the wedding, had contracted a case of chickenpox, and had blotches all over her face. Deborah performed her duties honorably, however, and then went back to bed and watched the rest of the festivities through the window.

Missing at Sheila's wedding was her maternal grandmother, Chaia. Chaia had married Ben Benewitz while they were both living in Florida. They lived together for quite a few years, but they were both getting older and frailer. They decided to move back to New York around 1978. They found an assisted-living apartment in the Bronx, where they were furnished their meals; and for a while, they were closer to Ben's children and Chaia's two daughters, who lived in New York. Unfortunately, they were only here about a year before Chaia took seriously ill and died. She had expressed a desire to be cremated, and her wishes were carried out. Some weeks after her funeral, a memorial service was held, and I was asked to deliver a eulogy for her. Here it is:

EULOGY FOR CHAIA BENEWITZ

IN OUR LIFETIMES, WE EXPERIENCE MOMENTS OF HAPPINESS OR PLEASURE, AND THESE MOMENTS ARE SUPERIMPOSED ON MOMENTS OF TRAGEDY OR SADNESS. AND SOMEHOW WE MUST BE ABLE TO EXPERIENCE BOTH SADNESS AND HAPPINESS AT THE SAME TIME.

WHEN PERSONAL TRAGEDY TAKES THE FORM OF THE DEATH OF A LOVED ONE AND WE ARE BROUGHT CLOSER TO THE REALITIES OF DEATH, IT IS DIFFICULT TO REMEMBER OR EXPERIENCE ANY REASONS FOR HAPPINESS. WE BECOME OBSESSED WITH SEEKING AN ANSWER TO THE QUESTION: WHAT IS THE PURPOSE OF LIFE? WHAT IS THE POINT IN SPENDING A LIFETIME, STRUGGLING, SACRIFICING FOR CHILDREN, STUDYING OR WORKING TO FURTHER ONE'S POLITICAL BELIEFS, WHEN THE END RESULT IS DEATH?

IF WE LOOK AT CHAIA'S LIFE, PERHAPS WE CAN BEGIN TO FIND AN ANSWER. HER LIFE IN EDWARDSVILLE, OPERATING A STORE AND RAISING THREE CHILDREN AT THE SAME TIME, MUST HAVE BEEN DIFFICULT ENOUGH. BUT SHE WAS ALSO ABLE TO DO MORE THAN HER SHARE TO FURTHER THE POLITICAL AND CULTURAL MOVEMENTS SHE SO STRONGLY BELIEVED IN.

AND SHE CONTINUED TO DO SO THROUGHOUT HER LIFE DESPITE MANY ILLNESSES AND MANY PERSONAL TRAGEDIES. SHE MAINTAINED, THROUGHOUT HER LIFE, A MORAL CODE THAT I HAVE SEEN IN FEW OTHER PEOPLE. MATERIAL POSSESSIONS NEVER PLAYED A MAJOR ROLE IN HER LIFE. AND SO, DURING WORLD WAR 2, WHEN BLACK MARKETING WAS SO PREVALENT AND THE OPPORTUNITY TO MAKE A GREAT DEAL OF MONEY PRESENTED ITSELF, SHE REFUSED TO DO IT BECAUSE IT CLASHED WITH HER MORAL CODE.

SHE NEVER BECAME BITTER. IN HER LIFETIME, SHE SUFFERED THROUGH THE MOST DEVASTATING EXPERIENCES. BESIDES LOSING MANY RELATIVES IN THE HOLOCAUST, SHE LIVED THROUGH PERSONAL LOSSES THAT MOST OF US ARE FORTUNATE ENOUGH NOT TO HAVE TO EXPERIENCE.

IN ADDITION TO THE LOSS OF A HUSBAND, SHE KNEW THE LOSS OF HER SON-IN-LAW PHILLIP. SHE HAD TO EXPERIENCE THE LOSS OF HER DAUGHTER JULIA, AND THEN EVEN THE LOSS OF HER GRANDDAUGHTER ELLEN.

AND THROUGH ALL THIS, SHE NEVER BECAME BITTER. AFTER EACH TRAGEDY, SHE CONTINUED TO MAKE HER POLITICAL AND CULTURAL CONTRIBUTION.

BUT EQUALLY IMPORTANT, SHE SET AN EXAMPLE FOR THOSE AROUND HER. AND THOSE AROUND HER DREW STRENGTH FROM HER. SHE BELIEVED THAT FOR AS LONG AS SHE WAS ABLE, SHE HAD THE RESPONSIBILITY TO LIVE HER LIFE MORALLY AND TO DO WHATEVER WAS IN HER POWER TO DO THAT

WOULD BE BENEFICIAL TO OTHERS. NO TRAGEDY IN HER LIFE SHOOK THAT BELIEF!

THIS, I BELIEVE, WAS THE SOURCE OF CHAIA'S STRENGTH. THIS PHILOSOPHY OF LIFE SHE PASSED ON TO EVERYONE SHE CAME IN CONTACT WITH.

AFTER JULIA'S DEATH, CHAIA'S STRENGTH HELPED ME THROUGH THE FEAR, UNCERTAINTY, AND DEVASTATION THAT PERMEATED MY LIFE AND THE LIVES OF MY CHILDREN. DESPITE HER OWN GRIEF, SHE WAS ABLE TO HELP US MUSTER THE STRENGTH NECESSARY TO CONTINUE LIVING OUR LIVES.

NOW CHAIA IS GONE. WE WILL MISS HER. WE WILL MISS HER BRILLIANCE. WE WILL MISS HER INTELLECT. WE WILL MISS HER WIT AND HER DEDICATION TO HER IDEALS. EACH OF US HAD A "SOMETHING SPECIAL" IN OUR RELATIONSHIP WITH CHAIA. WE WILL MISS THAT. NOW WE MUST TAKE STRENGTH FROM HER MEMORY. AND WHILE, AT THIS MOMENT, THERE IS SO MUCH TO BE SAD ABOUT, I AM HAPPY BECAUSE I HAD THE PRIVILEGE OF KNOWING HER AND BEING PART OF HER FAMILY.

MAY SHE REST IN PEACE.

When Chaia and Ben left Florida, my sister, Beatrice; her husband, Joe; and my mother migrated to the state. Beatrice and Joe sold their home in Flushing and moved to a two-bedroom condo, which they shared with my mother.

The family was no longer a closely knit group living in proximity to each other.

Shortly after Deborah graduated from college, she decided to move to California. Once there, she also decided to change her name to Deah instead of Deborah. She explained that she wanted to remove the "bor" from her name. I have never been able to fully accustom myself to the change since I have always referred to her as Debby or Deb; however, I can write her name as Deah. So henceforth in this writing, I will refer to her as Deah.

Trudy and I had been married more than eight years. For the first four years, she continued to work as a guidance counselor in the New York City school system. Then there was a "shakeup," which resulted in her losing her job. It was an excellent opportunity for her to go back to school to pursue a career as a psychotherapist. After a few years at Adelphi University, she received her Master's Degree in Social Work and then continued to study at the Blanck Institute for more specialized training in psychotherapy. She began to work again at various agencies, cutting her teeth on the treatment of patients. Her real goal was to go into private practice.

We thought about moving to another house where she could set up an office in our home. We looked at a number of houses on the North Shore of Long Island. One we saw I regret not buying to this day. It was located in Lloyd Harbor. The house was magnificent, overlooking the bay. It was ideal because it had the possibility for setting up an office for Trudy with a private entrance. The only shortcoming was that it was far from a main artery—namely, the Long Island Expressway or the Northern State Parkway. Trudy also felt that it was too large and had lots of rooms we would not use. I didn't have a problem with that, but Trudy felt uncomfortable with all the unused space. That home, which we could afford at that time, soon became out of financial reach.

After a while, we decided to investigate the possibility of renovating the house we were now occupying rather than buy a new one. We were referred to a husband-and-wife architect team, and we arranged to meet with them. Stan and Lorie Maurer, operating as Maurer and Maurer, convinced us that they were the right people for us to work with. This began a business relationship that lasted more than ten years.

In 1980, shortly after Sheila and Marty married, we began to plan the reconstruction of our home. The first stage consisted of an entire revamp of the downstairs. The kitchen and small den became Trudy's office with a private entrance. The new kitchen was moved and catered to Trudy's desire for a gourmet kitchen. A restaurant stove became the centerpiece. A skylight was installed, and the rest of the kitchen equipment (dishwasher, refrigerator/freezer) was exactly what Trudy wanted.

This first phase took more than a year to complete. We lived in the house the entire time. There were times we had no heat, but we managed. We set up a temporary kitchen in our old bedroom upstairs, and we cooked on a Coleman camping stove. It was uncomfortable, but it was also thrilling to watch the progress. When this first stage was complete, Trudy began to see patients in her new office. We were both delighted.

For the next ten years, we were constantly involved with construction. First, we installed a greenhouse directly outside our kitchen door. The fantasy was that I could pursue my hobby of raising begonias while Trudy could be experimenting with recipes in the kitchen, both of us in full view of each other as we worked. It was a very happy time for us.

Our next phase was to construct a swimming pool in our backyard. The fantasy here was that it was so difficult to go off on summer weekends. Neither of us relished the idea of fighting traffic to get to the mountains or to Eastern Long Island. We decided that with a swimming pool, our home would be as beautiful and comfortable as any resort we could visit.

We then embarked on building a sunroom off the dining room. Originally, there was a screened porch, but much of it became our new dining room, which had to be expanded because the new kitchen infringed on the old dining room space. This project was completed successfully. One more serious stage had to be completed. The master bedroom upstairs needed a master bathroom, and this entailed an addition to the second floor of the house. It turned out to be the most expensive part of the renovation project; but when it was complete, Trudy was so proud of it that she had a champagne party in our bathroom. That had to be a first in entertaining.

Designatronics's growth pattern continued despite the high cost of borrowing. Fiscal year ending August 31, 1981, once again a banner year, had sales of $13.5 million and net income of $870,000. Everyone was happy with the results, and the company was displaying a good deal of financial health. Our operations in Haiti were doing well, and we were able to expand there. Our successful operation attracted the attention of people from the Overseas Private Investment Corp. (OPIC). Their function was to encourage investment by US businesses in certain countries, ostensibly to help bring prosperity and commerce to these countries.

OPIC had a published list of which countries qualified. OPIC, a quasi-governmental organization, offered loans to qualified borrowers with the understanding that these funds would be invested in a foreign country with the purpose of creating jobs for the natives of that country. They were also in the business of selling insurance to the borrower to insure against any possible expropriation of the investment by the host nation. Haiti qualified for such an investment, and hence we were contacted and offered a substantial loan in order to expand our operations. It appeared to be an offer difficult to refuse, especially since we were in need of expanding our existing space.

We were beginning to offer a new service at our Haitian facility. We were searching for possible clients who would like to assemble or manufacture in Haiti the way we had originally started with Sidney Fields. We used his plant space and his employees, but we were responsible for our own productivity. We compensated him by paying him for as many "people hours" we used. Sidney Fields became wealthy that way without having any responsibility for the productivity. We eventually moved to our own facility when we felt that our cost of buying "people time" exceeded what it would cost if we hired our own people in our own facility. Hence, we set up a Haitian corporation, which permitted us to hire people directly. Now we were in a position to offer the same service to other companies.

I went through the bureaucratic process of applying for the loan, and after several months, I was successful in negotiating a loan in excess of $500,000. I then arranged to lease an additional 10,000- square-foot building adjoining the one we were already occupying, and we were in business. Shortly thereafter, one of our customers became interested in our proposal, and we began to provide them with several hundred workers whom they supervised on their own. It turned out to be a very profitable part of our business. Our next few years at Designatronics were blessed with continued growth. Fiscal year 1982 saw sales exceeding $14.5 million and a net income of $950,000.

However, a death in the family on May 27, 1982, put a damper on the elation I felt during that year. My cousin Raymond Tunkel, who lived with us during our formative years, became ill and died rather suddenly. Raymond and his wife, Irene, whom he married shortly after coming home from his World War II service, had moved to Florida after he retired. His death was a shock to our entire family. He left his wife, Irene, and two children, Lenore and Barry

In fiscal 1983, sales had increased to $15.9 million while net profits exceeded $1.1 million.

Over the years, the number of shares outstanding grew through a series of stock splits, stock dividends, and buyback of shares on the open market. By the end of fiscal 1983, the total number of outstanding shares had reached over two million. The marketplace was beginning to recognize Designatronics, and the stock was trading at $8 per share. We had decided that it was time to have a secondary offering of stock to the public so that we could help reduce our debt and increase our working capital. I also felt it was time for Joe and me, as well as our officers, to diversify our personal assets. We retained the services of Advest & Co. to arrange a public offering of 500,000 shares of stock; 320,000 from the company; and 120,000 from Joe, me, and other officers of the company. The public offering went off successfully, and my personal assets became a little more liquid and diversified. Until now, the stock was being traded over the counter; but in August 1983, Designatronics stock began to trade on the American Stock Exchange. And in November 1983, it was being traded on the Pacific Stock Exchange.

The year 1983 was the year I became a grandfather for the first time. Sheila and Marty's first child was born on December 20, 1983, and Trudy and I became the proud grandparents of Jacqueline, a gorgeous baby girl. Of course, that was my opinion, and I do not believe I was not objective. Now, as I write this, Jacqueline is in the process of deciding which medical school she will attend.

September 24, 1984, saw the demise of my only surviving uncle. Max Segall died, leaving his daughter Betty Freeman; her husband, Arthur Freeman; his younger daughter Sarah; and her husband, Sol Laperdon.

Not everybody was happy about fiscal 1984. It turned out to be all we could have hoped for at Designatronics. Sales increased to $18.5 million and profits reached $1.1 million. That represented $0.46 per share, yet the market price for Designatronics stock was only $4.50. We had hoped that it would be much higher with these results. However, perhaps Wall Street was more astute than we were. Perhaps the street anticipated that we would not be able to maintain the growth rate we were showing. If so, then they were correct because fiscal 1985 turned out to be very disappointing. There was a considerable drop in computer peripheral sales and in the extensive profitable sales of communication components manufactured in our Haiti facility, which resulted in considerable profit decreases. Although there was an increase in sales to $19.6 million, our income fell to $485,000 (or $0.19 per share).

During that year, we had acquired the assets of Accusonic Systems, a company that manufactured loudspeakers, microphones, earphones, and other devices we thought would be a welcome addition to our product lines. We were also making substantial investments into our Techno division in the area of robotics and automation equipment. These investments did affect our profit, but we felt the investments would pay off in future years.

The year 1985 was also the year Deah informed us that she was going to marry Bill Filler, a man she had been living with for several years along with a number of other friends. Trudy and I went out to San Francisco to meet Bill. We found him to be fairly intelligent but not the most social person. I felt that he was uncomfortable in our presence, but I was determined to be supportive of Deah's choice. Deah wanted to plan and carry out her own wedding. She neither asked for nor indicated that she wanted any of our help except for the financing. On April 21, 1985, Deah and Bill were married. It was a joyous occasion. The ceremony was unusual, and Deah made a beautiful bride. Bill was a handsome groom. Many of our relatives came from the East to attend, and it was nice to see how many people thought enough of us to come. In addition to relatives, my close friends and business associates Joe and Bea Rubenfeld and Martin and Shirley Hoffman came out for the wedding.

1985–1986

THE YEAR 1985 was truly an eventful year. It was the year Mom became my exclusive responsibility. Her tenure with my sister, Beatrice, and brother-in-law, Joe, came to an end. For years, Beatrice's eyesight had been deteriorating. She had a serious condition that the doctors felt called for the removal of one eye. It was ironic that she followed in our father's footsteps. Beatrice became the second member of our family to lose an eye. Her sight in her other eye continued to deteriorate. It became more and more difficult for her to care for Mom. In addition, Mom was beginning to lose it mentally. She began to accuse Beatrice and Joe of stealing her things, and she was becoming too much for them to handle.

I brought her back to New York. For a while, she stayed with Trudy and me, but it became difficult for us to care for her properly since I had to go to work and Trudy was involved with her practice. Periodically, when she was not in session, she would try to attend to Mom. We had a housekeeper, Annie, who had been with us for some years. Trudy and Annie got along very well. In fact, they were very close. However, Mom was having a hard time with Annie. Nothing could have been further from the truth. I began to feel Trudy's unhappiness with Mom living in our home. Tensions were rising between us, and I decided that it was necessary to make other arrangements for Mom. I searched senior citizen hotels in the area, and after some investigation, we settled Mom into a hotel in Long Beach. None of us was very happy with the arrangements. Mom felt we had abandoned her, and I felt guilty about not being able to properly care for her at home. I visited her frequently, took her out as often as I could, and saw to it that she participated in some of the activities provided by the hotel. She did manage to befriend several women, but she missed her home and felt useless. She was accustomed to being independent by providing for herself and for her husband and children. For a while, Beatrice, Joe, and their daughter, Susan, gave her some cause for being useful. She could do things for them around the house. Now, with no dependent husband, all her children grown and on their own, and even her granddaughter gone, she felt there was no purpose for her anymore. There was no way I could make her happy. She was accustomed to being with Beatrice and Joe, and now she did not see them on a daily basis. They were in no position to be helpful. Mom began to turn inward. I would frequently have to drive her to her doctors, and I often heard her verbalize to herself in Romanian, her native language that she had long ago abandoned. After one such soliloquy, she went from talking to herself in Romanian to English: "My son lives in a mansion, but he has no place for his mother." That was a devastating blow.

Traveling back in memory, I recalled how my cousin Daniel felt abandoned when his mother died and he had to be separated from his father and brother. He was helpless to do anything about it. I remembered how I felt when I returned from California and found that there was no room for me in the family home. I was capable of handling it by exerting my independence and moving into my own apartment.

I recalled how Chippy must have felt when her father abandoned her mother and her; she was helpless to do anything about that. And when her mother died years later followed by my marrying Trudy, Chippy felt totally abandoned even by me.

Now Mom felt abandoned by me. "My son lives in a mansion, but he has no place for his mother." Those words still haunt me. I began to understand the torture my father must have experienced when he had to choose between his family and his sister and ultimately made his sister leave our house. Now I was faced with making a similar difficult choice.

GEORGIA AND HEGEMAN AVENUES RECALLED

ONE DAY AT my office, I was reviewing our list of stockholders, and I came across a name: Sidney Rosen. As a boy, I knew someone by that name who had lived on Georgia Avenue. I wondered if it could be the same person. It also gave me cause to wonder about a lot of other boys I grew up with. I wondered where they were and what happened to them. I was sixty years old. The other boys and girls I grew up with ranged in age anywhere from fifty to eighty at that time. If they were alive, they had already lived the better part of their lives. In my spare time, I embarked on a search to see who I could locate from my "old gang." I started with telephone books and managed to find a few. We arranged to get together. When we did, it turned out to be such a pleasant and nostalgic reunion that we were encouraged to find more people. Through word of mouth and further research into suburban phone books, I managed to find even more. I took it upon myself to start a "Georgia and Hegeman Newsletter" in which I wrote about recollections of nostalgic value I recalled from our growing-up years, and I sent it out to everyone I found. Soon I was receiving the names of other people who had been contacted by those people I found.

The list of people receiving my newsletter had expanded to more than fifty people. Someone suggested that we call ourselves the Georgia and Hegeman Boys and Girls Club and that we have a reunion so that we could all meet and see if we recognized each other. That took some doing. We formed a committee to begin to investigate possible locations for the reunion. We ultimately settled on the Raleigh Hotel in South Fallsburg, New York. The date was set for the weekend of November 4–6, 1985.

The reunion turned out to be a smashing success. My recollections of the affair are reflected in the following newsletter:

DEAR FRIEND,

THE FIRST REUNION OF THE GEORGIA AND HEGEMAN BOYS AND GIRLS CLUB IS NOW HISTORY. FOR THOSE OF US WHO WERE THERE, IT PROVED TO BE A GREAT WEEKEND. ALMOST CONTINUOUS GREEK DANCING, TWO SHOWS A NIGHT FOR THOSE OF US THAT WERE NOT TOO TIRED TO STAY UP, AND ENOUGH FOOD TO FORCE SOME OF US BACK ON A DIET FOR AN ENTIRE MONTH. BUT THE HIGHLIGHT OF THE WEEKEND WAS THE SEEING OF OUR GUYS AND GALS. AMONG US, THERE WAS REUNITING WITH FRIENDS WE HAVEN'T SEEN IN A VERY LONG TIME. SINCE WE SAW EACH OTHER LAST, AS A GROUP, WE WERE MARRIED OR REMARRIED, REMAINED SINGLE, OR BECAME FATHERS, MOTHERS, GRANDFATHERS, GRANDMOTHERS, WIDOWS, AND WIDOWERS. WE HAD LIVED ENTIRE LIFETIMES IN DIFFERENT PARTS of the country, pursued careers, and even retired.

How did we relate to each other after all these years? After just a few moments of recognition, twenty, thirty, forty years melted away, and it was as if we were standing once again on the corner of Georgia and Hegeman shooting the breeze, reverting back to nicknames we haven't spoken in decades. We laughed—we cried. Some of us came together for what we named Nostalgia Hour, and we recollected childhood and adolescent experiences.

Trudy Schwartz asked, what is there about this group growing up around Georgia and Hegeman Avenues that was so special that so many of us enthusiastically participated in this reunion while so many more were terribly disappointed because they could not participate for lack of accommodations? Bobby Seigel responded by reading the letter he had written to Elaine Feldman, who is writing a book about growing up in Brooklyn.

Al Yuni recollected how, while he was jingling around a few coins, Butch Frank was in possession of "folding money." Not only did he have folding money, he had charge accounts at all the local merchants while we were busy hustling around trying to find or steal a few empty milk bottles, return them to Moishe, the grocer, so we could put

TOGETHER A NICKEL TO BUY A SPAULDING FLYER. BUTCH SINGLEHANDEDLY SUPPORTED THE PINBALL MACHINE IN THE CANDY STORE. WELL, PERHAPS THAT IS A SLIGHT EXAGGERATION. HE HAD A PARTNER NAMED MURRAY, WHO LIVED ON GEORGIA AVENUE NEAR LINDEN BOULEVARD. AND I RECALL MURRAY MASTERFULLY HANDLING THE PINBALL MACHINE WITH BODY ACTION SO BOLD THAT THE MACHINE WAS AFRAID TO SAY "TILT."

WE TALKED ABOUT STICKBALL GAMES, POOL ROOMS, ROCKAWAY, CONEY ISLAND, AND THE WAR YEARS. AND WHEN DID THE AIRPLANE CRASH INTO NAGELBERG'S HOUSE?

The weekend was too short. I realized after we left that there was so much I hadn't had time to learn about the group since, mainly, we were so involved with nostalgia. I, for one, would like to have learned more about their families. What has your life been like? What are your children doing?

I suspect that most of us felt the same way because we all expressed a desire to have a second reunion.

A second one was planned, and it turned out to be even more successful. We had almost a hundred people there.

My newsletter readership continued to increase. It contained an "In Memoriam" list of those who had died. We also published the names and addresses of all new people we found.

The newsletter flourished for more than ten years. During that time, we had annual reunions. We even had a reunion in Florida for those of us who had relocated there.

In January 1986, we were blessed with our second grandchild. Sheila gave birth to Rebecca.

Almost from the start, Rebecca, although a very beautiful child, was sickly. She came down with chickenpox at an early age, and she did not have a good start in life.

HAITI

In February 1986, with the assistance of the United States, Jean Claude Duvalier, his wife, and an entourage boarded a plane and flew out of Haiti. Jean Claude had finally been overthrown. Thus began a twenty-year history of upheaval and suffering for the Haitian people. One corrupt government after the other succeeded each other. Ultimately, Designatronics had to leave Haiti.

In June 1986, we received a letter from the White House inviting us to attend a briefing for senior executives of American firms with significant investments in Haiti. The letter read as follows:

DEAR MR. RUBENFELD,

THE WHITE HOUSE OFFICE OF PUBLIC LIAISON IS SPONSORING A BRIEFING FOR SENIOR EXECUTIVES OF AMERICAN FIRMS WITH SIGNIFICANT INVESTMENTS IN HAITI. RECENT CHANGES IN HAITI HAVE BROUGHT A NEW OPPORTUNITY FOR THE DEVELOPMENT OF A STABLE ECONOMY AND DEMOCRACY IN THAT CARIBBEAN NATION. US INVESTMENTS IN HAITI WILL BE ESSENTIAL TO THE SUCCESS OF THAT PROCESS.

> THE BRIEFING IS DESIGNED TO INFORM YOU OF THE CURRENT ECONOMIC AND POLITICAL SITUATION IN HAITI AND ITS IMPACT ON AMERICAN BUSINESS INVESTMENT THERE. SECRETARY OF STATE GEORGE P. SHULTZ WILL BE GIVING A BROAD OVERVIEW. ELLIOTT ABRAMS, ASSISTANT SECRETARY OF STATE FOR INTER-AMERICAN AFFAIRS; PETER MCPHERSON, ADMINISTRATOR OF THE AGENCY FOR INTERNATIONAL DEVELOPMENT; AND CRAIG NALEN, PRESIDENT OF THE OVERSEAS PRIVATE INVESTMENT CORPORATION, WILL DISCUSS THE DETAILS OF RECENT CHALLENGES AND OPPORTUNITIES FOR INVESTORS.

Joe Rubenfeld and I attended the briefing where Secretary of State George Schultz assured us that everything would be safe for us in Haiti. We were told how much we were needed by our government in Haiti. Later, we received a communication from the Haiti desk officer. The mailgram was sent from the US Department of Commerce. The mailgram read:

> I HOPE YOU WERE ABLE TO ATTEND THE WHITE HOUSE BRIEFING ON HAITI HELD ON JUNE 13. THIS MEETING PROVIDED THE US GOVERNMENT WITH THE OPPORTUNITY TO STATE OUR CONTINUED COMMITMENT TO DEMOCRACY IN HAITI. BECAUSE OF YOUR BUSINESS PRESENCE IN HAITI, YOU ARE A VITAL PART OF THAT FUTURE. AS THE DESK OFFICER FOR HAITIAN AFFAIRS AT THE DEPARTMENT OF COMMERCE, I AM AVAILABLE TO ANSWER YOUR QUESTIONS REGARDING HAITIAN ECONOMIC

INVESTMENT OR COMMERCIAL POLICIES. I MAY BE REACHED BY PHONE OR BY LETTER.

SINCERELY,
HAITI DESK OFFICER

If I had any trust or confidence in the bureaucracy of our government, this and subsequent events would drastically shake them.

By August 1986, I was faced with additional bad news. Designatronics's fiscal year produced reduced sales of $19.3 million but reflected losses of more than $500,000. We remained optimistic because we were introducing new innovative products, and we were in the process of producing on a contract for loudspeakers for the government, and we (hopefully) would be able to manufacture them at our Haitian facility, filling the gap for the severe cutbacks of business from our Israeli customer, Tadiran. In addition, the inflation that affected Israel at that time was so severe that it made it unprofitable to continue our operations in that country. We were forced to dissolve our Israeli partnership.

In November 1986, Mom was not feeling well, and I took her to see a doctor at a New York hospital. He had come highly recommended. He determined that, for some reason, she was bleeding internally. He indicated it was imperative that they operate immediately in order to stop the bleeding. I had no time to consult with my brother or sister. The decision had to be made immediately, and so I gave the doctor permission to operate. Shortly after the operation was in progress, he came out and informed me that Mom's blood pressure had dropped drastically and that in order to proceed, he had to put her on life support. Again, I gave my permission. I later learned that Mom had stopped breathing, although the doctor did not tell me that. I am not sure that I would have given him permission to proceed if I had known. The end result was the bleeding was stopped, but Mom never came off life support. I felt that she was suffering a lot as the result of not permitting her to die peaceably. I have never forgiven the doctor for not giving me accurate information.

It was a terribly emotional time for me. I had no one to consult with immediately, and I had to make the decision to allow the doctor to proceed with the surgery. I have never forgiven myself even though I acted in good faith based on the only information I had available to me.

Mom died on December 1, 1986, after a number of days during which time she remained on life support. I tried to reach the rabbi she knew when she lived in Flushing, but he was unable to handle the funeral arrangements, so we were forced to use a rabbi referred to us by the funeral home. He did not know Mom. I felt that, as her son, I wanted to do the eulogy rather than leave it to someone who had no knowledge of who she was. The following is the eulogy I delivered:

MOM'S EULOGY

IT IS DIFFICULT FOR ME TO BE UP HERE SPEAKING AT MOM'S FUNERAL, BUT IT IS IMPOSSIBLE FOR ME NOT TO. I DON'T FEEL THAT ANYONE ELSE CAN EXPRESS FOR ME WHAT I AM FEELING. I HAVE WATCHED MOM DURING THE PAST YEAR BECOMING MORE AND MORE

FRAIL. I HAVE WATCHED MOM DURING THE PAST YEAR BECOMING MORE AND MORE SENILE UNTIL IT WAS ALMOST IMPOSSIBLE TO RECOGNIZE HER AS THE WOMAN WE ALL KNEW. AND WITH MOM'S PASSING, IT IS, FOR ME, TRULY THE END OF AN ERA. MOM WAS THE LAST OF ALL HER SIBLINGS, SURVIVING OUR UNCLE MAX BY ONLY A VERY SHORT TIME. HER SIBLINGS, BROTHERS AND SISTERS, WERE OUR MOTHERS AND FATHERS, OUR UNCLES AND AUNTS, OUR GRANDMOTHERS AND GRANDFATHERS—AND YES, EVEN OUR GREAT-GRANDMOTHERS AND GREAT-GRANDFATHERS. MOM'S PASSING REMOVES OUR LAST LIVING FAMILIAL LINK WITH THE "OLD COUNTRY." AS A CHILD, I REMEMBER THE FREQUENT REFERENCE TO "IN DER HAIM" WHEN MOM WOULD BE REMINISCING ABOUT THE DAYS IN ROMANIA. THOSE OF US WHO ARE MOM'S CHILDREN AND THOSE OF US WHO ARE MOM'S NIECES AND NEPHEWS CAN RECALL WHEN, AS CHILDREN, FAMILY GATHERINGS WOULD TAKE PLACE USUALLY AROUND THE HOLIDAYS—SOMETIMES IN BROOKLYN, SOMETIMES IN LONG BRANCH. I CAN REMEMBER HOW THE EXCITEMENT OF THE ANTICIPATED GET-TOGETHER STARTED WEEKS IN ADVANCE. THE PREPARATION FOR THE LONG JOURNEY TO LONG BRANCH OR TO BROOKLYN WAS IN ITSELF AN ADVENTURE. I CAN RECALL THE ENDLESS QUANTITY OF FOOD AND, MOST OF ALL, THE WARM, LOVING FEELINGS THAT EXISTED. THOSE WERE DIFFICULT TIMES. OUR PARENTS COMING TO A STRANGE LAND, STRUGGLING TO ADJUST TO A STRANGE ENVIRONMENT, GETTING MARRIED AND BUILDING TO THE BEST OF THEIR ABILITY A HOME

ENVIRONMENT, FULL OF LOVE, IN WHICH TO RAISE THEIR CHILDREN.

MOM'S HOME WAS SOMEWHAT UNIQUE ALTHOUGH, AS A CHILD, I DIDN'T REALIZE IT. HER HOME WAS ALWAYS A HAVEN FOR RELATIVES IN NEED. I CAN'T EVER REMEMBER WHEN MOM WASN'T REACHING OUT TO MAKE A HOME FOR A RELATIVE IN NEED. AND I CAN'T REMEMBER THE TIME WHEN THERE WEREN'T OTHER RELATIVES LIVING WITH US. MOM WORKED LIKE NO ONE ELSE I EVER KNEW. SHE COOKED, BAKED, CLEANED, DID THE LAUNDRY, SHOPPED, AND TOOK US TO THE DOCTOR, THE DENTIST, TO HEBREW SCHOOL, AND THEN FOUND TIME TO GO TO SCHOOL TO IMPROVE HER ENGLISH. WHEN SHE WAS ALL THROUGH, SHE PUT ON A PAIR OF PANTS, LONG BEFORE IT WAS OK FOR A WOMAN TO WEAR PANTS, THEN PUT A SCHMATTA ON HER HEAD AND WENT UP ON THE ROOF WITH A PAIL OF TAR TO PATCH A LEAKY ROOF OR CLIMBED A LADDER WITH A PAIL OF PAINT TO PAINT THE CEILING. THE CURTAINS WERE WASHED, STRETCHED, AND REHUNG. CARPETS WERE PICKED UP, BEATEN CLEAN, AND PUT DOWN AGAIN. AND I CAN'T RECALL MOM HAVING ANY OUTSIDE HELP IN THE PERFORMANCE OF ANY OF THESE TASKS. MOM WORKED THIS WAY OUT OF A NEED TO DO SO—BUT ALSO OUT OF LOVE FOR HER FAMILY.

MOM DID NOT SURROUND HERSELF WITH MANY FRIENDS. SHE WAS MOST COMFORTABLE WITH HER FAMILY, AND ESPECIALLY WHEN SHE WAS PROVIDING US WITH FOOD. VISIT MOM AND PREPARE TO EAT. MOM WAS NOT MUCH OF A TALKER. SHE LACKED

THE VERBAL ABILITY TO EXPRESS HOW SHE REALLY FELT ABOUT HER FAMILY, AND IN THE PAST FEW YEARS, MOM WAS NOT ABLE TO EXPRESS HER LOVE IN THE WAY SHE FELT MOST COMFORTABLE DOING IT. IN THE PAST YEAR, MOM WOULD TELL ME HOW SORRY SHE WAS BECAUSE SHE WAS UNABLE TO MAKE SOMETHING FOR US TO EAT. "MOM," I WOULD SAY, "LET'S JUST TALK." AND SHE WOULD SADLY SHAKE HER HEAD.

AND NOW MOM IS GONE. AND LIKE MY COUSINS BEFORE ME, MY SISTER, MY BROTHER, AND I BECOME THE OLDEST LIVING GENERATION. THE FIRST GENERATION BORN IN "DER GOLDENER LOND." IT IS OUR TASK TO CONTINUE TO LIVE OUR LIVES TO THE FULLEST EXTENT OF OUR CAPABILITIES. THAT IS WHAT OUR PARENTS WANTED FOR US. IT IS WHAT WE WANT FOR OUR CHILDREN, GRANDCHILDREN, AND OTHER GENERATIONS TO FOLLOW. MOM, IT IS WITH BOTH GREAT SADNESS AND RELIEF THAT I SAY GOODBYE. WE WILL ALL MISS YOU GREATLY, BUT WE ARE RELIEVED THAT YOUR SUFFERING IS AT AN END. MAY YOU REST IN PEACE.

Shortly after Mom's death, Sheila presented me with her remembrances and feelings about her grandma. It was very touching and nostalgic, and I include it here because I treasure it.

SHEILA'S VIEW OF GRANDMA

SHE WAS A SMALL WOMAN, QUIET AND OLD-WORLD.

I WAS ALWAYS AMAZED AT THE SMALLNESS OF HER LIFE OR HOW IT WAS CONTAINED IN SUCH A SMALL SPACE.

A ONE-ROOM APARTMENT WITH A SMALL, TINY BEDROOM—NOT REALLY A BEDROOM, MORE AS AN AFTERTHOUGHT WITH A CURTAIN INSTEAD OF A DOOR.

NO DOOR.

I COULD NEVER UNDERSTAND WHY THERE WAS NO DOOR.

WAS IT BECAUSE SHE LIVED IN THE KITCHEN OR THE SIDE OF THE ROOM

THAT PLAYED THE PART OF THE KITCHEN?

OR WAS IT BECAUSE DOORS WERE NOT IMPORTANT?

WERE DOORS TOO MODERN?

WAS HER WHOLE LIFE SEPARATED BY CURTAINS?

WERE CURTAINS A WAY TO CLING TO HER PAST?

THE BEDROOM WAS SMALL AND DARK—AN INEXPENSIVE

WOODEN SET OF DRAWERS, A DARK ROOM THAT WAS UNINVITING.

I NEVER WANTED TO GO INTO THE BEDROOM.

I PREFERRED TO SLEEP ON THE SOFA BED, THE MUSTARD-YELLOW SOFA BED THAT WAS MUSTARD-YELLOW VINYL PRETENDING TO BE LEATHER.

I PREFERRED THE BIG ROOM.

I LIVED IN A HOUSE, A BIGGER HOUSE WITH LOTS OF SEPARATE ROOMS.

ALL THE ROOMS HAD A PURPOSE, AND ALL THE ROOMS HAD OBJECTS

SPECIFIC TO THE ROOMS.

Perhaps that is why I was so intrigued with a life that could

put all of those specific items of life in one room.

An end table, a couch, a table with a sewing machine,

an old armoire against a wall . . .

I remember a mirror over the armoire, but I don't really recall what it looked like. I remember it had an old feeling.

A large table, a small stove, so small I remember being amazed

that someone could have a stove with so few burners and a tiny oven, a doll oven, a sink to the right, and a small white cabinet for dishes.

Milky white dishes with a thin gold line. Dishes with white ridges. And the glasses— pineapple juice would be in the glasses.

Special glasses you did not see in Woodmere.

They were grandma glasses and the only place where pineapple juice tasted right.

A quiet, nervous woman who never seemed to think of herself

but seemed to take quiet enjoyment in the watching

and caring and "potchering after the kinderler."

My grandma was a grandma. She looked like a grandma,

she smelled like a grandma, and she pinched cheeks like

A GRANDMA. NOT SAYING MUCH, VERY QUIET,
BUT ALWAYS MUTTERING "BUTCHA, BUTCHA."

THERE WERE NO TOYS, NO COMMERCIAL TOYS,
BUT THE BUTTONS WERE CAPTIVATING.
JARS OR BOXES, I AM NOT SURE—
I WILL HAVE TO ASK MY SISTER.

WALNUTS ROLLING ON THE WOOD SLAB ON THE STOOP UNDERNEATH
THE BIG TREE ON THE CORNER HOUSE WITH THE GREEN FENCE.
A SPECIAL GREEN, DARK AND SHINY.
THE FENCE.
I KNEW WE WERE AT GRANDMA'S WHEN I SAW THAT GREEN.
I HAVE NOT SEEN THAT GREEN TOO OFTEN IN MY LIFE,
BUT ON THE OCCASION THAT ANOTHER HUE OR SHADE OR SWATCH OF
GREEN STIRS THE EMBERS,
IN MY GRANDMA'S MIND'S EYE,
THE GREEN SAYS, "WE ARE HERE. LET'S PLAY WALNUTS."

MY GRANDMA CHEATED ON PASSOVER.
SHE WOULD STEER MY COUSIN TO FIND THE AFIKOMEN.
WHEN MY SISTER AND I FOUND OUT AS ADULTS,
WE BOTH LAUGHED. "OH," WE SAID, "IS THAT WHY SUSAN ALWAYS WON?"

By August 31, 1987, the completion of another fiscal year for Designatronics, we managed to increase our sales to over $21.5 million. We were also able to reverse the tide of losses by generating $83,000 in profits. Conditions in Haiti were, at best, uncertain. I believed that productivity was affected by the emotional state of our Haitian workforce. They, like most people in the country, were uncertain of the future. Some people were elated with the opportunity for change. Others felt more comfortable with the status quo. We would maintain a wait and see approach. After all, our secretary of state assured us that all would be well.

By 1987, my urinary problems had become really bad. I found myself getting up many times during the night to go to the bathroom. Dr. Puchner, my urologist, finally recommended a transurethral resection (TURP) be performed. After he explained all I could expect from the surgery, I was really taken aback emotionally. One of the effects of the TURP was that, from that point on, I would have retrograde ejaculation. I was sixty years old in 1985, and I had no intention of having any more children. Yet the idea that I would experience orgasm but it would not be accompanied with ejaculation was very disturbing to me. I would have to deal with my emotional problem because the TURP had to be performed. It was, and I ultimately recovered and slowly began to accept the inevitable in exchange for relief of some of my urinary difficulties.

Meanwhile, despite the assurances we had from George Schultz, conditions in Haiti continued to deteriorate. We were concerned with interrupted production, shipping difficulties, and poor morale. We, like other companies, began to look for alternatives. Although we had no intention of leaving Haiti, we thought it might be a good idea to have a backup solution. We discussed this extensively with our board of directors. We ultimately settled on Costa Rica and proceeded to set up a small pilot operation there.

August 31, 1988, was another banner year for Designatronics, breaking all previous records in shipments and showing rather substantial increases in net profit after taxes. Sales reached $25.1 million, and profit was $727,000. However, what was more impressive to us was the growth of our backlog in orders—which reached $19.5 million, a record for the company. The officers were amply compensated in both salary increases and bonuses for turning in such a stellar performance. However, lurking in the background was a dark cloud that threatened to bring very bad times to our company.

Our Accusonic Systems Corp. subsidiary, a manufacturer of microphones and earphones, had an opportunity to bid on a large contract for the Department of Defense. The product was a helmet that contained, as part of its structure, earphones and a microphone. When we heard about the proposed procurement, we immediately informed the contracting officer handling the contract that we were interested in bidding. He attempted to discourage us by stating that we did not manufacture helmets. We answered that we could manufacture the earphones and the microphones and that we would find a subcontractor who was qualified to manufacture the helmets. We argued that previous awards were let to a manufacturer of helmets, and that company had to subcontract out the manufacture of the earphones and microphones. He had to admit the truth of our argument. I had the distinct feeling that this contracting officer favored the previous supplier. When I implied that I felt that our company could come forth with a bid that could save the government money, he immediately changed the rules of the game. He told me that the invitation to bid was going to be amended. The new terms would indicate that awards of contracts would be made to the three lowest qualified bidders. The lowest qualified bidder would receive 50% of the award, followed by 30% for the second lowest, and 20% for the third lowest. We found those terms acceptable.

After reviewing the contract terms, I arranged another meeting with the contracting officer and disclosed to him that we had plants in Haiti and Florida. I informed him that we intended to manufacture some of the earphone and microphone assemblies in Haiti and complete the process in our Florida plant. I was specifically told that as long as we complied with the Buy American Act, which required that at least 50% of the added value to the product originated in the United States, it was perfectly all right. With that assurance, we began to prepare our bid. First, we searched for and found Specialty Plastics, a qualified manufacturer of helmets in New Jersey. Coincidentally, they also intended to bid on the contract. We agreed that we would buy our helmets from Specialty Plastics and that they would buy their microphones and earphones from us, assuming our prices were competitive. Both companies went about preparing bids without any mutual communication with each other except to get each other's price quotation. As it turned out, Specialty's price to us was the lowest quote we were able to obtain from legitimate helmet manufacturers, and our price to them was the lowest they had received. We then bid on the contract, applying our own method of arriving at a selling price.

When the bidding period was over and the results published, Accusonic Systems was the lowest bidder, Specialty Plastics was the second lowest, and the old supplier, Gentec (which had a virtual monopoly on the product until we came along), was the third lowest bidder. This did not make the contracting officer very happy, and he was determined to make life as difficult for us as possible. He succeeded!

Shortly after the contracts were awarded, the contracting officer informed us that we could not manufacture any of the assemblies in Haiti. I reminded him that he was the one who had authorized it, and he denied it. I said that our bid was based on our ability to manufacture in Haiti, but he was not sympathetic. He said that our prototypes—which we were required to submit within an established period of time—would be rejected if any of our parts came from Haiti. In addition to that problem, Specialty Plastics was going to hold us responsible for delivery to them of acceptable microphones and earphones.

Our dilemma was further complicated by the fact that we did not have time to argue since we were required to obtain approval of our prototypes and begin delivery of the product within the time frame called for in the contract. We had no alternative but to manufacture in the United States. Our Florida facility was not large enough to accommodate the additional people we would need, so it became necessary for us to expand into larger space.

Ultimately, we were successful in meeting all our delivery requirements, but at tremendous excess cost that ran into several million dollars. We were left with no alternative but to once again take on the United States Government. We instituted a lawsuit that was to go on for more than ten years.

On May 26, 1989, Sheila gave birth to Stephanie, our third granddaughter. She was a delicious little girl whom I fell in love with immediately.

By August 31, 1989, we were licking our wounds as we reported the bad news to stockholders. Our sales for the year were $25.9 million, slightly better than the previous year; however, we generated a loss of $133,000. Our major difficulties emanated from our Accusonic Systems and Automatic Coil Co., Inc. subsidiaries. We continued to produce and deliver on the contract for helmets. We were losing money on each one produced, and this continued into our next fiscal year, when we finally completed shipments and halted the bleeding, which was affecting our other divisions. Continued growth and progress in product development in our Stock Drive Products, Sterling Instrument, and Techno Divisions stood in contrast. In this fiscal year, however, we absorbed most of the costs of setting up our Florida facility for production.

By August 31, 1990, our sales rose to $31.9 million while we had a net profit of $794,000. Our increased sales reflected the completed shipment on our government contract. We were busy licking our wounds while our lawsuit to reclaim our losses proceeded at a snail's pace through the court system.

My routine visit to see my urologist, Dr. Puchner, produced some concern. My PSA had risen, and when the test was repeated, the results proved to be the same. Dr. Puchner took a wait and see attitude and scheduled another appointment in six months. He didn't seem terribly concerned. We talked about the possibility that I had prostate cancer. He assured me that I was going to die one day, but not from prostate cancer. A very reassuring prediction.

I had reached my sixty-fifth birthday. I began to think about the Social Security System that had been set up years earlier. In their infinite wisdom, the government arrived at a retirement age of 65, when workers could start collecting Social Security payments. The age of 65 was set because few people would be fortunate to reach that age in order to collect. It was like a carrot you chase but fate plays a hand and prohibits you from reaching that point when you can retire and still receive a monthly paycheck.

Now here I was, 65 and eligible. However, I had long since passed the point where I could live on the proceeds of a Social Security check. We had built a house that we loved very much, but it was not cheap to maintain. If I retired, I would have to supplement my Social Security income with another source. Although I had been able to build a modest nest egg, the bulk of my assets was in the interest I had in Designatronics stock. Without those assets, I would be unable to sustain our current lifestyle. However, I was not yet ready to retire, so I put it out of my mind.

I was still looking toward the future, but I had reason to look seriously at how vulnerable we were. On March 13, 1990, Betty Freeman—the oldest daughter of my uncle and aunt, Max and Rose Segall—died of cancer. Reviewing my family history so far, quite a few of my relatives had died of cancer. I couldn't help thinking and believing that cancer was an epidemic. Death claiming members of my generation.

By August 31, 1991, sales at Designatronics dropped to $24.6 million while we sustained a net loss of $126,000. Many factors were in play at that time. First, we had completed shipments on our disastrous government contract through our Accusonic subsidiary with no new business to replace that contract. We continued to expand our spending on catalogs and advertising for our Techno Division, and to add to the mix, the turbulence caused by the buildup for Desert Storm brought about a recession. Conditions in Haiti were in turmoil due to a military coup. An executive order issued by President George H. W. Bush restricted the importation of Haitian-produced products. In addition, we were not able to bring raw materials into Haiti as the result of the boycott. We had commitments to our customers, and once again, our government's policy sabotaged our efforts. We were forced to halt all production in Haiti and produce our products at our Florida facility. We had no way of knowing how long this boycott would last, so we just had to keep our Haiti facility in a "wait and see" stance.

There were no apologies from our government for the assurances they had given us just a short time ago. Secretary of State George Shultz never came forward to offer us any explanations or any form of assistance. We were completely on our own. It gave me plenty of reason to stop and consider where I was in my life. I found, among my musings, the following thoughts:

SIXTY-SIX YEARS OLD (1991)

MY SIXTY-SIXTH BIRTHDAY HAS COME AND GONE. AND AFTER SIXTY-SIX YEARS, I STILL HAVEN'T BEEN ABLE TO FIGURE OUT WHAT THIS LIFE IS ALL ABOUT. FROM TIME TO TIME—USUALLY WHEN SOMEONE CLOSE DIES OR WHEN A NEW BIRTH TAKES PLACE—I LOOK FOR AN ANSWER. AND WHEN I FAIL TO FIND IT, I TELL MYSELF IT'S BECAUSE I LACK CERTAIN KNOWLEDGE. PERHAPS IF I STUDIED CHEMISTRY OR GREEK MYTHOLOGY, I WOULD FIND THE ANSWER I AM SEEKING. SOMEHOW I HAVE COME THIS FAR IN LIFE WITHOUT ANY REAL KNOWLEDGE OF CHEMISTRY OR GREEK MYTHOLOGY. I DON'T REALLY KNOW WHAT PANDORA'S CURIOSITY UNLEASHED WHEN SHE OPENED HER BOX, NOR DO I KNOW WHAT EXACTLY WAS WRONG WITH ACHILLES'S HEEL. SO I KEEP PROMISING MYSELF THAT WHEN TIME PERMITS, I WILL STUDY CHEMISTRY, GREEK MYTHOLOGY, PHILOSOPHY, AND PERHAPS FINALLY DISCOVER THE MEANING OF LIFE. BUT IN MY HEART OF HEARTS, I KNOW IT ISN'T THAT SIMPLE.

I DON'T KNOW HOW EXTENSIVE PHIL'S KNOWLEDGE IS OF GREEK MYTHOLOGY, BUT I DO KNOW THAT HE KNOWS A GREAT DEAL ABOUT CHEMISTRY, BOTANY, AND BIOLOGY. PHIL IS A FRIEND OF MINE WITH WHOM I SHARE A COMMON

HOBBY. WE BOTH GROW BEGONIAS—THAT IS TO SAY PHIL GROWS BEGONIAS AND I TRY TO GROW THEM. NOT ONLY DOES HE GROW THEM, HE PLANS THEIR DEVELOPMENT AND GUIDES THEIR GROWTH UNTIL THEY EMERGE AS BEAUTIFUL SPECIMENS JUST ON TIME TO ENTER THEM IN COMPETITION AND WALK AWAY WITH BLUE RIBBONS. IT IS RARE THAT PHIL'S ENTRIES DO NOT WIN FIRST PRIZE. AFTER WINNING, PHIL USUALLY LOSES INTEREST IN THE PLANTS AND GIVES THEM AWAY. FROM THAT MOMENT ON, THE RECIPIENT HAS THE CHALLENGING RESPONSIBILITY OF TRYING TO KEEP THE PLANT LOOKING AS BEAUTIFUL AS IT WAS WHEN PHIL GAVE IT TO HIM. OF COURSE, IT IS A LOSING BATTLE. THE PLANT WILL NEVER AGAIN LOOK THAT GOOD. PERHAPS IF PHIL KEPT THE PLANT, IT WOULD FADE ALSO BECAUSE ALL LIVING THINGS REACH THEIR APEX OF BEAUTY. AND BECAUSE HE LOVES HIS PLANTS, HE CAN'T STAND THE IDEA OF WATCHING THEM DETERIORATE, SO HE GIVES THEM AWAY.

In 1991, I became more discouraged with the consistent struggle I was having at Designatronics. I was feeling my age, and I was aware of frequent bouts of depression. I had an exam, and my PSA continued to rise, and Dr. Puchner was beginning to talk about the necessity for other examinations. However, Trudy and I had planned a trip to China, and I was not going to allow anything to interrupt it; so, for the time being, I put my urinary troubles out of my mind and concentrated on our forthcoming vacation. It was indeed a memorable trip. My notes on the trip may not be terribly interesting, but I include them here for the record.

OCTOBER 22, 1991—SAILING OR CRUISING THE YANGTZE RIVER

I'm not sure of the dynamics that prevented me from recording the events of this memorable trip to China until now. Perhaps the reasons will become clearer with time. In any event, we are presently on a ship called MV *Yangtse Paradise*, and I'm now sitting on the observation deck as we cruise through the third gorge we will encounter on this journey. The views are breathtaking. Mountains rising right out of the river. Along the riverbanks are hills terraced to permit farming, and there appears to be a good deal of it going on all along the riverbank. It is said that 50% of the Chinese people are dependent upon the Yangtze River for their survival, and China is populated by one billion people.

The ship is reasonably comfortable, although it leaves a great deal to be desired in cleanliness. As a matter of fact, throughout our trip so far, we have found that cleanliness does not appear to be a high priority. The carpets have been uniformly stained and dirty in each hotel room we have occupied so far. Our room aboard ship is understandably small. We find it necessary to store our suitcases with most of our belongings under the bathroom sink. Aside from two cubby holes in a very narrow closet that permits hanging of a few garments (but only diagonally or the closet door won't close), there is little other space for clothes storage. In the main, however, the room is reasonably adequate.

So far, the food aboard ship has been better than what we have experienced on land, but we didn't really expect this trip to be a gourmet experience. Perhaps our biggest concern before we left on this trip was how we would relate to our fellow tourists.

Our group consisted of twenty-nine people who first met at the Japan Airlines terminal at Kennedy Airport. When we arrived, a young lady gave us our airline tickets and instructed us to get on a line to check in. Almost immediately, we became aware of a group of eight people that appeared to be traveling together and were making their presence known by their very loud antics. The men were staking out their claim as part of their group with loud jokes and observations while the women cackled and laughed in appreciation to ensure their place. This group, although willing to open ranks to allow others in, mostly chose to form their own groups.

The first leg of our trip was a thirteen-hour flight to Tokyo Narita Airport, which we found rather pleasant except for the "gang of eight" that was overpowering in the noise they generated. We found the food reasonably good for airline food. It was certainly as good as the food we had on our last trip to the Orient, when we flew business class. We met a few of our group during this trip. Roberta, who is single, is traveling with her widowed aunt. She lives in Queens, and her aunt Helen lives in Florida. She appears to be a woman of some means since she has her own home equipped with a swimming pool. There are Chris and Frances, residing on Twenty-Second Street in Manhattan with a second home in

Upstate New York. They are actors of sorts, involved in doing commercials, although Chris has done some theater, playing a role in *Annie Hall*. They are both very colorful in their way, if a little weird.

Our schedule called for spending the first night in Japan, close to the airport so that we could conveniently make a morning flight to Beijing. We checked most of our baggage straight through to Beijing so we had no hassle with claiming them in Narita. With minimal difficulty, we came through customs and found the bus that would take us to our hotel. After settling into our room, we went down to dinner. It was far from memorable but adequate.

We then retired to our room. It was about 9:00 p.m., and we began the process of adjusting to the time change—some eleven hours' difference from home—by getting up at about 3:00 a.m. local time and being unable to fall back asleep.

In the morning, we found a message under our door indicating that our flight to Beijing would be delayed. So after a lovely Japanese breakfast consisting of miso soup and a vegetable dish, we took a taxi to visit the town of Narita, where there was a not very impressive Buddhist temple. Last year, we had seen many Buddhist temples in Japan and Thailand. This temple was not particularly outstanding. We then returned to our hotel and then on to the airport for our flight to Beijing.

Our arrival at the Beijing International Airport was a study in contrast. This airport was dreary, plain, and void of any attempts at making it attractive. Trudy felt it was like a scene when Humphrey Bogart escorted Ingrid Bergman to the airport for the flight out of Casablanca.

We found our luggage, passed through customs, and located our guide, whose first greeting was "Why did you come so late? I have been waiting for you over five hours." We didn't know it at the time, but that seemed to set the mood of our relationship with him. His name was Ming, but he settled on "Eddie."

Leaving the chaos of the airport, we boarded a bus that was to take us to our hotel; but first, we would stop for dinner at a restaurant. However, nobody in our group was particularly hungry, but our guide insisted on stopping there anyway, where some fruit and tea was served instead of dinner. We then proceeded to our hotel, where we were assigned rooms, and we gladly retired to ours. The accommodations were adequate.

Our night was again plagued with frequent awakenings or not being able to sleep at all, so we did a lot of reading. Breakfast was a pleasant surprise consisting of a buffet combining Chinese and Western foods—certainly more than adequate by any standard.

Our first day in China began with a bus trip to Tiananmen Square. In preparation for this trip, Trudy borrowed a number of video tapes on China from the library. We saw the film entitled *The Last Emperor* and various travel logs, several of which depicted Tiananmen Square, but the video didn't really show the size of the square. It is enormous, and in one of the buildings around the square, Chairman Mao's remains are on display, but time didn't permit our viewing them. We couldn't help thinking that two years earlier, a massacre had occurred here, but the exact extent of it remains evasive. As I continued to find as this trip proceeded, there were many places I would have liked to spend more time in, and other places were eminently missable. I would have liked more time here, but we were moved on to our next destination—the Imperial Palace, which is also known as the Forbidden City. The movie *The Last Emperor* was filmed here.

We then went to visit the summer palace where the emperor, his wife, and concubines would enjoy the benefits of being wealthy and people of position. There in the water near the palace is a stone boat where the empress would sit and enjoy entertaining their guests. The stone boat, of course, could not sail.

The "gang of eight," by this time, made their names known by loudly calling to each other. There is Howard and Arlene, Milton and Ruth, Arnold and Sandy, and Lenny and Marsha. Lenny came to China equipped with lots of ballpoint pens and lollipops to hand out. Individually, they are all nice; but as a group, they are very loud and are constantly competing for attention. Lenny, who refers to himself as the "round-eyed Buddha," has a sense of humor about his extreme size. "When a shark sees me, he says, 'Boy, there is my food for the next week.'"

No attempt was made to introduce members of the group to each other; but slowly and surely, we got to meet everyone.

Problems dealing with the relationship between Eddie and our group began to surface on the first day when he told a "joke" to pass the time while riding on the bus, and the joke was perceived as anti-Semitic. Nothing was said at that time, but after several jokes that were in bad taste, Eddie referred to our group as a "Jewish group." There was an eruption, which led to a frustrated attempt on Eddie's part as he tried to explain what he meant. Of course, no explanation could or would suffice. "We are an American group," observed Sheila, whose husband's name was Henry. The damage was done.

We then went to visit the Ming Tomb and the "Sacred Way," a rather long walk along a road that was lined with stone statues dating back to the sixteenth century. These statues were first of animals of all sorts, real and fantasy, and then of warriors that were placed there apparently to protect the tombs.

After lunch, we proceeded to the Great Wall of China. It is reported that the Great Wall is the only man-made object on the surface of the Earth visible from space. And of course, "you haven't been to China if you haven't climbed the Great Wall." So we climbed it. Up and up and up and up—untold numbers of steps and inclines. Walls were built around all important cities to protect them from invaders. Somewhere along the way, an emperor employed the labor of anywhere from 250,000 to 750,000 men for more than ten years just to connect all the walls. An enormous project by any standard.

Jet lag and little sleep the previous night were taking their toll. We had dinner and then were taken to the Beijing Opera, which after half an hour, we were only too glad to return to our hotel and go to sleep. It had been a full day.

Day 5. After another satisfying breakfast, which made up for the previous night's dinner, we were off to the zoo. The zoo was not on our itinerary, but our guide made special arrangements to go there, and it would cost "a little extra." Nobody minded paying a little extra, but we did feel it was uncalled for. The panda bear was delightfully entertaining, and we were glad we went to see him.

Our next destination was the Temple of Heaven, which we observed without too much enthusiasm. However, the temple is located in a park, and as we left, we proceeded along a sheltered walkway where many older men and women, retirees, were busy playing dominos and mah-jongg, playing homemade musical instruments, and singing delightful Chinese melodies. Everywhere we went, we were as much amusement to the people we encountered as they were to us. They were delightful, friendly, and in the main, seemed happy. I did not sense depression despite the feeling that these people worked very hard and had very little.

It was a full morning, and we were heading back to the airport for our flight to Xian, our next destination. There were signs at the hotel when we had first checked out indicating "thank you for helping us enforce our no-tipping policy." In the bus on the way to the airport, Eddie explained that the salaries of the servicepeople in the hotels, the bus drivers, and tour guides are low, and they really depend on tips. We must ignore the signs. A similar sign in the buses should also be ignored. The official unofficial practice is for each person to tip the bus driver $1 per day and each local tour leader $2 per day. Envelopes were passed out for us to make our contributions. This was another annoyance that many of us felt was uncalled for since we thought the price of the tour included all services and gratuities.

The flight to Xian was our first trip in a Chinese airplane. It was a relatively short flight, perhaps one and a half hours, during which time we were given a box lunch, small snacks, and finally, a gift of a cloth pocketbook, which looked like a panda bear.

A bus greeted us at the airport and took us to our hotel. Our assigned room was just too smelly and dirty, so we asked for another room, and this time, we were given a larger one with a double bed only a little less smelly. We opened the window to air out the place; but as it turned out, that room in Xian had been the best we'd experienced so far. Dinner was not memorable.

After breakfast the following morning, we visited Hot Springs (Hua Qing). We did not see any springs, hot or cold, so we will have to take their word for it. In any event, this is the place where Chiang Kai-shek was captured by the Communists in 1936 and forced to form an alliance in order to present a united front in China's fight against the Japanese. Historically, this is referred to as the Xian Incident.

Hot Springs was a summer residence of Hua Qing, and in front of the lovely building is the statue of Hua Qing's beautiful concubine, endowed with generous breasts.

That afternoon, we visited the sight of the warriors discovered in 1974 by peasants digging a well. The Terra-Cotta Army stood guard for over two thousand years over the tomb of the Emperor Qin Shi Huang, who is credited with starting construction on the Great Wall. It is believed that, although the excavation is not yet complete, they will ultimately uncover over eight thousand warriors, each one with different facial features and body positions.

OCTOBER 19, 1991

We flew to Chongqing and found it a very depressing and not a memorable city. It was, at one time, the capital headquarters for Chiang Kai-shek and was very mountainous.

OCTOBER 20, 1991

Our Yangtze river cruise began. We found the food aboard ship as good as we had while in China so far. We made a stop at Fengjie, where we visited the Temple of Heaven and Hell. It was necessary to climb nine hundred steps to reach the "Hell"—which, interestingly, was above the area designated "Heaven." Hell had scores of statues depicting positions of torture.

Our group continued to have difficulty becoming cohesive. The cliques remained, with each clique critical of the other's behavior. Our national tour leader remained insensitive to these goings-on and did nothing to bring the various factions together. Polarization of the groups was enhanced by the fact that, on the ship, the same people sat together during meals, limiting contact with members of the other "factions."

The young women serving as waitresses aboard ship were delightful, pretty, and charming. There was a set of beautiful twin girls that everyone would have liked to adopt and take home with them.

OCTOBER 21, 1991

This morning was one of the highlights of the trip when we boarded small boats at Badong and were propelled down Shennong Stream by river currents. We were assisted by six or eight oarsmen who frequently got out of the boat to pull it over a shallow spot. We traveled through some of the most beautiful natural sites we had ever seen. The highlight of this trip was passing through three gorges. We will probably never think of returning to China, but these views made this trip all worthwhile.

Getting into the small boats was an experience in itself. We left our vessel, MV *Yangtse Paradise*, and boarded a bus for a two-hour trip over precipitously narrow mountain roads scenically comparable to some Rocky Mountain crossings I recall from years ago. There were beautiful mountains and interesting scenes along the way. Mountain people were farming virtually vertical pieces of land and not leaving any piece of ground unplanted. Food appeared to be plentiful wherever we went in China, and one has to admire the fact that in forty years of Communist rule, starvation seems to have been eliminated despite the increase in population.

OCTOBER 23, 1991

This morning breakfast—consisting of a very loose oatmeal and medium-boiled eggs, toast, cake, tasteless coffee, and almost tasteless tea—was served at 7:30 a.m. so that we could go ashore to visit two cities called Jingzhou and Shashi. We found the cities very attractive. New structures architecturally different from the drab rectangular gray buildings we have seen so far. Our guide informed us that these cities—consisting of about 350,000 people—were better off economically because they enjoyed fertile soil, good rice, and a lot of fish; so the people had their eyes on a more luxurious life. We drove past a very beautiful park where the streets were lined with animals sculptured from the bushes. We visited a museum whose main feature was the remains of a 2,000-year-old man fully preserved, which was found in this vicinity. The body is on display in a case containing formaldehyde. It was found in a coffin entombed in another box, which was contained in yet another box. The containers were made of wood and treated with formaldehyde and buried some 30 meters in the earth, along with relics that indicated the man's name, position, and so forth. Also discovered in the area were beautifully designed silk garments that had somehow survived.

Lunch was at a local restaurant, where we found the food inedible, so we chose to go out for a walk while others remained to eat. In a local store, I was able to purchase a pair of tai-chi slippers for $2. Everywhere we go, we are a novelty. Many of the local people have never or had hardly ever seen Caucasians. Some people in our group came with balloons and lollipops, which they handed out to the children.

The last evening on the ship, there was a captain's banquet, which proved disappointing since it was a buffet and not too great, although there was much joviality with picture taking and fraternization with the crew. Photographs were taken with "our twins" and the captain, along with hugs and promises to send pictures. Earlier in the evening, Bill and Linda arranged a party and invited our entire ABC group.

Most of us attended, and some progress was made to integrate some of the people from other groups, although some were not interested. The evening came to a close with an amateur hour, where each group had to make a singing contribution to the show. ABC did its share with a song written by one of our group.

After the cruise, we visited Hong Kong, a sprawling city that can boast skyscrapers and modern structures without fear of being considered anything but "first world." My memories and notes come to an end here, and after reviewing notes, they don't seem to reflect or describe sufficiently what Trudy and I really experienced during that trip.

Shortly after we returned from China, Trudy and I went to California to meet our new grandson. Deah gave birth to Zachary, a bubbly bouncing red-headed boy on January 24, 1992. Zachary was unique, not only because he was red-headed at birth but because he was the only boy born in our family in two generations. All my children were girls, and until Zachary, all three of my grandchildren were girls. I was never unhappy about having girls. As a matter of fact, I was always partial to girls; but after three girl babies, it was kind of nice to have a grandson.

There was much trauma when we returned home from California. The inevitable fears that I had been living with for a long time were coming to pass. It was time for my next appointment with Dr. Puchner, who brought me face to face with my future, and it was not too appealing. After an examination, which included an ultrasound test, Dr. Puchner thought it was imperative that I have a consultation with another doctor because he had become suspicious of what he saw. An immediate appointment was arranged with Dr. Carl Olsson, head of Urology at Columbia Presbyterian. Dr. Olsson confirmed—after studying my records and the results of a cystoscopy that I underwent—that I had a malignant tumor in the prostate, and it was his recommendation that a radical prostatectomy be performed. He expressed some degree of urgency since it appeared as if the cancer may not be restricted to the prostate.

I was left with no time to evaluate the possibilities of alternative approaches to the resolution of this problem. Prior to the operation performed by Dr. Olsson, I was asked if I understood that the medical approach to the surgery was a lifesaving one. In the process of removing the cancer, it might be necessary to remove certain nerves, which would leave me impotent. I was in a state of shock, and I did not know or understand all the ramifications of what I was being told. Of course, I agreed to go ahead with the radical removal of my prostate.

After the surgery, Dr. Olsson informed me that although he had to remove one of the nerves, he was hopeful that I would not be left impotent. I was, however, left incontinent; and after a week in the hospital, I began the long process of regaining control of my urine flow. During this process, I was forced to wear diapers; and I did so for several months. Dr. Olsson was optimistic that he had removed all the cancerous tissue, but he cautioned me that we had to be ever watchful for a recurrence since the cancer had almost breached the prostate capsule. If it had, the cancer would have spread to other areas.

In the midst of my coping with cancer, "death by cancer" was very busy claiming another family member. My cousin Daniel, whom I was closest to, died after fighting cancer for more than a year. His death was devastating to me. We had been very close, and in his last days that he spent at Calvary Hospital, I visited him quite often and watched him—first slowly and then more rapidly—approach death. Daniel never married and never had children, but he had close ties to Barry and Lenore, his nephew and niece, as well as with his sister-in-law Irene Tunkel.

Coupled with the serious medical problems I was facing and family tragedies, problems at Designatronics continued to plague me. The company was being hurt badly because of the devastation inflicted on us as a result of the boycott in Haiti. The losses we were sustaining were eating away at the progress and growth we were experiencing in our electromechanical divisions and in our automation operations. I pondered over what should be done, and after much consultation with our board of directors, we decided to sell our operations in Haiti and Florida, close down our pilot operation in Costa Rica, and begin to stop the financial bleeding taking place. Then we made another very difficult decision. Joe Rubenfeld and I decided that, with the disposal of the electronic operations, there was really no useful position for Joe. Since I had in recent years devoted myself to the problems arising out of our Accusonic operations, my contribution to the other divisions was strictly managerial. Joe and I had always operated on an equal footing. We earned the same salary. We always received the same bonuses. Now if one of us had to leave the company, then both of us would. We were the highest-paid employees of the company, and if we could no longer make a viable contribution, then we should resign.

Over the years, I have always operated on the principle that a good parent was one that prepared his or her child to be independent. If the child grows up "not needing" the parent, then the parent has done a good job of raising the child. Similarly, a good administrator was one who made certain he could be replaced, if necessary, with minimum harm to the company. I felt that I set a good example in preparing Martin Hoffman and Frank Buchsbaum to take over if necessary. Either one was capable of filling my shoes. So after disposing of our electronic operations, Joe and I resigned as officers of Designatronics but remained on the board of directors of the company.

The new officers offered to make a retirement party for me, but I declined. I did, however, ask that our employees be assembled to permit me to address them. I told them that my leaving the company would not have any effect on them or their jobs. I tried to be as upbeat as I could, although inside, I was sad about leaving. It was a painful experience.

By August 31, 1992, after the restructuring, which eliminated the electronic component companies from the Designatronics balance sheet, net sales were $22.9 million for the continuing operations. Operating losses during the phase-out period were $2.4 million, all due to discontinued operations. Now Martin Hoffman assumed the role of president, and Frank Buchsbaum was executive vice president. Dr. Hitoshi Tanaka was senior vice president.

HAITI (1992)

IT WAS ANOTHER beautiful day. In the United States, they were celebrating Labor Day; but here in Haiti, it was just another Monday morning.

I—seated in a comfortable chair near the beautiful pool and shaded from the sun—was enjoying reading leisurely until the sun worked its way around the trees, raising the temperature considerably. I soon found it necessary to cool off. Under cover of a large beach towel, I removed an absorbent shield from inside my swim trunks and discreetly hid it in a bag next to my chair. If I hurried into the pool, the urine dripping that the shield was designed to absorb would not show on my dry swim trunks. The doctors and all the literature I read promised that incontinence would be a temporary condition, lasting anywhere from weeks to months. Now after eight weeks, I was not so sure. I would have felt better if I saw some improvement; but so far, none was apparent.

In the pool, the cool water refreshed me. I looked around and observed that set back on one side of the pool were a number of tables covered with white starched tablecloths. Trudy and I had enjoyed breakfast sitting at one of these tables a few hours earlier. We ate slices of fresh pineapple, melon, papaya, and warm croissants and drank strong Haitian coffee served by waiters in white coats. The bar was visible from where I stood in the pool, and a bartender was ready to create an array of exotic tropical drinks. Somewhere nearby, garlic was being roasted over a charcoal fire, and the aroma filled the air. Nostalgically, I recalled that my earliest recollections of Haiti were filled with these aromas constantly in the air. The surrounding vistas visible from the pool were green and hilly. I was alone, and I couldn't help appreciating the quiet and beautiful surroundings of the Villa Creole Hotel. In more than twenty years of coming to Haiti, this is the first time Trudy and I stayed at this hotel. For over fifteen years, we had a love affair with the Ibo Lele Hotel, which was higher up in the mountains overlooking Petionville, a suburb of Port-au-Prince. The hotel was perched on a cliff, and one could look down on Port-au-Prince and see the runway of the airport and know exactly when a flight was arriving from New York or Miami. At night, you could see the city lit up with man-made lights; and if you looked up, you could see untold millions of lights created by some supreme power.

The hotel was built by Robert Baussan, who was also the architect and owner. He lived in a large house located on the same mountain as the hotel, and it was only a short distance away. The house remained private and exclusive behind a stone fence and iron gates. Exotic vegetation contributed to the task of making the property invisible from outside the gates.

Robert Baussan was raised in that house, and his parents were people of means. He would follow in his father's footsteps and become an architect. Robert left Haiti for France when he was eighteen years old, and except for periodic visits home, he would not return to Haiti permanently until he became an architect.

Morris and Chaya Chernowsky had only one daughter, Tamara, and they were determined to have her rise above their station. Although they were not poverty-stricken by the standards of Jews living in Odessa in 1915, they had to sacrifice a great deal to accumulate the means to send Tamara to Paris to attend university. Tamara was never to step foot in Russia again.

In Paris, she became acquainted with many Bohemian artists, and she was encouraged to try her hand at painting. After her second attempt, she received a great deal of praise from them and decided she wanted to become a successful artist. She attended the university and spent as much of her spare time as possible painting.

Tamara and Robert became acquainted at the university and almost immediately fell in love. Robert would talk to Tamara about Haiti and how homesick he was for his beautiful country. He missed his family and longed for the day when he would return and contribute to his country's development through his newly acquired architectural knowledge. He spoke about the Haitian people, their culture, and the primitive works of religious art found in the churches of Haiti painted by untrained Haitians. Tamara became intrigued with the idea of living and painting in this primitive artistic environment, and when Robert pleaded with her to accompany him home during a summer recess at the university, she agreed. Tamara found Haiti to be all that Robert professed, and when he proposed that they marry after they graduate, she accepted. Shortly after they arrived back in Haiti, they were married in the garden of the Baussan home, where they were to take up residence.

Robert immediately began work on the design of a hotel which, when completed, was named the Hotel Ibo Lele, while Tamara, becoming more acquainted with Haiti, began to produce art that reflected the Haitian culture and its people.

The Hotel Ibo Lele became the most luxurious and beautiful hotel in Haiti. The Baussan family played host to visiting presidents, royalty, important dignitaries, and Hollywood stars. Photographs of the distinguished hotel guests lined the walls of the hotel lobby. The hotel had been built on several levels. Many of the larger and more luxurious rooms had balconies overlooking Port-au-Prince. Others had views of the mountains rising above Petionville. The kidney-shaped pool's fresh cool water circulated through the mouth of a flying dolphin. The mahogany bar had, as a backdrop, a wall depicting a Haitian peasant scene; and in the lower right-hand corner, in small print, was the name Tamara Baussan.

The room Trudy and I occupied at the Villa Creole had two doors on opposite ends, each leading to a balcony. One of these balconies offered complete privacy, and it was here that I came to sit after I came out of the pool. It was furnished with a sofa, a chair, and a footrest, which permitted me to sit comfortably in the chair while elevating my legs onto the footrest—a position I found tended to considerably reduce the dribble of urine and made me forget about the incontinence until I stood up.

What were we doing in Haiti? We had been coming here for the past twenty years, our last time two years ago when we thought it would be our last trip. My business interests in

Haiti would bring me here periodically, but it was Trudy and our love of the culture, arts and crafts, and the Haitian people that brought us so frequently. Everyone thought we were crazy for selecting Haiti as a vacation spot, but Trudy and I believed it was the best-kept vacation secret in the Caribbean. Hotel accommodations were extremely reasonable by comparison with other Caribbean islands, and the food could only be surpassed by exceptional restaurants in France. However, many changes had occurred, and I felt that the business climate was no longer conducive to profitable operations. The government was in turmoil, and many of our friends had left Haiti. So when we completed our vacation two years before, we thought it would be for the last time, and we said goodbye to a place where we shared so many exciting and stimulating experiences, a place where we were both thought of highly and respected.

Prior to my surgery, we had made plans to vacation in France and travel to regions we had not previously visited. We were really in need of a vacation. The stress, strain, and uncertainty that accompanied my illness had taken a serious toll on both of us. However, it was clear that the trip to France was unrealistic now, and Trudy thought going to Haiti would be more restful. We would feel more comfortable in a familiar environment despite the turmoil that existed in the country. We felt we could temporarily insulate ourselves while we rested and visited art galleries and craft shops.

The mountain framed by the balcony structure looked like an exquisite painting, I thought. I also thought about the discussion I had with Jim yesterday. He sat at the table next to where Trudy and I were having lunch in the hotel dining area overlooking the pool. Jim had arrived in Haiti just a few days before, and he would remain for about a month. He was here to study the problem relating to the large increase in the number of people fleeing Haiti in broken-down boats. I couldn't quite understand exactly what the study was about. In November 1991, President Bush embargoed materials from being shipped to Haiti by Americans while also preventing Americans from shipping materials out of Haiti to the United States. In addition, it became illegal to aid or abet the then Haitian government in any way. Translating this presidential order into practical terms, any American company operating in Haiti and leasing a building from the Haitian government was forbidden from paying rent. Since the electric utility was also owned by the Haitian government, an American-owned company was forbidden from paying its electric bill. How long would a US-owned utility continue to supply electric power essential to business operations to someone if he didn't pay his electric bill?

For all practical purposes, the embargo paralyzed our company. Production was brought to a standstill. In order to meet commitments to customers, machinery, equipment, and raw materials had to be returned to the United States. This had to be done within a very short time allowed by the terms of the embargo. New production facilities had to be developed and workers trained at tremendous cost. Our company was forced out of business in Haiti, and as a result, many Haitians were suddenly without jobs. The effect on the economy was catastrophic, and as bad as conditions had been for the poor Haitians before, it was now worse. Desperation drove many into unsafe boats in an attempt to seek asylum at Guantanamo in Cuba or any other port they could reach. Many never made it as their boats sank at sea. Those who did overburdened the facilities at Guantanamo and were returned to Haiti.

And Jim was now in Haiti for a month to study the problem as to why there were increasing numbers of boat people fleeing Haiti!

Then there was Bob, who had just arrived with his wife, Jean. Bob and Jean had a little boy about two years old who was being temporarily cared for by Jean's mother in Kentucky while they came to Haiti to look for a house. Bob indicated that in January 1993, they would come to live in Haiti. Bob was working for the US government, and his job would be to promote industry to come to Haiti.

"Are you working for the Overseas Private Investment Corporation?" I asked.

Bob had never heard of the organization. I explained that OPIC (as it was more commonly known) is a quasi-governmental organization whose purpose it was and had been for many years to promote private investments in certain qualifying countries. Haiti had become qualified some years ago, and OPIC had assisted my company in expanding its operations there. OPIC also sold insurance to these private investors, to protect them against loss due to expropriation by the host government. Unfortunately, they sold no insurance to protect an investor from the dastardly acts imposed on US companies that were forced to leave Haiti due to the US embargo. OPIC was the only government agency that operated at a profit—a concept foreign to government agencies. In fact, so foreign was the concept of profit that computer programmers for OPIC never factored in the need for recording profits. Profits had to be handled as negative losses.

Bob wasn't working for OPIC and remained rather vague about who he was working for. Could it be that he was involved with the CIA in some covert operation? Could Jim also be involved in some covert operation? Neither of their professed explanations made any sense to me, but nothing seemed to make any sense in Haiti anymore. How could Bob come to Haiti to promote investment in Haiti when the government had an embargo on operating there?

Father Aristide—a priest who was loved by the Haitian people and out of favor with the Catholic church—was the democratically elected president of Haiti, only to be overthrown against the will of the people, and nothing seemed to be able to reverse this injustice. The very boycott responsible for driving many companies out of business or out of Haiti was unsuccessful in reversing the overthrow of President Aristide. The boycott was successful in furthering the suffering of the poor, who had little enough as it was; while those people of means—the military, drug traffickers, and black marketers—managed to do just fine. As a matter of fact, they had no problem with the boycott continuing indefinitely. The United States policy with regard to Haiti was accomplishing exactly nothing. Nothing seemed to have changed in the last thirty years.

All these thoughts kept going through my mind as I comfortably relaxed on the balcony outside our room. It was beautiful, but I missed our days at the Hotel Ibo Lele. The

Hotel Ibo Lele had been on a steady decline for a number of years. Some years ago, Robert Baussan had died. When we went to offer our condolences to Tamara and their son, Jack, Tamara commented that in life, there are no happy endings. She was devastated at her loss but determined to go on with her art. The hotel management was left in the hands of her son, Jack. Misfortune struck again a few years later when Jack died suddenly. Now the hotel was left to be managed by Jack's daughter, who was really unable to manage it properly. The Hotel Ibo Lele deteriorated so badly that when I had visited Haiti, the hotel was occupied by several people who were renting their rooms by the month. The swimming pool was in a state of disrepair and inoperative, and there was no staff to handle the bar if one wanted a drink. No member of the Baussan family was visible when we went to visit. There was nobody for us to offer condolences to on the recent death of Tamara. Her grandchildren may have been around, but we didn't see them. I wiped an uncontrollable tear from my eye and studied the walls of the hotel, which were covered with Tamara's paintings. Trudy and I looked at each other and then bid the Hotel Ibo Lele goodbye. It was the end of an era.

I was also concerned about my future. I was hopeful that the structural changes we had made at Designatronics would result in the company moving ahead profitably now that the losing companies were out of the way. Indeed, the remaining entities continued to do well without having to carry the burden of the electronic companies. Justice moves very slowly. Our lawsuit against the Department of Defense was hung up in the courts and would remain there for a very long time. Although I had a good severance pay arrangement with the company in exchange for my resignation, I had to think about other sources of income. My greatest assets were still locked up in Designatronics stock. There was no way I could dispose of it on the open market except in small amounts. The best alternative was to seek out a buyer for the company.

During that year, ending on August 31, 1993, the positive results of our restructuring were gratifying. Net sales from continuing operations were $23.6 million while net profit, including the benefit of tax-loss carryforward, was $2.5 million. We began to seriously search for a buyer for the company.

I had lots of time on my hands now that I no longer went to work. Trudy continued to grow her practice, and she was very involved with her work. We had to plan our vacations around her professional time requirements, and we did. I spent more time in my greenhouse and devoted time to the Begonia Society, a group I joined a number of years earlier and was now its president. Our members were people of all ages that grew begonias. We met at each other's homes and viewed each other's progress with our plants. We exchanged information on how to grow better begonias and periodically entered our plants in contests to try to win a gold ribbon for the best plant in the show. I began to learn the ins and outs of my computer and began to think about going back to school to study subjects I had not studied during my formal education days. In so doing, I was thumbing through a Hofstra University brochure when I ran across a group called PEIR (short for Professionals and Executives In Retirement). The description of the group indicated that they were senior retirees made up of executives, business owners, lawyers, social workers, academics, doctors, librarians, pharmacists, volunteer community leaders, and other categories who were experiencing significant changes and voids in their lives as a result of retirement. Courses, lectures, presentations, and discussion groups reflected the diverse interests and areas of expertise of the members, who in addition to being students, also taught courses. The curriculum included subjects in literature, music and art appreciation, film, history, philosophy, psychology, economics, current events, and a host of other subjects.

I found the concept of this group intriguing, and after attending a number of their sessions, I decided to join. I have remained a member ever since.

AUGUST 1994

Some months before, I realized I was approaching my sixty-ninth birthday. I had no insurance policy as to how lucky I would be about my survival chances. I felt the need to reconnect with my surviving relatives. Recently, Barry Tunkel, my cousins Raymond and Irene's son, had become involved with tracing the family tree. It was a rather complex undertaking. From time to time, we talked about the family; and together, we made a list of people whom I was going to invite to a family reunion. The list consisted of the blood relations of Marcus Siegel and their spouses and children. It comprised quite a list of more than fifty people. In August, we assembled in our home in Hewlett Neck for a wonderful outdoor picnic. The kids, along with a number of adults, availed themselves of our pool since the weather was very cooperative. It was a wonderful opportunity for all of us to get together. There were some who never met others in the family and some who had not seen each other for many years. I was proud to be able to host such a gathering.

I had reached the age of sixty-nine. It had been several years since I had my radical prostatectomy, and so far, there had not been a recurrence of the cancer. But Dr. Olsson continued to alert me to the fact that he couldn't assure me that it would not recur. He just wasn't sure that the cancer had not spread outside the capsule of the prostate. We would just have to keep an eye on the situation. I interpreted that to mean "we will just have to wait for the other shoe to drop."

NOVEMBER 1994

I couldn't believe that Sheila had reached her fortieth birthday. For the occasion, instead of sending her the usual birthday card, I wrote the following poem and had it framed for her.

TO SHEILA ON THE OCCASION OF YOUR FORTIETH BIRTHDAY

IT WAS NINETEEN HUNDRED AND FIFTY-FOUR,
WE CARRIED YOU THROUGH THE FAR ROCKAWAY DOOR,
A RAVING BEAUTY WITH BIG DARK EYES,
AND A SET OF STRONG LUNGS TO VOCALIZE,
"KOSH ALL DE VINTERS AND SOPPETY WET,"
AND A "PHUNTA" YOU LOVED TO SHARE YOUR BED,

FROM INFANCY TO CHILDHOOD, YOU PASSED THROUGH,

AND EACH DAY IN YOUR LIFE BROUGHT SOMETHING NEW,

BOTH HAPPY AND SAD TIMES YOU DID KNOW,

YOU MOVED INTO ADOLESCENCE, YOU SURE DID GROW,

YOU STRUGGLED AND TOILED THROUGH YOUR TEENAGE YEARS,

FIRST HIGH SCHOOL THEN COLLEGE, YOU PERSEVERED,

AND THEN YOU MET MARTY AND THINGS SURE DID CHANGE,

YOU MARRIED AND NOW PLANS WERE BECOMING LONG-RANGE,

FIRST JAKI, THEN BECKY THEN STEPHANIE DID COME,

BUT BY NOW YOU HAD ALREADY BECOME SUPER MOM,

TURNING FORTY IS HARD, BUT LET ME TELL YOU,

THINK OF MARTY, WHO HAS ALREADY TURNED FORTY-TWO,

OR CHIPPY, WE WON'T EVEN MENTION HER AGE,

FOR FEAR IT MIGHT SEND HER INTO A RAGE,

SO LET'S JUST HAVE FUN AND CELEBRATE,

AND BE THANKFUL THAT YOU'RE NOT YET FORTY-EIGHT,

IF IT WILL MAKE YOU HAPPY, WE'LL STOP KEEPING SCORE,

BUT WISH YOU HAPPY BIRTHDAY AND MANY MORE.

We celebrated Sheila's birthday. It was a happy occasion. But now as I look back, who could have predicted the tragic events that were to follow?

DECEMBER 12, 1994

I wasn't much older than I had been on my birthday in August, but I certainly felt a lot older when I realized that my youngest child was thirty-eight and living far away from home with a new name. As difficult as all this was, and in keeping with the temporary practice of not just sending an ordinary birthday card, I wrote the following poem, placed it in a frame, and sent it to Deah.

TO DEAH ON THE OCCASION OF YOUR THIRTY-EIGHTH BIRTHDAY

YOU WAITED 'TIL ALMOST THE END OF THE YEAR,
BEFORE YOU SHOWED US YOUR FLAMING HAIR.
"FORGET IT, IT WON'T STAY THAT WAY,"
IS WHAT A LOT OF PEOPLE DID SAY.
THEY WERE ALL JEALOUS OF THE BEAUTIFUL HUE,
AND THEY EVEN FASHIONED WEE IMP AFTER YOU.

BY THE TIME YOU REACHED THOSE TERRIBLE TWOS,
YOUR ABILITY TO SPEAK WAS NO LONGER NEWS.
AND AS YOU GREW AND LEARNED SOME MORE,
YOU WERE READY FOR SCHOOL BEFORE YOU WERE FOUR.

GROWING UP WAS HARD, BECAUSE YOU COULDN'T WAIT—
YOU WANTED TO BE TWELVE BEFORE YOU WERE EIGHT.

YOU BEAT ON THE DRUMS, YOU ACTED AND SANG,
AND SURROUNDED YOURSELF WITH AN AWFULLY NICE GANG
OF NEIGHBORHOOD KIDS WHO HELD YOU IN AWE
AND SAW YOU AS PERFECT, NOT EVEN ONE FLAW.

WHEN TRAGEDY STRUCK, YOU WERE JUST THIRTEEN,
WITH NO LONGER A MOM ON WHOM YOU COULD LEAN.
GROWING UP FAST EVEN THOUGH IT WAS FRIGHTENING,
THROUGH HIGH SCHOOL AND COLLEGE LIKE A BOLT OF LIGHTNING.

YOU DIDN'T SLOW DOWN, NOT EVEN TO REST,
UNTIL YOU ARRIVED IN THE VERY FAR WEST,
WHERE YOU ACTED AND SANG AND ALSO TAUGHT,
AND FOR WORTHY CAUSES YOU CERTAINLY FOUGHT.

THEN ALONG CAME BILL, A KINDRED SOUL,
WITH WHOM YOU FOUND A COMMON GOAL.
YOU MARRIED AND THEN BABY ZACHARY CAME,
AND NOTHING WILL EVER BE JUST THE SAME.

SOL SCHWARTZ

> WORKING AND DIETING AND RAISING A SON MAY NOT ALWAYS BE THAT MUCH FUN.
> BUT GROWING AND MATURING IS THE ONLY WAY, WHILE WE ONCE AGAIN WISH YOU A HAPPY BIRTHDAY.

"Good and bad," "sadness and joy," "life and death"—they always seem to accompany each other. It is rare to find something to be joyful about without having sadness riding on its back. So it was on December 18, 1994, just after Deah's birthday and shortly before Trudy's and my wedding anniversary, we learned of the death of my cousin Bessy Alpert. She had been living in California, close to her sister Adele, the closest family relative she had. Of course, cancer was the culprit. I always found Bessy a person that had never really grown out of adolescence. I felt she went from adolescence to old age without really maturing into an adult. She never married and left no offspring.

On March 5, 1995, Trudy and I celebrated our twenty-third anniversary, and I composed these few lines to let her know how I felt about it.

> TO TRUDY ON THE OCCASION OF OUR TWENTY-THIRD ANNIVERSARY
>
> SO QUICKLY HAVE THE YEARS FLOWN BY, SINCE FIRST I SAW YOU THERE,
> MAGNIFICENTLY BEAUTIFUL—THE BELLE OF VAL D'ISERE,

WHERE DID I GET THE COURAGE TO MAKE THAT BOLD ADVANCE

ON ONE WHO COULD SO EASILY CLAIM ANY MAN IN FRANCE?

BUT I TURNED OUT THE LUCKY ONE, OUR YEARS TOGETHER DID SHOW

THAT YOUR BEAUTY, INSTEAD OF FADING, HAS INDEED CONTINUED TO GROW.

SO IF EVER I GIVE YOU CAUSE TO QUESTION, WHETHER OR NOT I CARE,

REMEMBER THAT IN ALL THIS WORLD, IT'S YOU I HOLD MOST DEAR.

SO ON THIS ANNIVERSARY OF THE DAY THAT WE WERE WED,

I REAFFIRM MY WEDDING VOWS, THOSE PRECIOUS WORDS I SAID,

AND FACE THE FUTURE BRAVELY, WHATEVER IT HAS IN STORE,

AS I WALK DOWN ITS UNCERTAIN PATH, WITH THE ONE THAT I ADORE.

AND I WILL CONTINUE TO VERBALIZE THAT WHICH IS MOST TRUE

ON THIS DAY, AS EVERY DAY, HOW MUCH I TRULY LOVE YOU.

HAPPY ANNIVERSARY

On April 17, 1995, Trudy celebrated her fifty-eighth birthday, and I acknowledged it with the following birthday wish.

TO TRUDY ON THE OCCASION OF YOUR FIFTY-EIGHTH BIRTHDAY

THE CHILDREN HAVE GROWN AND GONE THEIR OWN WAY,
 LEAVING US ALONE TO WORK AND PLAY.
 WE GREW OUR CAREERS AND REBUILT OUR NEST
 UNTIL IT REFLECTED THE VERY BEST
 OF HOW WE BOTH WANTED OUR HOME TO APPEAR,
 CONTAINING THE THINGS WE BOTH HELD VERY DEAR.
 WE TOOK TIME TO TRAVEL TO STRANGE DESTINATIONS,
 EASTERN EUROPE AND HAITI WITHOUT HESITATION,
 CHINA, JAPAN, ITALY, AND FRANCE,
 VAL D'ISERE AND THE BIRTH OF ROMANCE.
 COULD IT REALLY BE? DID IT GET SO LATE?
 THAT YOU HAVE ALREADY TURNED FIFTY-EIGHT,
 THE YEARS WERE SO GOOD, THOSE THAT ARE GONE,
 BUT THERE ARE BETTER ONES TO COME.
 LET'S LOOK TO THE FUTURE, BRAVE AND BOLD,
 BECAUSE, REALLY, WE'RE NOT SO VERY OLD.
 LET'S BE OPTIMISTIC, IT'S NOT TOO LATE.
 WE HAVE MANY MORE BIRTHDAYS TO CELEBRATE.
 AND MANY MORE TRIPS TO GET UNDER OUR BELT,
 WHILE BOTH OF US STILL LOOK VERY SVELTE.
 BUT YOU KNOW I WOULD BE VERY REMISS
 TO FORGET A DAY AS IMPORTANT AS THIS.
 SO FOR A SHORT TIME, PUT THE FUTURE AWAY,

AND CONCENTRATE FULLY ON THIS SPECIAL DAY.

THERE IS NOTHING MORE IMPORTANT I HAVE TO SAY

THAN "I LOVE YOU, I LOVE YOU, AND HAPPY BIRTHDAY."

I had framed the above ode to Trudy's birthday and presented it to her when we were comfortably seated in our favorite restaurant, Le Petit Bijou. Over cocktails, we reminisced about our years together, the trips we had taken. We talked about the fact that I was now retired and had lots of time to travel; but although Trudy was very interested in travel, she was also involved with her career and had no intentions of giving it up. Travel in the future would have to fit in with her work schedule. I was not entirely happy with that. No doubt, the twelve-year difference in our ages was a factor. I had had no intention of retiring when I was her age either. I began to resign myself to the fact that it was now my time to fit into Trudy's work schedule as she had done so many times in the past, fitting into mine. It was right then that we began to plan our trip to Poland and Lithuania.

JUNE 13, 1995, A POLISH-LITHUANIAN PILGRIMAGE

POLAND AND LITHUANIA! We had decided to go to Poland because we felt that we should see for ourselves, firsthand, the concentration camps. Trudy's grandmother came from Lithuania in 1904, and she wanted to see Vilnius. This wasn't our first trip abroad, but for days before we left, we were very nervous and had difficulty sleeping. We would wake at weird hours and be unable to fall back asleep. It's not as if we hadn't traveled to places most people would consider strange. We'd been to Czechoslovakia, Hungary, Yugoslavia, and Romania before the so-called Iron Curtain was lifted. We'd been to the Orient several times and to Haiti untold numbers of times.

"What way-out place are you going to this time?" we were asked.

"Poland," I answered. "Poland and Lithuania," I clarified.

"Why don't you go to some place where normal people go to, like the islands in the Caribbean or Las Vegas or on a cruise? What kind of vacation are you going to have in Poland?"

I responded, "It's not exactly a vacation we are going on. It's more like a pilgrimage. We're going to visit a number of concentration camps, cemeteries, and perhaps a surviving synagogue or two. If we are lucky, we may meet a few interesting people. We feel that by going, we are in some way making a statement that we have not forgotten and will not forget the horrible slaughter that humankind inflicted on millions of people."

Very few people understood why we were going. Our brother-in-law Joe Katz spent the war years hiding out in the forest with the Polish underground. It isn't easy to get Joe to talk about the time just prior to his joining the underground movement. On one occasion, we were able to get him to tell us about the day he left Makow Mazowiecki on some business. When he returned that evening, he found that his entire family—his wife, children, and father—were all taken away by the Nazis and killed. He later learned that his father, who was ninety-two years old, had been burned alive in Treblinka.

When we told him we were going to Poland, his first reaction was that we were out of our minds. His experiences were such that he couldn't conceive of anyone voluntarily going to Poland. We asked him to tell us a little about Makow Mazowiecki, the town he came from. He remembered it was a little resort town near a lake, and he lived on the second floor of a building on the square. His father was Yaacov the Schneider. There was no need for a second name. Joe spoke about his recollections with enthusiasm as he recalled long-lost pleasant days.

"If you go to Makow Mazowiecki, take a picture for me," Joe said. We promised that we would. This conversation took place on the phone, and when we were through, we hung up only to have the phone ring almost immediately. It was Joe again.

"Sol," he said, "do me a favor. Don't go to Makow Mazowiecki, and don't bring me any pictures. It is dangerous. You don't know those people."

"Joe," I said, "if we go, we will hire a private cab."

"Don't go in a private cab. That is the worst thing you can do. Only go if you can be surrounded by other people. Otherwise, you won't be safe."

We tried to comfort him and told him if we thought it wasn't safe to go, we wouldn't go.

My friend and partner, Joe Rubenfeld, spent the war years in Birkenau. He was the sole survivor of his immediate family. He made it to America in 1947, and for the next forty years or so, he had nightmares almost every night. Many years later, Joe went back to Poland and revisited Auschwitz and Birkenau; and somehow, he was able to get the horror out of his unconscious and get rid of the nightmares.

"Have a good trip," he told us, "but be careful. Those people are worse than the Germans."

Rebecca, the daughter of a friend of ours, was twenty-one years old. Five years earlier, she visited Poland as part of a group called "The March of the Living." She brought back an album full of never-to-be-forgotten photographs of the various concentration camps they visited.

"I know it is terrible to admit, but I returned from the trip hating the Polish people for what they did," she said.

We had trepidations about our decision to go to Poland. What were we letting ourselves in for? Could we really be placing ourselves in danger just because we are Jews?

The truth is we couldn't really explain why we felt compelled to go other than having a feeling that we should see the concentration camps. We should become familiar with what was left of our Eastern European heritage.

We were determined to take our chances. Trudy and I began to feel a little better about our decision when we came to the airport terminal and waited to board our flight; our destination was Warsaw. We looked around at our fellow passengers and tried to detect if there were any other Jewish people traveling to Poland. We were comforted when we saw a Hasidic man also waiting to board. Then Trudy struck up a conversation with a woman sitting next to her and found out that she was Jewish. She was born in Poland and managed to escape the Holocaust and had been going back to Poland each year for the past five years. She goes to visit friends and seems to know a great deal about Warsaw. She was extremely comforting about the concerns we were expressing regarding Polish anti-Semitism.

"You will be just fine," she said. "It will be no worse than what you experience in the United States."

We became aware of a group of people wearing badges identifying them as representing the United Jewish Appeal, so it was apparent we were not the only Jews on the flight.

We decided to relax and approach our adventure with a more positive attitude and to start by enjoying our flight. Perhaps, by the time our trip was over, I would be better able to explain why we felt compelled to go. Two glasses of wine later, I was certain I could.

MONDAY, JUNE 13, 1995

OUR FLIGHT TOOK us nonstop to Warsaw. I was in for an immediate surprise in that I had expected to find a less modern terminal. As we walked in the direction of customs and baggage claim, indicated by signs in English, we were aware that the nine-hour flight had taken its toll on us. We were ready to sleep and were feeling the first signs of jet lag. The flight was entirely full, and much to our surprise, the custom lines, although long, moved efficiently. So did the baggage-claim procedure. The moving belt was so quiet I could not hear it. I would not have been surprised to find that one of our bags was missing. Instead, our luggage appeared promptly and efficiently. Luggage carrying carts were available and free. Another surprise was that we were not required to fill out a duty declaration form.

When our turn to pass through customs arrived, our passports were taken, their numbers entered into a computer. Then they were returned to us, and we were on our way. There were two ways to exit—one way if you had something to declare and the other way if you didn't. We had nothing to declare, so we walked out into the main terminal. We were not asked how long we planned to remain in Poland or where we were staying, so unless Orbis (the tour company) had a copy of our itinerary reported to the Polish customs authorities, they had no idea of our planned or unplanned whereabouts.

In the main terminal, we went directly to the Orbis representative, who had arranged for a taxi to our hotel. The route took us through modern neighborhoods and lots of new construction. Warsaw was almost completely demolished during World War II and had virtually been rebuilt from the ground up. It was difficult to determine or see any remnants of the previous Socialist or Communist influence. Signs and buildings of foreign corporations were omnipresent: Coca-Cola, McDonald's, Taco Bell, Sony, and the Marriott were all alive and well and functioning in Warsaw.

The Hotel Jan III Sobieski is a beautiful and well-run modern hotel. We felt comfortable from the moment we stepped foot in the lobby and were equally satisfied with our nicely appointed accommodations. We unpacked quickly, and I went to bed and fell asleep. Before Trudy fell asleep, she discovered that the Moiseyev Ballet was in town and would only be here on Tuesday and Wednesday evenings. Of course, we had to go.

When we awoke some three hours or so later, about three o'clock in the afternoon, we dressed and went to speak to the concierge. He called and found that some tickets were still available, but it would not be possible to reserve them over the phone. By that time, Trudy had already decided where we were going to have dinner. It turned out that the opera house where the ballet would be performed was not far from the restaurant that was located in the Old Town. A taxi conveniently located outside the hotel drove us to the opera house. With the assistance of an English-speaking young man standing on the line behind us, we were able to make our wishes understood. We purchased tickets to the Wednesday-night performance since there were absolutely no worthwhile seats available for Tuesday night. Good seats were available for thirteen dollars each, and we snapped them up. We thanked the young man for his help and returned to our waiting taxi for the drive to the restaurant.

The restaurant was on the second floor of a very elegant old building that seemed to have survived the devastation that Warsaw had experienced. In reality, the entire building had been reconstructed identically to what the building had originally looked like. It retained the charm of what it must have been like before the war. We were seated next to a window that looked out onto the square, and we were able to see many outdoor tables shielded by umbrellas, where people were dining and drinking. It appeared pleasant and colorful, and if there were any underlying problems with the culture or the economy, they were not apparent here.

We ordered a plate of cold cuts that we thought would be our appetizer but determined, after it arrived, that it was plentiful enough to be our entire dinner. The plate contained four or five varieties, and they were exceptionally good in that they were not too salty. Accompanying the platter of meat was a basket of kaiser rolls, which were both fresh and crisp.

After dinner, we walked around. We looked in shop windows and were surprised at the availability of many beautiful things. We had not been back to places like Prague, Budapest, or Bucharest since our trip in 1988, which was before the Russians left in 1989, so I don't know how things may have changed since then. The kind of products now available in Warsaw were certainly not available in those cities then. Indeed, Warsaw may have had these things eight years ago also, but I do not know.

From one of the outdoor restaurants in the square, we heard music that could have emanated from New Orleans. At first, I thought I was hearing a recording being blasted over a loudspeaker; but as we came closer, we saw that a live band was producing this sound, and it made us feel at home. We sat at a table and ordered dessert and coffee; and at Trudy's request, the band played "When the Saints Go Marching In." We enjoyed our dessert and the music but felt that we had best return to our hotel because we had a big day planned for tomorrow. It was a very pleasant finale for our first day in Warsaw, and we were feeling more comfortable with our environment.

TUESDAY, JUNE 14, 1995

Breakfast at the hotel was a buffet with an amazing assortment of cereals, juices, fruit, meats, herring, cheeses, eggs, pancakes, pastries, and delicious breads and rolls. It was tough to maintain diet rituals.

The planned morning tour would take us to the Jewish area in a private car accompanied by an English-speaking guide. In the afternoon, we were scheduled to do a walking tour of the town, and we found it necessary to cancel it if we were going to squeeze in the visit to Makow Mazowiecki, Joe Katz's hometown. We learned that it was about one hundred kilometers from Warsaw and that we would have to allow at least four hours to drive there and back. Even if we spent no more than an hour in the town, we would still need at least a half day to make the journey. It was necessary to sacrifice our walking tour. Our concierge could arrange for the hotel taxi to take us there. We had already determined that on Monday, but we had another option.

Through Rabbi Stewart Geller, a friend of ours, we established contact with the Ronald Lauder Foundation in New York. This contact led to a chain of contacts who assisted in shaping our trip to Poland and Lithuania into the exciting experience it was turning out to be. In speaking to a representative of the Lauder Foundation in New York, Trudy explained that we were going to Poland and we wanted to meet some Jewish people there. They suggested that we must contact Rabbi Michael Schudrich, who could best help us when we reached Warsaw.

Rabbi Schudrich was described to us as a very modern person who knew everything there was to know about Jewish life in Warsaw. He could always be contacted since he had a car telephone. "No rabbi with a beard here," I thought to myself.

After returning from dinner Monday evening, I called Rabbi Schudrich, and he turned out to be very helpful. I told him we wanted to visit Makow Mazowiecki and explained our reason for wanting to go. He gave me Yaacov Szyc's phone number and assured me that he was very reliable and he had a good car. Yaacov was not Jewish, but his wife was, and the rabbi thought they were a very charming couple. Unfortunately, our schedule did not allow any time to meet the rabbi since he was leaving for vacation the next day. Had we known then that his vacation would take him to Kraków, we would have probably been able to arrange to meet him. I thanked him for his assistance and then called Yaacov. He seemed very personable on the phone and willing to drive us where we wanted to go. After speaking with him, I decided to hire him as our driver to escort us to Makow Mazowiecki. We arranged for him to pick us up at our hotel at 2:00 p.m. on Tuesday.

At 9:15 a.m., a man rushed into the lobby of our hotel and somehow knew immediately we were the people he was looking for. He introduced himself as Henryk Rummel and apologized for being late. Traffic conditions were horrible, and he was unable to park near the hotel. He then informed us that he was going to be our guide for the next three days.

Our tour began with a visit to the site of the Warsaw Ghetto, where little of the old neighborhood remains. It would be very difficult to picture what had really taken place there some sixty years ago. In the years between 1918 to 1939, Warsaw had the largest concentration of Jews in Europe, only exceeded by New York. The Jewish population (some 380,000 people) were almost 30% of the total population. The occupying forces isolated the ghetto from the rest of the city. That area consisted of approximately 307 hectares, and by November 1941, 450,000 Jews were crammed in as the result of resettlement of Jews primarily from territories annexed into the Reich. Under these overcrowded conditions, the death rate rose dramatically. Deaths climbed from 898 in January 1941 to 5,560 in January 1942. From October 1939 to mid-1942, 100,000 Jews died mainly from starvation and disease. From July 22 to September 21, 1942, 300,000 people were transported from the Warsaw Ghetto to Treblinka and murdered. Within the ghetto, acts of resistance were beginning to appear, and an organized uprising began to take shape.

ZOB, the Jewish fighting organization, provided the main force behind the uprising. ZOB was made up of 500 members. They were all under thirty years old. There were many heroic stories about the resistance forces fighting against overwhelming odds. However, on May 8, 1943, the Nazis surrounded the ZOB command bunker at 18 Mila Street and tossed in a gas bomb. The surviving members of the command took their own lives rather than surrender to the Nazis.

There are many monuments around the area that was the ghetto commemorating the bravery of the men and women who put up such a brave resistance. In walking from one monument to the next and reading about the fate of these young fighters, I wondered what the true cost their deaths were to our world. How many potential poets, doctors, scientists, and, yes, machinists, storekeepers, and attorneys had we lost? Had the cure for cancer gone to the grave with one of these fighters? Did new ways to prevent future wars die as well? I was both sad and angry with how destructive man can be.

We then visited the Jewish theater, where performances were being put on in Yiddish, but we were surprised to learn that most of the actors were not Jewish. Perhaps it should not have been such a surprise. The Jewish population left in all of Poland is only about four thousand. The director of the theater is not Jewish either, although his wife is. Yaacov, the guide who, later that day, escorted us to Makow Mazowiecki, informed us that the director was really anti-Semitic and a better politician than a director. He said that the director was able to hold on to his job through a number of political regimes because he managed to appease the "powers that be." Yaacov's wife is an actress, we learned, who managed to obtain a bit part in the movie *Schindler's List* and is also a member of the Jewish theater but rarely gets any work because she is not in favor with the director. We did not get to meet the director, but we did meet his wife, who gave us a very sterile history of the theater as it operates today.

We went on to the Nozyk synagogue, the only surviving synagogue in Warsaw. During World War II, it suffered severe damage when the Nazis used it to stable horses. During the Warsaw Ghetto uprising, it suffered disastrous damage. With the help of "American" money, the synagogue underwent a great deal of renovation and restoration over a six-year period. We were not fortunate enough to be able to attend a service. We did, however, get to meet Rabbi Pinchas Menachum Joskowicz, a Hasidic Jew who was very impressive with his long white beard and his ability to speak English. He told us that he returned from Israel in 1988 to become Poland's chief rabbi. The shammas took us around and was very helpful in explaining the history of the synagogue. When I asked him how things were for him during the war, since he was old enough to have been alive then, he said that he was one of the lucky survivors of the camps. He has children who left Poland and migrated to Denmark and are professionals. He didn't want to go to Denmark, so he stayed in Poland. Now he is old and sick. He told us that he is having prostate difficulties and has to wear a bag to gather his urine. His children want him to come to Denmark, but he has nobody to take over his responsibilities at the synagogue. Living conditions were not good now, he told us, since it is very difficult to get by on the small pension he receives. The shammas was better off when the Communists were in power because costs for necessities were controlled. Now if his children didn't send him money, he would not be able to live.

The shammas could easily have been seen attending services at the synagogue I remember as a child in East New York. He could have been the man who went through the congregation passing out snuff, as was the tradition. We talked in Yiddish, and I understood him very well. He spoke just like my father or uncle and could well have been either. He was a very familiar personality.

All too quickly, the morning fled, and we only barely scratched the surface of all there was to see and learn about Jewish life and history in Warsaw. We had an afternoon appointment with Yaacov, and so we asked Henryk to bring us back to our hotel. We arranged to meet again Wednesday morning.

Yaacov appeared promptly at 2:00 p.m. He is a very good-looking young man about thirty years old and sporting a gold earring. We learned that he had met Rabbi Michael Schudrich through the Lauder Foundation, for whom he also worked.

The trip to Makow Mazowiecki took us through the countryside, small towns separated by farms growing a variety of grains and vegetables. Yaacov had never been to Makow Mazowiecki. I don't believe he ever heard of it until I mentioned it to him, and he looked it up on a map. We told him that we were warned about going there and that we had trepidations about the people and how they would react to Jews. Yaacov did not feel we had anything to worry about.

The first indication we had that we were going in the right direction was a road sign that said we were nine kilometers from Makow Mazowiecki. Shortly thereafter, we came to a bridge. A sign noted we were crossing the Orzyk River, and I knew from Joe's description we were approaching the marketplace. On the other side of the bridge, Yaacov parked the car. In a moment, I pinpointed the location where Joe's house was. "The second house from the corner on the right,"

Joe had told me. On the ground floor of the house, there was a shop just as there must have been when Joe was there. The upstairs may be the living quarters for the people who run the shop downstairs.

I stared at the building and the street and tried to imagine Joe Katz walking along with his children. Were they boys or girls? I did not know. How hard was it for him to make a living in this community? Did he work in the building that he said was his father's shop, or did he work elsewhere within the marketplace? Did he get along well with his neighbors? Was he born in this town, or did he migrate here? So many questions rushed through my mind.

I wished that Joe were here so that I could ask him the questions directly. Perhaps if he were here, he would be more able to talk. At home, it is not easy to engage him to discuss his life in Poland. It must be extremely painful to remember; and yet perhaps, if he could verbalize his recollections, it might become easier for him to live with them. I thought about his daughter, Susan Green, and his grandchildren, who are the products of his new life in America. There will come a time when they will want to know more about Joe's past, and unless Joe speaks about it, they may never truly know who he was. I think about my father's parents and the lives they lived in Romania, and I wish that I could learn more about them. That knowledge went to the grave with my father, and I regret it.

The old marketplace is now a park-like square surrounded by two-story buildings with stores on the ground floor and probably apartments over the stores. I looked for some sign that Jews had lived here in the past, but there were none to be found. I took photographs as I promised Joe I would, and then we looked around for older people who could possibly remember Joe's father, Yaacov the Schneider.

There was an elderly cement worker repairing a section of sidewalk, and we approached him. With Yaacov as our interpreter, we asked the man if he lived here during or before the war. He said he did not. Then we saw an elderly lady sweeping the sidewalk about halfway down the block from Joe's old house. Yaacov asked her if she lived here before the war. She said she did. We learned that her name was Teresa Janiszewski. She was approximately 5 feet 2 inches tall and had a head of hair dyed auburn, a color we found quite common among the Polish women we met. She did not remember Yaacov the Schneider, but she did remember that many Jews lived here and occupied most of the houses around the square. Teresa could tell us where the synagogue used to be and where the remnants of the cemetery were. As a matter of fact, she was willing to escort us there. We could also meet her sister, who lived near the cemetery, but first she had to change her dress. She invited us into her house, but she preferred to get to the entrance from the back.

We followed Teresa around the corner to an alley. Soon we came to a gate that, when entering, placed us in a very pretty garden. Teresa was growing hollyhocks, lupine, and other colorful flowers. She also was growing strawberries, chives, and several other herbs. We then entered the house through a small foyer. To the left was a tiny kitchen that contained an undersized refrigerator, a coal stove, and an electric range. Off the kitchen was another somewhat larger room that served both as her living room and bedroom. On the wall was a crucifix and a picture of Pope Paul. Against one wall, there was a mantel with a collection of porcelain objects. Against another wall was a single bed. The room also contained an armchair.

Teresa was not embarrassed about changing her dress in our presence, and she did so as we talked and learned more about her. She had been widowed for three years. She was seventy-three years old. Teresa permitted me to photograph the inside of her house and her garden. There was a bush that Teresa said was planted by her husband, and she wanted a photo of herself in front of the bush. I took the photo and promised to send her a copy.

We left the house, and Teresa got into the front seat of the car with Yaacov while Trudy and I occupied the rear seat. She directed Yaacov to a dilapidated building and identified it as the old synagogue. There were several people sitting outside the building, and it was impossible to determine if it was presently being lived in or used for another purpose.

We drove on, perhaps a few more blocks, before we parked the car again. About fifty feet from the street and hidden by some trees was a monument constructed like a four-sided pyramid made from fragments of tombstones. Tears came to my eyes, and I wondered if any of these stones were from the graves of people Joe might have known. I tried to read some of them, but it was difficult. Teresa told us that the townspeople had erected the monument. Off to the right of the monument was a large flat space with several buses parked. This area, which used to be the cemetery, was now a bus station. I wondered if it was unreasonable to expect the world to forever honor the ground under which people were buried. Carried to the extreme, over many years, every inch of the Earth would eventually be a grave for someone. At some point, the ground has to be "recycled" and lived on. Perhaps the very ground on which our homes are built were once the burial grounds for people.

I photographed the monument and the bus station before we left. Teresa led us away, and we walked a short distance to a small dry goods shop that Teresa entered. Inside, the shop was stocked with not very fashionable garments. An old woman proprietor was introduced to us as Teresa's sister. She looked much older than Teresa but in fact was three years younger. She did not dye her hair. Teresa's sister did not remember Joe's father either, but she remembered the names of other Jewish families nostalgically. She spoke affectionately and sadly about some of the people she remembered. After a while, we bid her goodbye and left.

Teresa then guided us to a remote street and pointed out a small building that she identified as the mikvah (the ritual bathhouse). She said that the Nazis used it to inflict water torture on people as punishment. Were there any Jews living in the town now? She didn't think so. We drove back to her house. She was like a newfound friend. Teresa invited us in for tea, but we told her that we had to return to Warsaw. We kissed goodbye, and I promised to send her the photos she wanted.

On the way back, we again crossed the bridge over the Orzyc River, bid the town goodbye, and headed back to Warsaw. We wondered why we should have been afraid of the people of Makow Mazowiecki. It was very hard to picture

Teresa as a hateful anti-Semite Polish woman. We only met a few, but if they were typical of the people Joe thought we ought to be afraid of, it would only prove how banal evil is.

On the way back to Warsaw, we asked Yaacov how his life was affected since the Communists were no longer in power. He said that for him, things are not better now.

"For older people who have to live on the little pension they receive from the government, things are worse now. Prices have gone up, and now they have to pay for their medical costs, and it is very hard for them to get along. Young people are still hopeful that it will get better eventually, but I'm not so sure. Before, if I went to the dentist, she would take care of the problem and charge me a dollar. I would give her a dollar tip, and she was very happy. Now she charges me $50, and she doesn't even say thank you."

We began to feel very close and trusting of Yaacov. He also seemed to know a great deal about what was going on in what was left of Polish Jewish culture. We asked him if he knew anyone in Kraków who could act as our guide because we had some open time there that we would want to utilize to good advantage and to see as much as we could. He immediately mentioned a man named Henryk Halkowski and referred to him as "Mr. Jewish Kraków." He gave us Henryk's telephone number.

Yaacov dropped us off at our hotel. It had been a full day, and we were still feeling the effects of jet lag. It was almost 8:00 p.m. We were tired and hungry, so after a quick refresher, we went for dinner, after which we returned to our hotel and tried to go to sleep. I found my mind racing from one thought to another. There we were in a country where millions of our fellow Jews perished, and I was feeling that there was a lot to learn and discover. Did I have the right to do that? Should I not just hate this place and not even give it a second thought? Am I some kind of traitor to the Jewish people, spending money in Poland that, in some way, is ultimately helping the Polish government that is or was so blatantly anti-Semitic? Somewhere in this maze of questions, sleep finally overtook me.

WEDNESDAY, JUNE 14, 1995

AFTER ANOTHER DELICIOUS breakfast, we were ready for a new adventure. Henryk Rummel appeared promptly at 9:00 a.m. Today our tour would take us first to visit the Tykocin (Tiktin) synagogue. The little village of Tykocin near Bialystok in northeast Poland was owned by a noble family who invited ten Jewish families to settle there in 1522. By the nineteenth century, there was a Jewish majority in the village; and by the beginning of World War II, half the local inhabitants were Jewish.

On the way to Tykocin, I asked Henryk how things were for him now with the radical political changes that had taken place in Poland.

"In the old days," he said, "we couldn't get a passport to travel out of the country without being questioned extensively. To get a passport, you would have to undergo an interrogation to explain why you wanted to leave the country and then receive a lecture on how evil the West was and how they would try to corrupt you. Today everyone has a passport. You don't have to explain why you want to travel. But the problem is now that we can travel at will, we don't earn enough money to pay for it."

"How were things for you during the war?" I asked.

Color seemed to drain from his face as he reflected back to those days. "In 1939, we were living in the western part of Poland. And one day, Gestapo agents came through the town and, without any warning, gathered up all the professionals and those perceived as intellectuals and told them they had to move. Because my father was a teacher, we were among those who had to move. I was eight years old, and my sister was five years old. We were all gathered in a school and were forced to stay there for two days. Straw was put on the floor to sleep on, and there was no food or water given us on the first day.

"On the second day, we were given a cup of water that they called soup. There were about fifty people in each classroom, and we all slept like sardines. After two days, we were broken into groups and loaded into railcars, each group in a car. We were not told where we were going. The train began to move, and after a while, we came to a village train station, where we stopped, and a car full of people would be unloaded. Then the train moved on until it came to another village, and another car was unloaded. Then the train came to a village, and the people in the car, my family, and I were ordered to get out. All of us got off the train, and we were met by a Nazi who didn't know why we had come or what to do with us. He had not received any orders or instructions.

"About ten kilometers from the railroad station, there was an abandoned building that was partially occupied by a drunken shoemaker. In the days to come, we learned that the shoemaker would work one or two days, make some money, and then get drunk and stay drunk until his money ran out. Only such a man could live the way he lived in that building. All fifty of us occupied the building, and it was even worse than the conditions that we lived with in the classroom. We were all crowded into this small space and left to fend for ourselves. Gradually, people moved out as they found other places to live. We were the last to leave. Twice a week, my mother and I would go into town and sell dairy products that she bought from the local farmers. In town, we would buy coffee—well, something like coffee, but it was made from grain. We brought it back and sold it locally. My mother and I did that twice a week, and that is how we managed to stay alive. It was very dangerous because we were not allowed to go into the town. Eventually, we also moved out after finding a very small place to live. After the war, when we returned to our village, we found our house abandoned. During the war, it had been occupied by the daughter of a German family that had been a neighbor before we were evacuated."

"Are you Jewish?" I asked Henryk.

"No, I'm not Jewish. My father was a teacher, and the Nazis wanted to isolate all Polish professionals and intellectuals because they were afraid that these people would become leaders of an active rebellion against the Nazis, so they had to be isolated. Later, intellectuals and professionals were taken to concentration camps."

We arrived at Tykocin and found our way to the synagogue. It was built in 1642 in baroque style and had been completely restored internally and externally. It is now used as a Jewish museum. When you enter, you can immediately hear taped cantorial selections. The walls are covered with printed prayers—a pattern we saw repeated in other synagogues we visited. Perhaps it was a custom started a long time ago to assist those wishing to pray but unable to afford a prayer book.

We were surprised to see a large group of children, escorted by several adults, wandering through the synagogue. We asked Henryk to find out who they were and where they were from. Henryk asked the children, and they told him that they were on a class trip. Trudy asked Henryk to ask them if they know what a Jew is. In response to the question, one boy responded in English, "A Jew is just like anyone else except that they don't live here anymore."

In 1939, on the eve of World War II, half the population of Tykocin was Jewish.

We continued through the synagogue, studying the exhibits. There was a model of how the village used to look with the settlement grouped around two poles—the synagogue and the Jewish marketplace at one end and the church and the Christian marketplace on the other end. Other interesting exhibits, not necessarily emphasizing Jews, were to be found in a small building attached to the synagogue. This building, I believe, could have originally been the "shtibil," or the study house, that invariably accompanied every synagogue.

Our next destination was Treblinka, about fifty miles from Warsaw and the site of one of the most infamous Nazi extermination camps. When we arrived and entered, we were surprised to find that we were virtually the only visitors there. We were told that we would not see very much of what Treblinka used to be during the war years. Treblinka came into existence in the summer of 1941 near a gravel mine. It was surrounded by a barbed-wire fence, and its inmates included Jews and Poles, mainly from Warsaw. Few people who entered Treblinka survived to tell about their internment. Most were put to death. Until their death, the inmates were forced to work in the gravel mine and at loading railway cars at the Malkinia railway station. Some inmates were employed in the camp workshops. Women were put to work on the camp farm.

In the spring of 1942, inmates of the camp, known as Treblinka I, were used to build Treblinka II, the Holocaust factory. None knew then that the function of Treblinka II was to be implementation of the Nazi plans for the "Final Solution" of the Jewish people. Treblinka II was completely surrounded with barbed-wire fencing and entwined with pine branches in a manner that prevented anything going on in the camp from being seen from the outside. Only Jewish inmates were used to build the interior of the camp. According to the Nazi plan, no inmate who was a witness to the genocide that was to take place could remain alive as a witness. Therefore, those Jews used in the construction were exterminated.

On the inside, the camp was divided into two parts. In the first part, housing barracks for the Nazi crew, storehouses, and workshops were built. The second part, separated by a high hedge and fence, contained the gas chambers—thirteen in all. However, the Nazi plan was to deceive the victims into thinking that their fate was not extermination, and so a make-believe railway station was built by the platform within the camp. Signs pointing to nonexistent passages, other platforms, waiting rooms, cafeterias, ticket offices, and other railroad station installations gave the illusion of something other than the real reason why they were there. The first rail transports arrived in July 1942. It brought Jews from the

Warsaw Ghetto. In subsequent transports, they were brought from all over Poland and other countries as well.

Between 1942 and 1943, 800,000 Jews died at Treblinka. After the victims were gassed, the bodies were transported by a working squad of Jewish prisoners to a place where the bodies were interspersed with wood, doused with a flammable liquid, and then incinerated. It was later reported that not always were the victims dead before they were set on fire. This mass grave burned day and night. The stench and ashes of burned bodies covered the entire area. As many as 15,000 to 18,000 victims were gassed and burned daily. This method of cremation supplemented and preceded the installation of all thirteen crematoria.

There is only one monument to an individual hero. Janusz Korczak (Dr. Henryk Goldszmit), who ran a Jewish orphan asylum in Warsaw, chose to go to the gas chamber with his orphan children rather than abandon them.

Our guide, Henryk, was not a novice to Treblinka. While we wandered through the camp, he discreetly stayed on the side and permitted us to privately commiserate with the feelings that were being stirred up. How is it possible for human beings to deliberately plan the extermination of an entire people? How is it possible to plan, in such detail, the construction of barracks for the exclusive purpose of storing the belongings, clothes, shoes, furs, and jewelry of those who were going to be exterminated? Treblinka camp sent over 200 railway cars of shoes and clothes to Germany. Special trucks were used to transport gold, jewels, bank notes, and other valuables confiscated from the prisoners to Germany.

Were these people different from us? Did they have such horrible experiences in their contacts with Jews that they could, with clear conscience, plan and participate in the extermination process? Could they, in clear conscience, after participating in the extermination of 18,000 people in one day, go home to their families and enjoy having dinner with them and hearing about their children's activities that day at school? Could their families, smelling the stench and seeing the smoke rising from the crematoria, not ask what was going on there day after day? Could they really hide the truth from themselves? Could they really sleep at night knowing that the following day, they would repeat the same procedure?

And what about me, looking at my watch and seeing that it was getting late. We had tickets for the Moiseyev Ballet that evening, and I didn't want to be late for the performance. Was I going to be able to put aside all that I had seen and felt that day and go about enjoying dinner and then the ballet? Was that what the Nazi exterminators were doing when they went home to their families? Were they secretly saying to themselves that they were obeying orders and could do nothing to change matters, or were they in full agreement with the orders they were obeying?

Visiting Treblinka was a sobering experience. Some place, perhaps the very ground on which we walked, Joe Katz's father may have also walked before he perished more than fifty years ago. Treblinka was a sobering experience, but it was only a prelude to even worse sights.

We left Treblinka and returned to Warsaw. The drive back was again through the countryside, where we would periodically see stacks of hay on wooden frames that lent them support. Each stack stood six or more feet high. I now could understand the story Joe Katz told me about how, when he returned to his town and found that his entire family had been deported, he was hidden by a Catholic woman for a while. Then she felt it was too dangerous for her to do this since anyone found aiding or hiding a Jew would immediately be shot. Joe said that she helped him hide inside one of these haystacks, where he was forced to remain until she felt it was safe enough for him to leave. When Joe could finally leave, he noticed that from each stack on the farm, another Jew emerged.

Arriving at our hotel, we bid Henryk good night and arranged to meet him the following morning. We had just enough time to take a shower, get dressed, and go to the opera house.

The opera house was full, and the lobby was bustling with people, all of whom were well-dressed. I was glad I had decided to wear a jacket and tie. There was an air of excitement and anticipation. We found our seats and sat studying the audience. We observed that we were probably the only Americans there and had little hope of finding a familiar face. Suddenly, the young man who helped us with translation at the ticket office came by. He was like a long-lost friend, and we called to him. He came over and told us his name was Lajos. We chatted and learned that he had traveled to many countries in Africa, South America, and North America. He spoke English fluently. The curtain was about to go up, and we arranged to meet him during intermission.

We thoroughly enjoyed the Moiseyev dancers during the first half of the show. At the intermission, we again met

Lajos and enjoyed a delightful conversation, during which we shared experiences.

"Are you in the field of science that affords you the opportunity to travel so broadly?" Trudy asked.

"No. I am a Catholic priest," he said.

So much for stereotypes, I thought.

Following the performance, we found a restaurant and had an unremarkable dinner, after which we returned to our hotel. Some fears and myths that we came with were beginning to wear away. We were not afraid of being attacked on the street, and we were really excited about the experiences we were having. We found that we could enjoy our evening despite Treblinka.

THURSDAY, JUNE 15, 1995

HENRYK ARRIVED PROMPTLY. We had just finished another delicious breakfast. So far, breakfasts turned out to be our best meals. However, food did not play an overwhelmingly important role since there were so many other exciting things happening that we could overlook the fact our dinners were not exceptional.

Our itinerary today was to visit the Majdanek concentration camp, but there were several stops along the way. We first visited a small village named Gora Kalwaria, known as Ger in Yiddish. Gora Kalwaria is located about 20 miles from Warsaw, and in 1795, Jews were allowed to settle here. In the nineteenth century, Gora Kalwaria became the seat of the most famous and powerful Hasidic dynasties in Poland. There used to be a synagogue in this town, but unless you knew exactly where it had been, you could never find it. From the street, you have to enter through a set of iron gates into a courtyard, and only then could you see a building with a Star of David still visible over the doorway to the entrance. The building had been used as a furniture warehouse but was now being renovated and restored. The building appeared to have been a very impressive synagogue, but we were not able to enter it, so it was impossible to really appraise what it had been. Like the building, if there were any Jews left in the town, they were not visible.

We continued to our next stop, Kazimierz Dolny. Along the route, we were fortunate to observe a rare stork on a telephone pole. I do believe that this is the first time I have ever seen a stork other than in pictures.

Just outside Kazimierz Dolny, we stopped at the New Jewish Cemetery. The Old Cemetery, dating back to the sixteenth century, and the New Cemetery, established in 1851, were devastated by the Nazis, who used the gravestones as paving material. Just outside the New Cemetery, there is a very moving monument to the Holocaust victims. In mid-1980, hundreds of tombstones were recovered and built into a gigantic mosaic wall rising up on the hillside. There is a vertical jagged crack in the mosaic to symbolize the sudden extinction of the entire Jewish community. The crack is wide enough so that you can walk through it to the other side of the monument. There in the shade created by the many tall trees, you find yourself in a peaceful forest-like setting—the remnants of the New Cemetery. The contrast between this and the sunny environment on the other side of the monument is startling at first, but once you adjust to the serene and peaceful quiet "in the cemetery," it is possible to feel a spiritual connection with all that this monument represents. On the sunny side of the monument, some children were playing while the rest of their families were picnicking nearby. The significance of the area was completely lost on them until Trudy escorted them to the shady side of the monument and explained where they were and what the significance of this place was.

We came into Kazimierz Dolny to find the streets packed with people, and we had to park some distance from the center of the square. It was Corpus Christi day, and religious celebrations were going on.

Kazimierz Dolny is a lovely "arty" town and is a favorite tourist spot. It is in east central Poland and is located on the Vistula River, between Radom and Lublin. Jews settled here in the late fourteenth or early fifteenth century. By the sixteenth century, they were well established and had a synagogue and a cemetery. By 1830, the town's 1,200 Jews made up nearly 60% of the population. During the nineteenth century, a Hasidic court was established. There were 3,000 Jews living in Kazimierz before World War II, comprising 60% of the population. The town is centered on a square lined with very old Renaissance buildings. The former synagogue—dating to the eighteenth century—was devastated by the Nazis and was rebuilt to its original outer appearance in the 1950s. Now the building is being renovated into a cinema. There is a plaque, however, commemorating its original function and memorializing the 3,000 local Jews murdered by the Nazis.

In the market square, we met a group of young people who were teaching in Poland and were visiting Kazimierz that day. Angela was from Boston and was of Polish extraction. She was teaching English in a town not too far away and was also studying political history. Erik was from Florida and was Jewish. He was also teaching English and had attended a public seder at which Rabbi Schudrich, our Warsaw contact, had officiated. Erik said that they had expected about 50 people to attend the seder but were pleasantly surprised when 150 people showed up. We spent a little more time chatting with them, and then we were on our way to the Majdanek concentration camp.

Majdanek was unusual in that it was the first of its kind to perform a "double role." It was to be a mass extermination center for the Poles and was to provide slave labor on a massive scale. The original plan was for it to hold 50,000 prisoners. By November 1941, plans had been altered to expand the camp to handle 125,000 people; and in December 1941, the plan was again expanded so that the camp could contain 150,000 hostages. The expectations of having many more Soviet prisoners, after the initial successes during the invasion of the Soviet Union, resulted in the plans for Majdanek to yet again be expanded for the camp to hold 250,000 prisoners. The plan included necessary service buildings and workshops, a laundry, a delousing room, a crematorium, and large industrial plants.

The construction began in the autumn of 1941 and continued until the end of 1942, but due to difficulties encountered with transport of building materials followed by shortages of materials as the German war situation deteriorated after their advance into the Soviet Union was halted, only about 20% of the plan was completed by the time the camp had been liberated. During the three years that Majdanek existed, prisoners representing fifty-one nationalities were interned there. The number of Poles represented 38%, Jews 31%, and Russians 20.9%. Those prisoners that were not put to death immediately were engaged in construction work and worked at facilities that serviced the camp. Many prisoners were farmed out to firms outside the camp to perform slave labor in their factories.

It is estimated that about 500,000 prisoners passed through Majdanek. About 360,000 persons died. Of this number, 200,000 perished as the result of inhuman conditions in the camp while 160,000 were exterminated.

The Nazis abandoned Majdanek before they had an opportunity to completely dismantle the camp, as they had succeeded in doing in other places. Most of the mass murder installations were found in place when the Soviet Army liberated the camp.

During our tour, we visited barracks containing nothing but shoes taken from the victims before their extermination. Other barracks contained suitcases the victims brought with them, thinking that they were being relocated. Hair shorn from the victims and not yet shipped to the industrial establishments that used it for military purposes was contained in a barrack of its own, while untold pairs of eyeglasses filled another barrack. Outside the gas chamber, there is a room fitted with a dissection table. The victims' gold teeth were extracted before cremation.

It is difficult to imagine how human beings could place a greater value on suitcases, shoes, and other material things than they could on human life.

We visited the crematorium, and unless you see the installation in person, it is virtually impossible to appreciate the magnitude of the crimes perpetrated on the thousands of victims who died here and the millions who died in other camps such as this. These crimes were enacted in the ordinary course of "doing business as usual." Gas chambers had to be constructed with knowledge about the lethal devices to be used, so the Nazis went to their finest industrial companies and asked them to design and draw up plans for the construction of the crematoria and the production of the gas to be used for the "Final Solution."

Seeing Majdanek as we had, almost as it was left fifty years ago, was an experience that reinforced my feelings of the importance of understanding what it is that can make human beings capable of inflicting such heinous crimes against other human beings. I have heard it said that the Nazis knew that in order for them to carry out such a crime against humanity, it would be necessary to reduce the victims to something other than human beings. And so through starvation, torture, incredible cruelty, beatings, and living conditions unfit for the lowest form of animals, they were able to almost accomplish their goal of mass extermination, because the victims were not seen as humans anymore by their captors.

We had enough for that day. I really needed a break to sort out my feelings about what we had seen. We left Majdanek and returned to Warsaw. I wondered how we would feel about eating dinner that evening, but when we sat down, we ate. It was a nonevent as our dinners mostly were, but perhaps they would improve. In any event, we were more involved with the schedule for the following day. We had to get an early start because we were going to Vilnius for the weekend, and our flight was leaving at 7:00 a.m.

FRIDAY, JUNE 16, 1995

IT WAS NECESSARY to depart early for the airport, so we had breakfast in our room because the dining room was still closed. However, our breakfast was delivered by room service, available twenty-four hours a day. Although the continental breakfast (which was complimentary) was not as elaborate as the buffet breakfast available in the dining room, it was more than ample.

Our cab arrived and took us to the airport, where we checked in. Shortly after that, we boarded our flight to Vilnius. Everything had gone perfectly according to plan until we arrived in Vilnius. We had expected to be met at the airport and be taken to our hotel. After waiting for a half hour, we began to feel that a snag had developed. We had a tourist aide at the airport contact the Hotel Sarunas, where we had a reservation, but the hotel indicated it did not have any record of our reservation. They did have available space, however, and they would immediately send a car to pick us up.

While we were waiting, we struck up a conversation with another passenger, an American of Polish extraction. He told us about a Polish priest from Dansk (home of Lech Walesa and the place where the Solidarity movement began) who made blatant anti-Semitic remarks from the pulpit. The priest apparently was not criticized by the Pope or the church. Our fellow passenger was unable to give us any more details. We asked our informant what he was doing here, and he told us that he was visiting his aunt, who lived in a small Polish village. She showed him pictures of family members who had migrated to America that she kept all these years. He found this a very moving experience, and I could relate to that. I had a similar encounter with photographs that Aunt Salya kept in her apartment in Israel, when I went to meet her for the first time. Our fellow passenger—whose name we never learned—was an economist working for the United States government, and he was visiting friends in Vilnius.

Our car came, and when we arrived at the hotel, we continued to inquire about our reservation since we had paid for our hotel stay in advance. They insisted that they still could not find a reservation for us. They would continue to try to contact Orbis, which they seemed never to have heard of. I then inquired about the tour of the Jewish sites in Vilnius that we also had arranged for Saturday, the next day. They didn't know anything about that either, but they would contact the few tour companies and see if they knew anything. In any event, we were not to worry since they could arrange a tour for us if we wanted. We found the situation a bit unsettling, but we were determined not to let it spoil our weekend plans. After all, we did have a room to stay in and a tour could be arranged, so it really wasn't a terrible dilemma.

We settled into our room, and since we would not know anything about the hotel's research until later that afternoon, we decided to explore the Jewish quarter of Vilnius. From the guidebook, we learned about a Jewish museum and decided to visit. When we knocked at the door, no one answered at first, and it appeared as if nobody was there; but persistent knocking finally brought a woman to the door. We asked to see the museum, and she said that she would gladly give us a tour. Her name was Rachel, and she had lived in Vilnius all her life. She explained that the museum was being renovated. They received funding from the German embassy. The exhibits on display were about famous Jewish personalities from various walks of Jewish life in Vilnius. Vilnius had been an important seat of Jewish life before the Holocaust, and the Jewish population were a reformed intellectual group. For example, some noted Zionists came from Vilnius. Now, the Jewish community was probably not large enough to support a museum, and I wondered whether the community should contribute to its support. The building was modest, and it appeared that Rachel's struggle to reopen the museum could be alleviated with an influx of funds. After our tour, she asked for contributions to help carry the work forward.

After leaving, we walked along the street and came to a shop where we stopped for coffee and chatted with a young man who spoke some English. He fancied himself a "businessman." He was trying to get a business started. Everywhere we went, we met young people who were involved with trying to become entrepreneurs—a trend that started with the departure of the Communists in 1991.

When we left the coffee shop, we decided to find the restaurant we thought we would have dinner at that evening. In our Vilnius guidebook, Trudy had found Lietuvos Jerozale, a kosher restaurant listed, and we thought we would check it out. We walked along the street, following our map and having some difficulty finding a particular street that would take us to the restaurant. We met a man walking toward us who apparently could see that we were not natives. He asked whether he could be of any help. The man spoke excellent English. He introduced himself as Al Kanauka. He was a Lithuanian who had left the homeland many years before and who now lives in California. For the past three years, since the Russians departed, he had returned and was acting as a business consultant with some business interests of his own. We chatted for a while, and then he invited us to follow him to his office, where he had a better map to share with us. At first, we were a little skeptical about trusting him, but we decided to risk it. We accompanied him into a courtyard and then through a door that led to a hallway, where there was a series of doors. He entered one, and we followed him. The room was being set up as an office but had not yet been furnished, and there was scarcely any place to sit. Neither was there an abundance of light, but there was a computer and a telephone on the desk. He found the map and helped direct us to where we wanted to go. We then told him the story of how our hotel and tour arrangements were a problem. We told him we were interested in visiting the Jewish sites in Vilnius. He immediately suggested that we contact Irena Veisaite.

"Irena knows everything there is to know about Jewish life in Vilnius, and she surely could direct you to a tour guide who could probably help you."

Thanking Al for his wonderful assistance, we went on our way, feeling a little guilty about the fact that we had been wary about his wanting to help us.

After determining where the restaurant was, we returned to our hotel and called Irena. Fortunately, we found her at home. We told her about our dilemma and how our plans had run awry and that we were in need of a guide. She recommended Regina Kopilevich and gave us her phone number and told us that if Regina was not available, to call her back. We chatted for a while and learned that Irena lived part of the time in Vilnius and the rest in England. She worked for the Soros Foundation, but somehow I got the impression she was not working out of a need for money. I thanked Irena for the information and told her we would call her back and let her know how we made out with Regina.

I called Regina and again was fortunate to find her at home. I told her that we were interested in a tour of the Jewish sites in Vilnius, where 100,000 people were killed by the Nazis. Regina informed me that she was busy in the morning doing a morning tour with two other American visitors, but she was certain they would not mind if we joined them. In the afternoon, she could take us to the Paneriai Forest.

We were quite content with the arrangements, and before going out to dinner, Trudy called Irena back to thank her and to let her know that we had successfully established contact with Regina. Trudy asked Irena whether it would be possible to meet with her or if she would join us for dinner since we were anxious to meet Jews in Vilnius. Unfortunately, she had dinner plans, but perhaps we could meet after dinner.

Trudy felt that would not be a good idea. Saturday we were busy with a full-day schedule, and so was Irena, so we left the matter open. We said we would call her Sunday morning to see if we could possibly get together before returning to Warsaw.

Before leaving for dinner, we told the hotel clerk we had already made our own plans for our tour. The clerk informed us that so far, they had not been able to untangle the problem about why they did not have our hotel reservation and planned tour.

Dinner at the Lietuvos Jeruzale turned out to be a big surprise when we saw ham and bacon offered on the menu. I expressed my astonishment to the waiter, and he informed me that the restaurant used to be a kosher restaurant but was no longer one, although they did offer kosher-style food. For a while, we were the only occupants of the restaurant; but soon a big party of people entered. We were as curious about them as they appeared to be about us. Were they Jewish? Did they know that the restaurant no longer serves kosher food? Did they care?

I finally couldn't contain my curiosity and approached a young woman in the group and asked whether she spoke English. She pointed to a young man across the table and indicated that he did. When I talked to him, I learned that the group consisted of teachers except for him. He was a student, and they were just coming from a musical recital. He was a student at the school where these other people taught. It turned out he was the only Jew at the table. He then asked about us, and I told him we were American Jews visiting Vilnius for the first time and that Trudy's mother's family came from the city. Trudy's grandmother left Vilnius in 1904, and Trudy was the first member of her family to return to Vilnius.

After dinner, we returned to our hotel that was not nearly as nice as the Jan III Sobieski in Warsaw, but it was adequate.

SATURDAY, JUNE 17, 1995

Regina picked us up at 9:00 a.m. for our walking tour. She was perhaps thirty-five years old and spoke very good English. She was a native of Vilnius. As we walked, she told us that we were going to another hotel, where we would pick up the other people who would be joining us.

On the way, she gave us a little background of herself. She revealed she was a genealogist and had been working on the genealogy of the family of the other people who would be joining us.

We arrived at their hotel and found a young man waiting in the lobby. He was introduced to us as Andrew, and shortly, an older man joined us. He was Andrew's father and introduced himself as Dan. During the morning, while we visited the synagogue of Vilnius and the old ghetto section, we learned that Dan's family originally came from Kaunas, the second biggest town in Lithuania with a large number of Jews. The family name was Duberstein. Through a strange series of circumstances, Andrew discovered that his grandfather (his father's father) had compiled a book of Jewish folk songs, which had been published in Poland many years ago. This spiked Andrew's interest, and he somehow found Regina and retained her to research the Duberstein family in the town from where they originally came.

Andrew—who is a reporter for the *Philadelphia Inquirer*—was, I suppose, no novice to the task of research, and it probably was not unusual to hire someone to research a story. Regina had worked on the project for many months and was finally able to trace the family back a number of generations and to obtain the names and other pertinent data about members of the family. Now Dan and Andrew came to Vilnius to meet with Regina and be brought up to date on her research. I was delighted to hear a story like this. I was also envious and wished I could trace my father's family back a few generations. My grandfather may have been a carpenter, and that is all I know about my father's father.

The synagogue was a very impressive structure from the outside. We were unable to go in because it was closed; however, we did get the idea that it was quite beautiful. Before World War II, there were 96 synagogues in Vilnius; and today, only this one remained. It was constructed in 1894. The old town—where we had walked yesterday and returned to today—was a study in old buildings and narrow streets. In the remains of one building, virtually in ruins, a Star of David that had been engraved in the stone could still be seen. There were memorial plaques here and there commemorating the Jews of Vilnius who had perished at the hands of the Nazis.

At noon, Regina took us to a small restaurant for a snack. Andrew announced that he and Dan were going to the opera that evening. We had the same idea, but we heard that the acoustics in the opera house were not very good and neither was the opera company, so we decided not to go.

After lunch, Dan and Andrew took their leave. We bid them goodbye, not thinking that we would see them again.

They had arrangements to meet with Regina a number of times in the days ahead while they went over their genealogy.

Regina led us to a small street where a car was parked with a woman in the driver's seat. The woman was introduced to us as Regina's sister, who evidently owned the car, and we drove to Paneriai Forest. It was only about five kilometers outside town. "PANERIAI MEMORIALAS"—in very large letters engraved in stone—greet you at the entrance. Between July 1941 and July 1944, more than 100,000 people were murdered here. Of this number, 70,000 were Jews from Vilnius. In the first three months of occupation, 35,000 were slaughtered.

As we entered the forest and walked a little way, we were impressed with how beautiful and serene the surroundings were; and after a short walk, we came upon a large monument of white stone. Regina explained that the monument commemorated the death of 100,000 Soviet citizens at the hands of the Nazis. Another monument had been placed there when Lithuania became independent of Russia in 1991. This monument of black marble had a Star of David engraved at the top and commemorated the killing of 100,000 people, including 70,000 Jews. One could debate whether the motive of the Russians—in not making a distinction between Jews and other Soviet citizens—was an act of anti-Semitism. Or perhaps it was a policy of treating Jews as equals and recognizing them only as Soviet citizens.

As we walked deeper into the park-like forest, we came upon a grass-lined area circled by a marble ring, perhaps fifty feet in diameter. At one time, there was a pit into which victims were led, shot, and buried. Later, the Nazis exhumed the bodies and burned them to cover up the evidence. We then approached another and much bigger and deeper pit into which other victims were forced to remain while engaged in the task of pulverizing the bones of the dead. It is ironic that the Jewish prisoners were forced to attempt to cover up the murderous deeds of the Nazis.

Apparently, Paneriai Forest was the first extermination camp. The Nazis, however, found it inefficient since they could only exterminate 100 people a day. There were no crematoria here. The method used was to shoot the victims, create a pyre of the bodies interspersed with logs, and set them on fire. More efficient methods had to be found, and they were.

We continued our walk and soon met a young man and woman bending over a strawberry patch that was growing wild. The strawberries were tiny. Regina asked the young woman, and she offered some to us to taste. They were good. She and her husband were simply here for a walk and to collect strawberries. There didn't seem to be any awareness about the significance of where we were. Strawberries were growing, and they were there for the picking. I couldn't help thinking that these strawberries had grown and been fertilized by the ashes and bones of 100,000 people.

We left the forest, and during the drive back to our hotel, we learned that Regina was the product of a Jewish father and a non-Jewish mother. Her father had died, and when her mother remarried, she again married a Jewish man. The family was not particularly religious, but they were involved with the cultural aspects of Judaism. Regina considers herself a Jew, even though her mother isn't. She explained that the woman usually follows the religion of the man so that a non-Jewish woman marrying a Jewish man would usually result in the woman following the Jewish faith. This appears to differ from the way a Jew is defined in Israel, where if the mother is Jewish, then the offspring are Jewish. Obviously, there is a great deal to ponder over what makes a Jew a Jew.

We arrived at our hotel and bid Regina and her sister goodbye and thanked them for an enlightening experience.

That evening, we ate at a restaurant across from the opera house. We were about to order our dinner when Dan and Andrew came walking in and asked if they could join us. It appeared they had gone to the opera but had walked out after the first act because Andrew was hungry. I thought that it might be a polite way of saying that the performance had left a great deal to be desired, and I felt that our decision not to go had been a wise one. We enjoyed pleasant conversation, which compensated for the fact that the food was only so-so. Trudy commented that it was both ironic and pleasurable that in a place where there are so few Jews, we kept running into interesting Jews at every turn. After dinner, Trudy and I were tired enough to want to do nothing but go back to our hotel. Once again, we bid Dan and Andrew goodbye and hoped we would meet again.

SUNDAY, JUNE 17, 1995

Before breakfast, we called Irena to determine whether we would have an opportunity to meet her before we left for Warsaw on the afternoon flight. Unfortunately, she told us that a very important Jewish man passed away, and she had to attend the funeral, and it would be impossible for us to get together. Trudy and Irena chatted extensively on the phone, and Irena said it was important to remember that not only Jews perished in the Holocaust; and it was also important that millions of Poles, other than Jews, were also victims of the Nazis. Not all Poles were bad people, and it is imperative that we not continue to blame the Polish people for what the Nazis did in Poland. Trudy expressed our regrets that we would not get to meet Irena and hoped that one day, we would have an opportunity to meet since she was such an interesting woman.

After breakfast, we had several hours before we had to be at the airport, and we decided to spend the time by visiting the KGB Museum that we found listed in our guidebook entitled *Vilnius in Your Pocket: The Official City Guide*. Under the heading of "Museums," we found the following listing:

KGB Museum
(3-H-3) Gedimino 40, tel. 62-24-49.

Open 10:00–13:00, 14:00–17:00. Sat.; Sun. 11:00–17:00.

The prison cells in the basement of the former KGB building have been opened. In these cells, thousands of Lithuanians were interrogated before being deported to Siberia. Most tour guides are former inmates. Entrance from the right.

We thought it would be an interesting place to visit. A short taxi ride brought us to the building. It is an impressive, solidly built five-story stone structure that we later learned dated from Czarist days. As we neared the entrance, we found two policemen parading back and forth in front of the locked door. The policemen, through hand motions, informed us that the building was closed. We were trying to determine when it was going to open, but we were not able to get our question across intelligibly, nor could we understand any answers the police were attempting to communicate.

At that moment, a man and a woman were passing by, and we stopped them and asked if either of them spoke English. The man said he did. We explained to him we wanted to visit the museum, but the police seemed to be telling us that we couldn't and that it appeared closed. The man spoke to the policemen and determined the building was undergoing renovation and the museum was closed. We explained that we came from the United States and we wanted to see whatever there was to see of the exhibit since we would not have an opportunity to return. The young man communicated this message to the policemen, which motivated one of them to go to the door and knock. Through the closed door, he spoke to someone inside, and a moment later, the door was opened by a neatly dressed woman. Our newfound friendly interpreter repeated our dilemma to her. She quickly invited us in and escorted us up four flights of what appeared to be newly installed marble steps. On the way, she explained that the building was being renovated. After completion, it would be a courthouse and would also house the archives of the KGB.

At the top of the fourth flight, we went through a door into a corridor, where we found five or six people sitting. Also present was a lame cat. A small dish of food and another dish containing water was on the floor under a table around which these people sat. We were escorted past these people through a door that opened into an office and were offered seats. Soon, a number of the people seated in the hall came in to join us. Our interpreter, whose name I learned was Juozas Dauguila, and his wife, Jollita, explained for us our interest in the museum. The woman who answered the door originally said that the people sitting in the building were actually "on strike." They were protesting the appointment of an archivist who was supposed to set up the KGB Museum. The chosen archivist was a Communist, and the present government was also made up of old Communists. The protesters felt that the chosen archivist would not present the facts and that he would attempt to "rewrite history." They wanted to appoint their own archivist, and they had been sitting in on strike for the past two years and intended to stay until they were successful. The lame cat, we were told, was also on strike, and he had been sitting with them.

"The lame cat symbolizes a crippled Lithuanian people, but we are not broken," one protester said. The office we were sitting in was the one used by the old KGB official.

We thanked them for their courtesy, and as we left the office, I noticed a bulletin board on the wall with typewritten sheets hanging, none of which I could read. There was also a drawing posted with the faces of Marx, Lenin, Stalin, and Hitler. I could only conclude that these people would characterize all four of these men in a similar way and had no sympathy for either Nazism or Communism.

We left the building with Juozas and Jollita. We walked along the street, chatting with them, and Trudy observed that they were both nicely tanned.

"We just returned from a vacation in Turkey," one of them said.

I asked Juozas what he did for a living, and he said he used to be a biochemist. But now he was trying to go into business importing chemicals and equipment, and he had established contact with a company named Perkins Elmer in the United States.

"Have you ever been to the United States?" I asked.

"No, but I had an aunt living there. In 1970, my aunt, a Lithuanian, was visiting here, and she wanted to go to the US embassy before leaving for home. I escorted her, carrying her suitcase. When we approached the embassy, a guard asked for my identification. My aunt presented her US passport and was allowed to enter. I just wanted permission to enter so I could help her with her suitcase, but I was forbidden from entering. I was asked for my name, which the guard wrote down. Some days later, I was called down by the KGB and accused of trying to flee. If I wasn't trying to flee, didn't I know that I was in danger of being interrogated by US personnel in the embassy? Fortunately, they didn't press the matter any further."

Juozas said he became familiar with the KGB building during that interrogation, and he explained that there was an underground passage leading to the prison. Many people were taken into custody without any warning, on their way to or from work, and they have never been heard from again.

We asked if they had time to stop for coffee with us, but they said they really couldn't since they had to go to a funeral. I told them that an acquaintance, Irena Veisaite, whom we spoke to this morning, was also going to a funeral of a very important Jewish man. Juozas smiled and told us that they knew Irena and that they were going to the same funeral.

We bid our newfound friends goodbye and decided to walk back to our hotel. Yesterday, Regina had told us that there had been a Jewish cemetery in Vilnius, but it had been turned into a football stadium. We went in search of it and shortly came upon a monument that was all that remained of the Jewish cemetery. The monument sat outside Zalgiris Football Stadium, near the Hotel Sarunas, where we were staying.

"How ironic," I thought. "Even in death, signs of our having lived had to be obliterated."

We returned to our hotel, gathered up our bags, and left for the airport. On the short flight to Warsaw, a young man and woman kept staring at us. We couldn't understand why until the young man, speaking English, asked Trudy if she came from Jericho. Trudy's first reaction was that he meant the city of Jericho in Israel, so she said no, she was from the United States. He clarified that he meant Jericho, Long Island. He pointed out that I was carrying the book *Schindler's List* that had, on the cover, a label stating "Property of the Jericho Library." We had ordered the book through our home library in Woodmere, which borrowed it for us from the Jericho Library. When we told the young man that we were from Woodmere, he almost jumped in the air, saying that he came from Hewlett, the neighboring town. He now lives in Japan, although his parents still live in Hewlett. He was traveling with his girlfriend, who was also a distant cousin and who lives in Kraków. They explained that they meet every few months in different places, and this time, they visited Vilnius. He was on his way back to Japan, and his girlfriend, Eva, would be returning to Kraków. We told them that we were going to Kraków, and Eva then gave us her address, and we promised to contact her while we were there. The young man also gave us his parents' phone number, and we promised to call them when we returned home. There was an interesting story about these two young people somewhere, but there was not sufficient time to learn it.

 Our Warsaw guide, Henryk Rummel, met us at the airport, and it was like being greeted by an old friend. He drove us to the Hotel Jan III Sobieski, where we retrieved the luggage we had left there, and Henryk then escorted us to the railroad station for our nearly three-hour trip to Kraków. It was a smooth ride through the countryside, but I couldn't help thinking about other trains that may have traveled along these very same tracks, moving victims to their demise at a number of concentration camps. I looked around at my fellow passengers that shared our compartment and wondered if they ever felt strange about the route they were traveling. Did they ever give a second thought to the horrible use these tracks were put to fifty years ago?

At the Kraków railroad station, we were met and driven to the Hotel Forum. We had a nice room with a beautiful view of the Vistula River and the bridge that crossed over it, leading into the Old Town. The Wawel Castle, a historic structure sitting on top of a hill, was framed by our window as if it were a beautiful picture. The royal cathedral is located within the walls of the castle, and many Poles consider these structures the very heart of the nation. Polish kings and national heroes are buried here, including the country's patron saint, Bishop St. Stanislaus.

Jews probably lived here since the thirteenth century. Near the main market square, there is a street called Jewish Street, which has been there since 1304. For the next two centuries, the Jewish community was comprised of Jews who were craftsmen, moneylenders, and merchants. Anti-Jewish sentiment developed as the result of the preaching of St. John of Capistrano in 1454, touching off violent riots that left many Jews dead. By the fifteenth century, many Jews began to move south to the suburb of Kazimierz. Before World War II, more than 64,000 Jews lived in Kazimierz (the Old City).

We settled into our room, went out to dinner, returned, and retired since we had an early morning tour planned. We were excited about being in Kraków. We were looking forward to our visit to Kazimierz.

MONDAY, JUNE 19, 1995

Our guide for the morning tour we had arranged was waiting in the lobby of our hotel and introduced herself as Jane. She was accompanied by a driver. Among the sites we were to see was Schindler's factory, the one featured in the movie *Schindler's List*. I had hoped that we might gain entrance into the building, but it had a locked gate. We were told that it was no longer a factory that manufactured enamel ware. It was now an electronic components factory, but I was not able to determine what kind of components they manufactured. I would have been especially interested in visiting the facility since I had been in the electronic components business, but Jane said that she was not able to arrange that. It did not appear to be operating at the time we were there. Later, I learned from another of our Kraków guides that the company was in bankruptcy. We were then driven to a home that was the residence of Amon Goeth, the Nazi commandant of the Jewish district of Kraków who was hung after the liberation. This man was depicted as a cruel, sadistic, and power-crazy person who could kill a prisoner without any just cause simply because he felt like it. Yet he lived in a perfectly respectable home that did not appear ostentatious. I may have been able to rationalize his cruelty if he were something other than a man who lived in a manner that was unfamiliar to me.

I could have thought that here was a creature completely unknown to me, and therefore, he could be the kind of beast he was because he was not just an ordinary human being. But this creature would certainly not be living in an ordinary home that was not different enough from any other home a middle-class businessman would have lived in. How could this all have happened? How could ordinary people embark on the task of destroying an entire people? The questions were there but not the answers.

We then visited the site of the former Plaszow concentration camp, located a short distance southeast of the former Jewish ghetto in Kraków. From this concentration camp, Oskar Schindler was able to save the lives of 1,100 Jews in his employ by insisting that they were essential to the German war effort. So there was Schindler in contrast to Goeth. Was there hope for mankind?

Our next step was the Remuh synagogue, the oldest remaining synagogue in Kraków. It was built in 1553 and was still in use. It is the center of Jewish life in Kraków today. The synagogue is adjacent to a cemetery that was apparently covered over until recently. It is believed that at one time, Poland was in danger of being invaded by the Swedes, and in order to prevent the destruction of the cemetery, it was covered over so that the Swedes would not discover it. (I never learned how they covered it.) There are important scholars and Jewish leaders buried here, including the tomb of Moses ben Israel Isserles—known as Remuh, Poland's most famous Talmudic scholar.

In the synagogue, we met a group of Jewish girls who were praying. We talked to them and learned that they had just completed a year of study in Israel and were on their way home to the United States after spending some time touring through Poland. Some of these girls were from Long Island, and others were from Brooklyn. They were also in Kraków to participate in the Jewish Folk Festival that was going on all that week. We had no idea that such a festival was taking place, but we were interested in finding out about it.

Across from the synagogue and cemetery, we discovered a restaurant and small shop that sold Jewish artifacts. We learned that Tuesday evening, there was going to be a concert of klezmer music performed in the opera house. In addition, we learned that the Ariel Restaurant was having a group entertain that evening. They were going to play and sing Jewish and Russian songs. We decided that the Ariel Restaurant was the place to have dinner, and we further decided that we wanted to attend the klezmer concert, and we had to buy tickets.

Our guide then took us through the streets of the "Old Town," which was where Jews lived before the Holocaust, but she was not well versed and could not tell us much about Jewish matters. We decided we would have to find a guide who was Jewish—or at least "more Jewish"—if we were to maximize our visit.

After our guided morning tour, we bid Jane good day and arranged to see her the following morning as planned, and we returned to the Ariel Restaurant to see what we could find out about a good guide and to have some lunch. We did have the name of Henryk Halkowski given to us by Yaacov in Warsaw, and we would inquire about him also.

The Ariel Restaurant had several tables outside and also had inside seating. We sat outside, and while we were waiting to be served, we noticed much activity by people with cameras moving in and out of a small courtyard next to the restaurant. We couldn't detect exactly what was going on, but we were not sufficiently curious then to pursue the matter further. After finishing our lunch, we visited Remuh cemetery and found that the wall surrounding it consisted of fallen tombstones resurrected into a gigantic wall. Several Hasidim were near a grave praying, and we wondered who might be deserving of their attention, but we never found out.

We then went to the opera house to buy our tickets for the klezmer concert and then returned to our hotel for a short rest.

In reviewing our itinerary, we found Thursday was a day that had been left open. We decided that we would use that day to visit other Jewish villages if we could find a good guide to accompany us. With that task in mind, we dressed and returned to the Ariel Restaurant for dinner.

Seated at a small table, we ordered drinks and leaned back, prepared to enjoy the music. Shortly after that, three musicians took their places in a corner of the restaurant. The fiddler and accordion player were both young women, and they were accompanied by a man who was responsible for providing the rhythm. These were versatile musicians because during the performance, the fiddler resorted to other string instruments while the accordion player was proficient with wind instruments as well. The performance was extremely enjoyable and nostalgic. They played Jewish songs, some of which I had not heard since I was a child. The Russian and

Gypsy melodies were also familiar, and I remember hearing much of that kind of music on radio station WEVD in New York, which was always playing in our house while I was growing up.

Not everyone in the audience liked the music as much as we did. There was a group on a tour from Scandinavia who appeared completely unfamiliar with the music and continued to talk among themselves while the musicians were playing. Only a lack of appreciation for the music could have kept them distracted from the musicians.

I noticed that sitting at a table close to ours were a man and woman who seemed to enjoy the music. They applauded enthusiastically after each number, just as we did. After the performance, I approached them and introduced myself. They were Mr. and Mrs. Kirshenblatt from Toronto. Mr. Kirshenblatt was an artist who painted Jewish scenes. They were originally from Poland, and they were here to attend the Jewish Folk Festival. He was to give a slide presentation on Jewish art at the festival. Their daughter, Barbara K. Gimblett, taught Jewish history at New York University and would be in Kraków to teach a course for five weeks. Coincidentally, we had purchased a book entitled *A Tribe of Stones* by Monika Krajewska. The book is about Jewish cemeteries in Poland; and among the acknowledgments, Monika Krajewska recognized the assistance of Barbara Gimblett and Michael Schudrich, the rabbi who had been so helpful to us in Warsaw.

The Kirschenblatts told us about a concert that they had attended the previous night. "Several cantors sang for an audience of more than 1,000 people, and 95% were Polish non-Jews. The performance received a tremendous standing ovation, and the cantors returned time after time for encores. Their enthusiasm was contagious."

Mr. Kirschenblatt then took out a book entitled *Jews in America in Art and Literature*, written by Rabbi Karp, and proudly showed us that one of his paintings was in the book. We then took our leave and returned to our hotel, feeling remorseful that we had missed the concert the night before. Lying in bed and trying to fall asleep, my mind was racing with mixed emotions. Here we were in Kraków, a city that could only boast 200 Jews, and yet it was playing host to a Jewish Folk Festival with people coming from all over to attend it. I learned that this was the fifth Jewish Folk Festival being held, and they were getting larger each year. Why were they doing this? Why were these people not feeling that they should boycott Poland? I wondered if I would learn the answers to my questions.

TUESDAY, JUNE 20, 1995

BEFORE BREAKFAST, WE called Eva Mankowska, the young woman we had met on our flight from Vilnius, and asked her to recommend a tour guide. Without hesitation, she recommended Henryk Halkowski, the same person Yaacov had mentioned to us when we were in Warsaw. With two recommendations, we thought we probably could do no better. We called Henryk and fortunately found him at home. We told him we were looking for a tour guide who could show us around the Jewish sites in Kraków and the adjoining towns. He appeared receptive, and we arranged to meet him at 1:30 p.m. at the Ariel Restaurant.

"How will we recognize you?" I asked.

"I have a beard and will be wearing a straw hat," he said.

We assumed it was enough of a description.

After breakfast, Jane again appeared for our walking tour. She was a much more knowledgeable guide about matters non-Jewish in Kraków. She escorted us through the town. We visited the Wawel Castle and the cathedral, and she gave us an informed historical view of the city and the significance of the castle to the Polish people.

Jane took us to Rynek Glowny, the main market square in the city. St. Mary's Church was located within the square, and every hour on the hour, day and night, a trumpeter climbed to the top of the church tower and blew the beginning bars of a medieval hymn, the "Hejnal." He blew it four times, once each to the north, south, east, and west. The melody was cut off each time in the middle of a note in order to commemorate the moment when, in 1241, the Tartars, who invaded from the east, shot an arrow into the throat of the trumpeter as he was sounding the hymn. The Tartars destroyed the city. In 1257, a comprehensive plan of reconstruction was drawn up through the efforts of Duke Boleslaw. The plan centered on the square—that is 200 meters by 200 meters square—and apparently has survived to this day.

By this time, the morning had gone, and we left Jane and went to the Ariel Restaurant for our meeting with Henryk. When we arrived, we found there was a lot of activity going on, people rushing this way and that. Some had television equipment. Several trucks were outside the restaurant loaded with equipment, and much activity was centered in the courtyard next to the eatery. We entered the restaurant and asked a young woman what was going on and learned that Itzhak Perlman, the renowned violinist, was here, and he was going to play with a famous klezmer band. The young woman—whose name I later learned was Jan Gura—was the director of special projects for Channel 13-WNET New York, and they were there to record the session for a special airing at the station's next fund-raising drive.

We sat at a table outside the restaurant and ordered lunch. We began to look around for Henryk and saw a man who looked like he might be Henryk because he had a beard and was wearing a straw hat. It was Henryk.

Henryk approached and joined us. After exchanging introductions, we explained to him that on Wednesday, we had plans to go to Auschwitz and Birkenau with a guide arranged for us before we left for the United States. According to our schedule, we should return about 2:00 p.m. We were free Wednesday afternoon and Thursday, and we wanted to retain him as our guide to take us around to whatever Jewish sites he thought we would be interested in seeing. We arranged to meet him Wednesday afternoon, to tour some of the local sites, and again on Thursday for an all-day tour.

As we were talking, we saw Itzhak Perlman emerge from the restaurant followed by a group of people. They all went into the courtyard, and shortly after that, we heard klezmer music. I got up from the table and entered the courtyard and saw the group playing, the television cameras working, and many people scurrying around. I tried to get closer to where the band and Itzhak Perlman were, but so did many other spectators, and I understood why we were stopped from approaching too closely. Jan Gura, charged with the task of keeping people at a distance, did a remarkable job without alienating them. She understood why people wanted to get closer, and she truly cooperated to whatever extent she could without disturbing the televising of the performance. I took many photographs from as many different angles as I could and then left the courtyard and rejoined Trudy, who was finishing her lunch and still talking to Henryk. Henryk noticed that Trudy was holding the book that had been our constant companion throughout this trip. We found that *Jewish Heritage Travel: A Guide to East-Central Europe* by Ruth Ellen Gruber was an extremely valuable source, and it never left our hands. Henryk said that Ruth was around here somewhere, and did we know about the other book she wrote entitled *Upon the Doorposts of Thy House* in which he was quoted? Trudy said that she heard about the book but was unable to buy it before we left the United States. Henryk said that it could be purchased at Ariel and immediately went in and obtained a copy for us.

"If you are lucky, you can get Ruth to autograph the book because she is around here somewhere. I will be glad to autograph the chapter in which I am quoted," he said as he looked around. He got up from the table and went into the courtyard and emerged a few moments later accompanied by a woman whom he introduced as Ruth Gruber. She told us that she was there to interview Itzhak Perlman, and while she was waiting, she would be happy to autograph both of her books that were now in our possession. Trudy told Ruth that we had difficulty getting the book in the States and that we had to order it, and it would take several weeks before we would get it. Ruth said she had heard this before and asked us to please call the publisher and complain about it. We promised that we would.

Sitting at the next table while all this was going on was an attractive young lady with whom Trudy had struck up a conversation. Her name, we learned, was Evita, and she was here for the Jewish Folk Festival. She said she had just returned from spending a year in Israel, where she was an au pair for an Israeli family. Now she was at the Jewish Folk Festival and was dancing with a group. They were doing Hasidic dances. After the festival, she was returning home to Germany. Evita was born in Poland, but her family was forced to leave Poland when she was fourteen years old because her mother had "political difficulties." They now live in Germany. After the festival, she would go home for a few weeks, and then she would be leaving for England, where she was to study Yiddish at Oxford. Evita also wrote for a German Jewish publication, and she was covering the festival for them.

"Are you Jewish?" I asked.

She responded negatively, and she couldn't really explain why she was so interested in Jewish culture. We told her of our planned trip on Thursday with Henryk and invited her to come along. She accepted the invitation immediately.

These fascinating conversations were going on while Itzhak Perlman and the world-famous klezmer band were unknowingly entertaining us from the courtyard. We learned from Jan Gura that she had flown in with Itzhak Perlman from London, where he had been performing. He was accompanied by his father and stepmother and the Nussbaums. The Nussbaums, we learned, were rich; and they had acquired a fortune through many business ventures but now were known as "The Kosher Vodka King." Nussbaum bottled and marketed a line of kosher vodka that had achieved a good degree of success. Perhaps one day, I will learn what makes vodka kosher in contrast to vodka that is not.

WEDNESDAY, JUNE 21, 1995

MARIA, OUR GUIDE, arrived promptly, accompanied by Jon, our driver for the day. During the ride to Auschwitz, we learned that Maria was a linguist and had studied at Stoneybrook, so she was somewhat familiar with Long Island. She had not visited any other concentration camps, but she was thoroughly familiar with Auschwitz, and she didn't believe that the other camps would yield her any more insight into the horrors that had been inflicted on the victims.

The camps are located about forty miles west of Kraków. They are named after the nearby town, Oswiecim. Before the war, Oswiecim was a shtetl where Jews made up 50% of the population. As we approached the camp, I began to understand for the first time that although Auschwitz and Birkenau are frequently linked together, they are really two separate camps and are about three kilometers from each other. Birkenau is frequently referred to as Auschwitz 2, having come into existence after the original Auschwitz 1. Auschwitz 1 opened in 1940 and is the camp most often seen with the iron gate that has the sign "Arbeit Macht Frei" displayed prominently on it. Originally, this camp was for political prisoners, members of the resistance movement, and intellectuals, whom the Germans feared could lead the subjugated nations into rebellion. It is a much smaller camp than Birkenau or Auschwitz 2, whose purpose was to help carry out the Nazi Final Solution to the Jewish problem.

Birkenau was the biggest extermination camp in the area. Jews made up 90% of the victims, and they numbered anywhere from 1.5 to 2 million souls. Less known to most people is that there was an Auschwitz 3 set up in 1942, close to the I. G. Farben works that was located in a town named Dwory, near Oswiecim. Its purpose was to supply slave labor to the factory. Between 1941 and 1944, more than forty camps were set up principally near German industrial plants that exploited the prisoners as slave labor.

The entrance to Birkenau consists of train tracks going through a building tunnel as they enter the camp. The building above the tunnel was the office and guard posts. From the second-story windows, I could look out on the camp and see the tracks as they stretched toward a platform where Nazis inspected the incoming prisoners and decided whether to send them immediately to the gas chamber or to save them to do slave labor. Many barracks have disintegrated, and only lines of brick chimneys remain. They reminded me of skeletons that I felt were appropriate images for what had taken place here. We walked along, following the tracks deeper into the camp until we came to a large monument honoring the victims. Nearby were the destroyed remains of the gas chambers. The victims met similar fates as at other camps we visited, only in larger numbers.

While walking the grounds of Birkenau, I couldn't help thinking of Joe Rubenfeld, my friend and partner who survived Auschwitz 2. I tried to imagine him living in the barracks unfit for pigs, horses, or cows. Never enough food, scarcely enough clothing to protect him from the cold, and continuous vigilance not to do something or say something that would prompt some sadistic guard to shoot him or send him to the gas chamber. He was lucky. He survived. Millions of other people, including his entire family—mother, father, and siblings—did not.

When we entered Auschwitz 1, which we visited after Auschwitz 2, I was surprised to see that it appeared more as a college campus or a US Army training base than a concentration camp. The barracks had been restored and were in a park-like setting with trees and flowerbeds around. If I didn't really know where I was, I could almost get the feeling that this is a good place to picnic. However, upon entering the barracks, we saw the same crowded conditions as existed at Auschwitz 1 and at the Majdanek concentration camp. One barrack that was used as a "court" for trying prisoners had a gallows right outside the building; and after the "trial," the prisoner was immediately taken out and hung or shot. Torture chambers were located in the basement, along with cells used for solitary confinement.

I had read about Auschwitz and Birkenau a hundred times in a hundred different publications and books. I had seen many documentaries, including the eight-hour movie *Shoah*, but none of those experiences elicited the emotions I experienced in walking through each barrack—one filled with human hair, another with victims' suitcases, and still another with confiscated eyeglasses. The crematoria were intact. On one oven, there was a wreath bearing the Italian colors. It is ironic that the wreath was placed on the oven chamber. Where else?

The victim or victims probably had no other grave on which to place a wreath. The gas chambers had been destroyed, but the ruins were left. I tried to mentally resurrect it. I tried to envision the victims forced into the chambers, and I tried to find some understanding about what could have been going through the minds of the Nazis responsible for doing the final act of extermination. I could not! Is it possible that they were capable of completely cleansing their minds of any thought? Is it possible that they operated as a robot would, without any emotion at all? Who were they really? What were they?

We left Auschwitz and Birkenau in total silence, but I wondered if I would ever be able to clear my mind of what I saw. It was of some comfort to me to know that survivors—despite what they may think silently, privately—apparently can go on with their lives. If they could, I am sure I, who had not suffered or experienced anything of the Holocaust, will certainly be able to.

We returned to Kraków and had our driver drop us at the Ariel, where we were supposed to meet Henryk. We found him talking to Evita. Henryk was ready to escort us to the old and new Jewish cemeteries. Evita asked if she could come along; we had no objections. In the old cemetery, Henryk pointed out the tombs of prominent Hasidic leaders; and in the new cemetery, he showed us where his mother and father were buried.

"They are buried," he told us, "in a single grave, one on top of the other."

His father predeceased his mother, so he is on the bottom. Evidently, vertical burial is not uncommon. It was mostly brought about because cemetery space for Jews was usually limited in size by the kings or rulers, and hence graves were at a premium. Henryk's grandmother is also buried in this cemetery, and he showed us where the marble insert—which gave the details of the person who is buried here—was missing.

"What happened to it?" I asked.

Henryk shrugged his shoulders and said it was stolen.

"Why would anyone want to steal a piece of marble?" I asked incredulously.

"I don't know," he answered. "Perhaps to use it for another grave by engraving the other side."

When we left the cemetery, Henryk walked us through the old quarter, and it was an entirely different experience from the one we had with Jane, whose knowledge of Jewish culture was limited. Henryk showed us buildings that were previously occupied by Jews and streets that were important representations of the Jewish past that now was only alive in the minds of those few who were left and might remember.

"Kraków is a Jewish town without any Jews," Henryk said, shaking his head sadly. But then his face lit up as he continued, "But the Jewish Folk Festival brought many Jews here."

It was getting late, and we didn't want to miss the klezmer concert that evening. We bid goodbye to Evita and Henryk and arranged to meet at our hotel the following morning. Henryk had arranged to hire a taxi for us, and we were going to Tarnow and other small villages along the way.

When we arrived at the opera house, we found many people standing around outside, talking excitedly. There was an air of pleasant expectations. Everyone was looking forward to the performance, and so were we. We entered the opera house and found our seats with no difficulty and awaited the beginning of the concert. Looking around us, we saw Henryk enter. Then we saw the author Ruth Gruber, Evita, and Eve, the young woman we met on the plane returning from Vilnius. We were absolutely amazed. We hadn't been to Kraków more than a few days, and already, we knew four people attending the same concert as we were. We also learned that Rabbi Schudrich was in Kraków for the festival, and we regretted not knowing that he was planning to come here for part of his vacation. I would have loved to meet him, but as things turned out, that pleasure would have to await another time.

The concert was a nostalgic experience in that the music brought me back to my childhood, when klezmer music was an integral part of my life. I thoroughly enjoyed the concert, and judging from the applause and standing ovations the performers received, the audience enjoyed it as much as we did. The audience was made up mostly of young people, and I didn't know what percentage was Jewish since I had the impression that many non-Jews were attracted to klezmer music now.

THURSDAY, JUNE 22, 1995

WE AWOKE TO overcast skies and rain, perhaps befitting our sadness that the next day, we would have to leave Kraków and return to Warsaw. We had met so many wonderful people here and enjoyed ourselves so completely that we hated the idea of leaving. After breakfast, we found Evita already waiting for us. Shortly, Henryk arrived and ushered us into the waiting taxi. We were off to Tarnow, located forty miles east of Kraków. Jews settled here in the fifteenth century, and it became a large Hasidic community. Before 1939, there were about 25,000 Jews living in Tarnow, and they made up about 40% of the population. In 1942, Tarnow was made into a ghetto, and thousands of Jews from other places were forced to live there under crowded conditions. It had, in the past, been famous for its clothing industry, and the Nazis conscripted about 3,000 Jews to sew clothing for the German Army. On June 13, 1940, the first transport of some 700 political prisoners from Tarnow was forced to go to Auschwitz. Some of these were Jews. Ultimately, all but a few Jews were transported to Auschwitz and Belzec for extermination.

On the way, we also learned that Evita's plans would take her to Austria after her Jewish studies were complete at Oxford. She would be working on some television programming for three months and would then return to Germany "to settle down with her boyfriend," with whom she had been living for the past three years.

When we arrived in Tarnow, we learned that the old Jewish section was right off the market square, but we had difficulty finding a place to park the car there. We had to park some two blocks away and walk back. It was not too pleasant as it was drizzling, and it turned out that rainwear was the order of the day.

Henryk pointed out a street sign saying "ul Zydowska" (translated as "Jew Street"), which marked one of the streets in the old town. Many streets were very narrow, and the buildings were from the fifteenth and sixteenth centuries. We walked along ul Zydowska until we came to a small park-like area, where the old synagogue had been. The Nazis had destroyed the synagogue in 1939, and all that remained were the four brick posts of the bimah that stood in the center of the synagogue. A new roof had been constructed to preserve the site, and a plaque had been placed there to memorialize the synagogue.

To visit the Jewish cemetery, it was necessary to visit the local museum and obtain a key from the caretaker. Henryk arranged this, and as we were opening the gate, we were told that the gate is only a replica of the original one.

"The original," Henryk claimed, "was taken without permission and is now on display at the Holocaust Museum in Washington, DC."

We entered the cemetery and saw enough to indicate that we could probably spend a lot of time looking at the many tombstones. The problem was that the weather would not cooperate, and it was extremely uncomfortable walking through the mud. There was a monument to the Jews from Tarnow who were forced to march into the cemetery, where they were murdered. Many of the tombstones had been desecrated and vandalized, but there was also an attempt to resurrect some of them. A mason was busy at work building new foundations for them.

We left the cemetery and returned to the car as the drizzle had now turned into a real rainstorm. There was probably lots more to be seen in Tarnow, but it was not possible to do so today.

We decided to return to Kraków. Henryk asked if we had any objection to stopping along the way. He wanted to visit Adam Bartosz, a friend who was the director of a museum that had been converted from an old castle. He told us that Adam was a Gypsy. We did not have any objection.

On the way there, we expressed the fact that it was past lunchtime and we were getting a little hungry. Henryk found a small restaurant that we would never have stopped at if we were on our own. There I enjoyed what I consider the best meal I had on the trip, other than breakfasts at the Hotel Jan III Sobieski in Warsaw. I ordered pirogen that were delicious and were even better than what "Mother had made." Trudy only ordered a salad, and it looked enticing, while Henryk ordered soup and a plate of chicken livers and vegetables that looked very good, but I would only vouch for the pirogen. Beer was available, but Henryk said that he didn't drink and preferred tea. Evita, like me, had the pirogen, and the entire check was nine dollars.

When we arrived at the castle, we found that we had to park the car on the road outside. We had to cross a moat in order to gain access to the castle. At the door, a young woman greeted us and told us the museum was not really open to the public today since there was a private party going on. We learned that the castle was available for rental for special occasions; and today, descendants of the original owners of the castle were having a family reunion. Members of the family had come from afar to attend the reunion. Henryk asked to see Adam Bartosz, and the young woman found him and brought him to the door. He greeted Henryk like a long-lost brother, and after we were introduced, Adam arranged for us to have a tour of the castle. We also were invited to the party in progress and were offered glasses of wine. Henryk forgot that he did not drink and had several glasses of wine.

We were treated very well during the tour. We were told about the history of the family that originally occupied the castle. We spoke to a number of family members. We went from one floor to another, viewing the kitchen, bedrooms, storage rooms, and the wine cellar. There we were offered more wine. It was an unexpected treat.

When we had our fill of wine and castle, we took our leave, exchanging addresses with Adam and inviting him to contact us if he found himself in the United States.

We returned to Kraków and our hotel, where we bid farewell to Evita and Henryk. A feeling of depression came over me, and I believe Trudy had a similar reaction, knowing that we were leaving the following morning and this adventure was rapidly coming to a close.

We returned to Warsaw and went to the Hotel Jan III Sobieski. We had a walking tour of Jewish points of interest planned. Our guide turned out to be not so terribly cooperative, but perhaps he was reflecting our mood in some way. The tour seemed to be a repetition of the one we did with Henryk Rummel when we first arrived in Warsaw. We cut the tour short and decided to do some shopping before having our final Warsaw dinner. In a city that could no longer really boast a Jewish population, we bought a Hasidic doll.

SATURDAY, JUNE 24, 1995

On the flight home, I began to sort out all that we had experienced on this trip. Did I find any answers to the many questions I had, or did I return with more questions than I had answers? I knew that I was deeply moved, and I had to try to understand what it all meant to me.

When we arrived at Kennedy Airport, we had to pass through customs and passport control. When we presented our passports to the customs agent, she welcomed us back to the United States and then looked at where we had been and observed our names.

"Your name is Schwartz and you went to Poland?" she snarled. Before I had an opportunity to respond, she continued, "How can you go there? I wouldn't give them five cents."

I noticed that she wore a Star of David locket around her neck.

"I think I could explain why we went, but it would take more time than we have here at the moment to do so," I replied.

I was shaken by her inappropriate remarks, but I knew that her attitude was not uncommon. Many people we knew felt the same way she did. How can a Jew give any kind of aid to Poland, a country that had been responsible for the deaths of millions of Jews? I thought again about the reaction of Joe Katz and Joe Rubenfeld. Was there something wrong with me? Was I missing something in not feeling the way they felt? One thing was certain, I would have to spend a lot of time sorting out my feelings and determine why I didn't feel the way a lot of people felt about going originally and why I didn't feel that way after our return.

EPILOGUE

TWO MONTHS HAVE passed since we returned from our trip, and I have spent many hours thinking about it. It has left marked impressions on me. The reality of the concentration camps and all the suffering, death, and cruelty that marked that period in our history continue to haunt me. I ask myself many questions: the same questions that concerned people have already asked. How could such a thing have happened? How could a civilized people have gone along with a deliberate plan to exterminate an entire race of people? What can we do to ensure that such cruelty, inflicted on a people, does not happen again? I ask these questions at a time when there is a resurgence of anti-Semitism by groups such as the skinheads in the name of nationalism. I ask these questions when untold thousands of people are being slaughtered in the name of "ethnic cleansing."

These are some of my thoughts. I realize that I have not extensively researched the validity of the opinions I am about to express. I voice them more in the hope that these thoughts will be talked about and evaluated for merit.

Prior to World War II, more than 380,000 Jews lived in Warsaw. This number represented almost 30% of the population. The Warsaw Ghetto that the occupying forces set up and cut off from the remainder of the city consisted of approximately 307 hectares into which all Jews in Poland were forced to resettle. In addition, Jews living in the Polish territories occupied by the Nazis were forced to relocate to this district. As a result, the death rate in the ghetto increased dramatically due to overcrowded and unsanitary conditions. Gradually, the population in the ghetto was reduced as many were transported to Treblinka for extermination or to be used as slave labor.

Concentrating the Jews into the small area, I believe, helped expedite the Nazi plan for their "solution" to the Jewish question. They were almost successful. Over three million Jews lived in Poland before the war. Now there are only about four thousand. The Jews left their mark in places we visited, but their presence is lacking. It is true that not all Jews died in Poland. After the war, many migrated to other places. Many relocated to Israel, where they were welcomed. Some came to the United States. Kraków, a city that had, before the war, a significant Jewish population, can now only claim a population of about 200, most over 75 years old. There are continuing discussions going on about what to do with Kraków to preserve its Jewish heritage. Similar discussions are going on about Warsaw and probably dozens of other cities. What kind of monuments ought to be erected to commemorate the fact that Jews lived and died there?

I would rather see an increased Jewish population come to live in these towns and villages and bring back to life the rich Jewish culture that existed before the Holocaust. I would like to see the reestablishment of the Jewish influence in Poland so that they could again contribute to the enrichment of the culture. Israel is a very small "oasis" surrounded mostly by hostile people. I would not like to see an increased concentration of the world's Jewish population in Israel. Although I do not want to underestimate Israel's strength and its ability to defend itself, I fear that it is too dependent on the United States for its survival. I am not at all certain that Israel could rely on the United States if this country had to choose between its Middle Eastern oil supply and Israel's survival. Under those circumstances, Israel can become one self-contained enlarged version of the Warsaw Ghetto. It is for this reason that I would like to see a growing diaspora worldwide, and particularly in those places where Jewish culture once flourished. It would also send a message to the world that the Nazi-implemented Holocaust did not succeed.

I think it was important for us to visit Poland and Lithuania. We added our voices to those others who have returned to see and learn firsthand about the atrocities. It was important to meet these other people, Jew and Gentile alike, who are interested in not allowing the Holocaust to be forgotten. It was important to see that a common bond can be welded to work toward a world that would one day eliminate the possibility of a repetition of the horror.

BACK IN THE STATES

By August 31, 1995, our efforts to seek out a buyer for Designatronics were beginning to pay off. We found a merger candidate, DD&D-DI, which agreed to buy all the existing Designatronics stock for $6 per share. Their intention was to take the company private. Although I would have valued the company for more than $6 per share, circumstances were such that it made sense to accept the offer. Recently, Joe Rubenfeld had been diagnosed with prostate cancer. The diagnosis appeared to be such that the cancer had metastasized, and it was questionable as to how long Joe would live since it appeared that the cancer was aggressive. Were Joe to pass away while the company was still unsold, it would present a serious problem for sale in the near future since Joe's stock would be involved in estate problems. It would serve no purpose to pursue the technical difficulties we would have encountered. Suffice it to say, many difficulties would be avoided if we could consummate a sale while Joe and I were alive.

My own estate problems were a matter of concern to me, and it was necessary to deal with them immediately. My share of the proceeds of the sale of the company, based on the number of shares I owned, would have been $2.5 million. From those proceeds, I would have had to pay a considerable amount in capital gains taxes, probably in the neighborhood of $400,000. I would have been left with approximately $2.1 million. That certainly should have been enough to live on for the rest of my life, especially since I was already 70 years old and waiting for the other shoe to drop. I really did not think I had very much more time to live. What became a matter of concern for me was how I could best take care of Trudy financially and still leave an inheritance for my children.

I consulted with my accountant and my attorney and made what, for me, seemed to be very daring decisions. It was suggested that I donate half of the shares I owned to the United Jewish Appeal. In exchange, they would sell the stock, and the proceeds would be put into a charitable trust fund.

Each January 1, the trust fund would be evaluated, and I would receive 10% of that value in two semiannual payments. The advantage of doing that was that the United Jewish Appeal would have received a donation of approximately $1.2 million that would be invested, and I would receive 10% each year based on the entire $1.2 million since, as a charitable foundation, the fund was exempted from capital gains taxes. If I received the funds, I would net approximately $800,000. It seemed like a good idea, and it would guarantee that Trudy would be taken care of financially for as long as she lived. I was 70 years old and in questionable health. Trudy was 58 years old and in good health. It seemed apparent that I would predecease her, and all my plans were based on that assumption. If I had not gifted to the United Jewish Appeal, I would have an estate valued at an additional $1.2 million dollars. To compensate for the reduction as the result of the gift, we purchased the second-to-die policy, which would help the beneficiaries pay the required inheritance tax. Most of all, I was concerned not to burden Trudy or my children with the need to dispose of fixed assets in order to raise cash for tax purposes.

My donation to the United Jewish Appeal coincided with the sale of Designatronics, and although I thought the price was lower than I believed it was worth, I agreed to the sale because of the reasons mentioned above.

I was several months past my seventieth birthday, but Chippy celebrating her forty-seventh birthday was even more frightening. I acknowledged her birthday by writing the following birthday message.

TO CHIPPY ON THE OCCASION OF YOUR FORTY-SEVENTH BIRTHDAY

DOWN THE MIDVALE PATH YOU DID SCURRY,
YOU SEEMED TO BE IN AN AWFUL HURRY.
"WHY ARE YOU RUNNING?" I SAID TO YOU.
"BECAUSE I HAVE SO MUCH TO DO."
I WAS SMITTEN, CHIP, WHEN YOU STOPPED TO CHAT,
YOU TOLD ME ALL ABOUT THIS AND THAT.
AT AN EARLY AGE, YOU LEARNED TO TALK,
BUT SOMEHOW YOU NEVER LEARNED TO WALK.
YOU WERE SMART AS A WHIP, NO ONE COULD FOOL YA—
NOT MR. WHISTLEMAN, ME, NOT EVEN JULIA.
YOU HAD YOUR SHARE OF TROUBLES AND WOES,
BUT DESPITE IT ALL, YOU CONTINUED TO GROW.
YOU STUDIED AND STUDIED AND STUDIED AND THEN
YOU WENT BACK AND STUDIED ALL OVER AGAIN.
SPANISH, FRENCH, AND SOME ARABIC TOO,
SOME YIDDISH AND ITALIAN TO NAME JUST A FEW.
ALL YOUR ACCOMPLISHMENTS SURE WEREN'T BAD,
BUT DESPITE IT ALL, YOU STILL REMAINED SAD.
THEN SUDDENLY RICHARD CAME INTO YOUR LIFE;
HE BECAME YOUR HUSBAND AND YOU HIS WIFE.
AND TOGETHER YOU'RE BEAUTIFUL AND FULFILLING;
IT SEEMS YOUR MARRIAGE DESERVES TOP BILLING.
AND NOW IT'S YOUR BIRTHDAY, I'M SURE YOU KNOW.
YOU MOVE RIGHT AHEAD AND CONTINUE TO GROW

THROUGH LEARNING AND LOVING AND LIVING AND PLAY,

UNTIL NEXT YEAR WE'LL AGAIN WISH YOU A HAPPY BIRTHDAY.

Again death raised its ugly head on November 29, when Leon Gurnick, my cousin Adele's husband, died, leaving Adele a widow with two children: Linda Campbell and Lance Gurnick. I had been very close to the family way back when I lived in California. In fact, I lived with Adele and Leon for a while after they were married and before I returned to New York when my father became ill. I have many fond memories of our days together.

After the sale of Designatronics, Joe Rubenfeld and I no longer had any official connection with the company. We were now former members of the board of directors, and we were free to pursue any direction we chose. Joe, over the years, had returned to his roots in Orthodox Jewry. He had become a Sabbath observer again. He had given up his earlier attempts at experimenting with eating non-kosher food. He found solace in rebinding old books. However, shortly after we sold our interest in Designatronics, Joe lost his battle with prostate cancer. None of the treatments he was undergoing appeared to be helpful, and no amount of prayers from all the rabbis in his congregation, well-wishers, or family were able to stem the tide of that horrible, aggressive disease.

I couldn't help relating to Joe's experience and my own. I was still alive four years after my surgery, and I have tried to live my life without constantly thinking about my disease; but from time to time, I can't help being reminded that at any time, the other shoe can drop and I can face a recurrence of the disease.

That time arrived in December 1996 when one day, I discovered blood on my underwear. I phoned and arranged for an appointment with Dr. Olsson. He immediately scheduled a cystoscopy, and within a few days, he performed it. In the process, he removed a tumor from my bladder. The shoe had finally fallen, although Dr. Olsson did not know for sure that the tumor was malignant. He also seemed to think that this cancer was not related to my original problem.

My recollections of the following period I recorded in an attempted diary log, which I am now recording here.

DECEMBER 27, 1996—FRIDAY

I urinated blood for the first time since my cystoscopy the previous Tuesday. What does it mean? I would have expected that if there was going to be any bleeding, it would be right after the procedure and not three days later.

DECEMBER 28, 1996—SATURDAY

I awoke and found some blood on my underwear.

We had brunch with David and Vania today and dinner with Joel and Cess Weintraub last night. We saw the movie *La Cérémonie*. I was able to make an appointment to see Joel Weintraub professionally on Thursday, January 2, 1997. Calling his office, the earliest I was able to make an appointment to see him was at the end of February, although

I could have gotten an earlier appointment with one of the other doctors in his office, which I didn't want to do.

DECEMBER 29, 1996—SUNDAY

Last night, I experienced an extremely vivid dream about Joe Rubenfeld. I dreamed I was near our pool with several other people. I can't remember who they were. Only Julia's face was recognizable. It was the anniversary of her death on December 29, 1969. Suddenly, I saw Joe standing near the pool. I knew it must be a dream because Joe is dead, but it seemed so real and vivid. I decided to walk up to him and see if the image would disappear, but the closer I came to him, the more vivid the image became. I then tried to take his hand, and he reached out to take mine. We established contact, and that seemed to verify that it was not a dream. But that is all I remember about it because the images faded, and I woke up.

DECEMBER 30, 1996—MONDAY

I was pretty worried about what I would hear from Helen at Dr. Olsson's office about the results of the biopsies taken of my bladder last week. I was unable to speak to her until pretty late in the afternoon. She said that the report, although not yet officially confirmed, appeared to be negative with no cancer indicated. I was afraid to trust or believe the report. She said to call back about five o'clock. She might have the official report by then.

When I called back, she still didn't have anything in writing; but the report was already on the computer, and she said that once it was put on the computer, it was pretty much finalized. It still indicated no cancer or penetration through the wall. I still can't trust it since Dr. Olsson was pretty sure that what he saw was either cancerous or precancerous. Now we waited some more until Dr. Olsson saw the written report and determined what the next step should be. I was becoming more inclined toward doing the BCG (a chemo wash of the bladder) treatment as a precaution. The picture got more confusing, but at least there was no talk yet about removing a cancerous bladder. Reason to celebrate? Perhaps.

DECEMBER 31, 1996—TUESDAY

Obviously, our main preoccupation was still with the subject of bladder cancer and what to do about it. At about noon, I had called Helen to see if she had received the written report, and she said that she had and that Dr. Olsson was looking at it. I also told her that I had a number of bleeding episodes after I spoke to her yesterday. Helen said that she would speak to Dr. Olsson about it and call me back. We, of course, waited with bated breath. And finally, several hours later, she called back and reported that Dr. Olsson was not concerned at all with the bleeding. It apparently was not uncommon for bleeding to occur for a considerable period after the cystoscopy. As for his interpretation of the biopsy report, he was quite adamant that the report indicated no cancer present and called the tissue "atypia" as differentiated from "displaisure." He was not recommending BCG treatment at this time. He said that that treatment carried a certain amount of risk, such as irritation of the bladder along with other possible problems, and he saw no reason to take that risk now. His recommendation was simply to do another cystoscopy in three months. He said nothing would be lost by not starting the BCG treatment now.

For the first time in months, I felt a burden lifted from my shoulders. I think I will be able to enjoy New Year's Eve with a much lighter load perched on my shoulders. Happy New Year.

JANUARY 2, 1997—THURSDAY

Trudy wants to celebrate her forthcoming sixtieth birthday by buying herself a string of pearls and a fur coat besides going to France, Haiti, Israel, Jordan, and Italy. Why not? Live while we can. Dinner out tonight.

JANUARY 11, 1997—SATURDAY

We attended Kerry Cooperman's bar mitzvah, and the service at Temple Israel in Great Neck was everything that always turned me away from organized religion. The rabbi was as pompous as I stereotypically think most of them are, and he was as boring as usual—in contrast to the service that was performed at Jacqueline's bat mitzvah, which I thought was interesting. Jacqueline's rabbi was not too pompous and at least addressed some social issues and did not place himself on a pedestal. The party in the evening was certainly more elaborate than Jacqueline's luncheon, and the food was surprisingly not bad. Trudy and I danced for the first time in a long time because of her knee. This morning, she was feeling pain in her knee as a result. It was obviously a long way from being healed.

JANUARY 12, 1997—SUNDAY

Recapping the past ten days, I learned that Lesley Brittman had discovered that she had either cancer of the abdominal wall or of the ovaries and was already undergoing chemotherapy.

FEBRUARY 3, 1997

Mickey called to inform me that Maxie died.

We went to the theater with Al and Lois Alcosser and Joe and Jocelin Levy on Sunday, February 2, 1997, and saw a very good play. We then went out to a very pleasant dinner. I'm worried about Jocelin, whose liver implant is acting up and is giving some indications of wanting to reject. Up to now, she had a pretty good outlook and was fairly optimistic; but yesterday, she appeared to be losing faith. Al had this very funny phlegmy cough, which he said was from a mild case of pneumonia that he had. Health is certainly becoming a prominent problem among us.

FEBRUARY 5, 1997

Yesterday I was totally depressed and felt lonely and alone. It was the second day I traveled to Brooklyn to get the

Mazda fixed. I felt awful, and after the car was supposedly repaired for the second time, I was told to drive it around the neighborhood for about fifteen minutes before going home, just to make sure it was OK. Suddenly, I had an urge to visit the graves of Mom and Pop at Washington Cemetery. I drove in and parked adjacent to the cemetery plots and just stood at their graveside for a few minutes. I guess I felt an alienation from everyone and everything in this world and tried to reach something in "the other world." I was not successful. I studied some of the other tombstones in the vicinity and saw a number of stones that indicated the burial of Russians. I could tell this by the names and by the fact that they had the picture of the deceased on the tombstone. It was very eerie. It also felt strange because one of these graves had flowers on it. The Russian customs were obviously different from those I am accustomed to, and it felt as if "intruders" were being buried in the area supposedly belonging to the United Botashoner, a Romanian burial society. The Russian stones stuck out like sore thumbs.

PEIR

I'm working on a report for PEIR and am doing it on Senator Bilbo. When I went to the library, I had expected to find a lot of material on such an infamous man; but much to my surprise, I found only one book and a minor reference to him in another. However, I planned to get more information with help from the bibliography in this one book.

Perhaps this is a good time to explain PEIR, which is an acronym for Professionals and Executives In Retirement, but later was changed to Personal Enrichment In Retirement. PEIR is an organization that meets on the Hofstra University campus. It consists of retired senior citizens who have a keen interest in furthering their education. We are considered students of Hofstra, and we pay a tuition. However, we are responsible for preparing our own curriculum, and our members are responsible for acting as proctors or teachers as well as students. We volunteer to teach subjects that we may or may not know anything about. The lack of knowledge of a subject requires us to do research into the subject, and that certainly becomes a great learning experience. We cover a broad variety of subjects, including but not limited to history, chemistry, art, music, philosophy, and current events.

I joined PEIR when I found my hobbies were insufficiently stimulating for me in my days of retirement. PEIR became a wonderful outlet for me.

SATURDAY, DECEMBER 6, 1997

We were honored at St. Mark's Baptist Church. We had purchased tickets to attend a luncheon in honor of the twenty-sixth anniversary of the Reverend Walker's affiliation with the church. Annie Banks, at the end of the luncheon, introduced Trudy and me as her employers, sometimes friend, sometimes enemy, and noted that "everyone has their own angel. These two are my special angels." Then a lovely song was sung in Trudy's honor, and she was presented with a bouquet of roses. It was a nice afternoon, and after returning home, Trudy went to bed because she was in pain. The pain was constantly present, and for some reason, it was not being controlled yet by any medication.

SUNDAY, DECEMBER 7, 1997

It has been ages since I've attempted to keep this diary. I have been unable to get myself to write anything. Of late, I have been unable to read anything either. Trudy has suggested that I get medication to help me, and I think I will have to do that. I now have to admit to myself that I am unable to function properly and at a time when I will be called upon to function at my best. This morning, I discovered blood on my underwear—the same symptom I had which led to the removal of a bladder tumor in September 1997. It is an unhappy event to accompany the sadness I feel on this anniversary of the fifty-sixth anniversary of the day Pearl Harbor was bombed.

DECEMBER 23, 1997

I haven't thought much about my bladder cancer or my prostate cancer of late. These concerns have been superseded by more pressing problems relating to Trudy's cancer. Why am I writing this? Perhaps it is because I have to sort it all out in my mind. Perhaps if I go over the details of the last nine months, I will be better able to cope with what the future has in store. I have to put all this into some kind of order. I have to face the inevitability of Trudy's impending death.

I never thought that I would outlive her. I am 72 years old, and she is not quite 60. All our plans were conditioned on her outliving me. Perhaps it is too soon to make that assumption now with blood appearing again on my underwear, but I was told that with bladder cancer that was contained within the bladder, I would have to be married to my urologist. Every three months, he would perform a cystoscopy and remove any new tumors that may have grown; but as long as it remains contained, it is not particularly life-threatening. But this is the first time I have observed blood since the first tumor was removed. Even so, I don't think it is immediately life-threatening. Trudy's condition, on the other hand, is.

How our lives have changed in the last nine months. In February 1997, we were planning to go to Haiti. It would have been our first visit in almost five years, and we were looking forward to it. We were planning to visit art galleries and restaurants that were our favorites years ago (if they were still there) and just enjoy the sun. A week before we were supposed to leave, Trudy felt a gnawing pain in her back accompanied by a slight temperature. I suggested that since we were going to Haiti, it might be a good idea if she went to see the doctor. Her visit to Dr. Greenstein showed nothing, but he suggested that she have a CAT scan just to be sure. She immediately made an appointment, and on the following day, a CAT scan was done at Great Neck Radiologists. The shocking report indicated that a transitional cell carcinoma was suspected in the ureter and kidney, and she was advised to immediately see a urologist. Because of my previous experience with Dr. Carl Olsson, we were able to immediately arrange an appointment. He performed a cystoscopy and confirmed that the cancer had probably originated in the ureter and had advanced to the left kidney and that it was absolutely necessary to remove the kidney, the ureter, and a number of lymph nodes. He knew that the condition was very serious and that after surgery, chemotherapy would be necessary.

Our trip to Haiti was canceled, and instead, reservations were made at Columbia Presbyterian Hospital. Trudy wanted to stay in a private room that overlooked the Hudson River, and that was arranged. The private room enabled me to stay with her for as long as she remained in the hospital. I slept in the room on a chair bed.

Before leaving the hospital, Dr. Dan Petrylak visited. He is an oncologist, and he told us that chemotherapy was absolutely recommended. He told us that if Trudy did not take the chemotherapy treatments, there was a 90% chance of recurrence of the cancer within two years. The odds were reduced to 50% with chemotherapy. We talked about the seriousness of the disease and then made an appointment to see him in his office in a few days, but he cautioned against any long delay in proceeding with the treatment. When we met with him, he indicated that the treatment of choice was one known as MVAC, a combination of esoteric chemicals that was sure to be toxic in a number of ways. One of the chemicals in the "cocktail" was known to be damaging to the kidneys, and since Trudy only had one kidney, they would have to monitor the treatment very carefully to attempt to prevent any damage. Another chemical was damaging to the red blood cells and the white blood cells, and blood tests would have to be taken weekly to see if any damage was done to her blood. Of course, it went without saying that she was going to experience nausea and lose her hair, but Dr. Petrylak assured us that it would grow back.

The treatment would be administered over a two-day period. On the first day, one of the chemicals would be administered. That would only take a short time. On the next day, the combination of the other three chemicals would be administered intravenously over a four- or five-hour period, along with another drug to help stave off the nausea. The treatment would be done every three weeks for a total of four treatments, or maybe five or six—to be determined as they went along. He suggested that Trudy go into the hospital for the first treatment; and if she handled it well, she could take the remainder as an outpatient.

For the next three months, she experienced almost constant nausea, fatigue, and a loss of sensation in her fingertips and the soles of her feet. Her hearing was somewhat affected, and for some reason, her sense of smell became heightened. After the second treatment, a CAT scan showed that "nothing bad" was happening. She continued with two more treatments, after which another CAT scan showed no new problems. It was decided that no further treatments would be administered at this time and that another CAT scan would be done in August 1997, three months after the completion of the chemotherapy.

In July 1997, more than three months since the surgery had been performed, it was necessary for Dr. Olsson to perform a routine cystoscopy. The exam turned up a tumor in Trudy's bladder, which was removed. Dr. Olsson felt that this tumor was unrelated to the transitional cell carcinoma in the kidney and ureter. September found us back for another CAT scan, and this time, enlarged lymph nodes were found, and the cancer had possibly spread to the lungs and spine.

"Does that mean the MVAC was not effective?" I asked.

"Well, not necessarily," he answered.

"Well, what does it mean?" I asked.

"It may mean that the cancer would have spread more quickly if she hadn't had the treatments."

"Dr. Petrylak, why don't you give us the straight story. The MVAC didn't do a damn bit of good, did it?"

"No, not really," he responded.

"There is another group of chemicals that we will put her on. We're doing a trial, and she would have to agree to be part of a test group. I can have the papers ready today, and we can begin the therapy within a day or two."

Dr. Petrylak now indicated that this chemotherapy protocol would be two chemicals: Taxol and Carboplatin. This regimen would also produce nausea and loss of hair (which had begun to grow back after cessation of the MVAC treatments) and a condition known as neuropathy—which, I believe, can be described as nerve damage and, symptomatically, would be recognized by numbness in the fingertips and toes. Trudy was already experiencing neuropathy, which symptomatically shows up as numbness in the fingertips and toes as a result of the MVAC treatments. And now we were led to understand that the condition was not reversible, and there was a good chance that she would have the condition for the rest of her life.

The protocol called for a series of three treatments, three weeks apart, after which a CAT scan would be performed, followed by another three treatments. If we had no objections, Trudy would be part of a study, and accurate statistics would be kept. We had no objections, but we retained our right to drop out of the study anytime we saw fit, which was agreeable to Dr. Petrylak. Before Trudy would begin the new treatment, it was necessary for her to visit Dr. Casilda Balmaceda, a neuro-oncologist, to determine whether she was fit enough to withstand the onslaught of the new chemotherapy. After a series of tests, she was approved for the treatment. Our confidence in this new therapy was lacking, especially since we were told that there was only a 30% chance of its being effective.

Since the start of the MVAC treatment, we had become a little more sophisticated in deciphering the words of our oncologist. We learned that chemotherapy could not be counted on as a cure. The percentages quoted were really meant to indicate that the treatment had a 30% chance of effecting a remission. When they spoke of a 30% chance of being effective, what was really meant was that perhaps they could retard the disease for an undetermined period of time in 30% of the cases. We had to ask ourselves if the odds were worth all the suffering. In the meantime, we set up an appointment to begin the new therapy.

September 1997 also found me on Dr. Olsson's operating table for my routine three-month cystoscopy. I was lying on my back with my feet in stirrups. The various measuring devices were already connected to monitor my blood pressure, heartbeat, and who knows what else. Dr. Olsson then came in and said hello.

"How are you?" he asked.

"Dr. Olsson, you will tell me how I am after your examination," I replied. "But I need to talk to you about my wife. She has had a recurrence, and it appears to have spread to other lymph nodes and possibly to the spine and lung."

A horrible look of disappointment came over his face. "I have one more procedure to do after I have finished with you, and I will talk to you after I'm finished," he replied. He then called his nurse and instructed her to send up Trudy's file to his office.

The procedure indicated that a new tumor was in my bladder. He removed it. I was disappointed that a tumor was present so soon. Three weeks earlier, I had completed a series of BCG treatments that were supposed to help build up my immune system against recurring tumors. Apparently, the treatment was not successful.

When the procedure was finished, I met Trudy, who had accompanied me to the hospital, and told her that Dr. Olsson would see us as soon as he finished his next procedure. He was true to his word. We were ushered into a small office in the cystoscopy suite, and Dr. Olsson reviewed Trudy's chart. He was honest in that he indicated her condition was serious, and he classified it as a grade 4, the worst classification. However, as grade 4s go, she did not have the worst kind since the cancer had not yet spread to a major organ. We told him that we would like a second opinion, and he immediately suggested we see a Dr. Christopher Logothetis who practiced at the M. D. Anderson Medical Center in Houston, Texas.

"I have seen people who were treated by Dr. Logothetis alive when they had no business being alive," he said.

The following day, we had an appointment with Dr. Petrylak, who was going to familiarize us with the new protocol procedure, and we told him we would like to obtain a second opinion. He too suggested Dr. Logothetis. With both recommendations in hand, we went home and immediately tried to make an appointment in Houston. We were directed to Sherry Preston, the clinical referral specialist. We informed her of our desire, and as we acquainted her with Trudy's history, we mentioned that we were about to begin a new protocol. She immediately indicated that Dr. Logothetis would not see Trudy if she was on a treatment protocol. We tried to convince her that she was already set to take the first treatment the following day but that we wanted Dr. Logothetis to see her before the second treatment. She insisted that he would not see her if she was in the midst of an existing treatment. We were unsuccessful in convincing her to make the appointment. We were terribly disappointed because we did not want to delay the treatment.

I called Helen, Dr. Olsson's nurse, and told her what had taken place. Several hours later, Helen called us and told us that Dr. Olsson had spoken to Dr. Logothetis and that he had agreed to see us. We then called Houston and spoke to Sherry again, and now she appeared to be much more polite and considerate. An appointment was set for Monday, October 7, 1997.

Sherry told us that the hospital had special arrangements with Continental Airlines and that special airline rates could be obtained. She told us she would fax us all the instructions and suggested hotel and motel accommodations. Trudy felt that as long as we were going to Houston, we might as well go there a few days earlier and take advantage of a short weekend respite before seeing the doctor on Monday.

We flew to Houston on Friday, October 4, 1997, and checked into the Omni Hotel. It was a lovely hotel, and our accommodations were nice. Over the weekend, we ate in a number of nice restaurants, visited the NASA Space Center, and spent some time just resting by the pool. Sunday afternoon we checked into the Jesse H. Jones Rotary House, which is located just across the street from the hospital and caters exclusively to people coming to the M. D. Anderson Medical Center. They have a patient guest relations department, and the patient representative, Jasmine Amatong, couldn't have been more hospitable or cooperative. She furnished us with a lot of information that made it easier for us to get through the red tape of filling out the necessary forms.

On Monday, we appeared at the hospital for our appointment at twelve noon, and we were greeted by Pauline Dieringer, RN, who was Dr. Logothetis's nurse. She spent a great deal of time with us gathering Trudy's history, and when she was through, she said that the doctor would be with us shortly. While we waited, a young man introduced himself as Bryan Petter. He said that he was the patient advocate, and if there was anything he could do for us, to please let him know. We thanked him, never thinking that we would call on him or speak to him again. Shortly thereafter, Dr. Logothetis entered the room.

Dr. Logothetis asked Trudy to briefly go over her history. He had evidently read the report that Pauline had prepared because he was aware of certain facts about Trudy that neither of us had mentioned so far. Dr. Logothetis impressed us as being extremely friendly and sympathetic. He referred to himself as an optimist. "If one is not an optimist, one can miss opportunities," he said. Dr. Logothetis, during the entire interview and examination, never rushed or gave us the impression that he was too busy to pay attention to us. We liked him immediately.

He was honest with us in that he confirmed that what Trudy had was indeed a transitional cell carcinoma and that the condition was very serious, but he felt that the cancer could be stabilized through chemotherapy. He felt that subsequent surgery to remove the lymph nodes that were affected could reduce the chances of a recurrence. He indicated that the surgery was serious and would probably require a hospital stay of approximately two weeks. We asked if the surgery would be performed in Houston, and he said yes, but he was certain that Dr. Olsson could perform it as well. The main thing was to stabilize the cancer. He was aware that Trudy had already had one treatment of the Taxol-Carboplatin protocol, and it was his recommendation that we go back to New York and have a second treatment, after which a CAT scan should be performed. If there was any indication that the chemicals were producing positive results, he recommended that the treatment be continued. If not, he suggested that the treatment be abandoned in favor of a protocol he would recommend. We asked him about radiation therapy, and he explained that radiation was fine for a localized condition and that it could tend to reduce the size of the tumor; but chemotherapy worked systemically, and as long as Trudy was not experiencing a great deal of pain, he would defer radiation in favor of chemotherapy.

I can't emphasize enough how confident and comfortable Dr. Logothetis made us feel. We were ready to abandon all other treatments and come to Houston at the drop of a hat in order to have Dr. Logothetis treat Trudy. He, however, recommended that we continue to be treated in New York but that he would oversee the treatment. We made arrangements to send him the results of all tests performed so that he could consult intelligently with our New York doctors.

We left Houston thinking we had made a good friend and found a doctor that made us comfortable—something we had not felt with Dr. Petrylak, who we felt was always looking at his watch and in a hurry.

When we returned for our next appointment for the second round of chemotherapy on Thursday, October 9, 1997, Trudy was examined by Dr. Petrylak, who knew that we had just returned from Houston. He inquired as to what Dr. Logothetis had to say. We briefed him on the details, but we noticed a look of consternation came over his face. We asked him what the trouble was, and he said, "I'm in charge of this case. The protocol calls for three treatments and then a CAT scan will be performed."

I asked what would be the problem of having a CAT scan taken after the second treatment to see if the treatment was being effective.

"That is not the way the protocol is written, and I will get in trouble with the West Coast if I deviate." This reference to the West Coast apparently had to do with where the study emanated from, and he, Dr. Petrylak, was a part of the study. At that point, I indicated that I didn't care about the study. I was concerned about Trudy, and if the treatment was not working, I saw no point in continuing it; and apparently, Dr. Logothetis didn't think so either. From that point on, our relationship with Dr. Petrylak continued to deteriorate. I felt that I could not work with him as a family member, but Trudy was the patient, and she had to make the decision whether to continue with him or change her oncologist.

At some point, I believe Dr. Petrylak had a discussion with Dr. Logothetis, which may have convinced Dr. Petrylak to agree to the CAT scan after the second treatment. Several weeks after the second chemotherapy treatment, the CAT scan indicated that not only had the treatment done no good, there were indications of further spread of the disease. I obtained copies of the test results consisting of CAT scans, MRI, and bone density test and sent the information to Dr. Logothetis along with a series of questions as to how we should proceed. I also indicated that we had a serious problem with Dr. Petrylak, and we were considering using another oncologist recommended by Dr. Olsson. Would Dr. Logothetis have a problem working with another doctor in New York?

Medical politics must have raised its ugly head. Dr. Logothetis had made it clear to us he would respond to our inquiries, but we never heard from him again.

A visit to a recommended radiological oncologist, Dr. Ennis, resulted in a course of treatment that failed to stem the progress of the cancer. I asked him what he suggested we do next. He said, "Very honestly, if I were you, I would do as many of the things I have always wanted to do and not put it off for a better time."

In keeping with Dr. Ennis's advice, Trudy felt there were many things she always wanted to do; however, she was faced with many physical restrictions because of her increasing pain. She did decide she would want to visit a resort in Puerto Rico that we had been putting off for a long time. We made arrangements to go, but it was problematic whether we would get there because of Trudy's blood tests, which were being monitored almost daily. We did ultimately get an OK from the doctor, and we did go. It turned out to be our last vacation together. We had lovely accommodations, and we ate and drank well, but the trip was plagued with difficulties. The pills she was taking for pain only gave her minor and temporary relief.

Upon our return home from our trip to Puerto Rico, we kept an appointment with Trudy's oncologist. He recommended she be admitted to the hospital, where the pain could be better managed. At first, Trudy resisted because she felt that if she went to the hospital, she would never leave it alive. I promised her that I would not let that happen. I would see to it that she returned home.

I arranged for admission to the McKeen Pavilion at Columbia Presbyterian Hospital. This pavilion was an exclusive floor with luxurious private rooms overlooking the Hudson River. It was my wish that some degree of pain management would permit the development of an approach that would permit me to take Trudy home, where I could manage her pain control. I was very disappointed. I found that not only did the pain management physicians have very little to offer, but the nursing care on the floor was terribly insufficient. After a few days, I began to get the idea that the hospital management expected the patients in the pavilion to provide their own private nurses. Recognizing the situation, I moved into the room with Trudy. The room had a chair that opened up into a single bed. Sleep was a very rare option during the night. The chair bed was lumpy, and

I found myself sitting up most of the time. However, I was not concerned with my comfort. My purpose was to cater to Trudy's needs as best I could because a nurse's attention was almost impossible to obtain without waiting upward of thirty to forty-five minutes after notifying the nurses' station that Trudy needed something. I was tempted to hire a private nurse. But if I did that, I would not be able to stay in the room with Trudy, and I didn't want to be away from her side.

Trudy's stay in the hospital lasted six weeks. During that time, it became apparent to me that her condition was terminal. She was aware of that inevitability, and she arranged to have her friend and colleague, Cess Weintraub, come to visit her at the hospital. Together, Trudy acquainted Cess with her patient load and arranged to transfer them to other therapists.

Each day Trudy was hospitalized was filled with torture for me trying to get medical attention from doctors and nurses to ease Trudy's pain. Eventually, it was decided to implant a device that would administer morphine periodically, but that didn't seem to do much good. My emotional condition was tenuous, and I wasn't quite sure of my judgment, but I knew the hospital was no longer the place for Trudy. I had promised her that I would not let her die in the hospital, and I began to push the doctors to permit me to take her home. I prevailed and was put in touch with a social worker at the hospital who assisted in arranging for hospice care at home. Once those arrangements were in place, I whispered to Trudy that I was taking her home. Her eyes opened wide in a way that seemed to indicate to me that she approved. That was the last indication I had that any of my attempts to communicate with her were successful.

An ambulance took her home. A hospice nurse was there to greet us. The bed provided by hospice was in our sunroom—a room that Trudy and I both loved. The room was enclosed by glass doors and windows, with additional light available through a skylight. Trudy was settled into the bed. In addition to the hospice worker who came for several hours each day, I arranged for round-the-clock private nurses. We did all we could to make her comfortable, but pain was our enemy, and neither I nor any of the attending nurses could do very much to alleviate her suffering.

I began to wish for Trudy's death, but her heart was strong, and she held on. I stood by her bed and begged her to let go. I was tempted to accelerate the frequency and amount of morphine we were permitted to administer. I knew this would hasten her death, but I wasn't sure it would lessen her pain.

I did not have the courage to do that.

On the morning of the seventh day after I had brought her home, the attending nurse told me Trudy was running a rather high temperature and she would have to do something about it. I told the nurse that I was under the impression that a patient in hospice care would not be treated medically but only made comfortable. The nurse told me that she had to treat the high temperature, and she sent me out to the pharmacy to purchase suppositories to bring it down. I immediately went to purchase the suppositories, and when I returned home, the nurse told me Trudy had expired just moments ago. I was robbed of being at her bedside at that moment.

The day before she died, March 24, 1998, I stood by her bedside and read out loud several love poems I had written to her. I don't know how much she heard or was able to comprehend. It was my wish that she would know how much I loved her, how I would change places with her if only I could.

I felt cheated. It was not supposed to be this way. "The best-laid plans of mice and men," I thought. I was supposed to die first. I was twelve years older than Trudy. I felt that Trudy was a more valuable person. She could be more helpful to my children than I could. They had learned to trust and depend on her for advice. Her psychological and therapeutic training were more valuable than anything I could offer them. I was the sick one. I was fighting off various cancers. If anyone should die, it should be me.

The funeral home was crowded with friends and relatives. In addition to the eulogy presented by Rabbi Geller, two of Trudy's friends, Beverly Winston and Cess Weintraub, spoke. My daughter Sheila delivered a eulogy also. It was outstanding in that it was heart-wrenching as she described her sadness at having now lost two mothers.

SHEILA'S EULOGY FOR TRUDY

WHEN I WAS 15, I LOST MY MOTHER TO CANCER.
I AM 43; I HAVE LOST MY MOTHER TO CANCER.
TWO MOTHERS, TOO MANY, FAR TOO SOON.
WHEN I WAS 15, MY WORLD SHATTERED,

LOUD AND SHRILL—LIKE THOUSANDS OF STEEL-SHARP SHARDS OF GLASS

NO LONGER SHINING, NO LONGER BRILLIANT, BUT CRUEL IN THEIR ACUTENESS

CRUEL IN THEIR DEADLY SHARP EDGES,

CRUEL IN THEIR ABILITY TO PIERCE THE HEART.

WHEN MY WORLD SHATTERED, MY HEART BROKE.

A WRENCHING BREAK,

LIGHTNING-QUICK, EARTH-SHATTERING, BREATH-STOPPING,

REELING IN PAIN, THE SCREAMING INSIDE MY HEAD

SO LOUD IT HAD TO BE LEAKING THROUGH MY PORES.

YET

WHO COULD HEAR?

I WAS ALONE, STRANDED AND DESOLATE,

BARELY BALANCING ON THE PRECIPICES OF CRATERS

HERE ON EARTH

FATHOMLESS CRATERS UNSEEN BY THOSE AROUND ME

EVEN THOSE CLOSEST TO ME

CRATERS UNSEEN EVEN BY MYSELF

I SURFED ALONG THIS PRECIPICE SEEMINGLY UNTOUCHED,

TAKING AN OCCASIONAL STUMBLE IN BUT MANAGING TO PULL MYSELF OUT,

UNSCATHED, BUT NOT REALLY, FOR UNDERNEATH LIVED A BUBBLING TURBULENT WORLD OF CONFUSION AND DESPAIR.

WHO COULD QUENCH AND STILL THE CHURNING WATERS?

A ROSE APPEARED,
A BEAUTIFUL ROSE,
UNAFRAID OF THE TURBULENCE BEFORE HER.
NEW AND FRESH AND VIBRANT,
READY TO GIVE, READY TO LOVE,
WHO COULD SEE THE CRATERS AND THE PERSON TEETERING ON THE EDGE,
THE ROSE THAT COULD SEE THE CRATERS THAT NO ONE ELSE COULD,
NOT EVEN MYSELF.
"JULIA," SHE SAID, "I HAVE BROUGHT YOU YOUR DAUGHTER."
WHO BUT A ROSE, UNAFRAID OF TROUBLED WATERS, COULD
GUIDE ME THROUGH THE PUZZLING MAZE OF ADOLESCENCE
AND LIGHT THE WAY FOR THE ROADS AHEAD, ALLOWING ME TO SINK A LITTLE
BUT NEVER ALLOWING ME TO DROWN?

WHO ELSE BUT A ROSE COULD SAY, "SOL, CAN'T YOU SEE
YOUR DAUGHTER NEEDS YOU?"
ONLY A ROSE COULD SEE THE MUDDY WATERS AND BRING

THEM TO CLARITY AND, AT THE SAME TIME, CHANGE THEM TO A
SERENE, PEACEFUL EBB AND FLOW OF A GENTLE WAVE.

I AM 43 AND MY WORLD HAS SHATTERED AGAIN. LOUD AND SHRILL LIKE THOUSANDS OF STEEL-SHARP SHARDS OF GLASS,
NO LONGER SHINING, NO LONGER BRILLIANT BUT CRUEL IN
THEIR ACUTENESS, CRUEL IN THEIR DEADLY SHARP EDGES,
CRUEL IN THEIR ABILITY TO PIERCE THE HEART.

YOU CAME INTO MY WORLD AND HEALED A GAPING WOUND,
FILLED MY LIFE AND THE LIVES OF THOSE AROUND ME WITH
LAUGHTER AGAIN AND RENEWED SMILES LONG FORGOTTEN.
YOU OPENED OUR EYES TO SIGHTS WE'D NEVER SEEN BEFORE
AND FILLED OUR HEARTS WITH EMOTIONS WE NEVER KNEW EXISTED.
YOU TAUGHT US TO TALK.
YOU TAUGHT US TO FEEL.
YOU TAUGHT US TO TRUST WITH LOVE THAT WAS HONEST
AND PURE AND STRONG.
LOVE THAT WAS UNCONDITIONAL.
AND YET YOUR OWN FEARS OF BEING LOST, OF BEING ALONE

AND UNLOVED, KEPT YOU WONDERING,
"DO I BELONG? WILL I MAKE A DIFFERENCE?"

AND SO IT IS FOR ALL OF US,
THAT TURBULENCE AND UNCERTAINTY COMES AND GOES,
SOMETIMES IN VOLUMINOUS WAVES,
SOMETIMES IN A RIPPLE SOFT AND GENTLE,
SOMETIMES AS A MIGHTY STORM.
BUT ALWAYS THERE IS THE ROSE THAT STANDS STRONG AND TALL
AND SWEET—
A FRAGRANT AND BEAUTIFUL GIFT TO ALL WHO ARE LUCKY
ENOUGH TO HAVE BEEN TOUCHED BY HER WONDER.
SO YOU SEE, YOUR FEARS WERE UNFOUNDED.
YOU INDEED MADE A DIFFERENCE,
AN ENORMOUS DIFFERENCE IN MY LIFE,
IN ALL OUR LIVES.

THANK YOU, MOM.
AND, MOM, I AM WEARING RED SHOES.

I was unable to speak. I wasn't certain that I realized the whole funeral scene was real. I was numb. When Deah sang, accompanied by her friend Steve Kurtz on guitar, and when Annie Banks, our housekeeper of many years, sang "Amazing Grace," I was unable to relate it to a Jewish funeral, where music is totally absent. I know that Trudy had asked Annie Banks—who has a lovely voice and sang in a church choir—to sing "Amazing Grace" at her funeral. However, much of the service became more real to me when some time after the funeral, I listened to a tape recording Rabbi Geller had made, which he presented to me after the funeral.

Trudy was buried in a grave at Mount Ararat Cemetery. We had purchased the plots shortly after we married, but I never dreamed that she would be using her plot before me.

After the funeral, we sat shiva at home; and following the shiva period, I began the long trek back to some sort of a reality. Deah stayed on for a few more days, not wanting to leave me alone; but then she had to return to California because she had been neglecting her school work. She was in the midst of pursuing her doctorate, which Trudy and I had encouraged. Deah's departure left me alone to face the horrible unreal questioning of why I was still alive. I was of the frame of mind that there was really nothing to live for. I felt that I had lived a fairly successful life. I had enjoyed a certain level of success in my life's work. Trudy and I had traveled a lot. Life was no longer a precious commodity for me.

After Julia's death in 1969, I was left with the responsibility of two teenage daughters who had to be raised and a business that had to be run. These were motivations that kept me going. Now, almost thirty years later, I was retired and the children were grown and had families of their own. I really felt an absence of motivation to continue living. In addition, cancer of the bladder was a constant companion. My anger at how fate had dealt with us all contributed to my desire to die. After all, I had lived a long enough life, and now there was no real good reason to go on. Then how could I explain the fact that I continued to be treated for my bladder cancer? My only answer to that was that I wanted to be in charge of how I would face the end of my life, and dying from bladder cancer was not my chosen way, so I continued to accept Dr. Olsson's treatment. Shortly after Trudy's funeral, I underwent a urological exam, during which Dr. Olsson again found and removed several tumors in my bladder.

Emotionally, I was hitting rock bottom. I decided I had to get away from home. A trip to Haiti was my prescription. Perhaps I wanted to relive some of the experiences Trudy and I had shared. I asked my brother, Leonard, if he would join me since I did not want to go alone. He agreed. We had a very nice week together, visiting art galleries, eating in nice restaurants, visiting old friends, and in general, reliving times I had spent here with Trudy. The trip was both pleasurable and painful. I missed her terribly.

When Leonard and I left Haiti, he returned to Florida, and I went on to New York. As I entered my home in Hewlett Neck, I was immediately hit with the terrible prospect of occupying it alone. Everywhere I looked, I saw Trudy. I explored each room of the house. In the kitchen, I saw her happily working on some new recipe. In her office, where she treated her patients, I saw her sitting at her desk. In our bedroom, I saw her sleeping, and I had images of the times we made love and we held each other. In our greenhouse (a room I had taken such great pride in), I found I no longer had any interest in maintaining it. In our conservatory—the room in which she took her last breath—I saw her lying on her deathbed. I tried to tell myself that with time, I would be able to cope better with the devastation I felt. I hoped that the loneliness would dissipate even as I thought there was no longer any valid reason to live.

Annie Banks stayed on because she had promised Trudy she would take care of me, our dog Ti Chien (whom we nicknamed Mr. T), and our two cats. Annie also took over the task of watering the plants in the greenhouse because I began to neglect them.

However, there was one responsibility that I did not neglect, and that was to continue to visit Trudy's mother, Alice Ashendorff. Alice became a widow several years before I met Trudy. She lived in Brooklyn, the same apartment where she had lived with her husband, Louis, and their two children, Trudy and Arthur. Trudy lived there until she married, after which she and her new husband moved to their own apartment.

Trudy and I would visit Alice periodically and, on occasion, take her out to dinner. Alice did not seem to make any real demands on her two children, and the relationship, in later years, between Alice and her son, Arthur, was distant. As a matter of fact, even though Arthur lived in Manhattan, there was a period during which a year would pass without Arthur visiting with his mother. Trudy, on the other hand, saw to it that she visited her mother weekly, sometimes accompanied by me.

Around 1993, we began to notice that Alice was beginning to fail. She began to neglect her apartment, and she was not paying her bills. In addition, there were neighboring men who were taking advantage of her financially. We discovered this by auditing her checkbook. Trudy decided it was time to take over the responsibility of handling her money. We did that with Alice's blessings and arranged to give her an allowance. However, her deterioration continued, and we felt that it would be better if we could get her into a senior citizen hotel closer to where we lived so that I would be able to visit her and tend to some of her needs even if Trudy couldn't. By 1995, I was retired and had time on my hands, but Trudy was still very much involved with her practice. We found a senior citizen facility in Long Beach, which was much closer to our home and seemed to be appropriate for Alice's needs. There she lived for a while, but she continued to deteriorate mentally. Alzheimer's was beginning to take its toll, and she did not seem to recognize us sometimes.

One day we received a call from the home that Alice had fallen and had been taken to Long Beach Hospital. She had not broken any bones, but the doctor said she really should be in a nursing facility where she could receive more intensive care. We were fortunate, with the doctor's influence, to get her into the Long Beach facility associated with the hospital. Alice appeared to be happy there except she complained that her son, Arthur, had not visited her for months even though he had been there the previous day. She became progressively worse, and Trudy, even after her surgery, continued to visit her every few days. I often accompanied her.

After Trudy died, I went to visit Alice along with her son, Arthur. I did not know how we would handle the contingency of Alice asking about her daughter. On that first visit after Trudy's death, it was a blessing she did not ask about her. She accepted the fact that Arthur was her son, and I was not sure who she thought I was.

Alice died two years later. In that time, she never mentioned or asked about Trudy. I often wonder if she knew or sensed something that she didn't want to face and hence refrained from mentioning her. We buried her next to her husband, Louis, at Mount Ararat Cemetery, a short distance from where Trudy is buried. Alice had no living friends. We had a graveside funeral service attended by Arthur; his significant other, Rheva Myers; and just a few family members.

PEIR AND META

After Trudy became ill, I had become occupied with taking her to doctors and hospitals. Between her health problems and mine, it seemed that we were always involved with one medical appointment or another. Although I retained my membership in PEIR, I had not gone to many classes. On occasion, I would attend a class entitled Challenges in Retirement. This was a group of relatively new members of PEIR. The purpose was to attempt to help newly retired people cope with their altered lifestyle. We discussed the problems retirement presented and attempted to help each other find workable solutions. Through this group, I managed to make and retain a connection with at least some of the members.

Even though I had rarely attended during this period, a number of PEIR members came to Trudy's funeral. Meta Smith, Robert Ratner, Sid Wasserman, and others were there. Meta Smith attended sessions in the Challenges in Retirement group with me. Meta had become widowed two or three years earlier and found PEIR to be a lifesaving organization for her. Her husband had died of prostate cancer. When she came over to offer her condolences, I remember thanking her and saying that one day, I hoped we would have an opportunity to compare experiences.

Now I decided to resume my attendance at PEIR classes in the hope that it could be a distraction for me. I longed for an escape from my health problems and my loneliness. I could not stay around the house very much. I knew that I could not continue to live there, and yet I knew Trudy's death was still too fresh in my memory, and it was not wise to make any radical decisions at that time.

PEIR was a lifesaver for me to some degree. While I attended classes four days a week, it was fine. However, returning home to an empty house was extremely difficult, and it didn't seem to get any better with time. I had the nights to contend with, and I found myself getting into bed after an early meal and trying to sleep away the time. I had known depression, and the symptoms were familiar to me. I could not stand it for very long. I was not able to function effectively alone. I needed company.

One evening, completely on impulse, I called Meta Smith and asked her if she would have dinner with me. I was surprised when she quickly agreed. I was happy at the prospect of having company, and I told her that I would pick her up. Meta lived in Syosset. She countered with "Let's meet at Hofstra, where we attend classes." It was about halfway between Woodmere and Syosset. I was delighted that she had accepted and was elated that I would have company for dinner.

We met in the Hofstra parking lot, and Meta then joined me in my car. We drove to Aliana, a small French restaurant not far from my home. We enjoyed a few drinks, had a wonderful dinner, and talked until we were told that the restaurant was about to close. We hadn't realized how long we had been there talking. We were both hungry for human contact. I knew of my need, but Meta didn't realize until that evening just how much she also really missed talking to someone.

We left the restaurant, and I suggested we go to my home to continue our conversation. I also wanted to see how it felt being in the house with another woman. We spent another couple of hours there. Meta talked about her husband, Les, and their relationship; and I spoke of Trudy and our relationship.

It was getting late, and I had to drive Meta back to the Hofstra parking lot, where her car was. When we arrived, we both acknowledged that it felt good to be able to bare our souls, the many thoughts and feelings that were bottled up inside us.

I was still a long way from being enthusiastic about life. I knew that I missed Trudy. I continued to see her all around me. I was conscious of the fact that I was no longer married. Ironically, I now recalled being told after one of my frequent cystoscopies, "From now on, you are married to your urologist." That prediction was correct.

SEPTEMBER 1998

Another cystoscope exam found new tumors in my bladder. Now Dr. Olsson recommended I undergo a series of BCG treatments he heretofore had not recommended. The BCG treatment is a process that entailed injecting a cocktail of chemicals into the bladder, permitting the solution to remain there for an hour before evacuating it. This meant weekly visits to the hospital for the next six weeks, after which there would be a two-week respite before undergoing another cystoscopy exam.

OCTOBER 1998

October 1998 spelled the end of Deah's marriage to Bill, leaving in its wake all the usual problems relating to how much time their son, Zachary, should spend with each of them. Shortly after their divorce, Bill was in another relationship. Deah, after several years, met Ted, whom she has had a relationship with for the past eighteen years.

The divorce became final in November 1998. They had agreed that Zak would spend part of each week with each of his parents. The effects the breakup may have had on Zak are probably no different from that suffered by most children when parents decide to divorce. However, the divorce was relatively simple because there was no great issue over division of assets.

In 1998, I made another trip to Haiti—this time, with a specific goal in mind. It had to do with solar ovens.

In 1990, I had received a phone call from Gene Sullivan. He represented a company that manufactured solar ovens, and they were interested in finding a company in Haiti that might be interested in a partnership arrangement with an entity that would assemble solar ovens there for the local market. They believed that it would be a wonderful product for Haitians as a substitute for cooking over charcoal-burning fires. Haiti's environment is being destroyed as the result of deforestation. Trees are cut down to make charcoal, and they are being cut down more quickly than they are being replaced. As a result, the soil is being washed away. If Haitians could be weaned from open charcoal-burning fires and depend on solar cooking, it would be a good thing for the environment. The idea seemed plausible and, in my opinion, warranted further investigation. I arranged to meet with Mr. Sullivan and Thomas Burns, chairman of Burns-Milwaukee Inc., a company located in Wisconsin.

The meeting resulted in my suggesting that Mr. Burns send me one of his solar ovens so that I could arrange to see how successful it would cook and bake. He did, and after I verified that it was reasonably efficient, I began to do some further research into cost estimates for building the oven. At the time, I felt that in quantity, the oven could be built for around $50. I asked myself, how would the average Haitian who cooked over a charcoal fire be able to afford $50? I found that to be an obstacle, but not an insurmountable one. I remembered that for my brother Leonard's bar mitzvah, he received a gift from Mom and Pop—a beautiful bicycle. It cost $42. The method of payment for the bicycle was on the installment plan. Each week, Leonard would carry a payment to the department store until it was paid off.

I thought that some variation of that plan might be used by Haitians acquiring the solar oven. However, the insurmountable obstacle I encountered came from the need for a staff of "missionaries" who would go out to the villages to teach the people how to use the oven. The cost of this task would make the whole plan unworkable because I was not able to justify a price tag that would be affordable for the average Haitian. In addition, my company was publicly owned. I had to answer to the stockholders, who were looking to me to operate the company profitably. I ultimately decided that it was not a viable business proposition for my company, and I turned it down.

Now, some eight years later, I thought the idea of widespread use of solar ovens in Haiti could still do a great deal for the environment. I was prepared to return to Haiti and set up an assembly facility. However, the main problem still existed. There would still be a need for a team of people to go into the small towns and villages to teach the Haitians how to use the ovens. My thinking now was changed in that I was no longer restricted by the need to make a profit since the entity would not be part of a publicly owned company. I was not interested in making money from the venture, but I still could not privately finance the costs involved. I thought that the World Trade Organization or the International Monetary Fund or some such entity would be willing to finance such a venture. Hence, I returned to Haiti in the hopes of meeting with representatives of these organizations. Not wanting to go alone, I asked Meta if she would be interested in accompanying me. She agreed with some degree of hesitancy. I convinced her that it would be an interesting experience for her, and she finally agreed. I planned a two-week trip and set up some appointments and hoped that others I wanted to see would be available to me once we were in Haiti.

I managed to meet with a representative of the World Trade Organization. I found they were not interested in financing such a venture. They felt that Haiti was too unstable. I was unable to arrange an appointment with a representative of the International Monetary Fund, but a conversation on the phone with a representative proved to be equally unsuccessful.

Interspersed with these mostly failed attempts at obtaining financing, Meta and I spent time visiting art galleries and craft shops, and I escorted her through some of my old haunts. After about five or six days, I awoke to find my underwear covered with blood. I became frightened and knew that it was necessary to cut our trip short and return home. I immediately called Dr. Olsson and reported what had happened, and he told me to come home as quickly as possible and come to see him.

DECEMBER 1998

More tumor growth. The BCG appeared to act as a fertilizer instead of an inhibitor. Dr. Olsson then tried another chemical concoction for the next three months. He sat me down after this unsuccessful treatment and told me that he was concerned that the tumors were growing too fast; and although they had been contained in the bladder so far, he was concerned that if the cells were to break through the bladder lining, we would be in very bad shape. He recommended that the bladder be removed. I was in a state of shock when I heard this. Until now, I was not overly concerned about staying alive, but I was absolutely opposed to suffering or remaining ill for a long period of time.

Dr. Olsson made an appointment for me with an aide who explained what life would be like for me after my bladder was removed.

During my preoperative meeting with Dr. Olsson, I explained to him that I would have difficulties being a patient at Columbia Presbyterian Hospital. I explained that my experiences with Trudy made it impossible for me to be a patient here. He seemed to understand and arranged for the surgery to take place at the Allen Pavilion, an annex some distance from the main hospital.

After the surgery, I had the overwhelming task of adjusting to living without a bladder. The adjustments were emotional as well as physical. When I returned home, I was fortunate to have Leonard and Cynthia stay with me—at great sacrifice to themselves—to lend me both physical and emotional support. Meta was also wonderful during that time. I believe that her being there for me kept me from contemplating suicide.

Trudy had died on March 25, 1998. I thought about her every day. On the twenty-fifth of each month since her death, I became especially depressed. Sometimes during the year, I found myself depressed without even realizing that it was the twenty-fifth of the month. In early June 1999, I arranged for the unveiling of Trudy's tombstone. My remarks at the unveiling follow:

TRUDY'S UNVEILING

I SUPPOSE THAT UNVEILING TRUDY'S TOMBSTONE IS SUPPOSED TO BRING ABOUT SOME KIND OF CLOSURE, BUT I'M NOT CERTAIN WHAT THAT CLOSURE IS SUPPOSED TO BE. IS IT SUPPOSED TO SIGNIFY THE END OF MOURNING HER? IS IT SUPPOSED TO SIGNIFY THE TERMINATION OF MY grief over the end of my marriage—the end of the devastation I feel over the loss of a friend, partner, lover, and confidant? Should it be the termination of the grief I feel over the end of a relationship that was more important to me than life itself? As of this moment, I am unable to acknowledge any closure. I have not been able to overcome the anger that permeated my every thought about why she met such an untimely death. I have been unable to overcome my rage over the irony that Trudy predeceased me. I cannot put to rest the fact that there was still so much she had to offer to our children, grandchildren, friends, and her patients.

During this 1 year, 2 months, and 19 days, I have tried to tell myself that if Trudy were able to communicate with me, she would tell me that it is time to get on with my life, whatever that is. I have tried and will continue to try as long as I am able, but getting on with my life carries with it the all-too-frequent burden of remembering images of her suffering. Images of hopefulness and helplessness during the last year of her life. Images of her never crying or complaining about why this was happening to her. Only observations about how the cancer went about its merry way, progressing despite all attempts to stop or slow it. Why didn't she cry? Why didn't she cry, at least once?

My life with Trudy was all I could ever have hoped for in a marriage. We shared twenty-seven wonderful years. For that, I am grateful beyond words. I know she loved and cared for me. As for our children and grandchildren, I believe she was a wonderful mother, grandmother, and friend. She was there for them whenever they called on her.

I loved Trudy as I have loved no other human being. I continue to love her as if she were still here with us. I don't suppose that will ever change; nor am I able to say that I will ever be able to laugh and smile again the way I did because I was fortunate to have had Trudy share my life.

I try to remember the wonderful aspects of our life together whenever the horrible images of her illness crash into my mind. I try to recall our intimate conversations, our exchanges of ideas, the beautiful and exciting trips that we shared. I try to superimpose these thoughts on the images of her last weeks of horrible suffering. It is often an unsuccessful battle. But I try.

Trudy was the most honest person I know. She was not capable of telling a lie. She was not capable of knowingly hurting anyone or taking advantage of anyone to benefit herself. She was dedicated to her friends, patients, and family. She was sincere in everything she undertook. She was meticulous in the way she dressed and even more so in how she prepared

FOOD FOR A DINNER PARTY AS WELL AS A SIMPLE MEAL FOR JUST THE TWO OF US.

AT TRUDY'S FUNERAL, I WAS UNABLE TO EXPRESS MY GRIEF. IN FACT, I WAS NUMB THROUGH MOST OF IT. BUT I WAS TOLD BY MANY PEOPLE HOW MEMORABLE AND UNUSUAL A FUNERAL SERVICE IT WAS. I WAS TOLD BY PEOPLE THAT WHEN IT IS THEIR TIME TO GO, THEY WOULD LIKE NOTHING BETTER THAN TO BE REMEMBERED AS TRUDY WAS. I HAVE HAD OPPORTUNITIES TO RELIVE HER FUNERAL SINCE IT HAD BEEN RECORDED BY RABBI GELLER. I THINK SHE WOULD HAVE BEEN PLEASED TO BE REMEMBERED THE WAY SHE WAS.

I HOPE THIS CEREMONY OF UNVEILING THE STONE WHICH MARKS HER GRAVE WILL RESULT IN BRINGING ABOUT SOME REALITY FOR ME—SOME ACCEPTANCE OF THAT WHICH I CANNOT REVERSE. AND I HOPE THAT IT, IN SOME WAY, BRINGS SOMETHING POSITIVE FOR ALL WHO ADMIRED, CHERISHED, AND LOVED HER.

I returned home and went about trying to accept the reality of Trudy's untimely death. Coping with my emotional problems was constantly hampered by the physical difficulties that persisted in haunting me.

I had not fully adjusted to life without a bladder when it was discovered that the cancer had spread to my urethra. Once again, I was destined to undergo surgery. I was back in the hospital less than a year after my bladder had been removed. This time, the surgery kept me in the hospital for about a week. After returning home, I was in a great deal of pain and running temperatures that should not have occurred. I returned to the hospital to investigate the source of the difficulty. I underwent test after test and finally was readmitted for the purpose of undergoing large doses of antibiotics. Ultimately, the diagnosis was that I had contracted a staph infection. I was forced to remain in the hospital for an additional two weeks, during which time I was given large doses of antibiotics intravenously. Once again, my emotional state had deteriorated to a dangerous level, and life just held little value for me. Meta visited me daily, and she was the only bright light of the day. Finally, the infection was brought under control, and I was permitted to leave.

Returning home, I was again faced with living in a house that I loved and which held so many pleasant memories for me. Yet I saw Trudy everywhere. It was a home we built together over many years. It was Trudy's home and my home. I could not continue to live there alone or with anyone else. Suddenly, the house seemed too large. There were rooms I did not enter for months at a time. Only Annie went in to clean them. Trudy's old office and waiting room stood empty and cold. Our living room, where we sat on so many winter evenings in front of the fireplace, remained empty and closed. Our beautiful conservatory, where we spent so many pleasant hours, only brought back images of Trudy's last days in a hospice bed in that room which she loved so much. Our gourmet kitchen—which featured a professional Garland stove in which Trudy took so much pride—now stood cold and virtually unused. Our greenhouse was displaying signs of neglect because even though Annie tried to tend to it, she was not able to care for the plants or propagate new ones, and I no longer had the disposition to show her what to do. That first summer after Trudy's death, our swimming pool remained unused.

I became aware that if I were going to get on with my life, I could not continue to live in this house. I decided to put it up for sale. I did not have any idea where I would go or what I wanted to do. I had been advised that I should make no major decisions while I was in a state of mourning. Well, I did not really know when the state of mourning would end. I was trying to go on with living, even building a close friendship with Meta, but I was still mourning. Selling my home was a major decision, and I would just have to trust in my own instinct that it was the right thing to do at this time, even if my mind was not as clear as it might be some time later.

Bolstering my decision to put the house up for sale was Annie's announcement to me that she would like to leave because she wanted to return to North Carolina. She had continued to stay on because of her promise to Trudy to "take care of me." She felt that she really wasn't needed because she spent most of her time sitting around watching television. I agreed that it was OK and that her promise to Trudy had already been met. Annie's leaving was convenient because it gave me the impetus to move ahead with my decision.

Selling the house, however, was not as simple as I had thought. I discovered that the way we designed the house was ideal for Trudy and me, but it was not as appealing for new people coming in with larger families. We had virtually turned our home into a two-bedroom house from what had originally contained five. We now had to find the right buyer who could see the many advantageous luxuries but who didn't need more bedrooms.

When I announced to my children and grandchildren that I was selling, it triggered a number of responses (some poetic) that moved me, so I include them here:

PERSONAL ODYSSEY—BECKY COOPERMAN

AS I THREW THE FLOWERS ONTO THE GRAVE, TEARS DRIPPING DOWN MY FACE, I THOUGHT OF MY GRANDMOTHER, MUCH LIKE THE FLOWER THAT FELL FURTHER AWAY FROM ME OVER TIME. SAYING MY LAST GOODBYE, I REMEMBER MY JOURNEY THAT LED UP TO THAT MOMENT, INCLUDING BOTH THE SORROWFUL AND GOOD TIMES.

MY ODYSSEY STARTED WHEN MY MOTHER INFORMED ME THAT MY GRANNY WAS SICK, AND THAT SHE AND MY GRANDFATHER WOULD NOT BE GOING ON VACATION. WE WOULD NOT BE ABLE TO TAKE CARE OF THEIR DOG, WHOM I LOVED HAVING, LIKE WE DO EVERY TIME MY GRANDPARENTS GO AWAY ON VACATION. I WAS ANGRY AT FIRST. I REMEMBER MY FIRST REACTION CLEARLY, AND MY EXACT WORDS WERE "JUST BECAUSE GRANNY IS A LITTLE SICK, WHY CAN'T THE DOG COME ANYWAY?" IT WASN'T UNTIL LATER THAT DAY, WHILE IN THE CAR, MY MOTHER SPILLED TO ME THAT MY GRANDMOTHER HAD CANCER. MY BREATH STOPPED FOR A QUICK SECOND. I WAS SPEECHLESS. DIFFERENT THOUGHTS WERE FLOWING THROUGH MY HEAD. I DIDN'T UNDERSTAND HOW THIS WAS happening. I felt terrible for the way I had acted prior to finding out just how sick she really was. The very first words that came out of my mouth were "Is Granny going to die?" My mother answered with confidence, yet with a mournful look on her face, "No. I don't think she is going to die." I sat back with a little relief but still had a worried feeling inside of me. I needed something to overcome how I felt about my poor reaction, when I heard she was just sick. As soon as I went home, I called up my grandmother, not mentioning the cancer, just talking. Talking about school, talking about sports, talking about my life—to make her happy.

Happy as she sounded then, time passed, and my grandmother became more ill, even after her treatments. It wasn't being told about her condition that made me realize things were not well, but it was the changes that began to occur in my life, such as the less frequent visits.

Going to the theater for my birthday is a tradition I have had for a long time with my grandparents. A great part of my journey was seeing my last show with both my Granny and Grandad. We were off to see *The King and I*, and I remember before we left, I watched my Granny tie a colorful scarf around her head and place on an elegant-looking hat. I admired the fact that she wasn't intimidated by her loss of hair, even though she was a person who was always concerned with her looks. At that moment, I hoped I could be like her, to be able to overcome a loss with pride and dignity. From that night on, I tried to keep hope alive.

My grandmother's favorite time of the year was Thanksgiving. She always put so much effort into making everyone feel comfortable and welcome. Tables of home-cooked food, beautiful flower pieces on each table . . . everything matched. Even the napkins she folded so beautifully added to the perfect picture. Being there on Thanksgiving was always a very special time for me, but this year, it had much more significance than it ever had before. Before the meal, my grandfather made a toast, as he does every year. This year, however, his speech took a different meaning in my heart. For as long as I can remember, my grandad would end his toast by wishing our family a good year to come. But this year, his words changed. As he raised his glass, he said wistfully, "And hopefully, we will all be gathered here together next year, to celebrate another fabulous Thanksgiving." As he spoke those final words, I watched him look over at my grandmother, raising his eyebrow, clearly showing who he was referring to. It was then I realized, she wasn't getting better and that death could soon fall upon us. Even though I knew she wasn't getting better, I believed she would. What fed this discrepancy? I didn't believe . . . I couldn't accept that somebody so wonderful, so generous, so caring—who never did anything in her whole life to harm anybody—could be struck down so young and unfairly and taken away from me.

As winter's fingers gripped us, death started to tighten its fingers around my granny. The closer death came to my grandmother, the farther my mother seemed from me. When my granny's illness took her from her own home, into the hospital, it took my mother too. My mother's frequent visits to the hospital left me and my sisters on our own for many days and nights. Forced to struggle with my loneliness, my fear, my sadness, and feeling abandoned by my mother, I became a stronger person and began to reach out to other family members and friends, because my mother was losing her own mother and had her own odyssey to travel.

When my mother would speak about her visits to my grandmother, I wanted to go myself, to be able to have my final memories with her. Concerned how we would react to a face that no longer belonged to her, she preferred we not visit and be left with a better memory. Even though I was angry and wanted to see her so dearly, I respected her wish. I never did get to see her alive again.

Sitting in my sixth-grade science class, listening to the attendance being called, I heard my name and I responded I was in class. Not being heard by the substitute teacher, she stated softly, "Oh, Becky is not here. Her grandmother passed away." A shock of sadness and misery went through my whole body. Even through her last week, I believed my granny would pull through. Having to find that out from a teacher who didn't even realize she was talking to me—all my hope came crashing down. Tears started to fall, and the teacher took me out of the class and apologized for my having to find out that way. I walked back into the class to get my stuff, knowing that twenty sets of eyes were staring at me, yet I looked at no one. Too many thoughts were going through my mind to be able to focus. I talked to my family about my feelings, and I thought that I might make myself feel better if I would just write . . . write what I was feeling. Write my thoughts or write poetry for my grandmother. My granny loved my poetry, and I put as much effort as I possibly could into writing a special poem to read to her about a rose.

Before I knew it, I was at my grandfather's house, waiting for the black limousine to take us to her funeral. Old friends and distant family all gathered together to say goodbye also. I wasn't allowed to see her in the hospital, so I wanted to say my last goodbye in person. My family had preferred I

NOT GO, BUT I KNEW I HAD TO. AND WHEN I DID, I WAS ABLE TO SAY MY FINAL GOODBYE.

AS I THREW MY FLOWER ON TOP OF HER GRAVE, TEARS DRIPPING DOWN MY FACE, I KNEW MY GRANDMOTHER COULD SEE THE STRONGER PERSON I HAD BECOME AND COULD HEAR ME SAY "I LOVE YOU."

Becky wasn't through expressing how she felt. She penned these thoughts sometime later.

TO GRANNY,

IT'S BEEN THREE YEARS SINCE YOU PASSED AWAY,
TEARS AND SMILES HAVE FLOWN FROM DAY TO DAY,
WHEREVER I AM, I'M THINKING OF YOU,
BECAUSE YOUR SPIRIT SURROUNDS ME THROUGH AND THROUGH.
YOUR EYES TWINKLING DOWN FROM THE STARS UP ABOVE,
OR YOUR HAIR SWAYING IN THE GRASS, GIVING OFF LOVE.
SURROUNDED BY THE SWEET FLOWERS, I FEEL YOUR SMELL,
IN THE CLOUDS I SEE YOUR FACE—IT'S EASY TO TELL.
THE WAVES IN THE OCEAN CARRYING YOU EVERYWHERE,
NOW YOUR HAPPY SPIRIT IS SPREAD FOR ME TO SHARE.
I BREATHE THE AIR IN WHICH YOUR SPIRIT REMAINS,

BUT I CANNOT REACH YOU—IT'S LIKE BEING HELD BACK BY CHAINS.

BUT NO MATTER WHERE YOU ARE . . . THE STARS . . . THE GRASS . . .

THE FLOWERS . . . THE CLOUDS . . . THE AIR . . . OR THE WAVES FAR APART.

MOST IMPORTANTLY, YOU HOLD A SPECIAL PLACE IN MY HEART.

LOVE,
BECKY

And this is from Stephanie:

FOR SALE

THIS IS NO HOUSE. THIS IS A HOME. I WALK IN THE DOOR TO THE DELIGHTFUL FACE OF MY GRANDAD. THE ODOR, WARM AND WELCOMING. THE JUMPING UP AND DOWN WITH JOY. I FEEL SAFE IN THIS WONDERFUL PLACE CALLED A HOUSE.

AS A LITTLE GIRL, I WADDLE DOWN THE STAIRS INTO THE BASEMENT. TO MY LIKING, I FIND IT FILLED WITH TOYS. MY FAVORITE IS ANTS IN MY PANTS. PUPPETS AND STUFFED ANIMALS FILL MY EYES WITH GLEE. BUT YEARS GO BY, AND SOON, THAT BASEMENT IS JUST A BASEMENT.

AS I STAGGER UP THOSE BASEMENT STAIRS, I START TO NOTICE THE HOUSE FOR WHAT IT REALLY IS. THE DINING ROOM WITH THE STONE FLOOR AND THE DINING TABLE WITH ITS GLOSSY TORTOISE TOP. THE WALLS WRAPPED IN PRIMITIVE HAITIAN ART.

The dog always silently sleeping on his pink mat by the side door. The conservatory filled with windows and skylights that allow me to see the beautiful plants my grandmother kept. Pots blooming with flowers and small trees. The bird feeders with birds of all kinds fluttering around in search of treats they like. I become aware of everything, from the little glass candies in the glass bowls of the living room to the Jacuzzi bathtub in the bathroom with the marble floor.

More and more, I appreciate the little things. My granny's collection of every little knickknack you can think of—souvenirs, figurines of little cats and birds, stones, and little wooden boxes. And who could forget the famous rooster collection? Roosters lined every nook and cranny of the hallways. But now, this is no longer my home. It is far too big for a simple man I call Grandad. So my house of dreams, my palace, my place of comfort, was being sold.

I feel betrayed, cheated. My memories were being stolen away from me, like ocean waves that destroy a child's sandcastle in the blink of an eye. I did not live in this house. Even though this is no longer my home, the memories I possess will last forever.

MARCH 2000

Less than two years after Trudy's death, my brother-in-law Joe Katz passed away. Just a short time before, Joe and Beatrice Katz had decided to leave Florida and relocate to Scottsdale, Arizona, in order to be close to their daughter, Susan; their son-in-law, Brian Green; and their two grandchildren, Helene and Ross. By this time, Beatrice—who had been losing her eyesight for many years—was reaching a point where she was really no longer able to take care of a home. Their moving to a senior citizen hotel in Scottsdale relieved both Beatrice and Joe of many household responsibilities. Unfortunately, Joe became ill rather suddenly and passed away in March 2000.

I experienced an inordinate amount of difficulty in selling the house. Each day that went by without a willing buyer was torture because it meant that I had to return home to the reminders of days gone by. The many happy times Trudy and I shared in this home. Now I had to convince myself that this was no longer a home. It was just a house—just another house. It was excruciatingly difficult for me to see potential buyer after potential buyer come through, only to find the house unsuitable for their purposes. It hurt that they could not see the love and care that went into making an ordinary house a home in which love was shared.

I was also becoming aware of the fact that I am not the kind of person who can live alone. I have seen many people make the adjustment to living alone, some even preferring it, after becoming single following a divorce or separation or after a mate passes away. I was not such a person. I could never be happy not having someone to share my life. I was not such a person who could happily adjust to sleeping alone—to not waking up next to someone I loved. I could perhaps continue to live a life by participating in PEIR or finding some way to perform constructive activities, contribute to the community—but it would never be a totally satisfying experience. Could I contemplate entering into another relationship? Could I do that while I still felt such strong emotional ties to Trudy's memory? Would I be able to care enough for someone else and truly participate in a new relationship so that I would not feel that I was "shortchanging" her? Equally important, could she feel that I was really into this new relationship? Was she capable of entering into a relationship that she could give herself to emotionally?

These were the thoughts that permeated my thinking as I attempted to sell my house. Of course, I also wondered where I would go if I were successful. Did I want to stay in Woodmere or perhaps move to a senior citizen development somewhere? Should I consider buying a condominium or rent an apartment? What would I do with the accumulation of dishes, furniture, and an extensive Haitian art collection? The obvious answer seemed to be to give much of this to my children—that is, if they wanted it.

I would have to worry about these material things after I find someone to buy the house. Until then, everything was on hold—except my growing friendship with Meta Smith. Meta lived in her large house with her divorced daughter, Jordana, and her two children, Gabrielle and Chase. Meta and I found each other great company and a source of comfort.

Meta had been born and raised in a small Pennsylvania coal-mining town called Shamokin. Her parents ran two shoe stores that provided them with a meager existence. Meta was the oldest of five children, and in her earlier years, she had to help raise her younger siblings. At age sixteen, she was ushered off to pharmacy school at Temple University, where she met Lester Smith, also a student of pharmacy, whom she eventually married.

Lester's father, who was also a pharmacist, had a store on Long Island; and after Lester's graduation, he went to work at his father's pharmacy, as did Meta after she finished school. This was Meta's physical departure from Shamokin, but emotionally, she is still a child of that coal-mining town.

I can't help mentioning the similarity between Meta's and Julia's upbringing. Julia also came from a small coal-mining town in Pennsylvania called Wilkes-Barre, where her parents operated a dry goods store. Julia's mother encouraged her to leave as soon as she finished high school because she saw no future for her if she remained in Wilkes-Barre.

Meta and I had been dating. She was at my bedside throughout my various surgeries. I was learning to like her a great deal. I was beginning to enjoy her company; and most of all, even though we disagreed about a lot of issues (mostly political), I found that I wanted to be with her. She was excellent company, and we seemed to get along well together.

Meta concluded it was time for her to sell her home about the same time I did. Her house needed a great deal of repair, and she found that the upkeep was more than she needed. I thought it might not be a bad idea if Meta and I decided to live together in a rented house or apartment after we both sold our homes, and we could share the rent and other expenses. It would certainly be economically advantageous for both of us. We were not considering any long-term commitment, and it would give us both an opportunity to see how we got along together. Since neither of our homes was sold yet, it gave us ample time to consider the idea while we continued to see each other at PEIR and in our spare time.

Of course, there were other factors to consider. How would my children and grandchildren take to the idea of my living with a woman out of wedlock? How would Meta's six children take to the same idea? How would her siblings and grandchildren take to the idea? Meta and I talked about it amusingly because, in truth, we really didn't care what they thought as long as we thought it was a good idea. Besides, we didn't really think there would be any objections.

In May 2001, I went to Oakland, California, to attend Deah's graduation and to see her receive her doctorate degree. I was very proud of her accomplishment. I was aware of how hard it had been for her. She had to overcome many obstacles. Her education was interrupted by the death of Trudy. Despite all this, she managed to complete her studies and her dissertation. She had been living through stress for so long that it finally took its toll. In September 2001, she developed difficulties with her back, which virtually kept her in a state of paralysis for a long time. To this day, she is still partially disabled as a result.

Until now, I was unable to find a buyer for my house. I listed it with one broker after another, and I tried multiple listings and taking out newspaper ads on my own with no success. Finally, a middle-aged couple, the Bartons, fell in love with the house. They liked everything about it. They had no children living with them, so they had no need for more bedrooms. They were collectors of Haitian art, and I had Haitian art all over the house, displayed in nooks and crannies, which made the house very colorful. We could agree on the price, but there was just one hitch. They had to sell their house first. They asked me to hold the house for them. They were even ready to put down a deposit. I readily agreed since I did not have any other potential buyers breaking my door down. I did not realize that they had some serious problems with selling their house.

Months went by, and the Bartons kept insisting that they wanted the house if I would just be patient a little longer. Finally, one day, I received a phone call asking me if it would be possible for them to come with their daughter, who was an architect, to go over renovation plans. I readily agreed, and the following Sunday, they appeared. I hadn't seen them in months. I recognized Larry Barton immediately, but his wife was not recognizable. She was obviously quite ill, but no one mentioned anything about it. They went through the house while their daughter took notes and measurements. They said that they were ready to set a closing date. They told me their attorney would call mine to accomplish that. The date was set for two or three weeks later, sometime around September 2002, and the closing would take place in my attorney's office.

On the day of the closing, I appeared at my attorney's office, and so did the attorney for the Bartons, along with Larry Barton. His wife was not present. At this meeting, in our presence, the buyer's attorney tried to discourage the buyer from going through with the purchase, even if he had to lose the deposit. For the first time, it was disclosed to us that the buyer's wife had become terminally ill. However, Larry Barton insisted on going ahead and even insisted we move the date up for him to occupy the house. This put a great deal of pressure on me because I didn't have a place to move to, and I expected that I would have at least three months to vacate the house. That was cut down to six weeks. I agreed because I did not want the deal to fail.

The papers were signed, money changed hands, and I immediately threw myself into the task of finding some place to go and the idea of disposing of things. I knew that wherever I went, I would not have the same amount of room that I had here. I had to get rid of lots of things. Of course, my first attempt was to gather my three children and have them select what they wanted. There was furniture, artwork, dishes, and trinkets of all sorts. After their selections, I gathered together lots of things and contributed them to local charities. Still, there were mountains of possessions that I could not emotionally part with. I would just not fit into a small apartment. I would have to find a small house with a basement or other places for storage.

Meta and I searched for a place. My geographical criteria was governed by wanting to be conveniently close to Hofstra University and our PEIR group. That gave us a pretty wide range of towns on the South Shore of Long Island and even some on the North Shore. We looked at apartments and houses in Oceanside, Long Beach, Rockville Center, Baldwin, Roslyn, and Great Neck, just to name a few. We finally found a house in Great Neck that was affordable. We retained movers and set a date for the relocation. These two moves were coordinated rather efficiently, and Meta and I took up residence at 5 Edgewood Place in Great Neck.

I turned over the Hewlett Neck house to Larry Barton on time. Some days later, I learned that he had moved in immediately, but Mrs. Barton never did. Although I have no details, I learned she died of cancer. Larry Barton hadn't even unpacked his belongings, but he and his family sat shiva in the house.

Meta and I began the adjustment to our new home. It wasn't long before our garage was laden with possessions that neither Meta nor I could "possibly live without." We set up housekeeping on the upstairs level, where there were three bedrooms. We quickly decided which room would be our master bedroom and then allocated the other two rooms—one as an office, which we would share, and the other as a den. I must confess that it took quite a lot to adjust to our new master bathroom. I had really become spoiled after living with a master bathroom that was able to host a champagne party after Trudy and I had it built.

As Meta and I continued to live together, participate in PEIR together, and get to gradually know each other's families, I found that my original feelings of friendship had gradually developed into fondness, affection, and ultimately, love. I began to realize that I could love another woman without feeling disloyal to Trudy. My feelings for Trudy remain. Meta has similar attachments to her deceased husband, Les. We have talked about it, and we have both concluded that we can love each other without feeling any disloyalty to our previous spouses.

Each year, we go together to visit the graves of Les, Trudy, and Julia. Meta lights a candle for Les on the anniversary of his death. She calls each of her children to remind them of the anniversary. She has not lost contact with her past devotion to her husband and family. Nor have I. For as long as I live and am able, I will continue to remember and cherish the years I spent with Trudy. For as long as I live, I will continue to remember and cherish the years I spent with Julia.

FEBRUARY 4, 2003

Another tragedy befell our family when, once again, cancer claimed another victim. My youngest cousin, Sarah Laperdon, passed away after being ill for a short time. Sarah had always watched her diet, exercised regularly, and as far as I know, never lived a life of excess. She and Sol Laperdon worked and raised three children. Sarah and Sol were devoted to each other, but death showed no mercy.

I have continued to remain under the watchful eye of Dr. Carl Olsson. Every six months, I was required to have x-rays and CAT scans taken. So far, as of this writing, the second shoe has not dropped. I will not look a gift horse in the mouth. I am thankful for each day I am able to wake up and function. I am thankful for the relationship Meta and I have been able to develop.

In early 2004, Meta's family began to plan a reunion of the Moskowitz clan. *Moskowitz* was Meta's maiden name, so although most of her family were Smiths, Karns, and any number of other married names, they still felt a part of the

Moskowitz clan. The only Moskowitzes actually remaining are Meta's two brothers, their wives, and offspring—namely, her brother Myron; his wife, Joan; and son, Michael, and family. And there is her brother Rollie; his wife, Pita; and son and daughter, Josh and Cara. All in all, Meta has a rather large family in contrast to mine. I had met most of her family by that time, but my children and siblings mostly had not met them. I discussed with Meta the idea of combining their family reunion with an official recognition of our relationship. Neither of us felt that marriage was an advantageous arrangement. However, we were both comfortable with a ceremony entitled "A Declaration of Love." At the ceremony, Meta would declare her love and devotion to me; and I, in turn, would declare my love and devotion to her. We would make the reunion a weekend affair and invite our two families, brothers, sisters, grandchildren, nephews, nieces, cousins, aunts, and uncles—if there were any—to a weekend bash at the Nevele Hotel in the Catskills. This affair would allow all the relatives to mix and become acquainted. We both thought it was a great idea, and we then went about planning the event, which took place the weekend of August 20–22, 2004.

The weekend, despite the fact that it rained, turned out to be really successful, and almost everyone had a great time. The following are the "Declarations of Love" that Meta and I vowed.

DECLARATION OF LOVE BY SOL

META,

BEFORE THIS ESTEEMED GATHERING OF THE CLAN OF MOSKOWITZES, SMITHS, AND A SPRINKLING OF SCHWARTZES, WE HAVE DECIDED TO MAKE OUR DECLARATION TO EACH OTHER PUBLIC.

OUR SECRET IS OUT AND KNOWN. BUT WHAT IS PERHAPS NOT SO WELL KNOWN IS WHAT THIS DECLARATION MEANS TO ME.

WHEN TRAGEDY STRUCK IN MY LIFE, LEAVING ME A WIDOWER FOR A SECOND TIME, LIVING NO LONGER HELD ANY MEANING FOR ME. I FELT THAT I HAD LIVED A FULL LIFE. I HAD DONE IT ALL, SEEN IT ALL, AND NOW THERE WAS NOTHING MORE TO LOOK FORWARD TO. YES, THE GRANDCHILDREN WERE NOT YET GROWN. THERE WERE BAS AND BAR MITZVAHS AND WEDDINGS IN THE FUTURE. BUT THE DAY-TO-DAY LIVING DURING THE LONG INTERVALS OF THOSE HAPPY OCCASIONS SEEMED UNBEARABLE—UNTIL YOU!

ONE EVENING, SITTING AT HOME ALONE, I COULD NO LONGER TOLERATE THE LONELINESS. SO ON IMPULSE, I CALLED YOU AND ASKED IF YOU WOULD CARE TO JOIN ME FOR DINNER; AND MUCH TO MY SURPRISE, YOU SAID YES. AND THAT EVENING, I FOUND SOMEONE WHO COULD REOPEN THE WINDOW TO LIFE FOR ME.

DINING IN A SMALL, WARM, INTIMATE FRENCH RESTAURANT, ACCOMPANIED BY KAMIKAZES (OUR FAVORITE DRINK) AND WONDERFUL WINE, WE TALKED FOR HOURS, SHARING OUR RESPECTIVE tragedies and joys. We probably would have talked into the early morning hours if the restaurateur hadn't signaled that they wanted to close. The restaurant was close to my home, and we were not through talking, so we went to my home and continued to talk.

Earlier that evening, when you agreed to join me for dinner, I offered to come and get you like normal people our age used to do when going out on a date. To my surprise, you declined my offer and instead suggested that we meet in the Hofstra parking lot. "Women's Lib," I thought, so I agreed. I regretted my decision when it was time to take you home, and instead, I was forced to deliver you back to your car. At least you had agreed to ride to the restaurant in my car. Perhaps you thought that riding in your car would be too intimidating for me. It could have been. Who wouldn't be intimidated by a woman who sports a license plate that reads "Meta Says"? However, after spending our first evening together, any intimidating fears were quickly replaced with feelings that I had found someone who was compassionate, caring, and sincere.

It was pretty late, and Women's Lib and "Meta Says" notwithstanding, I was unhappy about dropping you back at the Hofstra parking lot. But there was no alternative,

AND WE WENT OUR SEPARATE WAYS HOME—YOU TO SYOSSET AND I BACK TO WOODMERE.

UPON ARRIVING HOME, I IMMEDIATELY CALLED TO FIND OUT IF YOU HAD ARRIVED HOME SAFELY, AND MUCH TO MY CHAGRIN, YOU HADN'T YET ARRIVED. IT SHOULD HAVE TAKEN ME MORE TIME TO GET HOME THAN YOU. AT THAT MOMENT, I KNEW I HAD MADE A MISTAKE IN NOT BEING MORE INSISTENT THAT I PICK YOU UP. ULTIMATELY, YOU ARRIVED HOME. HEAVY TRAFFIC WAS THE CULPRIT, AND WHEN YOU CALLED ME BACK TO TELL ME THAT YOU HAD ARRIVED SAFELY, I WAS SO RELIEVED THAT I HAD TO MAKE ANOTHER DINNER DATE IMMEDIATELY WITH YOU. BUT THIS TIME, I INSISTED ON PICKING YOU UP AT YOUR HOME; AND THIS TIME, YOU GRACIOUSLY AGREED.

NEITHER OF US WAS THAT FAR REMOVED FROM OUR RECENT TRAGEDIES—YOUR LOSS OF LES AND MY LOSS OF TRUDY. WE FOUND THAT WE COULD SHARE THESE TRAGEDIES WITH EACH OTHER WITH COMPASSION AND UNDERSTANDING. BUT AFTER A WHILE, I ALSO FOUND IT WAS POSSIBLE TO CARE FOR ANOTHER PERSON WITHOUT FEELING DISLOYAL TO TRUDY OR NEGATING THE WONDERFUL RELATIONSHIP THAT WE HAD HAD. AS YOU AND I SHARED MORE TIME TOGETHER, AS YOU AND I SHARED MORE INTIMATE DETAILS OF OUR LIVES TOGETHER, WE MOVED CLOSER, AND I FOUND THAT MY CARING FOR YOU GREW. I DISCOVERED THAT MY CARING HAD TURNED TO AFFECTION.

WHEN, FOR PRACTICAL REASONS, WE DECIDED TO SHARE A COMMON ABODE AFTER DISPOSING OF OUR

RESPECTIVE HOMES, WE HAD THE OPPORTUNITY OF SPENDING MORE CONCENTRATED TIME TOGETHER, AND I FOUND MY AFFECTION FOR YOU TURNING INTO LOVE AND A DESIRE TO SPEND MORE AND MORE TIME WITH YOU. THE MORE TIME WE SPEND TOGETHER, THE STRONGER MY FEELINGS OF LOVE FOR YOU BECOME.

YOU MAKE MY WORLD ALL THAT IT IS. OUR LOVE DEFINES MY LIFE, AND IT IS WHAT I AM MOST THANKFUL FOR.

I LOVE YOU EVEN AS WE STRUGGLE TO BE OUR OWN INDIVIDUALS.

I LOVE YOU WHEN YOU STAND FIRM WHEN YOU FEEL YOU ARE ABSOLUTELY RIGHT, EVEN WHEN I KNOW I AM ABSOLUTELY RIGHT.

SOMEHOW, OUT OF ALL THE TWISTS AND TURNS OUR LIVES COULD HAVE TAKEN, AND OUT OF ALL THE CHANCES WE MIGHT HAVE MISSED, IT ALMOST SEEMS LIKE WE WERE GIVEN A MEANT-TO-BE MOMENT— TO MEET, TO GET TO KNOW EACH OTHER, AND TO SET THE STAGE FOR A SPECIAL TOGETHERNESS.

WHEN I AM WITH YOU, I KNOW THAT I AM IN THE PRESENCE OF SOMEONE WHO MAKES MY LIFE MORE COMPLETE THAN I DREAMED IT COULD BE.

I LOOK TO YOU FOR INSPIRATION AND FOR ENCOURAGEMENT, AND YOU NEVER LET ME DOWN. YOU LIFT MY SPIRITS UP AND TAKE MY THOUGHTS TO PLACES WHERE MY TROUBLES SEEM MUCH FARTHER AWAY AND MY JOYS FEEL LIKE THEY'RE GOING TO STAY IN MY LIFE FOREVER.

IT IS NO SECRET TO ANYONE WHO KNOWS US THAT WE LIVE TOGETHER, BUT IT MAY NOT BE AS

WELL KNOWN HOW WE REALLY FEEL ABOUT EACH OTHER. AND SO WE CHOSE THIS OCCASION TO PUBLICLY DECLARE OUR MUTUAL LOVE FOR EACH OTHER.

META, AS I GAZE INTO YOUR EYES, I PUBLICLY DECLARE THAT I LOVE YOU VERY MUCH, AND I LOOK FORWARD TO SPENDING WHATEVER TIME IS LEFT FOR ME ON THIS EARTH RESPECTING YOU, HONORING YOU, CARING FOR YOU, AND LOVING YOU.

DECLARATION OF LOVE BY META

AS I DECLARE MY LOVE AND DEVOTION TO YOU TODAY, I REALIZE FORTUNE HAS SMILED ON ME AND GRANTED ME A NEW BEGINNING AND A NEW MEANING IN MY LIFE. YOU WALKED INTO MY LIFE WHEN, IN MY WILDEST DREAMS, I COULD NOT IMAGINE MEETING ANYONE AS WONDERFUL AS YOU. OUR RELATIONSHIP IS A RARE GIFT. WE ARE CONNECTED IN A WAY THAT DEFIES EXPLANATION.

AS YOU NOW KNOW, I DO NOT ENJOY TRAVELING. AND WHEN YOU INVITED ME TO GO TO HAITI—OF ALL PLACES, HAITI—AND I DID NOT HESITATE, I KNEW THERE WAS SOMETHING THERE. IT WAS A DEFINING MOMENT.

HEALTH PROBLEMS AROSE, AND WHEN I FOUND MYSELF WORRYING AND CARING ABOUT YOU, I FOUND MYSELF THINKING ABOUT YOU ABOVE ALL ELSE.

WHEN YOU INVITED ME TO SHARE YOUR HOME AND LIVE WITH YOU, MY LOVE HAD ALREADY DEEPENED.

AND LOOKING BACK, I KNOW THAT WAS THE BEST DECISION OF MY LIFE. WE ARE SO HAPPY TOGETHER. MY LIFE IS MORE COMPLETE WITH YOU THAN I EVER DREAMED IT COULD BE.

I LOVE YOU WHEN OUR MOODS VARY AND WHEN OUR OPINIONS ARE IN OPPOSITE DIRECTIONS.

I LOVE YOU WHEN YOUR IDEAS AREN'T QUITE THE SAME AS MINE AND OUR BELIEFS CLASH.

I LOVE YOU WHEN YOU TAKE A STAND ON WHAT YOU FEEL IS ABSOLUTELY RIGHT, EVEN IF I DON'T FEEL THE SAME WAY.

I LOVE YOU FOR WHAT YOU BELIEVE, FOR THE EMOTIONS YOU FEEL, AND FOR THE IDEAS THAT HELP ME OPEN MY OWN MIND TO POSSIBILITIES I HAVEN'T YET EXPLORED.

WE DELIGHT IN KNOWING EACH OTHER WELL ENOUGH TO LAUGH TOGETHER AND KNOW WHAT EACH IS THINKING WITHOUT THE BENEFIT OF WORDS.

ROMANTICS WE BOTH ARE—FAVORITE RESTAURANTS WITH SPECIAL TABLES IN QUIET CORNERS, WHERE THE WAITERS KNOW US AND SMILE AT US WITH WARMTH. WE ORDER WINE AND EXCHANGE LOVING GLANCES. THESE ARE INTIMATE MOMENTS THAT WE CAPTURE AND HOLD ON TO TIGHTLY AS WE NEVER KNOW WHAT TOMORROW BRINGS. AND FOR EACH SUCH MOMENT, WE GIVE THANKS FOR WHAT WE HAVE.

HOW I LOVE THE MANY TIMES YOU SANG TO ME— SONGS THAT WE BOTH ASSOCIATED WITH YEARS GONE BY, EACH RECALLING OUR OWN SEPARATE MEMORIES WITH NOSTALGIA.

HOW DEEPLY I FEEL YOUR COMPASSION AND SENSITIVITY WHEN YOU HEAR MELODIES OF YOUR CHILDHOOD THAT BRING TEARS TO YOUR EYES AS TOUCHING MEMORIES ARE RECALLED.

THE LONGER WE ARE TOGETHER, THE MORE ENDURING MY LOVE. I HAVE LEARNED TO APPRECIATE YOUR QUALITIES. JUST TO NAME A FEW—YOUR TENDERNESS, UNDERSTANDING, IDEALISM, GENEROUS SPIRIT, AND DEVOTION TO FAMILY. FOR ME, YOU ARE A TOWER OF STRENGTH—SOMEONE I CAN ALWAYS DEPEND ON.

I AM SO VERY LUCKY TO HAVE FOUND YOU, WHOM I ADMIRE AND RESPECT. MY FRIEND, COMPANION, CONFIDANT, AND LOVER. I OPEN MY HEART TO YOU AND KNOW YOU WILL UNDERSTAND THE BOND OF TRUST BETWEEN US THAT HAS GROWN STRONGER WITH EACH AND EVERY DAY.

YOU ARE SO PRECIOUS TO ME—A DIAMOND AMONG MEN—AND I HAVE BEEN TRULY BLESSED.

I HAVE MET YOUR FAMILY AND TRULY LOVE THEM ALL, AND IT IS SO GRATIFYING TO KNOW THAT THEY SINCERELY LOVE ME IN RETURN. MY FAMILY, AS LARGE AS IT IS, JOINS ME IN THE DELIGHT AND JOY OF SEEING US TOGETHER AND LOVING YOU.

NO LONGER ARE WE SIGNIFICANT OTHERS TO THE WORLD, BUT "GIRLFRIEND AND BOYFRIEND."

MAY YOU NEVER DOUBT THAT I WILL ALWAYS BE BESIDE YOU, CARING FOR YOU, LOVING YOU WITH ALL MY HEART. YOU ARE THE WIND BENEATH MY WINGS.

The ceremony did not have the benefit of a rabbi. Instead, the task of "master of ceremonies" was assigned to Meta's brother Myron, who officiated over a spontaneous desire of many of our guests to get up and speak in our honor. My children, Meta's children, my siblings, and hers—and even Simone and Eve, Meta's grandchildren—all honored us with their recollections and good wishes. The only fly in the ointment that I observed was a strange distance I thought I noticed between my daughter Sheila and her husband, Marty. My observation, which I did not give a lot of thought to at that time, was the omen of bad things to come.

I do not intend to deal with the subsequent dissolution of their marriage except to say that in the interim years, both Marty and Sheila have found other mates and have both remarried.

OCTOBER 31, 2004

Once again, death came knocking at our family's door. My cousin Adele Alpert didn't answer her phone when her son Lance called her. Several attempts to reach her failed, which prompted him to go to her apartment. He found her dead on her bed in a manner that seemed that it happened quickly and suddenly. She was fully dressed. What consolation could I take from this loss? Something other than cancer caused her demise.

EPILOGUE II

JANUARY 9, 2018

FOURTEEN YEARS HAVE elapsed since Meta and I declared our love and devotion to each other. During those years, so much has transpired. First and foremost, both Meta and I have survived beyond our ninetieth year. We still live together happily and harmoniously, but now we live in a ranch that can boast "no steps" in Melville, Long Island. My battle with cancer is still ongoing even after being diagnosed with lung cancer, a new entry in 2013. With the surgical removal of part of my lung, I have thus far not had a recurrence.

I have been more fortunate than my sister, Beatrice Katz, who succumbed to multiple myeloma on December 24, 2006. Beatrice was living at a senior citizen facility in Phoenix, Arizona, having moved there from Florida to be close to her daughter, Susan. I maintained telephone contact with her several times a week. Together, we were able to reminisce about our younger years in Brooklyn. We would talk to each other in Yiddish just for the fun of remembering the language.

Meta and I went out to Phoenix to visit with her shortly before she died. We were able to observe her loneliness since her husband, Joe Katz, passed away. Beatrice consoled herself with doting on her parakeet, Tweety. She fed and played with Tweety. She worried about the bird when she left the house.

That visit was the last time I saw Beatrice alive. At her funeral, Leonard and I spoke with an awareness that he and I were the only remaining members of our immediate family.

On August 31, 2011, after several months of horrible suffering with a bad case of shingles and diverticulitis that left him weak and vulnerable to infection, Leonard succumbed. He and his wife, Cynthia, were living in Connecticut at a senior citizen facility closer to their children, Sheldon and Steve. Meta and I went to visit when Leonard was taken to the hospital. We spent several days at the hospital. I think we were in a state of denial as to how ill he was. He complained about a pain in his shoulder. The physician suggested a surgical procedure to alleviate the pain. The surgery was done in the evening. The next day, we came to the hospital early and sat next to his bed. I could see he was suffering and in pain. At one point, a nurse came in and administered an injection that I assumed was to help relieve the pain. Moments later, she called the doctor, who arrived quickly; and after examining Leonard, he pronounced him dead.

I was in a state of shock! I did not believe he passed away as I sat next to his bed. His passing left me as the sole surviving member of our family.

Never to be forgotten were my cousins Nate and Betty Seigal, Lesley Brittman, and Lester Schwartz, who have since passed away.

I, however, cannot terminate this writing without looking at the bright side of my life. My eldest granddaughter, Jacqueline, married Matt Jossen. Jacqueline gave birth to my first great-granddaughter and is pregnant with their second child.

My granddaughter Becky is engaged to marry Ryan Freed.

My granddaughter Stephanie is engaged to Scott Glucksman.

WHO AM I?

Having passed my ninety-second birthday, it is not unrealistic to be aware that I have more days behind me than I have to look forward to. I consider myself fortunate to have survived many life-threatening illnesses, but they have left their mark. I realize that my ability to travel to places I would have loved to visit is no longer possible. Travel has always been, for me, the best learning experience. There is no substitute for the experiences encountered and the people you meet.

I have no intention to stop living and learning each day, but I have to do so differently. My activities are limited to "close to home" places. My circle of friends are those I encounter in groups, who, like myself, are still interested in living and learning.

Lest I leave the impression that I no longer am interested in having fun, forget it. I still love to party and will welcome any opportunity to get together with friends and family for a celebration and to lift up a glass of wine to "shekka de nop."

I look around my home surrounded by photographs of my parents, my children, my grandchildren, and now even my great-grandchild, and I ask myself, "Of what importance has my life been until now?" What part of who I am can I attribute to my parents' influence? What legacy can I claim credit for when I look into the faces of my children and grandchildren?

My parents tried hard to instill in me a belief in the basic tenets of Judaism. They raised me in a Jewish home and tried to encourage me to follow in their footsteps. They were partially successful. I identify culturally as a Jew, even as I question the concept of God.

My thirst for education is endless. I have been fortunate to have been married to two women who had encouraged and assisted me in pursuing educational opportunities. Now in the twilight of my days, I am still fortunate to have Meta, my soul mate, participate with me in seeking out educational endeavors.

My three daughters followed in their mother's footsteps by choosing education in various forms as vocations. They have all been teachers. Chippy, before she retired, had been the principal of several schools. Sheila and Deah have earned their doctorate degrees in their chosen fields of education. I couldn't be more proud of them and their accomplishments.

I am no less proud of my grandchildren. Jacqueline is now a medical doctor, while Becky and Stephanie are making their way in the business world. Zachary, the youngest of my grandchildren, has just completed his bachelor's degree in music and is investigating opportunities to pursue a career in teaching. My pride extends to the fact that all my children and grandchildren know that they have a responsibility to contribute to their society, and they do so by volunteering time and effort, whenever possible, to worthy causes. I can only hope that I, in some way, contributed to making them the kind of people they turned out to be.

END

Descendants of Rose Siegel

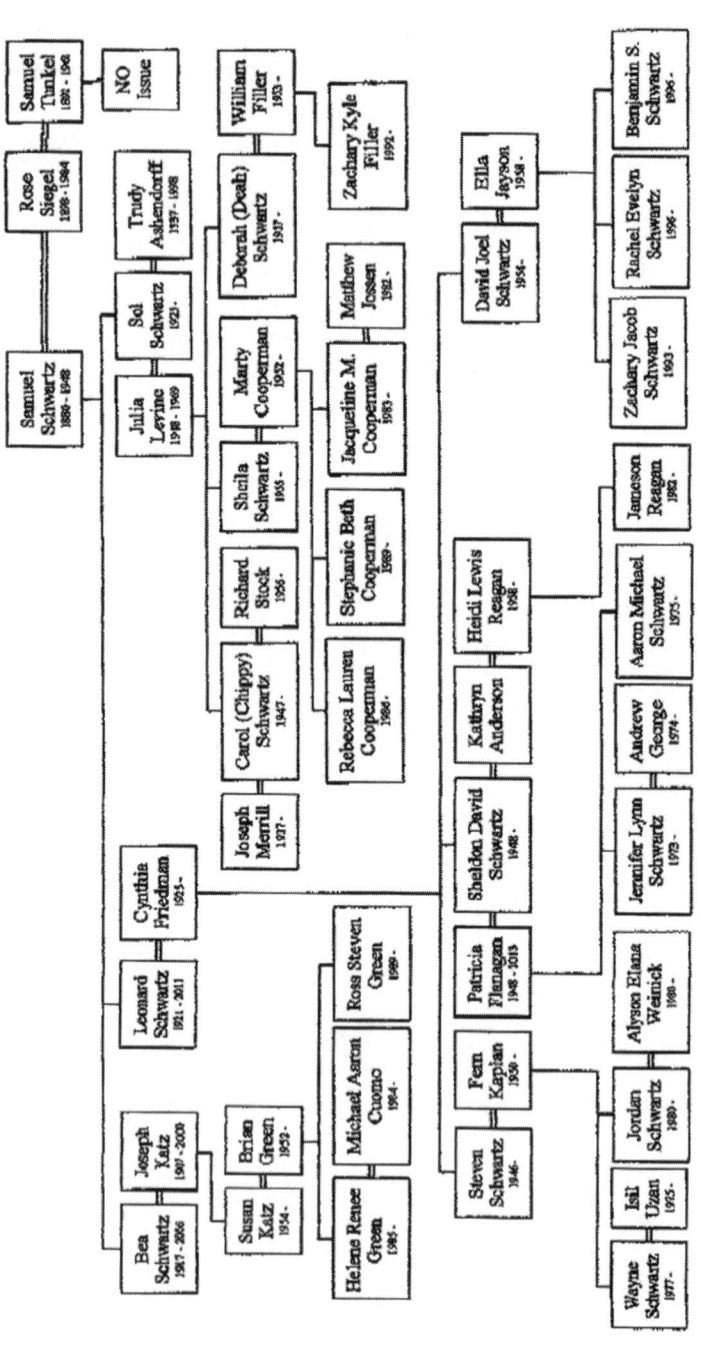

Children and Grandchildren of Marcus Siegel

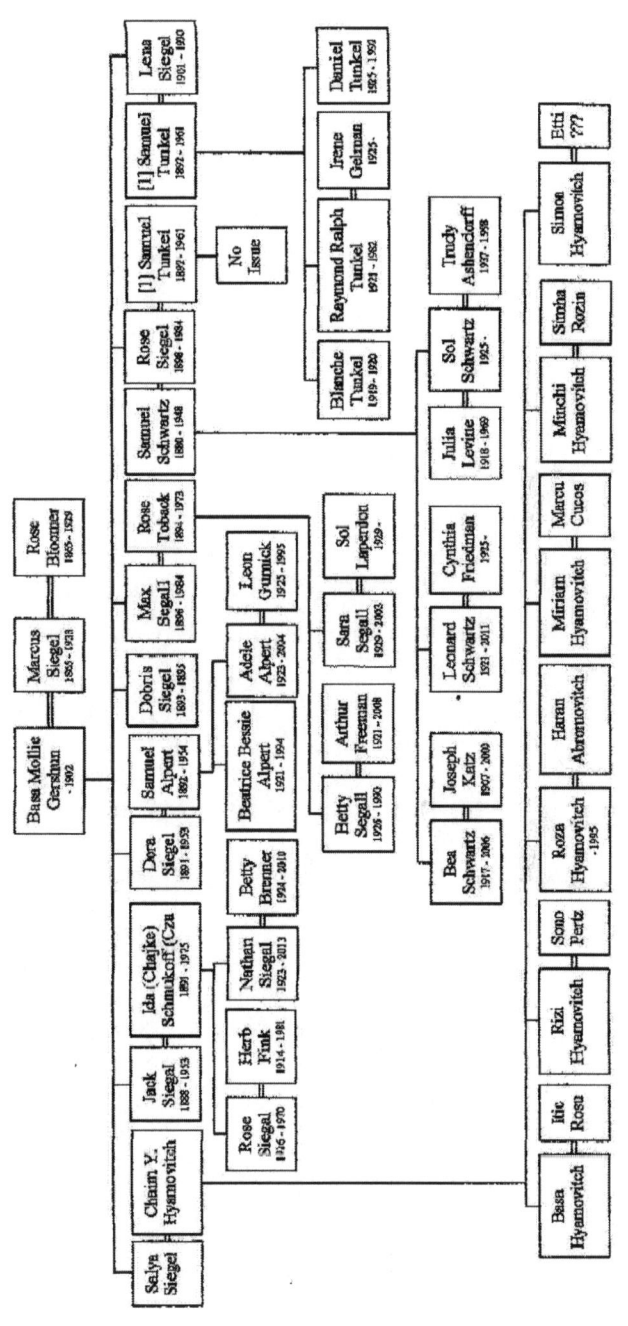

Children and Grandchildren of Leibish and Rebecca Schwartz

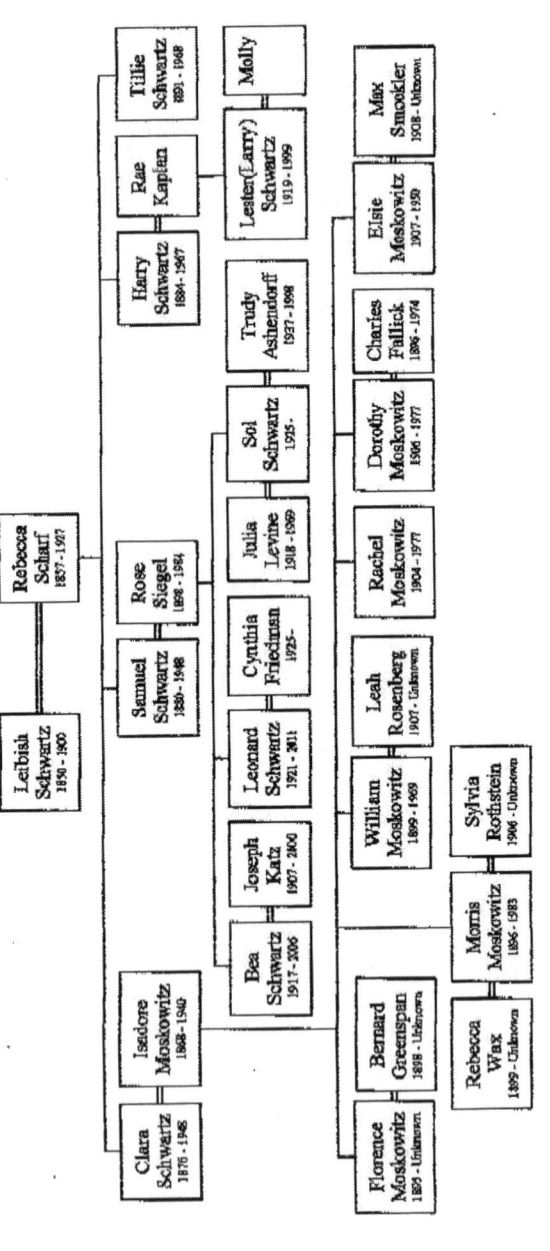

Family from Israel
Bottom Row (L-R): Chaim Hyamovitch,
Rose Schwartz (Tunkel),
Salya (Siegel) Hyamovitch

Front Row (L-R): Jake Siegal, Marcus Siegel, Rose Bloomer (Siegel) Sam Alpert
Top Row (L-R): Ida Siegal, Rose Schwartz (Tunkel), Max Segall, Lena Siegel (Tunkel), Dora Alpert

Sol Schwartz, Julia Schwartz

Rose Bloomer (Siegel), Marcus Siegel

Rivka (Rebecca) Schwartz

Hot Diggety Dog Stand

Front Row (L-R): Sol Schwartz, Bea Katz
Top Row: (L-R): Leonard Schwartz, Rose Schwartz (Tunkel), Sam Schwartz

Sol Schwartz, Meta Smith

492 Hegeman Aveuue as it appears today

Trudy Schwartz and Dolly (Cat)

Beatrice and Joe Katz

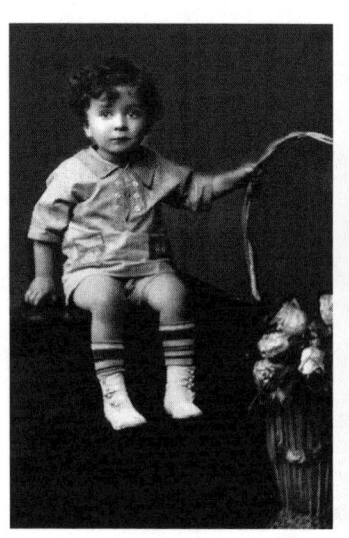  

Sol Schwartz as baby, Sol Schwartz (Bar Mitzvah),
Sol Schwartz (Elementary School Graduation)

INDEX

A

Accusonic Systems, 215, 235, 237–38, 240, 256
Ace Design, 121, 127
Adelphi University, 209
Advest & Co., 213
Alcosser, Al, 53, 56, 70, 100, 110, 113
Alcosser, Lois, 366
Alexandria, Egypt, 189
Aliana (restaurant), 394
Allen Pavilion, 400
Alpert, Adele, 6, 19–20, 31, 37, 61–65, 70, 93, 273, 361, 430
Alpert, Bessy, 31, 69, 93, 273
Alpert, Dora, 6–7, 31–32, 61, 92, 167, 440
Alpert, Sam, 6, 31, 93, 440
Altman, Amos, 154
Amatong, Jasmine, 377

American Coil Company, 77, 80–81
American Labor Party, 73
American Stock Exchange, 120, 144, 214
Andrew (reporter), 319–20, 323
Angela (teacher), 308
Anne (classmate), 11
anti-Semitism, 11, 60, 280, 321, 355
Ariel Restaurant, 333–34, 337–38
Aristide, 265
Armed Services Procurement Regulations, 156
Ashendorff, Alice, 170, 391
Ashendorff, Arthur, 391–92
Ashendorff, Louis, 391, 393
Athens, Greece, 189
Atlantic Sash and Door Company, 3

Auschwitz, 71, 279, 339, 342–45, 348
Automatic Coil Co. Inc., 81, 85, 88, 92, 94–95, 98–99, 120, 124, 139, 146–47, 153–55, 166–67, 192, 195, 198, 204, 238
Avnet, Charles, 55

B

B., Ruth, 17
Badlands, the, 138
Badong, China, 252
Balmaceda, Casilda, 374
Banks, Annie, 216, 391, 404–5
bar mitzvah, 14, 37, 39–41, 365, 397, 423, 450
Barton, Larry, 418–20
Bartosz, Adam, 350–51
bat mitzvah, 365
Baussan, Jack, 266
Baussan, Robert, 259, 266
Baussan, Tamara, 260–61, 266
BCG Radio, 49–50, 53
BCG treatment, 364–65, 375, 395, 399

Becky (grandchild), 270, 410–12, 434
Bedford Avenue, 88, 92, 96
Begonia Society, 267
Behar (businessman), 37, 57–58, 61
Beijing, China, 245, 248
Beijing Opera, 248
Belafonte, Harry, 54
Benewitz, Ben, 176, 205
Benewitz, Chaia, 91, 94–95, 176, 205, 208
Benjamin (teacher), 40–41
Birkenau, 279, 339, 342–45
Bitto (friend), 29
Blanck Institute, 209
block parties, 56
board of directors, 99, 122–24, 128, 130, 140, 144, 156, 235, 256–57, 361
Bob (government employee), 264–65
Boleslaw, Duke, 338
Bosporus Sea, 187
Boston, 160, 308
Boulder Oaks, 157–58, 171
Boyle Heights, 61, 63
Brittman, Lesley, 164–65, 366, 432
Brittman, Marvin, 164–65

Broadway, 77, 88
Brooklyn, 1, 12, 32, 44, 47, 53, 66–67, 77, 88, 93, 96–97, 99, 120, 170, 333, 366, 391, 431
Brooklyn Polytechnic Institute, 53
Buchsbaum, Frank, 144, 153, 257
Bullock (teacher), 38
Burns (superintendent), 50–53, 397
Burns, Thomas, 397
Burns-Milwaukee Inc., 397
Bush, George H. W., 240

C

C., Estelle, 17
C., Lenny, 17–18, 26
Cairo, Egypt, 189
California, 59–62, 65–66, 68, 70, 84, 92, 138–39, 150, 192, 195, 205, 208, 217, 254, 273, 315, 361, 389, 417
Calvary Hospital, 256
Camp ABC, 74–75, 87
Campbell, Linda, 361
Camp Midvale, 85–86

cancer, 92–93, 95, 239–40, 255–56, 269, 273, 288, 358, 361–64, 366, 369–73, 375, 378, 380, 384, 389–90, 393, 401, 403, 406–7, 420–21, 430–31
Cap Haitian, Haiti, 183, 193
Carl (cabdriver/spy), 103–4, 111–19
Casablanca, 48, 90
Cascade Inc., 78
Catano (schoolboy), 38
CAT scan, 370, 372–73, 378–80
Catskills, 3, 16, 422
Center Harbor, 172
Challenges in Retirement, 393
Channel 13-WNET, 338
Charlie (tourist), 164–65
Charlie (trolley operator), 16
Chase (Meta's grandchild), 415
Chava (tourist), 185–88
chemotherapy, 366, 371–74, 378–80
Chiang Kai-shek, 250–51
Chicago, Illinois, 62

China, 242–43, 246–48, 250–52, 254
Chongqing, China, 251
Chris (tourist), 244–45
CIA (Central Intelligence Agency), 265
City College, 44, 46–47, 67, 72
Cohen, Bess, 150
Cohen, Sid, 23–24
Columbia Presbyterian Hospital, 196, 371, 381, 400
Comedians, The (Greene), 111
Comerio, Puerto Rico, 146–48, 153, 155
Communists, 73, 250, 252, 282, 289, 295, 314, 326
concentration camps, 277, 279–80, 299, 329, 342, 355
Continental Airlines, 376
Control Parts Inc., 48
Cooperman, Kerry, 365
Cooperman, Marty, 204
crematoria, 302–3, 311, 322, 344
Cuba, 264

cystoscopy, 255, 362, 364–65, 370, 372, 374–75, 396

D

Daily News, 23
Dan (tourist), 319–20, 323
Dansk, Poland, 312
Dauguila, Jollita, 326–27
Dauguila, Juozas, 326
Davis, Joe, 138–39, 195
Deah (daughter), 209, 215, 254, 271, 273, 388–89, 396, 417, 434
Debevoise Street, 85, 88–89, 93
DeLuca, Peppino, 59–60, 65
Democratic Party, 73
Denis (tenant), 135–37
Denton Avenue, 157
Denver, Colorado, 138
Department of Defense, 141–43, 149, 151, 156, 235, 266
Desert Storm, 240
Designatronics Inc., 99, 121–22, 124–25, 127–30, 133, 139, 145, 182, 195, 211, 213–14, 224, 226, 234–35, 239–40,

242, 256–57, 266–67, 357, 359, 361
Dieringer, Pauline, 377
Duvalier, Jean Claude, 106, 111, 115, 137, 224
Duvall, Philippe, 113
Dwory, Poland, 343

E

East New York Vocational High School, 38
Eddie (tour guide), 246–47, 249
Edelberg, Donald, 71
Edelston (businessman), 71
Egypt, 189
El Capitan, 62
Electronic Instrument Co. Inc., 66–67, 70, 97
empire state college, 190–91
Englewood Cliffs, New Jersey, 15
Erik (teacher), 308
espionage, 72
ethnic cleansing, 355
Etienne, Jean Robert, 112–13
Europe, 185, 287
Evita (tourist), 340–41, 345–48, 350–51

Exact Precision Corp., 97–99

F

F., Dorothy, 17–20
Fallsburg (village), 3, 220
Far Rockaway, 93–94, 132, 134–35, 176, 269
Fengjie, China, 251
Field, Normy, 23–24
Fields, Sidney, 154, 192, 212
Filler, Bill, 215, 396
"Final Solution," 301, 311, 343
Finn, Lillian, 91
Florida, 70, 91, 95, 176, 192, 195, 198, 204–5, 208, 213, 222, 236–38, 240, 244, 256, 308, 390, 414, 431
Fomento, 146
Forbidden City, 247
Frances (tourist), 244
Francois (guide), 107–9, 112
Frank (government employee), 109–10, 117
Fred (Shana's son), 157–59
Freed, Ryan, 433
Freedom Singers, 54, 92
Freeman, Arthur, 214

Freeman, Betty, 214, 239
Freida (realtor), 133–37
Freidman, Cynthia, 57–58, 91, 400, 432
French Alps, 162
Friedman, Fanny, 93
Friedman, Harry, 93
Friedman, Martin, 77, 81, 94–95
Fuchs, Estelle, 55

G

G., Harold, 14
Gabrielle (Meta's grandchild), 415
"gang of eight," 244, 247
GAO (General Accounting Office), 141–42
Garbelli (neighbor), 27
gas chambers, 301, 310, 343, 345
GC&G Jewelers, 44
Geller, Stewart, 285, 384, 389
General Electric, 142
Geneva, Switzerland, 164–65
Gentec, 237
George, Lake, 171, 174
George Washington Bridge, 15
Georgia and Hegeman Boys and Girls Club, 220
Georgia and Hegeman Newsletter, 219
Gerty (housekeeper), 159, 167, 171–72, 174
Gimblett, Barbara K., 335
Glucksman, Scott, 433
Goeth, Amon, 331
Gold, Marian, 164
Golub, Roz, 87
Gonusky, Billy, 27
Goodman (therapist), 161
Gooz, Carl, 25
Gora Kalwaria, Poland, 306
Grand Canyon, 66, 138
Great Depression, 16, 46
Great Neck Radiologists, 370
Great Wall of China, 248, 250
Greece, 182, 189
Greene, Graham, 111
Greenglass, David, 72
Greenstein (doctor), 370
Gruber, Ruth, 340, 347
Gruber, Ruth Ellen, 339–40
Gura, Jan, 338–39, 341
Gurnick, Lance, 361
Gurnick, Leon, 63–64, 361

gypsies, 33

H

Haftorah, 41
haiti, 100–101, 103, 106, 108–11, 116–17, 119, 148, 154–55, 165–67, 183–84, 192–95, 198, 204, 211–12, 215, 224–25, 234–37, 240, 256, 258–66, 370–71, 390, 396–98
Halkowski, Henryk, 295, 333, 337
Hanson, Phil, 155
Hegeman Avenue, 1, 17, 27–29, 32, 35, 68–69, 219, 221
Hejnal, 338
Helen (government employee), 109–10, 117
Helen (nurse), 363–64, 376
Helen (tourist), 244
Heller, George, 100, 122, 140
Henry Avenue, 133–35
Hewes, Peter, 124, 128
Hewlett Neck, 133
Heywood, Roger, 124, 128
Hialeah, Florida, 192, 198, 204

Hirsh, Sam, 59
Hitler, Adolf, 327
Hoffman, Martin, 140
Hoffman, Shirley, 215
Hoffman, Trudy. *See* Schwartz, Trudy
Hofstra University, 267, 368, 394–95, 419
Hollywood, California, 48, 59–60, 62, 90, 261
Holocaust, 69, 73, 168–69, 280, 301, 307, 314, 324, 333, 345, 349, 356–57
Holocaust Museum, 349
Hong Kong, 254
Horowitz, Ephraim, 59
Hot Diggety Dog, 63, 444
Hotel Forum, 330
Hotel Jan III Sobieski, 282, 329, 350, 352
Hotel Oloffson, 100, 103
Hotel Sarunas, 312, 328
House Armed Services Committee, 141
Houston, Texas, 375–76, 378–79
Hudson River, 371, 381

I

Ibo Lele Hotel, 114–15, 155, 193, 259, 261, 265–66
Ida (aunt), 14, 195
I. G. Farben, 343
International Monetary Fund, 398–99
"In the Mood" (Miller), 29
Iron Curtain, 277
Israel, 100, 166–67, 169, 182, 184–85, 189, 195, 226, 289, 313, 323, 329, 332–33, 340, 356–57, 365, 439
Isserles, Moses ben Israel, 332
Istanbul, 185
Istanbul Hilton, 185

J

Jack (supervisor), 50–52
Jack (tourist), 185–88
Jacmel, Haiti, 193
Jacqueline (grandchild), 214, 365, 432, 434
Jacques (Haitian), 102–3, 117
Jamaica, 103, 117, 119, 148
Jane (guide), 331, 333, 337–38, 346
Janiszewski, Teresa, 292–95
Japan, 244–45, 329
Jean (Bob's wife), 264
Jericho Library, 329
Jesse H. Jones Rotary House, 377
Jewish cemetery, 307, 328, 349
Jewish Folk Festival, 333, 335–36, 340, 346
Jewish Heritage Travel: A Guide to East-Central Europe (Gruber), 339
Jewish National Fund, 11
Jewish Street, 330
Jews, 27, 51, 60, 94, 260, 279–80, 287, 290, 292, 294, 296, 300–303, 306–9, 316–17, 319–21, 323–24, 330, 332–33, 335–36, 342–43, 345–48, 350, 354–56
Jews in America in Art and Literature (Karp), 336
J. H. Bunnell & Co., 53, 55
Jim (tourist), 262–65
Jingzhou, China, 252
John of Capistrano, Saint, 330
Jolicoeur, Aubelin, 111, 117
Jones (teacher), 10, 12

Jordana (Meta's daughter), 415
Joskowicz, Pinchas Menachum, 289
Jossen, Matt, 432
Judaism, 322, 434

K

K., Harold, 13, 15
Kanauka, Al, 315
Karp (rabbi), 336
kashrut, 73
Katz, 278
Katz, Joe, 69, 278, 285, 291, 303–4, 354, 414, 431, 449
Kaunas, Lithuania, 319
Kazimierz Dolny, 307–8, 330
Keith, Joe, 166, 168
Kelly, F., 128
Kennedy Airport, 244, 353
Kenol, Jacque, 115
KGB (Komitet gosudarstvennoy bezopasnosti), 324–28
KGB Museum, 324, 326
kibbutz, 185
Kingston, Jamaica, 119
Kirshenblatt (tourist), 335–36

Kiryat Shmona (town), 168–69
Kopilevich, Regina, 316, 319–23, 328
Korczak, Janusz, 302
Korea, 88
kosher, 15, 314, 317, 341, 361
Krajewska, Monika, 335
Kraków, 286, 295, 329–33, 335–37, 342, 345–48, 350–51, 356
Krepp, Sylvia, 24
"kuchalaine," 3
Kuras, Roz, 54
Kuras, Victor, 54, 67, 81, 83–85, 87–88, 144

L

Lajos (friend), 304–5
Laperdon, Sarah, 421
Laperdon, Sol, 214, 421
Last Emperor, The, 246–47
Lauder Foundation, 285, 290
left-wing, 48, 94
Lemurt, Jack, 30
Lena (aunt), 33, 167
Lenin, Vladimir, 327
Lenny (tourist), 247
Le Petit Bijou, 276
Lerner (teacher), 23–24

Levin, Ed, 88–89, 92
Levine, Charles, 71, 76
Levy (homeowner), 133–34
Levy, Jocelin, 366
Levy, Joe, 366
Lietuvos Jerozale, 314
Linden Boulevard, 29–30, 32
Lindy, the, 29
Lithuania, 276–77, 285, 319, 321, 357
Lloyd Harbor, 209
Logothetis, Christopher, 375–80
London, England, 180, 341
Long Beach, 217, 392, 419
Long Beach Hospital, 392
Long Island, 16, 36, 97, 133, 141, 145, 176, 209, 211, 329, 333, 342, 416, 419, 431
Long Island Expressway, 209
Long Island Trust Company, 145
Los Angeles, California, 61–62, 69, 92–93, 138
Louvre, 180

M

M., Leo, 17, 19
Majdanek concenration camp, 306, 309–11, 344
Makow Mazowiecki, Poland, 278–79, 285–86, 288, 290, 294
Manhattan, New York, 1, 67, 87, 89, 164, 181, 244, 391
Mankowska, Eva, 329, 337
Mann, Joe, 166–67
March of the Living, 279
Maris, Peter, 196–97
Marx, Karl, 327
Mathews, Doris, 173
Mathews, Matt, 172–73
Maurer and Maurer, 210
Maxie (friend), 29–30, 366
McBride Street, 94, 134
McKeen Pavilion, 381
McKesson & Robbins, 28
M. D. Anderson Medical Center, 375, 377
Meshover, Teresa, 56, 62, 67
Mick (neighbor), 25
Mickey (friend), 29, 366
Miller, Bert, 66, 97
Miller, Glen, 29, 54
Ming. *See* Eddie (tour guide)
Ming Tomb, 248

Minter, Chippy. *See*
    Schwartz, Chippy
Minter, Julia. *See* Schwartz,
    Julia
Moiseyev Ballet, 282, 303
Monadnock, Mount, 172,
    174
Monroe Street, 89, 92–93
moshav, 194
Moskowitz clan, 421–22
Mount Ararat Cemetery,
    389, 393
Mozlin, Paul, 67
Mr. T (dog), 391
Mr. Whistleman (imaginary
    friend), 90–91
multiple myeloma, 431
Munston Manufacturing
    Corp., 70–71
Muse, Ed, 54, 91–92
MVAC, 371–74
Myers, Rheva, 393
myopia, 9

N

Narita Airport, 244
NASA Space Center, 377
NASDAQ, 144
Nazis, 278, 287–89, 294,
    298–301, 303, 307–8,
    310–11, 316, 320–22,
    324, 331, 343, 345,
    348–49, 356–57
Nevele Hotel, 422
New Cemetery, 307
New Hampshire, 141, 157–
    59, 162, 171
New Hyde Park, 157, 192,
    198
New Jersey, 14–15, 63, 85,
    91, 177, 196, 236
New Lots Avenue, 9, 15,
    27–28, 30, 43
New York Hospital, 149
New York Stock Exchange,
    55
New York University, 190, 335
Niagara Falls, 138
Northern State Parkway,
    209
Nozyk synagogue, 289
Nussbaums, 341
NYA (National Youth
    Administration), 46–
    48, 90

O

Ochos Rios, 119
Old Cemetery, 307

Olsson, Carl, 255, 269, 362–64, 370, 372, 374–76, 378, 380, 390, 395, 399–400, 421
Omni Hotel, 376
OPIC (Overseas Private Investment Corp.), 211–12, 264–65
Oram Mfg. Co. Ltd., 166–67
Orbis, 281–82, 313
Orient Express, 185, 187
Orthodox, 7, 34, 73, 361
Orzyc River, 294
Oswiecim, Poland, 342–43
Oxford University, 341, 348

P

Pacific Stock Exchange, 214
Paneriai Forest, 316, 321–22
Paris, France, 19, 180, 260
Pearl Harbor, 43, 369
Pector (pharmacist), 28
PEIR (Professionals and Executives In Retirement), 267, 367–68, 393–94, 415, 417, 419–20
Pennsylvania, 65, 106, 416
Pennsylvania Avenue, 29

Pep's Vesuvio, 59–60
Perfect Gear and Instrument Corp., 139–40, 192, 195, 198
Peristyle, 115, 117–18
Perkins Elmer (company), 327
Perlman, Itzhak, 338–41
Petionville, Haiti, 112–13, 155, 259, 261
Petrylak, Dan, 371, 373–75, 379–80
Petter, Bryan, 377
Philadelphia Inquirer, 320
Phoenix, Arizona, 431
Pierre (spy), 116, 137
Pike, Otis, 141–43
pirogen, 350
Polakoff, Abe, 159
Polakoff, Ethel, 159
Poland, 276–81, 285–86, 288–89, 291, 296–98, 302, 306, 308, 319, 324, 332–33, 335–36, 340, 353, 356–57
Pontrelli's Ballroom, 64
Port-au-Prince, Haiti, 101, 104, 114, 193, 259, 261
Portugal, 180

Port Washington, 121, 123, 129, 131
Precise Electronics Inc., 98, 121
Preston, Sherry, 376
PS 190, 9, 15, 17
PS 202, 9, 11, 13, 17, 27, 37, 42
Puchner, Peter, 196, 234, 238, 242, 254
Puerto Rico, 100, 146–49, 151, 153–54, 380–81

Q

Qin Shi Huang, 250
Queens, New York, 32, 244

R

Rachel (curator), 314
radiation, 378
Raines, Jack, 174
Raines, June, 174
Raleigh Hotel, 220
Ratner, Robert, 393
Rebecca (family friend), 279
Rebecca (granddaughter), 223
Reibman, Zwe, 53, 56
Remuh, 332, 334
Roberta (tourist), 244

Robeson, Paul, 54, 74–75
Romania, 7, 60, 167–69, 277, 291
Roosevelt, Franklin, 68, 73
Rosen, Sidney, 219
Rosenberg, Ethel, 72
Rosenberg, Julius, 72
Rosner, Nathan, 60–65, 196
Rosner, Rifka, 60–63
Rubenfeld, Bea, 215
Rubenfeld, Joe, 73, 76, 88, 124, 151, 166, 192, 198, 225, 256, 279, 343, 354, 358, 361, 363
Rubenfeld, Joseph, 71, 140
Rummel, Henryk, 286, 297, 329, 352
Rynek Glowny, 337

S

Sabbath, 7, 34, 41, 73, 167–68, 361
"Sacred Way," 248
Sadie (cousin), 59
Salt Lake City, 138
Salya (aunt), 7, 167–68, 184, 313, 439
San Francisco, 138, 215
Schindler, Oskar, 332

Schindler's List, 288, 329, 331

Schudrich, Michael, 286, 290, 308, 335, 347

Schultz, George, 225, 234

Schwartz, Beatrice, 3, 6, 9, 12, 15–16, 69–70, 91–92, 159, 208, 216–17, 414, 431–32, 449

Schwartz, Chippy, 86–87, 89–92, 94, 151, 162–64, 181–82, 204, 218, 359, 434

Schwartz, Deborah Anne (*see also* Deah (daughter)), 95, 132–33, 150–51, 157–61, 164, 172, 175, 177, 180, 205, 208–9

Schwartz, Harry, 3–4, 64, 68, 70, 77

Schwartz, Julia, 87, 89–95, 99–100, 102–7, 109–10, 114–15, 118, 122, 124, 131–32, 134, 137–38, 140, 148–51, 157–58, 161–62, 169, 175–76, 182, 192, 363, 416, 421

Schwartz, Julia Minter, 87, 89–95, 99–100, 102–7, 109–10, 114–15, 118, 122, 124, 131–32, 134, 137, 148–51, 157–58, 169, 175–76, 182, 192, 363, 416, 421

Schwartz, Leonard, 3, 6, 9, 12, 15–16, 19, 32, 49, 55, 57–58, 77, 84, 91, 390, 400, 432

Schwartz, Lester, 432

Schwartz, Rebecca, 3–6, 33

Schwartz, Rose Siegel, 3, 30, 34, 84, 155, 216–18, 226–30, 272, 367, 388, 397

Schwartz, Sam, 1, 3, 8, 11–12, 16, 19, 22, 25, 35–37, 50, 59, 65–66, 68–69, 218, 290–91, 298–99, 320, 361, 445

Schwartz, Sheila Jane, 94, 132–33, 150–51, 157–59, 161, 164, 172, 180–81, 204–5, 210, 214, 223, 230, 238, 269, 430, 434

Schwartz, Trudy, 164–65, 169–72, 174–77,

180–87, 192–94, 209–
11, 214–16, 245–46,
254, 261–62, 273–74,
276–77, 316–18, 323–
24, 327–28, 339–40,
358–59, 368–84,
388–95, 400, 403–5,
414–15, 420–21
Securities and Exchange
Commission, 138
seder, 308
Seeger, Pete, 54
Segall, Max, 7, 167, 191, 214, 239
Segall, Rose, 191, 239
Seigel, Jake, 7, 14, 167
Seigel, Marcus (Zayde), 6–7, 24, 33–35, 59–60, 268, 440
Seine, 180
Seitz, Al, 105, 110, 117
Shamokin (town), 416
Shana (housekeeper), 157–59
Shashi, China, 252
Sheid (neighbor), 22–23
Sheila (tourist), 248
Shennong Stream, 252
shiva, 151, 389, 420
"shlug kapoorus," 34
"shtibil," 300
shul, 24, 34, 40
Siegal, Jack, 93
Signal Corps, 71
Siwek, Reuben, 96, 125, 128, 131, 133, 140
skinheads, 355
Skinny (trolley operator), 16
Smith, Lester, 395, 420–21
Smith, Meta, v, 393–95, 398–400, 404–5, 415–17, 419–22, 430–32, 434
solar ovens, 396–98
Soros Foundation, 316
Soviet Union, 94, 309
Specialty Plastics, 236–37
Stalin, Josef, 94, 327
Stalory (teacher), 10, 12, 37–38
Stanislaus, Saint, 330
staph infection, 404
Starlite Precision, 120–21, 124, 145
Star of David, 306, 320–21, 353
Steiny (neighbor), 25
Stephanie (grandchild), 238, 412, 433–34

Sterling Instrument, 123, 139, 141, 144–45, 175, 198, 238
stickball, 18, 21, 25, 222
St. Mark's Baptist Church, 368
St. Mary's Church, 337
Stock, Richard, 182
Stock Drive Products, 145–46, 153, 157, 165, 175, 192, 198, 238
Stoneybrook University, 151
strawberries, 322
subway, 1, 12, 15–16, 27, 36, 47, 66–67
Sullivan, Gene, 396–97
Sylvia (classmate), 48, 90
synagogue, 7, 278, 289, 292–93, 297, 299–300, 306, 308, 319–20, 332–33, 349
syosset, 394
Szyc, Yaacov, 278, 286, 288, 290, 292–93, 295, 333, 337

T

Tadiran Corp., 165–66, 226
Tanaka, Hitoshi, 257
tap-tap, 193
Tartars, 338
Technicolor, 60
Techno division, 215, 240
tefillin, 41
Tel Aviv, Israel, 166, 169, 184
Temple of Heaven, 249
Temple of Heaven and Hell, 251
Temple University, 416
Terra-Cotta Army, 250
Thailand, 245
Thomas Jefferson High School, 38–39
Tiananmen Square, 246
Tillie (aunt), 3–6, 8–11
Tonton Macoute, 115
Tornel, L., 128
Trafalgar Square, 180
transitional cell carcinoma, 370, 372, 378
transurethral resection (TURP), 234
Treblinka, 278, 287, 300–303, 305, 356
Treptau (instructor), 48
Tribe of Stones, A (Krajewska), 335
Truman, Harry, 67, 73
Tunkel, Barry, 213, 256

Tunkel, Daniel, 6, 14–15, 30–33, 42, 49, 55, 57, 68, 92, 217, 256
Tunkel, Harry, 3–4, 64, 68, 70, 77
Tunkel, Irene, 57, 213, 256, 268
Tunkel, Lenore, 213, 256
Tunkel, Raymond, 6, 31–32, 55, 57, 213
Tunkel, Sam, 6, 22, 37, 57, 68–69
Turkey, 23, 182, 185–86, 327
Tweety (parakeet), 431
Tykocin (village), 297, 299–300

U

Union Station, 63
United Botashoner, 367
United Electrical Union, 124
United Electrical Workers Union, 80
United Jewish Appeal, 280, 358–59
United States, 110, 117, 154, 184, 192, 224, 236–37, 258, 263, 280, 313, 325, 327, 329, 333, 339–40, 351, 353, 356–57
Upon the Doorposts of Thy House (Gruber), 340
US Army, 173, 344
US Department of Commerce, 225
US Navy, 71
USSR, 72

V

Val d'Isere, 162, 165, 169, 171
Valentino, Rudolph, 60
Veisaite, Irena, 315–17, 324, 328
Villa Creole Hotel, 259, 261
Vilnius, Lithuania, 277, 311–21, 324, 328–29, 337, 347
Vilnius in Your Pocket: The Official City Guide, 324
Vistula River, 308, 330
voodoo, 115, 118, 193

W

Walesa, Lech, 312
Wallace, Henry, 67, 73

Warsaw, 280–87, 289–90, 294–95, 300, 302–3, 306, 308, 311, 317–18, 324, 328–29, 333, 335, 337, 348, 350, 352, 355–57
Warsaw Ghetto, 287, 289, 302, 355, 357
Washington Cemetery, 367
Wasserman, Sid, 393
Watnick, Beverly, 74
Wawel Castle, 330, 337
Weintraub, Cess, 362, 382, 384
Weintraub, Joel, 362
Wellin, Martin, 53, 56
Western Components, 195
WEVD, 335
White, Josh, 54
White House, 224
Wilkes-Barre, Pennsylvania, 106, 416
Winnipesaukee, Lake, 171
Winston, Beverly, 384
Woodmere Academy, 132–33
World Trade Organization, 398
world war II, 60, 189, 213, 282, 289, 297, 300, 308, 320, 330, 355
Wurlitzer, 54

X

Xian Incident, 249–50
XYZ Coil Co, 70–71, 73, 75–76, 80, 97

Y

Yaacov the Schneider, 292
Yangtse Paradise, 243, 252
Yangtze, 243, 251
Yellowstone National Park, 66, 138
Yiddish, 24, 41, 168–69, 184, 288, 290, 306, 341, 431
Young Progressives of America, 67

Z

Zachary (grandson), 254, 396, 434
Zalgiris Football Stadium, 328
Ze'ev (agronomist), 194
Zimmerman, Arthur, 81, 96
ZOB, 287

Edwards Brothers Inc.
Ann Arbor MI. USA
March 19, 2018